A SERIES OF CONDUCT BOOKS

THOEMMES

ACKNOWLEDGEMENTS

I should like to thank my husband, R. A. Waldron, and my friends in the London Women's Studies Group, for their help and encouragement during the preparation of this Introduction, especially in the tracing of Hannah More's often erratic quotations. Special thanks in this regard are due to Carolyn Williams, whose wide knowledge and untiring persistence are beyond praise.

Portrait of Mrs Hannah More reproduced by kind permission of Bristol Central Library.

CŒLEBS IN SEARCH OF A WIFE

Hannah More

With a new Introduction by
Mary Waldron

THOEMMES PRESS

© Thoemmes Press 1995

Published in 1995 by

Thoemmes Press
11 Great George Street
Bristol BS1 5RR
England

ISBN 1 85506 383 2

This is a reprint of the 1808–9 Edition
© *Introduction* by Mary Waldron 1995

Publisher's Note

INTRODUCTION

Although Hannah More (1745–1833),[1] the remarkable
daughter of an obscure schoolmaster of Stapleton, near
Bristol, wrote with unrelenting energy for most of her
life and was first published at the age of twenty-one, she
was sixty-three before she produced her first and only
novel in 1808, here reprinted for the first time for more
than a century. Her early favoured genre was the
drama; in 1766 a dramatic representation – hardly a
play – of moral and didactic import entitled *The Search
After Happiness* (I)[2] was published. It had been written
some five years earlier for private performance by the
girls of the boarding-school run by More and her sisters
in Park Street, Bristol, but proved popular and was a
modest commercial success. She next turned to tragedy
for performance on the public stage. With the approval
of the Dr Johnson/Blue-stocking circle, of which she
was by this time a part, and the support of David
Garrick, to whom she had been introduced by their
mutual friend and the Mores' neighbour in Bristol, Dr
John Stonhouse (sometimes 'Stonehouse'), she became
known as a successful playwright. *The Inflexible
Captive* (II) was produced in Bath in 1775, with an
epilogue by Garrick; and in 1777, with Garrick's active

---

[1] See M. G. Jones, *Hannah More* (Cambridge: CUP, 1952) for detailed
treatment of her life and work.

[2] The works referred to may all be found in the eleven volumes of More's
Collected Works (London: Cadell and Davies, 1830). Volume numbers
are noted in text.

co-operation in the writing, *Percy, a Tragedy* (II) was put on at Covent Garden to considerable acclaim, running for twenty-one nights. *The Fatal Falsehood* (II) followed in 1779, but by the time of its production Garrick was dead, and More stricken with grief at the loss of her friend and mentor. This, combined with comparative failure of the play and the added injury of an accusation of plagiarism by Hannah Cowley,[3] led to disillusionment on the part of More with the theatre. In any case, she had always been a woman of strongly puritanical Christian views, who had had to make large allowances for the worldliness of the theatrical scene. Only Garrick, who in his later years came to believe in the drama as a potent moral force, had reconciled her to it, and without him her more characteristic reactions reasserted themselves – she saw even tragedy (as she says much later in a preface to her own plays) as 'in direct opposition to the spirit of religion'. She renounced it.

More was only satisfied with tragedy while she could convince herself that it was upholding the kind of morality she believed in, for her real bent lay in the social and moral reform of a society in which she saw much to condemn. It was out of this that *Cœlebs* was finally born. In the same year as *Percy* she produced her first educational work, *Essays on Various Subjects, principally designed for Young Ladies*,[4] and from that time this kind of publication forms the bulk of her work, notwithstanding the contemporary prominence given to her light and occasional verse (I). She left

[3] Recounted in William Shaw ('Sir Archibald MacSarcasm'), *Life of Hannah More with a Critical Review of her Writings* (London: T. Hurst, 1802), p. 44.

[4] Replaced in 1799 by *Strictures on the Present System of Female Education* (V) and omitted from the *Works*.

drama with reluctance, though, for in 1782 she compromised by composing *Sacred Dramas* (I), adaptations of the scriptures for use in schools.

Two things happened at about this time to enable More to come into her own as a reformer. She became involved, from about 1787, in the movement for the abolition of the slave trade led by William Wilberforce; and also, through Wilberforce and others, with Anglican Evangelicalism and the Clapham Sect.[5] The origins and activities of the latter movement are too complex to be detailed here, but certain of its tendencies were particularly attractive to More. She had always believed, with the Evangelicals, that if it was sincere, Christianity would pervade and penetrate the ordinary concerns of daily life, and not be a marginal matter of church-going and ritual Sunday observance; she also subscribed to a second, perhaps less clearly articulated, view that the social hierarchy as it then existed was ordained by God and that radical politics was the work of the devil. Put together, these two tenets added up to an insistence on the enhanced acknowledgement of their moral and religious duties by all ranks in the interests of the stability of the existing order. To the Evangelical way of thinking this was becoming increasingly urgent in England as France moved through the major upheaval which began in 1789. In particular, the nobility and gentry were felt to be corrupt and unmindful of their duty to set a good example of pure living to the underclass; moreover, they were handing them over in large numbers to the more populist religious movements, such as Methodism, seen then to be overtly politically subversive. In More the

---

[5]   See Ford K. Brown, *Fathers of the Victorians* (Cambridge: CUP, 1961) for a detailed study of this movement.

Evangelicals had a perfect propagandist. She had shown her paces by her poem against the slave trade, published in 1788; the titles of two pamphlets published in 1788 and 1790 respectively speak for themselves – *Thoughts on the Importance of the Manners of the Great* and *Estimate of the Religion of the Fashionable World* (XI). As the Revolution in France got under way, further material of this kind was required, now aimed at the lower ranks, who might be suspected of wishing to emulate their French counterparts. *Village Politics* (III) in 1792 was a deliberate counterblast to Tom Paine and parallels Burke's *Reflections* in simple and rustic terms; later (1795–8) she was part author of the *Cheap Repository Tracts* (III and IV), an unparalleled effort at mass propaganda, in the direction of quietism and stasis.

All these publications sold remarkably well and raised More's public profile. But the education of girls was really her dominating concern, and in 1799 she was able to build on her reputation as a safe and respectable social reformer in *Strictures on the Present System of Female Education* (V). Here she argues for serious education for girls instead of the curriculum of useless and decorative 'accomplishments' common at the time; and also for the encouragement of a robust Christianity, which, she insists, will conquer by example without undue female assertiveness. This is all connected with her overarching concern with social stability and the effectiveness of women in their proper domestic spheres. The whole message of this, as well as of the earlier *Essays*, is against the Rousseauesque idea of the passivity of women and in favour of their acceptance as moral and intellectual beings – but she has no use for the doctrine of 'rights'; duties are her central concern, and in this she radically parts company with Wollstonecraft.

It is in the *Strictures* that we can discover the polemical basis for *Cœlebs*. But why More turned so late in life to fiction is something of a puzzle. She was sternly contemptuous of the contemporary novel, which was being produced in ever-growing numbers by such organizations as the Minerva Press, and lent in its thousands to young women of all ranks and conditions through the circulating libraries. More considered them downright dangerous – in the *Strictures* (p. 140) she denounced them as 'a most pernicious source of moral corruption' in their moral relativity and presentation of 'mixed' characters. Her decision to write one herself is typical – she simply believed that she could transform the genre. Accepting that she could do nothing to stop the flow, More thought she could purify the waters. 'A little to raise the tone of that mart of mischief', she writes to William Weller Pepys in 1809, a year after publication, 'and to counteract its corruption I thought was an object worth attempting.'[6] This was her declared intention, but we might beg to add that she rather hankered for the creative mode after her long divorce from playwriting; the tracts had not quite satisfied this predilection; and she also undoubtedly thought that her ideas might acquire more credibility and a wider audience if presented through a long work of fiction.

But there were other, perhaps not so conscious, factors involved in the genesis of *Cœlebs*. The years leading up to its publication are significant. 1805 was

---

[6] More to Pepys, 13 December 1809. Printed in William Roberts, *Memoirs of the Life and Correspondence of Mrs. Hannah More* (London: Seeley and Burnside, 1834), Vol. III, p. 313.

a rather special year for More, for she had just emerged from a crisis which might easily have destroyed her as a public figure. This is usually known as the 'Blagdon Controversy' and it raged from 1798 to 1803. As a result of a project to institute Sunday and evening schools for the poor in her neighbourhood in the Mendip area More had been accused of everything from closet Methodism to outright sedition in a series of competing pamphlets, egged on by the great reactionary journal of the war years, the *Anti-Jacobin Review*.[7] More confessed herself prostrated by this episode, and was beset by what we would now recognize as stress-related illness for two years. But 1805 saw a great change in the fortunes of England in the conflict; war-hysteria was no longer looking for the enemy within; the Blagdon affair had been more or less forgotten; public attention turned to domestic affairs, particularly the succession to the throne. With characteristic pragmatism, More was ready to take the opportunity to complete her rehabilitation. With the encouragement of an entourage of mildly Evangelical bishops she published *Hints towards forming the Character of a Young Princess* (VI). This was typically confident and almost impudent considering that it was addressed to the royal family. It sold six editions very quickly; public anxiety about the succession was rising; Charlotte, only child of the Prince of Wales, was clearly in direct line to the throne. From all accounts her education did not seem to be fitting her for her exalted position.[8] More

---

[7]   See Brown, Chapter 6, and Jones, Chapter VIII, for more details of this episode.

[8]   Daughter of the Prince and his estranged wife, Caroline of Brunswick, Charlotte was being brought up by Lady Elgin and was said to be somewhat wild and undisciplined. She died at the age of twenty-one in childbirth (1817).

realized at once that her own public image had suffered
no lasting damage, and she prepared her pen for
something more ambitious. Forming the character of
one special young woman was all very well – but
More's target was all young women, and anyone else
she could cram into the novel she planned. It moreover
gave her scope to answer her critics without naming
names, at the same time showing how orthodox she
really was. It was an ideal vehicle for her at this time.

Cœlebs is built on the 'quest' structure, and takes its
cue from any number of traditional narratives in which
a young man sets out on a journey to find his ideal
mate. This young man, whose real name is Charles
('Cœlebs' simply means 'bachelor') is eminently eligible,
and, one suspects, conceived as an antidote to such
heroes as Tom Jones, the archetypal 'mixed' character.
It becomes immediately obvious that More's essentially
didactic aims impede her as a novelist; she forgets how
important it is that readers should be able to engage
positively in some way with the central character.
Charles is quickly revealed as a self-occupied prig, with
whom only other prigs could possibly identify. At
twenty-four he is without fault, knows his own mind,
has an exact tally of the qualities he expects in a wife,
and is able to nose out such vices as hypocrisy, moral
laxity, insincerity, and worldliness in others with
unerring exactitude. As More's twentieth-century
biographer aptly remarks 'As an ironical study of an
insufferable egoist much could have been done with
Cœlebs,'[9] but More's treatment is perfectly serious, and
the result often unintentionally comic. However, other
persons in the narrative, whose moral and social
perfection are not required, are presented with spirit

[9] Jones, Chapter IX, p. 194.

and realism. Clearly More had a talent for fiction – it is a pity that her moralism impeded its freer operation.

We are left in no doubt as to what standards 'Cœlebs' is about to apply in his search as early as the first chapter, which is devoted to the excellences of Milton's *Eve*, with extensive (and inaccurate) quotation, as well as rebukes to those critics who have seen fit to censure her. Charles wants a wife who will submit to her husband, take a subordinate place and 'study household good', and yet show evidence of 'intellectual worth' (I:12). There is some slight, if clumsy, attempt at humour – Charles admires Eve's entertainment of Raphael in *Paradise Lost*, saying 'I am afraid I know some husbands who would have had to encounter very ungracious looks, not to say words, if they had brought even an angel, *unexpectedly*, to dinner. Not so our general mother…' (I:10). This does nothing much to temper the heavy uncompromising complacency of the narrator; his cards are on the table from the beginning. It is interesting to note the assumption about contemporary opposition to his concept of the whole duty of women '…methinks I hear some sprightly lady, fresh from the Royal Institution, express her wonder why Eve should be banished by her husband from Raphael's fine lecture on astronomy…' (I:11).

Charles's parents are recently dead; both have been anxious for his finding a suitable wife; both have given him advice. His mother has advocated consistency:

> Be not taken in by strictness in one point, till you are assured there is no laxity in others…I call education, not that which is made up of shreds and patches of useless arts, but that which inculcates principles, polishes taste, regulates temper, cultivates reason, subdues the passions, directs the feelings, habituates

to reflection, trains to self-denial, and...that which refers all actions, feelings, sentiments, tastes, and passions to the love and fear of God' (II:13).

One cannot help feeling that a girl thus educated might turn out a paragon, but would hardly be fun to live with. Charles's father has emphasized intelligence and domestic habits over accomplishments, and referred him to Mr Stanley, of Stanley Grove in Hampshire, for advice.

Charles departs for London on his way to Hampshire, and visits several recommended families while he is there. More's obsession with social criticism leads her further to damage her hero by causing him to find continual fault with even the best of them, so that added to his priggishness is a carping habit of mind. (His attitudes are in fact much more appropriate to a 63-year-old woman than a young and inexperienced man. Charles is an imperfectly fictionalized stand-in for the author.) The marriageable girls he meets are either too flighty and ignorant, too learned, over-dressed, or worse, under-dressed; they talk too much, or else are dumb and awkward in company. The general neglect of 'household good' on the part of the ladies leads to inelegant table-arrangements and uneatable dishes. Religious attitudes are either too superficial or too narrowly pious – sometimes even both these things. Of a certain Mrs Ranby he meditates that though she may be keen to display her piety and is very strict in her views, her lifestyle is not consistent with them: '...it is not enough', he thinks, 'that the doctrines of the Gospel furnish a subject for discussion if they do not furnish a principle of action' (VI:30). Mrs Ranby believes in 'faith without works' – a potent sign at this time of a leaning towards Calvinism. This is one of many places in the novel where More is seeking to defend Anglican Evangelicalism from the common charge of Calvinism, and to put her hero – and herself – on the right side of the fence doctrinally. Nevertheless, the portrayal of Mrs Ranby is fictionally more satisfactory than that of Charles, particularly in her exchanges with her rather timid husband – see for instance V:27, where Mr Ranby ventures disastrously to agree that his wife may share in the general sinfulness of mankind. It is a pity that More does not more often use her talent for satire.

Sir John and Lady Belfield, with whom Charles stays when in London, are clearly the best of a bad bunch, but even they fall from grace by his exacting standards. They are sincerely religious, but too inclined to adapt themselves to the materialist notions of London society. Both agree that in religion 'things can be carried too far' and Sir John (according to Charles's estimate) 'found...that in the society in which he lived, the reputation of religion detracted much from that of talents; and a man does not care to have his understanding questioned by those in whose opinion he wishes to stand well' (VII:33). Charles keeps his opinions strictly to himself, but the narrative is effective enough for the reader to be acutely conscious of his probable facial expression as he judges his hosts; an example of this is the scene in IV:21–22 when the Belfields' spoiled and noisy children invade the dining-room after dinner.

Other propensities of the fashionable world come in for criticism, particularly among the women. The marriage-market and the manoeuvrings of mothers to recommend their daughters to eligible males is particularly distasteful to Charles, but he is predictably proof against any efforts to catch him. Mrs Fentham is so ambitious for her daughters to move upward in the social scale that her subtle schemes and intrigues invariably fail (IX:38–41). (She is punished at the end of the novel by losing her husband and all her money, and by being deserted by her friends – XLV:231–32.) Lady Bab Lawless, on the other hand, is 'far from shielding her designs behind the mask of decency' and is more successful as she gives the impression of 'artless simplicity' (IX:42). Charles is not imposed upon however; modestly, he professes not to consider himself rich enough for Lady Bab's ambition. In any case, he says, 'there is no part to the appendage of a wife which I have ever more dreaded than a Machiavellian mother' (IX:43). When not plotting to get their daughters married, women are failing in their duty to give generously to the poor and unfortunate, as are Lady Denham and her granddaughter (X:44–5), while patronizing undeserving opera singers like Mr Squallini, who eventually (XXIII:113) repays their patronage by eloping with Miss Denham. Silly wives are corrupting decent men like Mr Stanhope (X:46), and generally the religion practised is spasmodic and superficial. Charles decides to use these terrible examples as lessons: 'I beheld the miscarriages of others not only with concern for the individual but as beacons to light me on my way' (X:48). His self-complacency and tendency to pontificate are unconvincing in a callow young man on his first excursion from home – this is the voice of Hannah More, instructing, as usual, the young and old of both sexes in their proper paths of duty.

Perhaps the most heinous of the evils of the fashonable society described is its habit of not paying bills. Lady Melbury has ruined a respectable trader's family by failing to pay a debt. The daughter of the family comes into the orbit of the Belfield family as the maker of artificial flowers much in demand by fashionable ladies. Lady Melbury, not recognizing Fanny, proposes to increase her debt to the struggling family by a substantial order which she subsequently admits she can't pay for. The father is dead from grief and anxiety, but the dying mother recognizes Lady Melbury and the story comes out. Lady Melbury is presented rather as young and thoughtless than actually venal. This tale is given some prominence (XI:51–53 and XII:54–58), and its resolution, in which Fanny Stokes is taken into the Belfield family as governess and Lady Melbury's reformation begins, is deferred until later in the novel (XLVIII:249–255). Meanwhile Charles betakes himself to Hampshire.

The earlier part of the book concentrates on the iniquities of London; in Hampshire, More, through her central character, gives herself a wider frame of reference; the rest of the book is really a series of disquisitions upon her favourite topics, leavened by a little love-interest. Those favourite topics divide themselves roughly under five headings. By far the most important of these is religion, and this pervades all the rest. Subordinate to it, but related, are education, marriage and charitable activities. All these are, in their turn, connected to and concerned with the whole duty of women.

The positive and approved side of all these issues is to be found in the Stanley family, which consists of mother, father, and six daughters, the two eldest of whom are nineteen and sixteen. Not only do they avoid the pitfalls of the metropolis, but have achieved a perfect balance between religious duty and the enjoyment of the good things of life. They are landed gentry, with an assured position in society and no financial problems. An assortment of neighbours and family visitors provides the contrasting deluded and error-prone individuals who spark off the debates. Some of these benefit from their contact with the Stanleys; others are too far sunk in their own predilections for reform to be possible. A somewhat desultory narrative link for this series of moral discussions can be found mainly in the courtship by Charles of the eldest daughter, Lucilla. The continuing but spasmodic reference to Fanny Stokes, the London sempstress, and the visit of the Belfields to Stanley Grove while Charles is there also help to give the novel a sort of fictional unity.

Mr Stanley is the perfect type of Evangelical Christian, and is immediately regarded by Charles as the fount of all wisdom. He and the rector, Dr Barlow, are in total harmony, and together, politely but firmly, oppose any straying from the 'straight gate and the narrow way' of true religion. Further detailed exploration of the errors touched upon in the London section follows.

Few in the neighbourhood of Stanley Grove measure up to the ideals postulated by the book. Lady Aston, a good woman and exemplary mother, is too narrowly scrupulous and drives herself and her daughters into timidity and depression (XVI:71–5); the Belfields (as we have seen in London) are too concerned about the opinion of the world (XIX:88–92). Mr Tyrrel is in a more serious state of error (XXI). He is a reformed rake who has taken up 'antinomian' religion – he has been persuaded that he need do nothing to ensure his salvation except believe in God. This is the ultimate in the 'faith without works' creed which exercised such a hold over so many, and was perpetuated by popular 'hellfire' preachers, who claimed to be the inspired messengers of God. Mr Flam (XXVa:130–32)[10] is his direct opposite – the man who believes in 'works without faith', the good chap, who, according to Mr Stanley and Dr Barlow cannot be saved, for his morality does not stem from divine authority, but from generalized human benevolence. Phoebe, Mr Stanley's second daughter, dares to criticize Dr Barlow's sermon as 'too severe'; she is kindly but strongly castigated for setting up her own judgement against clerical authority (XXIV:114–15).

The chief message in all this is recognizable as More's own strongly-held conviction – that religion must come from the heart but avoid extremism. The conflicts of the Blagdon episode seem close to the surface as Mr Stanley exhorts Sir John Belfield not to regard charges of Methodist sympathies as he tries to strengthen his commitment to Christianity (XL:208 and XLV:234); and his insistence on the supremacy of the clergy in moral questions seems to represent a rejection of the central charge against More during that period – that of 'intrusion', or the usurpation of clerical authority. Mr Stanley and Dr Barlow seem eminently sensible, balanced and benevolent – until, perhaps, we realize that they are prepared to consign the pleasantest, kindliest people (like Mr Flam) to the everlasting bonfire for doing good actions from secular rather than religious motives. Mr Tyrrel and Mr Carlton, another reformed sinner, who have in the past done more evil than Mr Flam with his real good nature could encompass, are by this system much more certain of

---

[10] An error in the setting-up of this edition has led to the duplication of Chapter XXV. 'XXVa' refers to the second of the two.

salvation because their reformation is rooted in religion. Mr Tyrrel, dying of a paralytic stroke, and finally conscious of the falseness of his antinomian religion, is in better case than Mr Flam (XLVI:243).

That is not to say that good works are unimportant. Mr Stanley emphatically believes in faith *and* works as a means to salvation. The charitable activities of Lucilla and her sisters are given much space. One principle is clear – all charity should be directed at rewarding the upright and moral, but not at tempting them to look outside their station in life. The clothes that the poor are given are 'coarse' – quite unlike the donors'; and their stock with their benefactors is measured by their self-denial and biddableness. At an alfresco party given by the Aston girls (now relaxed and cheerful after their contacts with the Stanleys) for Lucilla and Phoebe, presentations are made to certain of the deserving poor in the neighbourhood. Three young women who have done their daughterly, and other, duties, even to the point of putting off their own marriages, are each presented with 'a handsome Bible, and a complete plain, but very neat, suit of apparel'. It is emphasized that 'all three had been exemplary in their attendance at Church, as well as in their general conduct' (XXXIV:173). It seems that Lucilla and her friends, though younger than they, have the right of rank to judge them.

The Evangelical opposition to indiscriminate charity is insisted upon. Sir John has always considered himself generous to the poor, but Charles feels that he is insufficiently concerned about the objects of his charity: 'Nor had he ever considered, as every man should, because every man's means are limited, how the greatest quantity of good could be done with any given sum.'

The kind of 'good' he has in mind is then explained by Mrs Stanley: 'the noblest charity [is that] which cures, or lessens, or prevents, sin' (XXVIII:139–40).

Training in charitable works is of course part of education in More's scheme, especially that of girls whose wealth and position define them as 'ladies'. 'Charity is the calling of a lady; the care of the poor is her profession', says Mrs Stanley (XXVIII:138). But the novel has a good deal to say about other aspects of education, and much criticism of what More saw as undesirable modern trends. There is some comment about child-rearing in general, but the Stanleys having lost their only son, the examples of good practice are almost all female. More seems to have eschewed discussion of the education of boys beyond infancy.

The more fashionable forms of education for girls are dismissed by Mr Stanley as 'Mahometan' – a charge not unfamiliar to readers of Wollstonecraft. By this is meant training which dwells exclusively on 'making woman an object of attraction'. Mr Stanley would have 'the understanding, the temper, the mind and the manners of [his] daughters, as engaging as these Circassian parents endeavour to make the person'. Charles stands by and admires all this, as it conforms so exactly with his dead mother's opinion and his own (XIV:67).

The Stanleys do not believe in prolonging childhood. At the age of eight, Kate declares to Charles 'today I give up all my little story-books, and am now going to read such books as men and women read'. This is her father's policy – 'too great a profusion of [children's books] protracts the imbecility of childhood'. Predictably, he considers the Bible, unabridged and unsimplified, as the best learning text for children older than eight or nine (XXV:121–2).

There is direct challenge to fashionable permissiveness – what we would now term 'child-centredness' – in the dialogue which takes place as Charles, his hosts, and their other house-guests go about visiting neighbours. Mrs Stanley laments the lack of respect for elders among children and regrets the 'harmless formality' of address, now replaced by 'an incivility, a roughness, a want of attention' (XXVa:127). In the same chapter we are shown the terrible results of family indiscipline and over-indulgence in the children of the Reynolds family (XXVa:127–8). But much more important than the inconvenience and disorder caused is the effect of indulgence on their hopes of salvation. In Chapter XXXII Mr Stanley mildly punishes one of his younger daughters for 'prevarication'; Miss Sparkes, an 'advanced' intellectual woman, brimful of the new ideas, warns him that he may 'break the child's spirit'. Mr Stanley will have none of this – he is sure that such tendencies must be checked early or they will proliferate. 'I feel myself answerable in no small degree for the eternal happiness of these beloved creatures' (XXXII:159). Willingness to discipline, for him, constitutes the reality of fatherly affection.

There is the inevitable discussion about whether girls should be taught the ancient languages, as all boys of a similar rank were. Mr Stanley is teaching Lucilla Latin, but he does not by any means consider this as normal; he has perceived a special aptitude in her, but 'only one girl out of six has deviated from the beaten track' (XXXIX:201). He will probably not do the same for Phoebe (Phoebe clearly has no say in the matter). In the next chapter Charles perceives to his intense satisfaction that Lucilla's Latin has not spoiled her domestic economy; he knows from Mrs Comfit, the housekeeper, that Lucilla is responsible for most of the smooth running of the household, and 'I felt no small delight in reflecting that all this order and propriety were produced without the smallest deduction from mental cultivation' (XL:214). A true latter-day embodiment of Milton's *Eve*.

This leads to other aspects of the ideal woman whom Charles feels he has found in Lucilla. He watches delightedly as her perfections unfold. Her most important attribute is silence. She hardly ever says anything, and when she by chance does venture an opinion she always blushes, fearing that she has said too much (XVIII:82); (one can't help wondering from time to time whether Hannah More ever thought she had said too much, or was somehow exempt from her own strictures). Charles discusses this with Sir John:

> During these conversations, I remarked that Lucilla, though she commonly observed the most profound silence, had her attention always riveted on the speaker. If that speaker was Dr. Barlow, or her father, or anyone whom she thought entitled to particular respect, she gently laid down her work, and as quietly resumed it when they had done speaking.
>
> I observed to Sir John Belfield, afterwards, as we were walking together, how modestly flattering her manner was when any of us were reading! How intelligent her silence! How well-bred her attention! (XXII:105)

Sir John goes on to castigate the habit of some ladies of forcing their 'little employments' – netting, sewing etc. – to the notice of the assembled company. Both gentlemen here evince the most amazing arrogance, considering that most of the garments on their backs were of home manufacture, but we have to assume that Hannah More approved of her invention – there is no detectable ironic slant. Charles agrees:

> It would be difficult to determine…whether this inattention most betrays want of sense, of feeling, or of good breeding. The habit of attention should be carefully formed in early life, and then the mere force of custom would teach these ill-bred women.…

This must be another instance of More's loss of grip on her character – even in the cause of education she could hardly have stomached such pomposity from a youth of twenty-four.

Lucilla certainly preserves a decorous silence, and her speeches are few but fluent – indeed, sometimes as sententious as Charles's own; (they will make a pretty pair). Her most protracted conversation is with him in Chapter XXXIII, and concerns her own efforts to keep her motives pure. She evinces a hair-splitting precisianism which seems very self-occupied to the non-Evangelical (though Charles enthusiastically approves):

> As to my very virtues, if I dare apply such a word to myself, they sometimes lose their character by not keeping their proper place. They become sins by infringing on higher duties. If I mean to perform an act of devotion, some crude plan of charity forces itself on my mind; and what with trying to drive out one, and to establish the other, I rise dissatisfied and unimproved, and resting my sole hope, not on the duty which I have been performing, but on the mercy which I have been offending.

Two whole pages of this sort of thing follow, to much mutual satisfaction. Lucilla's moral sophistry also appears later in the same chapter, when her mother reports on her near-decision to give up gardening because she finds it so absorbing and enjoyable. Her scruples are ultimately satisfied by the suggestion that her watch should be prominently displayed on the scene of her labours in order that she might contain her pleasure within the proper limits.

She is also well able to trounce her unsuitable suitor, Lord Staunton, who through much of the book is feared by Charles as his well-heeled rival, in a few well-chosen words (reported by Mrs Carlton): 'She was then driven to the necessity of confessing, that his principles were not those of a man, with whom she could venture to trust her own.' (How unlike poor Fanny Price, struck dumb by moral and social complexities!)

Charles's courtship is properly prudent and cautious, and altogether lacking in spontaneity and generosity: 'I felt that imagination, which misleads so many youthful hearts, had preserved mine...I had early formed a standard in my mind...I now seemed to have found the being of whom I had been in search.' This is falling in love by numbers – theory rather than practice, and very unlikely in real life.

Lucilla's foils at Stanley Grove are the flighty Miss Flams, the 'accomplished' Miss Rattle, and the masculine Miss Sparkes, who amongst other things, shocks everybody by doing something as unfeminine as examining her horse's hoof (XXXII:160). Lucilla's younger sister Phoebe is also set against her as less than perfect – she sometimes gets into trouble, and is as a result, a more well-realized fictional character. It is she who defends Miss Sparkes, but one feels some regret that she is gradually being persuaded out of her lively ways and will end up as wife to the stick, Sir George Aston.

Charles is inevitably successful in his courtship, but not before his creator has discussed a number of marriages, good and bad. That of the Stanleys is, of course, ideal, except that, as Mrs Stanley seems to have been rendered completely functionless by the domestic perfections of her eldest daughter, it is a wonder that she doesn't bore herself to death, or run off with Mr Flam, who seems to have more fun than anyone else in the novel. Mr and Mrs Belfield are a harmonious couple, united in their earnest desire to emulate the Stanleys in every way. Mr and Mrs Carlton have had their troubles, for theirs was an arranged, mercenary marriage, and Carlton an erstwhile rake, only called from evil by the piety and pathetic loyalty of his long-suffering wife (XVIII:82–87). Mr and Mrs Reynolds don't agree about anything, but are particularly at odds about how to rear their family (XXV:124–25), and the Hamiltons (XVII:80–81) are so affectionately unwilling to upset each other that their concealments are causing a completely unnecessary rift between them. These all help to form Charles's blueprint for his own marriage.

The reasons for the extraordinary success of this novel are quite complex. The first and main attraction was probably its moral and social didacticism. A shifting society in which so many people were upwardly mobile produced uncertainties which were soothed by the complacent assurance of More's 'good' characters. The fictional mode was easier to assimilate than the straightforward polemic of the *Strictures*, and parents were happy to be able to present their adolescent girls with an example of this popular form in which they could, unusually, feel complete confidence. This consideration overrode what turned out to be a not altogether favourable response from critics – and also, surprisingly, from some prominent Evangelicals.

There were some panegyrics, of course. The Reverend John Venn, of the Church Missionary Society, thought it 'one of the most useful works that has ever been written for the purpose which it was intended to answer';[11] William Weller Pepys, literary connoisseur and long-standing friend of the author, thought it equal to the writings of Burke.[12] But Alexander Knox, who became one of the pioneers of the Oxford Movement (the main reaction against Evangelicalism in the later nineteenth century) thought it purveyed an 'odd kind of redivived religious courtship' of which he was 'puzzled how to speak'.[13] The family of Henry Thornton, pillars of the Clapham Sect, did not believe that the author was Hannah More at all (it was published anonymously). A family friend, in a letter to Mrs Thornton, thought the author 'vain, coarse and somewhat presumptuous'. Far from believing the report that it had been written by More, this writer confided 'I earnestly hope it may be written by someone I have already thought disagreeable'.[14] The *Edinburgh Review* gave it to Sydney Smith who predictably tore it to pieces on both moral and literary grounds:

> Events there are none; and scarcely a character of interest...the book abounds with marks of negligence and want of skill.... Mrs Moore [sic] is too severe upon the ordinary amusements of mankind...this

[11] Venn to More, 30 April, 1810 (Roberts, III, 323).

[12] Pepys to More, 14 March, 1809 (Roberts, III, 295).

[13] Rev. Charles Forster, ed., *Thirty Years Correspondence: John Jebb and Alexander Knox* (London, 1834), p. 527. Cited in Jones, p. 196.

[14] Forster Papers (unpublished documents relating to the Thornton family and the Clapham Sect, currently held by the Victoria and Albert Museum in London), 30 December 1808. Cited in Jones, pp. 196–7.

good lady wants to see men chatting upon the Pelagian heresy – to hear, in the afternoon, the theological rumours of the day – .[15]

The *London Review* was more seriously critical, actually accusing More of defending 'what the world calls a Methodist' in her portrait of Mr Stanley, and thus of attacking the Established Church. The reviewer, clearly with the approval of the editor, Richard Cumberland, ends with the words 'caveat emptor'.[16] But the most unkindest cut of all was delivered by the *Christian Observer*, the official organ of the Evangelicals. Apparently lagging behind everyone else in identifying the author, their reviewer declared it 'apt to be vulgar' and discovered 'some want of taste and moral delicacy'.[17] Nothing could have been more embarrassing. In a letter to the editor, her close friend Zachary Macaulay, More furiously threatened to force the journal to make good its criticism; almost immediately she withdrew; she might suggest, but was 'far from *intending* to do it...I, who have never defended myself against my enemies, shall certainly not do it against my friends'.[18] But she wrote no more novels.

However, *Cœlebs* is important, because of its effect on at least one fellow-novelist. Jane Austen was ambivalent about Hannah More and the Evangelicals generally. She famously did not 'like the Evangelicals' but thought 'those who can, from reason and feeling' be Evangelicals, might be 'happiest and safest'. The

[15] *Edinburgh Review*, April (1809), pp. 146–7, 150.

[16] *London Review* No. 2, February (1809), pp. 424–44.

[17] *Christian Observer*, February, 1809. Cited in Jones, IX, p. 198.

[18] A. Roberts, ed., *Letters of Hannah More to Zachary Macaulay Esq. Containing Notices of Lord Macaulay's Youth*, (London: James Nisbet and Co., 1860), pp. 27–30.

thought of *Cœlebs* repelled her, but, she says 'Of course I shall be delighted when I read it, like other people'.[19] She did read it, for it is clear that *Mansfield Park* (published six years later) embodies her reaction to it. Mansfield Park is a more credible Stanley Grove, where lip-service to Evangelical pieties has little effect on Sir Thomas Bertram's family and are of no help at all to Fanny, who would like to emulate Lucilla. But her silences conceal ordinary human desires, and her self-examination cannot extinguish her love for Edmund and her jealousy of Mary Crawford; Edmund is by no means as in command of his passions as Charles, and falls for a girl quite unlike the Evangelical ideal. Several passages in *Mansfield Park* recall *Cœlebs*; Charles's inner monologue as to his feminine ideal parallels Edmund's self-deception about Mary; Mrs Norris's domestic fussiness would, one feels, not be acceptable to the Mrs Comfits of the early nineteenth-century world; unlike Lucilla, Fanny gets no support for her rejection of Crawford, and cannot explain her objections to him as Lucilla can to Staunton; when she drops her work as she listens to Crawford reading Shakespeare, it is against both her inclination and her principles, and turns Charles's pompous admiration of Lucilla's silence and attention on its head. The world of *Mansfield Park* is, perhaps unfortunately, the real world, where people have to suffer for their mistakes and put up with second-best.[20]

Lucilla Stanley went on providing an unreal model for realistic heroines. In Dorothea Brooke we hear a faint

---

[19] R. W. Chapman, ed., *Jane Austen's Letters* (Oxford: OUP, 1964), pp. 256 and 410.

[20] See my essay 'The Frailties of Fanny: *Mansfield Park* and the Evangelical Movement', *Eighteenth-Century Fiction*, April (1994), pp. 259–81 for a more detailed exploration of these ideas.

echo of Lucilla when she determines to give up riding because she enjoys it too much – and she disastrously marries Casaubon. Alice Vavasor and Isabel Archer show us how unlikely is Lucilla's survival in the real world of the nineteenth century – Eliot, Trollope and James demonstrate the real difficulty, and the tragedy, of woman's efforts to lead what was regarded as the virtuous life and yet do some good in the world.

But More's version competed with theirs for many years. Such was her literary skill that she was able to bring her moral theories to monstrous birth; Charles lives on the page, rather as Frankenstein's creation does, and one can only hope that one will not meet him round the next corner; Lucilla is sufficiently believable to have given many a young woman a feeling of hopelessness in the face of life as it is really lived. That many educators believed in the efficacy of the models set up here is evidenced by the novel's long publication history up to the final decades of the Victorian period. But some writers were determined to comfort the afflicted young female reader with more credible representations; Louisa May Alcott's Jo March in *Little Women* and Katy in the three stories of Sarah Chauncey Woolsey ('Susan Coolidge') are perhaps the best known. In *What Katy Did at School* (1874) Woolsey clearly indicates that she has Lucilla in mind as the true begetter of her girl-characters when she makes Elsie, on a dull visit to an elderly couple, fall asleep over the only story-book she can find – *Cœlebs in Search of a Wife*:

> It was about a young gentleman who wanted to get married, but who didn't feel sure that there were any young ladies nice enough for him; so he went about making visits, first to one and then to another; and

when he had stayed a few days in the house, he would always say, 'No, she won't do', and then he would go away. At last he found a young lady who seemed the very person, who visited the poor, and got up early in the morning, and always wore white, and never forgot to wind up her watch or do her duty; and Elsie almost thought that now the difficult young gentleman must be satisfied, and say 'This is the very thing'. When, lo! her attention wandered a little, and the next thing she knew she was rolling off the lounge for the second time in company with Mrs Hannah More. (*What Katy Did at School*, Chapter 1.)

This pleasantly disrespectful account makes a fitting conclusion to an introduction to *Cœlebs* and demonstrates how much tastes and expectations had changed during the sixty-odd years that had elapsed since its first publication. Those changes were permanent, as we can see from the continued relevance and popularity of the *Katy* books to this day, while *Cœlebs* has become simply an amusing, informative, sometimes slightly horrifying, historical curiosity.

Mary Waldron
1995

LITERARY REFERENCES

Like most of Hannah More's writing, *Cœlebs in Search of a Wife* abounds in quotation from and allusion to works of literature which were familiar to her. Almost every page of the text contains some reference to English, French, and classical authors, with Milton, Dryden, Addison, Johnson, Akenside, Cowper, Pascal, Cicero, and Horace predominating. Full annotation is not possible here, but some indication of the breadth of her reading may be found in the following list of major references which it has been possible to trace to their sources. (It is interesting in passing to note how often she refers to the drama, despite her frequent denunciation of the stage.) She quoted from memory, and is often inaccurate to the point of paraphrase; where necessary a correct version is added. Reference is made to chapter and page number, with quotations in the order in which they appear. I have not attempted to attribute the numerous biblical quotations and allusions, nor the passing references to authors and their works within the text.

CHAPTER I
(p. 9) Milton, *Paradise Lost*, IX.233–4
(p. 10) Milton, *Paradise Lost*, VIII.601–2
(p. 10) Milton, *Paradise Lost*, XI.617
  'Woman's domestic honour and chief praise'
(p. 10) Milton, *Paradise Lost*, V.331–3

'So saying, with dispatchful looks in haste
She turns, on hospitable thoughts intent
What choice to choose for delicacy best...'
(p. 10) Milton, *Paradise Lost*, V.338
(p. 10) Milton, *Paradise Lost*, V.343–4
(p. 11) Milton, *Paradise Lost*, V.334–6
(p. 11) Milton, *Paradise Lost*, V.398–9
'These bounties from our Nourisher, from whom
All perfect good, unmeasured out, descends.'
(p. 11) Milton, *Paradise Lost*, VIII.39–40
'So spake our Sire, and by his count'nance seemed
Entering on studious thoughts abstruse;'
(p. 11) Milton, *Paradise Lost*, VIII.48–51
(p. 11) Milton, *Paradise Lost*, VIII.84
'Cycle and epicycle, orb in orb.'
(p. 12) Milton, *Paradise Lost*, IV.298
(p. 12) Milton, *Paradise Lost*, IV.660
(p. 12) Milton, *Paradise Lost*, IV.490–1
'How beauty is excelled by manly grace'

CHAPTER II
(p. 14) Cowper, *The Task*, III.41–2
'Domestic happiness, thou only bliss
Of Paradise that has survived the fall!'

CHAPTER IV
(p. 20) Pope, *Imitations of Horace* II, Satires, I.127
(p. 21) Milton, *Paradise Lost*, II.880

CHAPTER V
(p. 26) Addison, *Cato*, I.i.47

CHAPTER VII
(p. 32) Pope, *Imitations of Horace*, Epistle II.25–26

CHAPTER VIII
(p. 36) Milton, *Lycidas*, 11
(p. 36) Akenside, *Pleasures of the Imagination*, I.481–6
(p. 36) Akenside, *Pleasures of the Imagination*, I.528
(p. 36) Akenside, *Pleasures of the Imagination*, I.532-3
    'Nor the powers
  Of genius and design,'
(p. 36) Akenside, *Pleasures of the Imagination*, I.488
(p. 37) Akenside, *Pleasures of the Imagination*, I.503–4
    'Is aught so fair
  As virtuous friendship?'
(p. 37) Akenside, *Pleasures of the Imagination*, I.504–5
(p. 37) Akenside, *Pleasures of the Imagination*, I.507
(p. 37) Akenside, *Pleasures of the Imagination*, I.506
(p. 37) Akenside, *Pleasures of the Imagination*,
    I.487–500

CHAPTER IX
(p. 39) Shakespeare, *A Midsummer Night's Dream*,
    I.i.100
  'Chanting faint hymns to the cold, fruitless moon.'
(p. 40) Edward Young, *Love of Fame*, Satires, IV.188
(p. 41) Scott, *Marmion*, V.XI
(p. 41) Milton, *Comus*, 561-2
  'And took in strains that might create a soul
  Under the ribs of death.'
(p. 42) Milton, *Paradise Lost*, IV.266
(p. 42) Gray, 'Elegy Written in a Country Churchyard', 76
  'They kept the noiseless tenor of their way.'

CHAPTER XII
(p. 56) Pope, *Rape of the Lock*, 30
(p. 57) Milton, *Paradise Lost*, IV.96–7

CHAPTER XIII
(p. 59) Cowper, *The Task*, I.265
(p. 60) Milton, *Paradise Lost*, VIII.43–4
  'And grace that won who saw to wish her stay'

CHAPTER XIV
(p. 64) Donne, *Progress of the Soul*, 'The Second Anniversary', 244–6

CHAPTER XV
(p. 68) Shakespeare, *Hamlet*, I.iii.61

CHAPTER XVI
(p. 75) No source identified
(p. 75) Akenside, *Pleasures of the Imagination*, III. 489–93

CHAPTER XIX
(p. 89) Addison, *Cato*, I.iv

CHAPTER XX
(p. 93) Nicholas Rowe, *Jane Shore*, II.i.279–80
(p. 95) No source identified.
(p. 95) Akenside, *Pleasures of the Imagination*, I.473–75

CHAPTER XXIII
(p. 109) Dryden, Epilogue to Etherege's *Man of Mode*, 16

CHAPTER XXV
(p. 120) Milton, *Paradise Lost*, IV.248
(p. 124) Milton, *Paradise Lost*, IV.626
(p. 128) Thomson, *The Seasons*, 'Spring', 1151
  'Progressive virtue and approving heaven.'

CHAPTER XXVII
(p. 135) Dryden, *Absalon and Achitophel*, 99

CHAPTER XXIX
(p. 140) Pope, *Rape of the Lock*, 30
 'Of twelve vast French Romances, neatly gilt'
(p. 143) Pope, *Essay on Man*, II.137

CHAPTER XXXII
(p. 157) Thomson, *The Seasons*, 'Autumn', 575

CHAPTER XXXIII
(p. 162) Pope, *Epistle to a Lady*, 8
(p. 164) Cowper, *The Task*, VI.140–1

CHAPTER XXXIV
(p. 168) Shakespeare, *A Midsummer Night's Dream*,
      V.i.100

CHAPTER XXXV
(p. 178) Milton, *Paradise Lost*, IV.241
 'Flowers worthy of Paradise'

CHAPTER XXXVII
(p. 193) Shakespeare, *Hamlet*, I.iv.17

CHAPTER XXXIX
(p. 204) Milton, *Lycidas*, 63
(p. 205) No source identified.

CHAPTER XLI
(p. 216) Milton, *Paradise Lost*, VIII.618–9
      'with a smile that glowed
  Celestial rosy-red, Love's proper hue,'

CHAPTER XLIII
(p. 221) Milton, *Comus*, 262–4
  'But such a sacred and home-felt delight,
  Such sober certainty of waking bliss,
  I never heard till now.'

CHAPTER XLV
(p. 231) Addison, *Cato*, III.i.8
(p. 234) Milton, *Paradise Lost*, VII.22
  'Within the visible diurnal sphere.'

CHAPTER XLVIII
(p. 252) Rowe, *The Fair Penitent*, V.i.54
  'Spectatress of the mischief which she made.'

CHAPTER XLIX
(p. 258) Milton, *Paradise Lost*, IV.657–8
  'But wherefore all night long shine these? for whom
  This glorious sight, when sleep hath shut all eyes?

OTHER CONDUCT-BOOKS
BY HANNAH MORE

(This does not constitute a complete list of her works, which can be found in M. G. Jones, *Hannah More* (Cambridge: CUP, 1952) p. 274.)

Essays on Various Subjects, Principally Designed for Young Ladies (London: Cadell and Davies, 1777)

Thoughts on the Importance of the Manners of the Great (London: Cadell and Davies, 1788)

An Estimate of the Religion of the Fashionable World (London: Cadell and Davies, 1790)

Village Politics (London: Cadell and Davies, 1792)
Cheap Repository Tracts 1795–1798. For a complete list see G. H. Spinney, *The Bibliographical Society* (London, 1940)

Strictures on the Modern System of Female Education (London: Cadell and Davies, 1799)

Hints on Forming the Character of a Young Princess (London: Cadell and Davies, 180)

Practical Piety (London: Cadell and Davies, 1811)

Moral Sketches (London: Cadell and Davies, 1819)

A NOTE ON THE TEXT

The volume from which the present text is reprinted was produced in 1880 by James Blackwood and Co., London. It is only one of a large number of editions (I use the word here to cover both separate imprints and impressions from existing type) which appeared during the nineteenth century. It has not been possible to examine the full range, but those copies which are available demonstrate the sustained viability of the work over a very long period. There were no fewer than twelve editions published by the end of 1809. For comparison I have consulted an 1808 copy (probably a first edition) and a twelfth edition from 1809 held by the British Library; copies from 1813, 1826, 1837, 1838 and 1879 are also present there. The novel is included in the various collections of More's works in 1818, 1830, 1834 and 1853. Fifteen editions are recorded in the *National Union Catalog Pre-1956 Imprints* as having appeared in the USA between 1809 and 1887, ten in New York, four in Philadelphia and one in Cincinnati.

After the first edition in 1808, some alterations were made, the principal one being the addition of Chapter XXVII, a disquisition on the portrayal of clergymen in literature. Another was the result of a very acrimonious exchange of letters between More and the Pope's Vicar-General in England, Monsignor Joseph Berington (printed in William Roberts, *Memoirs of the Life and*

Correspondence of Mrs Hannah More (London, 1834) pp. 280–291). This concerned some ill-advised remarks about 'popery' to be found in X:46 of the present reprint. More agreed that her comments might be ambiguous (merely) and suggested the substitution of a full-stop for the semi-colon after the word 'humiliation'. Both alterations had been made by the twelfth edition in 1809. The reader will note that the semi-colon has been restored in the present edition, suggesting that the editor used an early 1809 copy, before the resolution of the dispute with Berington, but after the addition of Chapter XXVII. By 1880 spelling and punctuation has come into line with current usage and there are other minor changes of no great significance; we have here substantially the version that More finally approved in 1809.

M^{RS} HANNAH MORE.

From an original Picture by E. BIRD, *of Bristol, in the Possession of*
MESS^{RS} CADELL & DAVIES.

Engraved by J. Godby.

CŒLEBS

IN SEARCH OF

A WIFE.

ILLUSTRATED.

LONDON
JAMES BLACKWOOD & CO., LOVELL'S COURT,
PATERNOSTER ROW.

CONTENTS.

—◦—

CHAPTER XLII.

CHAPTER XLIII.

CHAPTER XLIV.

CHAPTER XLV.

CHAPTER XLVI.

CHAPTER XLVII.

CHAPTER XLVIII.

CHAPTER XLIX.

CŒLEBS IN SEARCH OF A WIFE.

Chapter I.

 HAVE been sometimes surprised, when in conversation I have been expressing my admiration of the character of Eve in her state of innocence, as drawn by our immortal poet, to hear objections raised by those, from whom of all critics I should have least expected it—the ladies. I confess, that, as the Sophia of Rousseau had her young imagination captivated by the character of Fenelon's Telemachus, so I early became enamoured of that of Milton's Eve. I never formed an idea of conjugal happiness, but my mind involuntarily adverted to the graces of that finished picture.

The ladies, in order to justify their censure, assert that Milton, a harsh domestic tyrant, must needs be a very inadequate judge, and of course a very unfair delineator, of female accomplishments. These fair cavillers draw their inference from premises, from which I have always been accustomed to deduce a directly contrary conclusion. They insist that it is highly derogatory from the dignity of the sex, that the poet should affirm, that it is the perfection of the character of a wife,

> To study household good,
> And good works in her husband to promote.

Now, according to my notion of ' household good,' which does not include one idea of drudgery or servility, but which involves a large and comprehensive scheme of excellence, I will venture to affirm that, let a woman know what she may, yet, if she knows not this, she is ignorant of the most indispensable, the most appropriate branch of female knowledge. Without it, however she may inspire admiration abroad, she will never excite esteem, nor of course durable affection at home, and will bring neither credit nor comfort to her ill-starred partner.

The domestic arrangements of such a woman as filled the capacious mind of the poet, resemble, if I may say it without profaneness, those of Providence, whose under-agent she is. Her wisdom is seen in its effects. Indeed, it is rather felt than seen. It is sensibly acknowledged in the peace, the happiness, the virtue of the component parts ; in the order, regularity, and beauty of the whole system, of which she is the moving spring.   The perfection of her character, as the divine poet intimates, does not arise from a prominent quality, or a showy talent, or a brilliant accomplishment, but it is the beautiful combination and result of them all.   Her excellences consist not so much in acts as in habits, in

> Those thousand decencies which daily flow
> From all her words and actions.

A description more calculated than any I ever met with to convey an idea of the purest conduct resulting from the best principles.   It gives an image of that tranquillity, smoothness, and quiet beauty, which is of the very essence of perfection in a wife ; while the happily chosen verb *flow* takes away any impression of dulness or stagnant torpor, which the *still* idea might otherwise suggest.

But the offence taken by the ladies against the uncourtly bard, is chiefly occasioned by his having presumed to intimate that conjugal obedience

> Is woman's highest honour and her praise.

This is so nice a point, that I, as a bachelor, dare only just hint, that on this delicate question, the poet has not gone an inch farther than the apostle.   Nay, Paul is still more uncivilly explicit than Milton.   If, however, I could hope to bring over to my side critics, who, being of the party, are too apt to prejudge the cause, I would point out to them that the supposed harshness of the observation is quite done away by the recollection, that this scrupled ' obedience ' is so far from implying degradation, that it is connected with the injunction to the woman, ' to promote good works ' in her husband ; an injunction surely inferring a degree of influence that raises her condition, and restores her to all the dignity of equality ; it makes her not only the associate, but the inspirer of his virtues.

But to return to the economical part of the character of Eve.   And here she exhibits a consummate specimen and beautiful model of domestic skill and elegance.   How exquisitely conceived is her reception and entertainment of Raphael !   How modest, and yet how dignified !   I am afraid I know some husbands who would have had to encounter very ungracious looks, not to say words, if they had brought home even an angel, *unexpectedly*, to dinner.   Not so our general mother :

> Her dispatchful looks,
> Her hospitable thoughts,—intent
> What choice to chuse for delicacy best,

all indicate not only the ' prompt ' but the cheerful ' obedience.' Though her repast consisted only of the fruits of paradise,

> Whatever earth, all-bearing mother, yields ;

yet of these, with a liberal hospitality,

> She gathers tribute large, and on the board
> Heaps with unsparing hand.

The finest modern lady need not disdain the arrangement of her
table, which was

> So contrived as not to mix
> Tastes not well joined, inelegant, but bring
> Taste after taste, upheld by kindliest change.

It must, however, I fear, be conceded, by the way, that this 'taste
after taste' rather holds out an encouragement to second courses.

When this unmatched trio had finished their repast, which, let it be
observed, before they tasted, Adam acknowledged that

> These bounties from our *Nourisher* are given,
> From whom all perfect good descends,

Milton, with great liberality to that sex against which he is accused of
much severity, obligingly permitted Eve to sit much longer after dinner
than most modern husbands would allow.   She had attentively listened
to all the historical and moral subjects so divinely discussed between
the first angel and the first man ; and perhaps there can scarcely be
found a more beautiful trait of a delicately attentive wife, than she
exhibits by withdrawing at the exact point of propriety.   She does not
retire in consequence of any look or gesture, any broad sign of impatience, much less any command or intimation of her husband ; but
with the ever watchful eye of vigilant affection and deep humility :

> When by his countenance he seemed
> Entering on thoughts abstruse,

instructed only by her own quick intuition of what was right and
delicate, she withdrew.   And here again how admirably does the poet
sustain her intellectual dignity, softened by a most tender stroke of
conjugal affection :

> Yet went she not, as not with such discourse
> Delighted, or not capable her ear
> Of what was high—such pleasure she reserved,
> Adam relating, she sole auditress.

On perusing, however, the tête-à-tête which her absence occasioned,
methinks I hear some sprightly lady, fresh from the Royal Institution,
express her wonder why Eve should be banished by her husband from
Raphael's fine lecture on astronomy which follows ; was not she as
capable as Adam of understanding all he said of

> Cycle and epicycle, orb on orb ?

If, however, the imaginary fair objector will take the trouble to read
to the end of the eighth book of this immortal work, it will raise in her
estimation both the poet and the heroine, when she contemplates the
just propriety of her being absent before Adam enters on the account
of the formation, beauty, and attractions of his wife, and of his own love
and admiration.   She will farther observe, in her progress through this
divine poem, that the author is so far from making Eve a mere domestic
drudge, an unpolished housewife, that he pays an invariable attention
even to external elegance, in his whole delineation, ascribing grace to

her steps, and dignity to her gesture.   He uniformly keeps up the same combination of intellectual worth and polished manners :

> For softness she, and sweet attractive grace.

And her husband, so far from a churlish insensibility to her perfections, politely calls her,

> Daughter of God and man, *accomplished* Eve.'

I will not, however, affirm that Adam, or even Milton, annexed to the term *accomplished* precisely the idea with which it is associated in the mind of a true modern-bred lady.

If it be objected to the poet's gallantry, that he remarks :

> Her beauty is excelled by manly grace,
> And wisdom, which alone is truly fair ;

let it be remembered that the observation proceeds from the lips of Eve herself, and thus adds to her other graces the crowning grace of humility.

But it is high time that I should proceed from my criticism to myself. The connexion, and of course the transition, will be found more natural than may appear, till developed by my slight narrative.

Chapter II.

AM a young man, not quite four-and-twenty, of an ancient and respectable family, and considerable estate in one of the northern counties.   Soon after I had completed my studies in the University of Edinburgh, my father fell into a lingering illness.   I attended him with an assiduity which was richly rewarded by the lessons of wisdom, and the example of piety, which I daily received from him.   After languishing about a year, I lost him, and in him the most affectionate father, the most enlightened companion, and the most Christian friend.

The grief of my mother was so poignant and so lasting, that I could never prevail on myself to leave her, even for the sake of attaining those advantages, and enjoying those pleasures, which may be reaped by a wider range of observation, by a more extended survey of the multifarious tastes, habits, pursuits, and characters of general society.   I felt, with Mr. Gray, that we can never have but one mother, and postponed from time to time the moment of leaving home.

I was her only child, and though it was now her sole remaining wish to see me happily married, yet I was desirous of first putting myself in a situation which might afford me a more extensive field of inquiry, before I ventured to take so irretrievable a step, a step which might perhaps affect my happiness in both worlds.   But time did not hang heavy on my hands ; if I had little society, I had many books.   My father had left me a copious library, and I had learnt from him to select whatever was most valuable in that best species of literature, which tends to form the principles, the understanding, the taste, and the character. My father had passed the early part of his life in the gay and busy world ; and our domestic society in the country had been occasionally enlivened by visits from some of his London friends, men of sense and learning, and some of them men of piety.

My mother, when she was in tolerable spirits, was now frequently describing the kind of woman she wished me to marry. ' I am so firmly persuaded, Charles,' would she kindly say, ' of the justness of your taste, and the rectitude of your principles, that I am not much afraid of your being misled by the captivating exterior of any woman who is greatly deficient either in sense or conduct ; but remember, my son, that there are many women against whose characters there lies nothing very objectionable, who are yet little calculated to taste or to communicate rational happiness. Do not indulge romantic ideas of superhuman excellence. Remember that the fairest creature is a fallen creature. Yet let not your standard be low. If it be absurd to expect perfection, it is not unreasonable to expect *consistency.* Do not suffer yourself to be caught by a shining quality, till you know it is not counteracted by the opposite defect. Be not taken in by strictness in one point, till you are assured there is no laxity in others. In character, as in architecture, proportion is beauty. The education of the present race of females is not very favourable to domestic happiness. For my own part, I call education, not that which smothers a woman with accomplishments, but that which tends to consolidate a firm and regular system of character ; that which tends to form a friend, a companion, and a wife. I call education, not that which is made up of the shreds and patches of useless arts, but that which inculcates principles, polishes taste, regulates temper, cultivates reason, subdues the passions, directs the feelings, habituates to reflection, trains to self-denial, and, more especially, that which refers all actions, feelings, sentiments, tastes, and passions to the love and fear of God.'

I had yet had little opportunity of contrasting the charms of my native place with the less wild and romantic beauties of the south. I was passionately fond of the scenery that surrounded me, which had never yet lost that power of pleasing which it is commonly imagined that novelty can alone confer.

The Priory, a handsome Gothic mansion, stands in the middle of a park, not extensive, but beautifully varied. Behind are lofty mountains, the feet of which are covered with wood, that descends almost to the house. On one side a narrow cultivated valley winds among the mountains ; the bright variegated tints of its meadows and cornfields, with here and there a little white cottage embosomed in trees, are finely contrasted with the awful and impassable fells which contain it.

An inconsiderable but impetuous river rushes from the mountains above, through this unadorned but enchanting little valley, and passes through the park at the distance of about a hundred yards from the house. The ground falls beautifully down to it ; and on the other side is a fine wood of birch overhanging the river, which is here crossed by a small rustic bridge. After being enlarged by many streams from the neighbouring hills, it runs about half a mile to the lake below, which from the front of the house is seen in full beauty. It is a noble expanse of water. The mountains that surround it are some of them covered with wood, some skirted with cultivation, some rocky and barren to the water's edge ; while the rugged summits of them all present every variety of fantastic outline. Towards the head of the lake a neat little village ornaments the banks, and wonderfully harmonises with the simple beauty of the scene. At an opening among the hills, a view is caught of the distant country, a wide vale richly wooded, adorned everywhere with towns, villages, and gentlemen's houses, and backed by sublime mountains, rivalling in height, though not in their broken and alpine forms, those that more immediately surround us.

While I was thus dividing my time between the enjoyment of this exquisite scenery, my books, the care of my affairs, my filial attentions, and my religious duties, I was suddenly deprived of my inestimable mother. She died the death of the righteous.

Addison has finely touched on the singular sort of delicate and re-fined tenderness of a father for a daughter ; but I am persuaded that there is no affection of the human heart more exquisitely pure than that which is felt by a grateful son towards a mother who fostered his infancy with fondness, watched over his childhood with anxiety, and his youth with an interest compounded of all that is tender, wise, and pious.

My retirement was now become solitude ; the former is, I believe, the best state for the mind of man, the latter almost the worst. In complete solitude the eye wants objects, the heart wants attachments, the understanding wants reciprocation. The character loses its tender-ness when it has nothing to love, its firmness when it has none to strengthen it, its sweetness when it has nothing to soothe it, its patience when it meets no contradiction, its humility when it is surrounded by dependants, and its delicacy in the conversation of the uninformed. Where the intercourse is very unequal, society is something worse than solitude.

I had naturally a keen relish for domestic happiness, and this pro-pensity had been cherished by what I had seen and enjoyed in my father's family. Home was the scene in which my imagination had pictured the only delights worthy of a rational, feeling, intellectual, immortal man :

sole bliss of Paradise
Which has survived the fall.

This inclination had been much increased by my father's turn of conversation. He often said to me, 'I know your domestic propen-sities ; and I know, therefore, that the whole colour of your future life will be, in a particular manner, determined by the turn of mind of the woman you may marry. Were you to live in the busy haunts of men, were you of any profession, or likely to be engaged in public life, though I would still counsel you to be equally careful in your choice, yet your happiness would not so immediately, so exclusively, depend on the in-dividual society of a woman, as that of a retired country gentleman must do. A man of sense who loves home, and lives at home, requires a wife who can and will be at half the expense of mind necessary for keeping up the cheerful, animated, elegant intercourse which forms so great a part of the bond of union between intellectual and well-bred persons. Had your mother been a woman of an uninformed, inelegant mind, virtuous and pious as she is, what abatement must there have been in the blessings of my lot! The *exhibiting*, the *displaying* wife may entertain your company, but it is only the informed, the refined, the cultivated woman who can entertain yourself; and I presume, whenever you marry, you will marry primarily for yourself, and not for your friends. You will want a COMPANION ; an ARTIST you may hire.

'But remember, Charles, that when I am insisting so much on mental delicacy, I am assuming that all is right in still more essential points. Do not be contented with this superstructure, till you have ascertained the solidity of the foundation. The ornaments which decorate do not support the edifice! Guarded as you are by Christian principles, and confirmed in virtuous habits, I trust you may safely look abroad into the world. Do not, however, irrevocably dispose of your affections till you have made the long-promised visit to my earliest, wisest, and best friend, Mr. Stanley. I am far from desiring that your friend should direct your choice—it is what even your father would not do; but he will be the most faithful and most disinterested of counsellors.'

I resolved now for a few months to leave the Priory, the seat of my ancestors, to make a tour not only to London, but to Stanley Grove in Hampshire, the residence of my father's friend—a visit I was about to make with him just before his last illness. He wished me to go alone, but I could not prevail on myself to desert his sick-bed for any scheme of amusement.

I began to long earnestly for the pleasures of conversation, pleasures which, in our small but social and select circle of cultivated friends, I had been accustomed to enjoy. I am aware that certain fine town-bred men would ridicule the bare mention of learned and polished conversation at a village in Westmoreland, or indeed at any place out of the precincts of the metropolis; just as a London physician, or lawyer, smiles superciliously at the suggested merits of a professional brother in a provincial town. Good sense, however, is of all countries, and even knowledge is not altogether a mere local advantage. These, and not the topics of the hour, furnish the best raw materials for working up an improving intercourse.

It must be confessed, however, as I have since found, that for giving a terseness and a polish to conversation ; for rubbing out prejudices ; for correcting egotism ; for keeping self-importance out of sight, if not curing it ; for bringing a man to condense what he has to say, if he intends to be listened to ; for accustoming him to endure opposition ; for teaching him not to think every man who differs from him in matters of taste a fool, and in politics a knave ; for cutting down harangues ; for guarding him from producing as novelties and inventions what has been said a thousand times ; for quickness of allusion, which brings the idea before you without detail or quotation—nothing is equal to the miscellaneous society of London. The advantages, too, which it possesses, in being the seat of the court, the parliament, and the courts of law, as well as the common centre of arts and talents of every kind—all these raise it above every other scene of intellectual improvement, or colloquial pleasure, perhaps in the whole world.

But this was only the secondary motive of my intended migration. I connected with it the hope that, in a more extended survey, I might be more likely to select a deserving companion for life. ' In such a companion,' said I, as I drove along in my postchaise, ' I do not want a Helen, a Saint Cecilia, or a Madame Dacier ; yet she must be elegant, or I should not love her ; sensible, or I should not respect her ; prudent, or I should not confide in her ; well informed, or she could not educate my children ; well-bred, or she could not entertain my friends ; *consistent*, or I should offend the shade of my mother : pious, or I should not be happy with her, because the prime comfort in a companion for life is the delightful hope that she will be a companion for eternity.'

After this soliloquy, I was frightened to reflect that so much was requisite ; and yet, when I began to consider in which article I could make any abatement, I was willing to persuade myself that my requisitions were moderate.

Chapter III.

HAD occasionally visited two or three families in our own country, who were said to make a very genteel appearance on narrow fortunes. As I was known not to consider money as a principal consideration, it had often been intimated to me what excellent wives the daughters of these families would make, because on a very slender allowance their appearance was as elegant as that of women of ten times their expectations. I translated this respectable appearance into a language not the most favourable, as I instantly inferred, and afterwards was convinced, that this personal figure was made by the sacrifice of their whole time to those decorations which procured them credit, by putting their outward figure on a par with the most affluent. If a girl with a thousand pounds rivals in her dress one with ten thousand, is it not obvious, that not only all her time must be employed, but all her money devoted to this one object? Nothing but the clippings and parings from her personal adornments could enable her to supply the demands of charity ; and these sacrifices, it is evident, she is not disposed to make.

Another inducement suggested to me was, that these young ladies would make the better wives, because they had never been corrupted by the expensive pleasures of London, and had not been spoiled by the gay scenes of dissipation which it afforded. This argument would have weighed powerfully with me, had I not observed, that they never abstained from any amusement in the country, that came within their reach.

I naturally inferred, that she who eagerly grasped at every petty provincial dissipation, would with increased alacrity have plunged into the more alluring gaieties of the metropolis, had it been in her power. I thought she had even less apology to plead than the town lady ; the fault was equal, while the temptation was less : and she who was as dissipated as her limited bounds permitted, where there was little to attract, would, I feared, be as dissipated as she possibly could be, when her temptations were multiplied, and her facilities increased.

I had met with several young ladies of a higher description, daughters of our country gentlemen, a class which furnishes a number of valuable and elegant women. Some of these, whom I knew, seemed unexceptionable in manner and in mind. They had seen something of the world, without having been spoiled by it, had read with advantage, and acquitted themselves well in the duties which they had been called to practise. But I was withheld from cultivating that degree of intimacy which would have enabled me to take an exact measure of their minds, by the injunction of my father, that I would never attach myself to any woman till I had seen and consulted Mr. Stanley. This direction, which, like all his wishes, was a law to me, operated as a sort of sedative in the slight intercourse I had had with ladies ; and, resolving to postpone all such intimacy as might have led to attachment, I did not allow myself to come near enough to feel with interest, or to judge with decision.

As soon as I got to town, I visited some of my father's friends. I was kindly received, for his sake, and at their houses soon enlarged the sphere of my acquaintance. I was concerned to remark, that two or three gentlemen, whom I had observed to be very regular in their attendance on public worship in the country, seldom went to church in London ; in the afternoon, never. 'Religion,' they said, by way of apology, 'was entirely a thing of example ; it was of great political importance ; society was held together by the restraints it imposed on the lower orders. When they were in the country, it was highly proper that their tenants and workmen should have the benefit of their example, but in London the case was different. Where there were so many churches, no one knew whether you went or not ; and where no scandal was given, no harm was done.' As this was a logic which had not found its way into my father's religion, I was not convinced by it. I remember Mr. Burke, speaking of the English, who were so humane at home, and whom he unjustly accused of wanting humanity in India, says, 'that the humanity of Britain is a humanity of points and parallels.' Surely the religion of the gentlemen in question is not less a geographical distinction.

This error, I conceive, arises from religion being too much considered as a mere institution of decorum, of convention, of society, and not as an institution founded on the condition of human nature, a covenant of mercy for repairing the evils which sin has produced. It springs from the want of a conviction that Christianity is an individual as well as general concern : that religion is a personal thing, previous to its being a matter of example ; that a man is not infallibly saved or lost as a portion of any family, or any church, or any community ; but that, as he is individually responsible, he must be individually brought to a deep and humbling sense of his own personal wants, without taking any

2

refuge in the piety he may see around him, of which he will have no benefit, if he be no partaker.

I regretted, even for inferior reasons, the little distinction which was paid to this sacred day. To say nothing of the elevating views which the soul acquires from devoting itself to its proper object, the man of business, methinks, should rejoice in its return ; the politician should welcome its appearance, not only as a rest from anxiety and labour, but as an occasion of cooling and quieting the mind, of softening its irritation, of allaying its ferment, and thus restoring the repaired faculties and invigorated spirits to the demands of the succeeding week, in a frame of increased aptitude for meeting its difficulties and encountering its duties.

The first person whom I visited was a good-natured friendly man, whom I had occasionally seen in the North. As I had no reason to believe that he was religious, in the true sense of the word, I had no intention of looking for a wife in his family. I, however, thought it not amiss to associate a little with persons of different descriptions, that by a wider range I might learn to correct my general judgment, as well as to guide my particular pursuit. Nothing, it is true, would tempt me to select a woman on whose pious dispositions I could not form a reasonable dependence ; yet to come at the reality of those dispositions was no easy matter.

I had heard my father remark, that he had, more than once, known a right-minded girl, who seemed to have been first taught of Heaven, and afterwards supported in her Christian course under almost every human disadvantage ; who boldly, but meekly, maintained her own principles, under all the hourly temptations and oppositions of a worldly and irreligious family, and who had given the best evidence of her piety towards God, by her patient forbearance towards her erring friends. Such women had made admirable wives when they were afterwards transplanted into families where their virtues were understood, and their piety cherished. While, on the other hand, he had known others, who, accustomed from childhood to the sober habits of family religion, under pious but injudicious parents, had fallen in mechanically with the domestic practices, without having ever been instructed in Christian principles, or having ever manifested any religious tendencies. The implantation of a new principle never having been inculcated, the religious habit has degenerated into a mere form, the parents acting as if they thought that religion must come by nature or infection in a religious family. These girls, having never had their own hearts impressed, nor their own characters distinctly considered nor individually cultivated, but being taken out as a portion from the mass, have afterwards taken the cast and colour of any society into which they have happened to be thrown ; and they who before had lived religiously with the religious, have afterwards assimilated with the gay and dissipated, when thus thrown into their company, as cordially as if they had never been habituated to better things.

At dinner there appeared two pretty-looking young ladies, daughters of my friend, who had been some time a widower. I placed myself between them, for the purpose of prying a little into their minds, while the rest of the company were conversing on indifferent subjects. Having formerly heard this gentleman's deceased wife extolled as the mirror of managers, and the arrangements of his table highly commended, I was surprised to see it so ill appointed, and everything wearing marks of palpable inelegance. Though no epicure, I could not forbear observing that many of the dishes were out of season, ill-chosen, and ill-dressed.

While I was puzzling my head for a solution, I recollected that I had lately read in a most respectable periodical work, a paper (composed, I believe, however, by a raw recruit of that well-disciplined corps) which insisted that nothing tended to make ladies so useless and inefficient in the *ménage* as the study of the dead languages. I jumped to the conclusion, and was in an instant persuaded that my young hostesses must not only be perfect mistresses of Latin, but the *tout ensemble* was so ill arranged as to induce me to give them full credit for Greek also.

Finding, therefore, that my appetite was balked, I took comfort in the certainty that my understanding would be well regaled : and after secretly regretting that learning should so effectually destroy usefulness, I was resolved to derive intellectual comfort from this too classical repast. Turning suddenly to the eldest lady, I asked her at once if she did not think Virgil the finest poet in the world. She blushed, and thus confirmed me in the opinion that her modesty was equal to her erudition. I repeated my question with a little circumlocution. She stared, and said she had never heard of the person I mentioned, but that she had read 'Tears of Sensibility,' and 'Rosa Matilda,' and 'Sympathy of Souls,' and 'Too Civil by Half,' and the 'Sorrows of Werter,' and the 'Stranger,' and the 'Orphans of Snowden.'

'Yes, sir,' joined in the younger sister, who did not rise to so high a pitch of literature, 'and we have read " Perfidy Punished," and " Jemmy and Jenny Jessamy," and the " Fortunate Footman," and the " Illustrious Chambermaid."' I blushed and stared, in my turn ; and here the conversation, through the difficulty of our being intelligible to each other, dropped ; and I am persuaded that I sunk much lower in their esteem for not being acquainted with their favourite authors, than they did in mine for having never heard of Virgil.

I arose from the table with a full conviction that it is very possible for a woman to be totally ignorant of the ordinary but indispensable duties of common life, without knowing one word of Latin ; and that her being a bad companion is no infallible proof of her being a good economist.

I am afraid the poor father saw something of my disappointment in my countenance, for when we were alone in the evening, he observed that a heavy addition to his other causes of regret for the loss of his wife, was her excellent management of his family. I found afterwards that, though she had brought him a great fortune, she had had a very low education. Her father, a coarse country esquire, to whom the pleasures of the table were the only pleasures for which he had any relish, had no other ambition for his daughter but that she should be the most famous housewife in the country. He gloried in her culinary perfections, which he understood ; of the deficiencies of her mind he had not the least perception. Money and good eating, he owned, were

the only things in life which had a real intrinsic value ; the value of
all other things, he declared, existed in the imagination only.

The poor lady, when she became a mother, and was brought out into
the world, felt keenly the deficiencies of her own education. The dread
of Scylla, as is usual, wrecked her on Charybdis. Her first resolution,
as soon as she had daughters, was, that they should *learn everything*.
All the masters who teach things of little intrinsic use were extravagantly paid for supernumerary attendance ; and as no one in the family
was capable of judging of their improvements, their progress was but
slow. Though they were taught much, they learnt but little, even of
these unnecessary things, and of things necessary they learnt nothing.
Their well-intentioned mother was not aware that her daughters' education was almost as much calculated to gratify the senses, though in
a different way, and with more apparent refinement, as her own had
been ; and that *mind* is left nearly as much out of the question in
making an ordinary artist as in making a good cook.

Chapter IV.

ROM my fondness for conversation, my imagination had been
early fired with Dr. Johnson's remark that there is no pleasure
on earth comparable to the *fine full flow of London talk*. I,
who, since I had quitted college, had seldom had my mind
refreshed but with the petty rills and penurious streams of knowledge
which country society afforded, now expected to meet it in a strong
and rapid current, fertilising wherever it flowed, producing in abundance the rich fruits of argument, and the gay flowers of rhetoric. I
looked for an uninterrupted course of profit and delight. I flattered
myself that every dinner would add to my stock of images ; that every
debate would clear up some difficulty, every discussion elucidate some
truth ; that every allusion would be purely classical, every sentence
abound with instruction, and every period be pointed with wit.

On the tiptoe of expectation, I went to dine with Sir John Belfield,
in Cavendish Square. I looked at my watch fifty times ; I thought it
would never be six o'clock. I did not care to show my country breeding
by going too early, to incommode my friend ; nor my town breeding by
going too late, and spoiling his dinner. Sir John is a valuable, elegant-
minded man, and, next to Mr. Stanley, stood highest in my father's
esteem, for his mental accomplishments and correct morals. As I
knew he was remarkable for assembling at his table men of sense,
taste, and learning, my expectations of pleasure were very high. ' Here,
at least,' said I, as I heard the name of one clever man announced after
another, ' here, at least, I cannot fail to find

The feast of reason and the flow of soul :

here, at least, all the energies of my mind will be brought into exercise.
From this society I shall carry away documents for the improvement

of my taste ; I shall treasure up hints to enrich my understanding, and collect aphorisms for the conduct of life.'

At first there was no fair opportunity to introduce any conversation beyond the topics of the day, and to those, it must be confessed, this eventful period gives a new and powerful interest. I should have been much pleased to have had my country politics rectified, and any prejudices which I might have contracted removed or softened, could the discussion have been carried on without the frequent interruption of the youngest man in the company. This gentleman broke in on every remark by descanting successively on the merits of the various dishes ; and, if it be true that experience only can determine the judgment, he gave proof of that best right to peremptory decision by not trusting to delusive theory, but by actually eating of every dish at table.

His animadversions were uttered with the gravity of a German philosopher, and the science of a French cook. If any of his opinions happened to be controverted, he quoted, in confirmation of his own judgment, *l'Almanac des Gourmands*, which he assured us was the most valuable work that had appeared in France since the revolution. The author of this book he seemed to consider of as high authority in the science of eating, as Coke or Hale in that of jurisprudence, or Quintilian in the art of criticism. To the credit of the company, however, be it spoken, he had the whole of this topic to himself. The rest of the party were, in general, of quite a different calibre, and as little acquainted with his favourite author as he probably was with theirs.

The lady of the house was perfectly amiable and well bred. Her dinner was excellent, and everything about her had an air of elegance and splendour. Of course, she completely escaped the disgrace of being thought a scholar, but not the suspicion of having a very good taste. I longed for the removal of the cloth, and was eagerly anticipating the pleasure and improvement which awaited me.

As soon as the servants were beginning to withdraw, we got into a sort of attitude of conversation—all except the eulogist of *l'Almanac des Gourmands*, who, wrapping himself up in the comfortable consciousness of his own superior judgment, and a little piqued that he had found neither support nor opposition (the next best thing 'to a professed talker), seemed to have a perfect indifference to all topics, except that on which he had shown so much eloquence with so little effect.

The last tray was now carried out, the last lingering servant had retired. I was beginning to listen with all my powers of attention to an ingenious gentleman who was about to give an interesting account of Egypt, where he had spent a year, and from whence he was lately returned. He was just got to the catacombs,

> when on a sudden open fly,
> With impetuous recoil and jarring sound,

the mahogany folding-doors, and in at once, struggling who should be first, rushed half a dozen children, lovely, fresh, gay, and noisy. This sudden and violent irruption of the pretty barbarians necessarily caused a total interruption of conversation. The sprightly creatures ran round the table to choose where they would sit. At length this great difficulty of courts and cabinets, the *choice of places*, was settled. The little things were jostled in between the ladies, who all contended who should get possession of the *little beauties*. One was in raptures with the rosy cheeks of a sweet girl she held in her lap. A second exclaimed aloud at the beautiful lace with which the frock of another was trimmed, and which she was sure mamma had given her for being good : a profitable, and doubtless a lasting and inseparable, association was thus formed in the child's mind between lace and goodness. A third cried out, ' Look at the pretty angel !—do but observe—her bracelets are as blue as her eyes. Did you ever see such a match ?' ' Surely, Lady Belfield,' cried a fourth, ' you carried the eyes to the shop, or there must have been a shade of difference.' I myself, who am passionately fond of children, eyed the sweet little rebels with complacency, notwithstanding the unseasonableness of their interruption.

At last, when they were all disposed of, I resumed my inquiries about the resting-place of the mummies ; but the grand dispute who should have oranges, and who should have almonds and raisins, soon raised such a clamour that it was impossible to hear my Egyptian friend. This great contest was, however, at length settled, and I was returning to the antiquities of Memphis, when the important point who should have red wine, and who should have white, who should have half a glass, and who a whole one, set us again in an uproar. Sir John was visibly uneasy, and commanded silence. During this interval of peace, I gave up the catacombs, and took refuge in the pyramids. But I had no sooner proposed my question about the serpent said to be found in one of them, than the son and heir, a fine little fellow just six years old, reaching out his arm to dart an apple across the table at his sister, roguishly intending to overset her glass, unluckily overthrew his own, brimful of port wine. The whole contents were discharged on the elegant drapery of a white-robed nymph.

All was now agitation and distress, and disturbance and confusion ; the gentlemen ringing for napkins, the ladies assisting the dripping fair one ; each vying with the other who should recommend the most approved specific for getting out the stain of red wine, and comforting the sufferer by stories of similar misfortunes. The poor little culprit was dismissed, and all difficulties and disasters seemed at last surmounted. But you cannot heat up again an interest which has been so often cooled. The thread of conversation had been so frequently broken that I despaired of seeing it tied together again. I sorrowfully gave up catacombs, pyramids, and serpent, and was obliged to content myself with a little desultory chat with my next neighbour, sorry and disappointed to glean only a few scattered ears where I had expected so abundant a harvest ; and the day from which I had promised myself so much benefit and delight passed away, with a very slender acquisition of either.

Chapter V.

WENT almost immediately after, at the invitation of Mr. Ranby, to pass a few days at his villa at Hampstead. Mr. and Mrs. Ranby were esteemed pious persons, but, having risen to great affluence by a sudden turn of fortune in a commercial engagement, they had a little self-sufficiency, and not a little disposition to ascribe an undue importance to wealth. This I should have thought more pardonable under their circumstances, had I not expected that religion would in this respect have more than supplied the deficiencies of education. Their religion, however, consisted almost exclusively in a disproportionate zeal for a very few doctrines. And though they were far from being immoral in their own practice, yet in their discourse they affected to undervalue morality.

This was, indeed, more particularly the case with the lady, whose chief object of discourse seemed to be to convince me of her great superiority to her husband in polemical skill. Her chaste conversation certainly was not coupled with fear. In one respect she was the very reverse of those Pharisees who were scrupulously exact about their petty observances. Mrs. Ranby was, on the contrary, anxious about a very few important particulars, and exonerated herself from the necessity of all inferior attentions. She was strongly attached to one or two preachers, and discovered little candour for all others, or for those who attended them. Nay, she somewhat doubted of the soundness of the faith of her friends and acquaintance who would not incur great inconvenience to attend one or other of her favourites.

Mrs. Ranby's table was 'more than hospitably good.' There was not the least suspicion of Latin here. The eulogist of female ignorance might have dined in comfortable security against the intrusion and vanity of erudition. She had three daughters, not unpleasing young women. But I was much concerned to observe, that they were not only dressed to the very extremity of the fashion, but their drapery was as transparent, as short, and as scanty, there was as sedulous a disclosure of their persons, and as great a redundancy of ornaments, as I had seen in the gayest circles.

'Expect not perfection,' said my good mother, 'but look for *consistency.*' This principle my parents had not only taught me in the closet, but had illustrated by their deportment in the family and in the world. They observed a uniform correctness in their general demeanour. They were not over-anxious about character for its own sake, but they were tenderly vigilant not to bring any reproach on the Christian name by imprudence, negligence, or inconsistency, even in small things. 'Custom,' said my mother, 'can never alter the immutable nature of right ; fashion can never justify any practice which is improper in itself : and to dress indecently is as great an offence against purity and modesty, when it is the fashion, as when it is obsolete. There should be a line of demarcation somewhere. In the

article of dress and appearance, Christian mothers should make a
stand. They should not be so unreasonable as to expect that a young
girl will of herself have courage to oppose the united temptations of
fashion without, and the secret prevalence of corruption within ; and
authority should be called in where admonition fails.'

The conversation after dinner took a religious turn. Mrs. Ranby
was not unacquainted with the subject, and expressed herself with energy
on many serious points. I could have been glad, however, to have
seen her views a little more practical, and her spirit a little less cen-
sorious. I saw she took the lead in debate, and that Mr. Ranby
submitted to act as subaltern ; but whether his meekness was the
effect of piety or fear, I could not at that time determine. She protested vehemently against all dissipation ; in which I cordially joined
her, though I hope with something less intemperance of manner, and
less acrimony against those who pursued it. I began, however, to think
that her faults arose chiefly from a bad judgment, and an ill-regulated
mind. In many respects she seemed well-intentioned, though her
language was a little debased by coarseness, and not a little disfigured
by asperity.

I was sorry to observe that the young ladies not only took no part in
the conversation, but that they did not even seem to know what was
going on ; and I must confess, the *manner* in which it was conducted
was not calculated to make the subject interesting. The girls sat
jogging and whispering each other, and got away as fast as they
could.

As soon as they were withdrawn—' There, sir,' said the mother, ' are
three girls who will make excellent wives. They never were at a ball
or play in their lives ; and yet, though I say it, who should not say it,
they are as highly accomplished as any ladies at St. James's.' I cordially approved the former part of her assertion, and bowed in silence
to the latter.

I took this opportunity of inquiring what had been her mode of
religious instruction for her daughters ; but though I put the question
with much caution and deference, she looked displeased, and said she
did not think it necessary to do a great deal in that way ; all these
things must come from above ; it was not human endeavours, but
divine grace, which made Christians. I observed, that the truth
appeared to be, that divine grace, blessing human endeavours, seemed
most likely to accomplish that great end. She replied that experience
was not on my side, for that the children of religious parents were not
always religious. I allowed that it was too true. I knew she drew her
instances from two or three of her own friends, who, while they discovered much earnestness about their own spiritual interests, had
almost totally neglected the religious cultivation of their children ; the
daughters, in particular, had been suffered to follow their own devices,
and to waste their days in company of their own chusing, and in the
most frivolous manner. ' What do ye more than others ?' is an interrogation which this negligence has frequently suggested. Nay, professing serious piety, if ye do not more than those who profess it not,
ye do less.

I took the liberty to remark, that though there was no such thing as hereditary holiness, no entail of goodness, yet the Almighty had promised in the Scriptures many blessings to the offspring of the righteous. He never meant, however, that religion was to be transferred arbitrarily like an heirloom ; but the promise was accompanied with conditions and injunctions. The directions were express and frequent, to inculcate early and late the great truths of religion ; nay, it was enforced with all the minuteness of detail, ' precept upon precept, line upon line, here a little, and there a little '—at all times and seasons, ' walking by the way, and sitting in the house.' I hazarded the assertion, that it would generally be found that where the children of pious parents turned out ill, there had been some mistake, some neglect, or some fault, on the part of the parents ; that they had not used the right methods. I observed, that I thought it did not at all derogate from the sovereignty of the Almighty, that He appointed certain means to accomplish certain ends ; and that the adopting these, in conformity to His appointment, and dependence on His blessing, seemed to be one of the cases in which we should prove our faith by our obedience.

I found I had gone too far. She said, with some warmth, that she was not wanting in any duty to her daughters ; she set them a good example, and she prayed daily for their conversion. I highly commended her for both, but risked the observation, ' that praying without instilling principles, might be as inefficacious as instruction without prayer. That it was like a husbandman who should expect that praying for sunshine should produce a crop of corn in a field where not one grain had been sown. God, indeed, could effect this, but He does not do it ; and the means being of His own appointment, His omnipotence is not less exerted, by His directing certain effects to follow certain causes, than it would be by any arbitrary act.' As it was evident that she did not chuse to quarrel with me, she contented herself with saying coldly, that she perceived I was a *legalist*, and had but a low view of divine things.

At tea I found the young ladies took no more interest in the conversation than they had done at dinner, but sat whispering and laughing, and netting white silk gloves till they were summoned to the harpsichord. Despairing of getting on with them in company, I proposed a walk in the garden. I now found them as willing to talk, as destitute of anything to say. Their conversation was vapid and frivolous. They laid great stress on small things. They seemed to have no shades in their understanding, but used the strongest terms for the commonest occasions, and admiration was excited by things hardly worthy to command attention. They were extremely glad, and extremely sorry, on subjects not calculated to excite affections of any kind. They were animated about trifles, and indifferent on things of importance. They were, I must confess, frank and good-natured, but it was evident, that as they were too open to have anything to conceal, so they were too uninformed to have anything to produce ; and I was resolved not to risk my happiness with a woman who could not contribute her full share towards spending a wet winter cheerfully in the country.

The next day, all the hours from breakfast to dinner were devoted to the harp. I had the vanity to think that this sacrifice of time was made in compliment to me, as I had professed to like music ; till I found that all their mornings were spent in the same manner, and the only fruit of their education, which seemed to be used to any purpose, was, that after their family devotions in the evening, they sung and played a hymn. This was almost the only sign they gave of intellectual or spiritual life. They attended morning prayers, if they were dressed before the bell rang. One morning, when they did not appear till late, they were reproved by their father. Mrs. Ranby said, 'she should be more angry with them for their irregularity, were it not that Mr. Ranby obstinately persisted in reading a printed form, which she was persuaded could not do anybody much good.' The poor man, who was really well disposed, very properly defended himself by saying, that he hoped his own heart went along with every word he read ; and as to his family, he thought it much more beneficial for them to join in an excellent composition of a judicious divine, than to attend to any such crude rhapsody as he should be able to produce, whose education had not qualified him to lead the devotions of others. I had never heard him venture to make use of his understanding before ; and I continued to find it much better than I had at first given him credit for. The lady observed, with some asperity, that where there were *gifts* and *graces*, it superseded the necessity of learning.

In vindication of my own good breeding, I should observe that, in my little debates with Mrs. Ranby, to which I was always challenged by her, I never lost sight of that becoming example of the son of Cato, who, when about to deliver sentiments which might be thought too assuming in so young a man, introduced his admonitions with this modest preface :

Remember what our *father* oft has taught us.

I, without quoting the son of the sage of Utica, constantly adduced the paternal authority for opinions which might savour too much of arrogance without such a sanction.

I observed, in the course of my visit, that self-denial made no part of Mrs. Ranby's religious plan. She fancied, I believe, that it savoured of works, and of works she was evidently afraid. She talked as if activity were useless, and exertion unnecessary, and as if, like inanimate matter, we had nothing to do but to sit still and be shone upon.

I assured her that though I depended on the mercy of God, through the merits of His Son, for salvation, as entirely as she could do, yet I thought that Almighty grace, so far from setting aside diligent exertion, was the principle which promoted it. That salvation is in no part of Scripture represented as attainable by the indolent Christian, if I might couple such contradictory terms. That I had been often awfully struck with the plain declarations, 'That the kingdom of heaven suffereth violence' —' Strive to enter in at the strait gate '—' Whatsover thy hand findeth to do, do it with all thy might '—' Give diligence to make your calling sure '—' Work out your own salvation.' To this labour, this watchfulness, this sedulity of endeavour, the crown of life is expressly promised, and salvation is not less the free gift of God, because He has annexed certain conditions to our obtaining it.

The more I argued, the more I found my reputation decline ; yet to argue, she compelled me. I really believe she was sincere, but she was ill-informed, governed by feelings and impulses, rather than by the plain express rule of Scripture. It was not that she did not read Scripture, but she interpreted it her own way ; built opinions on in-sulated texts ; did not compare Scripture with Scripture, except as it concurred to strengthen her bias. She considered with a dispropor-tionate fondness those passages which supported her preconceived opinions, instead of being uniformly governed by the general tenor and spirit of the sacred page. She had far less reverence for the perceptive than for the doctrinal parts, because she did not sufficiently consider faith as an operative influential principle ; nor did she conceive that the sublimest doctrines involve deep practical consequences. She did not consider the government of the tongue, nor the command of her passions, as forming any material part of the Christian character. Her zeal was fiery, because her temper was so ; and her charity was cold, because it was an expensive propensity to keep warm. Among the perfections of the Redeemer's character, she did not consider His being 'meek and lowly' as an example, the influence of which was to extend to her. She considered it indeed as *admirable*, but not as *imitable;* a distinction she was very apt to make in all her practical dissertations, and in her interpretation of Scripture.

In the evening Mrs. Ranby was lamenting, in general and rather customary terms, her own exceeding sinfulness. Mr. Ranby said, ' You accuse yourself rather too heavily, my dear ; you have sins, to be sure.' 'And pray what sins have I, Mr. Ranby ?' said she, turning upon him with so much quickness that the poor man started. ' Nay,' said he meekly, 'I did not mean to offend you—so far from it that, hearing you condemn yourself so grievously, I intended to comfort you, and to say that, except a few faults——' 'And pray what faults ?' in-terrupted she, continuing to speak, however, lest he should catch an interval to tell them. 'I defy you, Mr. Ranby, to produce one.' ' My dear,' replied he, ' as you charged yourself with all, I thought it would be letting you off cheaply by naming only two or three, such as——' Here, fearing matters would go too far, I interposed, and, softening things as much as I could for the lady, said, ' I conceived that Mr. Ranby meant that, though she partook of the general corruption——' Here Ranby, interrupting me with more spirit than I thought he pos-sessed, said, ' General corruption, sir, must be the source of particular corruption. I did not mean that my wife was worse than other women.' ' Worse, Mr. Ranby, worse ?' cried she. Ranby, for the first time in his life, not minding her, went on, ' As she is always insisting that the whole species is corrupt, she cannot help allowing that she herself has not quite escaped the infection. Now, to be a sinner in the gross, and a saint in the detail—that is, to have all sins, and no faults—is a thing I do not quite comprehend.'

After he had left the room, which he did as the shortest way of allaying the storm, she apologised for him, said ' he was a well-meaning man, and acted up to the little light he had ;' but added, 'that he was unacquainted with religious feelings, and knew little of the nature of conversion.'

Mrs. Ranby, I found, seems to consider Christianity as a kind of freemasonry, and therefore thinks it superfluous to speak on serious subjects to any but the initiated. If they do not *return the sign*, she gives them up as blind and dead. She thinks she can only make herself intelligible to those to whom certain peculiar phrases are familiar ; and though her friends may be correct, devout, and both doctrinally and practically pious, yet if they cannot catch a certain mystic meaning, if there is not a sympathy of intelligence between her and them, if they do not fully conceive of impressions, and cannot respond to mysterious communications, she holds them unworthy of intercourse with her. She does not so much insist on high moral excellence as the criterion of their worth, as on their own account of their internal feelings.

She holds very cheap that gradual growth in piety which is, in reality, no less the effect of divine grace than those instantaneous conversions which she believes to be so common. 'She cannot be persuaded that, of every advance in piety, of every improvement in virtue, of every illumination of the understanding, of every amendment in the heart, of every rectification of the will, the Spirit of God is no less the author, because it is progressive, than if it were sudden. It is true, Omnipotence can, when He pleases, still produce these instantaneous effects, as He has sometimes done ; but as it is not his established or common mode of operation, it seems vain and rash presumptuously to wait for these miraculous interferences. An implicit dependence, however, on such interferences is certainly more gratifying to the genius of enthusiasm than the anxious vigilance, the fervent prayer, the daily struggle, the sometimes scarcely perceptible though constant progress, of the sober-minded Christian. Such a Christian is fully aware that his heart requires as much watching in the more advanced as in the earliest stages of his religious course. He is cheerful in a well-grounded hope, and looks not for ecstasies till that hope be swallowed up in fruition. Thankful if he feel in his heart a growing love to God, and an increasing submission to His will, though he is unconscious of visions, and unacquainted with any revelation but that which God has made in His word. He remembers, and he derives consolation from the remembrance, that his Saviour, in His most gracious and soothing invitation to the 'heavy laden,' has mercifully promised 'rest,' but he has nowhere promised rapture.

Chapter VI.

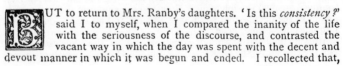BUT to return to Mrs. Ranby's daughters. 'Is this *consistency ?*' said I to myself, when I compared the inanity of the life with the seriousness of the discourse, and contrasted the vacant way in which the day was spent with the decent and devout manner in which it was begun and ended. I recollected that,

under the early though imperfect sacred institution, the fire of the morning and evening sacrifice was never suffered to be extinguished during the day.

Though Mrs. Ranby would have thought it a little heathenish to have had her daughters instructed in polite literature, and to have filled a leisure hour in reading to her a useful book that was not professedly religious, she felt no compunction at their waste of time, or the trifling pursuits in which the day was suffered to spend itself. The pianoforte, when they were weary of the harp, copying some indifferent drawings, gilding a set of flower-pots, and netting white gloves and veils, seemed to fill up the whole business of these immortal beings, of these Christians, for whom it had been solemnly engaged that they should manfully fight under Christ's banner.

On a farther acquaintance, I was much more inclined to lay the blame on their education than their dispositions. I found them not only good-humoured, but charitably disposed ; but their charities were small and casual, often ill-applied, and always without a plan. They knew nothing of the state, character, or wants of the neighbouring poor ; and it had never been pointed out to them that the instruction of the young and ignorant made any part of the duty of the rich towards them.

When I once ventured to drop a hint on the subject to Mrs. Ranby, she dryly said there were many other ways of doing good to the poor besides exposing her daughters to the probability of catching diseases, and the certainty of getting dirt by such visits. Her subscription was never wanting when she was *quite sure* that the object was deserving. As I suspected that she a little overrated her own charity, I could not forbear observing that I did not think it demanded a combination of all the virtues to entitle a poor sick wretch to a dinner. And though I durst not quote so light an authority as Hamlet to her, I could not help saying to myself, ' Give every man his due, and who shall 'scape whipping ?' Oh ! if God dealt so rigidly with us—if He waited to bestow His ordinary blessings till we were good enough to deserve them, who would be clothed ? who would be fed ? who would have a roof to shelter him ?

It was not that she gave nothing away, but she had a great dislike to relieve any but those of her own religious persuasion. Though her Redeemer laid down His life for all people, nations, and languages, she will only lay down her money for a very limited number of a very limited class. To be religious is not claim sufficient on her bounty ; they must be religious in a particular way.

The Miss Ranbys had not been habituated to make any systematic provision for regular charity, or for any of those accidental calamities for which the purse of the affluent should always be provided, and, being very expensive in their persons, they had often not a sixpence to bestow when the most deserving case presented itself. This must frequently happen where there is no specific fund for charity, which should be included in the general arrangement of expenses, and the exercise of benevolence not be left to depend on the accidental state of the purse. If no new trinket happened to be wanted, these young ladies were liberal to any application, though always without judging of its merits by their own eyes and ears. But if there was a competition between a sick family and a new brooch, the brooch was sure to carry the day. This would not have been the case had they been habituated to visit themselves the abodes of penury and woe. Their flexible young hearts would have been wrought upon by the actual sight of miseries, the impression of which was feeble when it reached their ears at a distance, surrounded as they were with all the softnesses and accommodations of luxurious life. 'They would do what they could ; they hoped it was not so bad as was represented.' They fell into the usual way of pacifying their consciences by their regrets, and brought themselves to believe that their sympathy with the suffering was an atonement for their not relieving it.

I observed with concern during my visit how little the Christian temper seemed to be considered as a part of the Christian religion. This appeared in the daily concerns of this high professor. An opinion contradicted, a person of different religious views commended, the smallest opposition to her will, the intrusion of an unseasonable visitor, even an imperfection in the dressing of some dish at table—such trifles not only discomposed her, but the discomposure was manifested with a vehemence which she was not aware was a fault ; nor did she seem at all sensible that her religion was ever to be resorted to but on great occasions, forgetting that great occasions but rarely occur in common life, and that these small passes, at which the enemy is perpetually entering, the true Christian will vigilantly guard.

I observed in Mrs. Ranby one striking inconsistency. While she considered it as forming a complete line of separation from the world that she and her daughters abstained from public places, she had no objection to their indemnifying themselves for this forbearance by devoting so monstrous a disproportion of their time to that very amusement which constitutes so principal a part of diversion abroad. The time which is redeemed from what is wrong is of little value if not dedicated to what is right ; and it is not enough that the doctrines of the Gospel furnish a subject for discussion if they do not furnish a principle of action.

One of the most obvious defects which struck me in this and two or three other families, whom I afterwards visited, was the want of companionableness in the daughters. They did not seem to form a part of the family compact, but made a kind of distinct branch of themselves. Surely, when only the parents and a few select friends are met together in a family way, the daughters should contribute their portion to enliven the domestic circle. They were always ready to sing and to play, but did not take the pains to produce themselves in conversation, but seemed to carry on a distinct intercourse, by herding, and whispering, and laughing together.

In some women, who seemed to be possessed of good ingredients, they were so ill mixed up together as not to produce an elegant, interesting companion. It appeared to me that three of the grand inducements in the choice of a wife are, that a man may have a directress for his family, a preceptress for his children, and a companion for himself.

Can it be honestly affirmed that the present habits of domestic life are generally favourable to the union of these three essentials? Yet which of them can a man of sense and principle consent to relinquish in his conjugal prospects?

Chapter VII.

RETURNED to town at the end of a few days. To a speculative stranger, a London day presents every variety of circumstance in every conceivable shape of which human life is susceptible. When you trace the solicitude of the morning countenance, the anxious exploring of the morning paper, the eager interrogation of the morning guest; when you hear the dismal enumeration of losses by land, and perils by sea, taxes trembling, dangers multiplying, commerce annihilating, war protracted, invasion threatening, destruction impending, your mind catches and communicates the terror, and you feel yourself ' falling with a falling state.'

But when, in the course of the very same day, you meet these gloomy prognosticators at the sumptuous, not 'dinner but hecatomb,' at the gorgeous fête, the splendid spectacle; when you hear the frivolous discourse, witness the luxurious dissipation, contemplate the boundless indulgence, and observe the ruinous gaming, you would be ready to exclaim, 'Am I not supping in the antipodes of that land in which I breakfasted? Surely this is a country of different men, different characters, and different circumstances. This at least is a place in which there is neither fear, nor danger, nor want, nor misery, nor war.'

If you observed the overflowing subscriptions raised, the innumerable societies formed, the committees appointed, the agents employed, the royal patrons engaged, the noble presidents provided, the palace-like structures erected, and all this to alleviate, to cure, and even to prevent every calamity which the indigent can suffer or the affluent conceive— to remove not only want, but ignorance—to suppress not only misery, but vice, would you not exclaim with Hamlet, ' What a piece of work is man ! How noble in reason ! how infinite in faculties ! in action how like an angel ! in compassion how like a God !'

If you look into the whole comet-like eccentric orbit of the human character; if you compared all the struggling contrariety of principle and of passion, the clashing of opinion and of action, of resolution and of performance ; the victories of evil over the propensities to good ; if you contrasted the splendid virtue with the disorderly vice ; the exalted generosity with the selfish narrowness ; the provident bounty with the thoughtless prodigality ; the extremes of all that is dignified, with the excesses of all that is abject, would you not exclaim, in the very spirit of Pascal, ' Oh ! the grandeur and the littleness, the excellence and the corruption, the majesty and the meanness, of man !'

If you attended the debates in our great deliberative assemblies ; if you heard the argument and the eloquence, ' the wisdom and the wit,' the public spirit and the disinterestedness ; Curtius's devotedness to his country, and Regulus's disdain of self, expressed with all the logic which reason can suggest, and embellished with all the rhetoric which fancy can supply, would you not rapturously cry out, This is

Above all Greek, above all Roman`fame?

But if you discerned the bitter personality, the incurable prejudice, the cutting retort, the suspicious implication, the recriminating sneer, the cherished animosity ; if you beheld the interests of an empire standing still, the business of the civilized globe suspended, while two intellectual gladiators are thrusting, each to give the other a fall, and to show his own strength ; would you not lament the littleness of the great, the infirmities of the good, and the weaknesses of the wise? Would you not, soaring a flight far above Hamlet or Pascal, apostrophize with the royal psalmist, ' Lord, what is man that Thou art mindful of him, or the son of man That thou regardest him ?'

But to descend to my individual concerns. Among my acquaintance, I visited two separate families, where the daughters were remarkably attractive, and more than usually endowed with beauty, sense, and elegance ; but I was deterred from following up the acquaintance, by observing, in each family, practices which, though very different, almost equally revolted me.

In one, where the young ladies had large fortunes. they insinuated themselves into the admiration, and invited the familiarity, of young men, by attentions the most flattering, and civilities the most alluring. When they had made sure of their aim, and the admirers were encouraged to make proposals, the ladies burst out into a loud laugh, wondered what the man could mean ; they never dreamt of anything more than common politeness ; then petrified them with distant looks, and turned about to practise the same arts on others.

The other family in which I thought I had secured an agreeable intimacy, I instantly deserted on observing the gracious and engaging reception given by the ladies to more than one libertine of the most notorious profligacy. The men were handsome, and elegant, and fashionable, and had figured in newspapers and courts of justice. This degrading popularity rather attracted than repelled attention ; and while the guilty associates in their crimes were shunned with abhorrence by these very ladies, the specious undoers were not only received with complaisance, but there was a sort of competition who should be most strenuous in their endeavours to attract them.—Surely women of fashion can hardly make a more corrupt use of influence, a talent for which they will be peculiarly accountable. Surely, mere personal purity can hardly deserve the name of virtue in those who can sanction notoriously vicious characters, which their reprobation, if it could not reform, would at least degrade.

On a further acquaintance, I found Sir John and Lady Belfield to be persons of much worth. They were candid, generous, and sincere. They saw the errors of the world in which they lived, but had not resolution to emancipate themselves from its shackles. They partook, indeed, very sparingly of its diversions, not so much because they suspected their evil tendency, as because they were weary of them, and because they had better resources in themselves.

Indeed, it is wonderful that more people from mere good sense and just taste, without the operation of any religious consideration, do not, when the first ardour is cooled, perceive the futility of what is called pleasure, and decline it as the man declines the amusements of the child. But fashionable society produces few persons who, like the ex-courtier of King David, assign their fourscore years as a reason for no longer ' delighting in the voice of singing men and singing women.'

Sir John and Lady Belfield, however, kept up a large general acquaintance ; and it is not easy to continue to associate with the world, without retaining something of its spirit. Their standard of morals was high, compared with that of those with whom they lived ; but when the standard of the Gospel was suggested, they drew in a little, and thought *things might be carried too far.* There was nothing in their practice which made it their interest to hope that Christianity might not be true. They both assented to its doctrines, and lived in a kind of general hope of its final promises. But their views were neither correct nor elevated. They were contented to generalize the doctrines of Scripture ; and though they venerated its awful truths in the aggregate, they rather took them upon trust than laboured to understand them, or to imbue their minds with the spirit of them. Many a high professor, however, might have blushed to see how carefully they exercised not a few Christian dispositions ; how kind and patient they were ! how favourable in their construction of the actions of others ! how charitable to the necessitous ! how exact in veracity ! and how tender of the reputation of their neighbour !

Sir John had been early hurt by living so much with men of the world, with wits, politicians, and philosophers. This, though he had escaped the contagion of false principles, had kept back the growth of such as were true. Men versed in the world, and abstracted from all religious society, begin, in time, a little to suspect whether their own religious opinions may not possibly be wrong, or at least rigid, when they see them so opposite to those of persons to whose judgment they are accustomed to look up in other points. He found, too, that, in the society in which he lived, the reputation of religion detracted much from that of talents ; and a man does not care to have his understanding questioned by those in whose opinion he wishes to stand well. This apprehension did not, indeed, drive him to renounce his principles, but it led him to conceal them ; and that piety which is forcibly kept out of sight, which has nothing to fortify, and everything to repel it, is too apt to decline.

His marriage with an amiable woman, whose virtues and graces attached him to his own home, drew him off from the most dangerous of his prior connections. This union had at once improved his character and augmented his happiness. If Lady Belfield erred, it was through excess of kindness and candour. Her kindness led to the too great indulgence of her children ; and her candour, to the too favourable construction of the errors of her acquaintance. She was the very reverse of my Hampstead friend. Whereas Mrs. Ranby thought hardly anybody would be saved, Lady Belfield comforted herself that hardly anybody was in danger. This opinion was not taken up as a palliative

3

to quiet her conscience on account of the sins of her own conduct, for her conduct was remarkably correct ; but it sprung from a natural sweetness of temper, joined to a mind not sufficiently informed and guided by Scriptural truth. She was candid and teachable, but as she could not help seeing that she had more religion than most of her acquaintance, she felt a secret complacency in observing how far her principles rose above theirs, instead of an humbling conviction of how far her own fell below the requisitions of the Gospel.

The fundamental error was, that she had no distinct view of the corruption of human nature. She often lamented the weaknesses and vices of individuals, but thought all vice an incidental not a radical mischief, the effect of thoughtlessness and casual temptation. She talked with discrimination of the faults of some of her children ; but while she rejoiced in the happier dispositions of the others, she never suspected that they had all brought into the world with them any natural tendency to evil ; and thought it cruel to suppose that such innocent little things had any such wrong propensities as education would not effectually cure. In everything the complete contrast of Mrs. Ranby—as the latter thought education could do nothing, Lady Belfield thought it would do everything ; that there was no good tendency which it would not bring to perfection, and no corruption which it could not completely eradicate. On the operation of a higher influence, she placed too little dependence ; while Mrs. Ranby rested in an unreasonable trust on an interference not warranted by Scripture.

In regard to her children, Lady Belfield was led by the strength of her affection to extreme indulgence. She encouraged no vice in them, but she did not sufficiently check those indications which are the seeds of vice. She reproved the actual fault, but never thought of implanting a principle which might extirpate the evil from whence the fault sprung ; so that the individual error and the individual correction were continually recurring.

As Mrs. Ranby, I had observed, seldom quoted any sacred writer but St. Paul, I remarked that Lady Belfield admired almost exclusively Ecclesiastes, Proverbs, and the historical books of the Bible. Of the Epistles, that of St. James was her favourite : the others she thought chiefly, if not entirely, applicable to the circumstances of the Jews and Pagans, to the converts from among whom they were addressed. If she entertained rather an awful reverence for the doctrinal parts, than an earnest wish to study them, it arose from the common mistake of believing that they were purely speculative, without being aware of their deep practical importance. But if these two ladies were diametrically opposite to each other in certain points, both were frequently right in what they assumed, and both wrong only in what they rejected. Each contended for one half of that which will not save when disjoined from the other, but which, when united to it, makes up the complete Christian character.

Lady Belfield, who was, if I may so speak, constitutionally charitable, almost thought that heaven might be purchased by charity. She inverted the valuable superstructure of good works, and laid them as her foundation ; and while Mrs. Ranby would not, perhaps, much have blamed Moses for breaking the tables of the law, had he only demolished the second, Lady Belfield would have saved the second, as the more important of the two.

Lady Belfield has less vanity than any woman I ever knew, who was not governed by a very strict religious principle. Her modesty never courted the admiration of the world, but her timidity too much dreaded its censure. She would not do a wrong thing to obtain any applause, but she omitted some right ones from the dread of blame.

Chapter VIII.

THE house of Sir John Belfield was become a pleasant kind of home to me. He and his lady seldom went out in an evening. Happy in each other and in their children, though they lived much with the rational, they associated as little as they thought possible with the racketing world. Yet being known to be generally at home, they were exposed to the inroads of certain invaders called fine ladies, who, always afraid of being too early for their parties, are constantly on the watch how to disburthen themselves, for the intermediate hour, of the heavy commodity *time ;* a raw material which, as they seldom work up at home, they are always willing to truck against the time of their more domestic acquaintance. Now, as these last *have* always something to do, it is an unfair traffic, ' all the reciprocity is on one side,' to borrow the expression of an illustrious statesman ; and the barter is as disadvantageous to the sober home-trader, as that of the honest negroes, who exchange their gold-dust and ivory for the beads and bits of glass of the wily English.

These nightly irruptions, though sometimes inconvenient to my friends, were of use to me, as they enabled me to see and judge more of the gay world than I could have done without going in search of it— a risk which I thought bore no proportion to the gain. It was like learning the language of the enemy's country at home.

One evening, when we were sitting happily alone in the library, Lady Belfield, working at her embroidery, cheerfully joining in our little discussions, and comparing our peaceful pleasures with those pursued by the occupiers of the countless carriages which were tearing up the ' wheel-worn streets,' or jostling each other at the door of the next house, where a grand assembly was collecting its myriads, Sir John asked what should be the evening book. Then, rising, he took down from the shelf Akenside's ' Pleasures of Imagination.'

' Is it,' said he, as soon as he sat down, ' the rage for novelty, or a real degeneracy of taste, that we now seldom hear of a poet who, when I was a boy, was the admiration of every man who had a relish for true genius ? I cannot defend his principles, since in a work, of which *Man* is professedly the object, he has overlooked his *immortality*—a subject which one wonders did not force itself upon him as so congenial to the sublimity of his genius, whatever his religious views might have been. But to speak of him only as a poet : a work which abounds in

3—2

a richer profusion of images, and a more variegated luxuriance of expression, than the 'Pleasures of Imagination,' cannot easily be found.
The flimsy metre of our day seems to add fresh value to his sinewy
verse. We have no happier master of poetic numbers, none who better
knew

> To build the lofty rhyme.

The condensed vigour so indispensable to blank verse, the skilful
variation of the pause, the masterly structure of the period, and all the
occult mysteries of the art, can perhaps be best learnt from Akenside.
If he could have conveyed to Thomson his melody and rhythm, and
Thomson would have paid him back in perspicuity and transparency
of meaning, how might they have enriched each other !'

'I confess,' said I, 'in reading Akenside, I have now and then found
the same passage at once enchanting and unintelligible. As it happens
to many frequenters of the opera, the music always transports, but the
words are not always understood.' I then desired my friend to gratify
us with the first book of the 'Pleasures of Imagination.'

Sir John is a passionate lover of poetry, in which he has a fine taste.
He read it with much spirit and feeling, especially these truly classical
lines :

> *Mind, mind* alone, bear witness earth and heaven,
> The living fountains in itself contains
> Of beauteous and sublime : here hand in hand
> Sit paramount the graces ; here enthroned
> Celestial Venus, with divinest airs
> Invites the soul to never-fading joy.

'The reputation of this exquisite passage,' said he, laying down the
book, 'is established by the consenting suffrage of all men of taste,
though, by the critical countenance you are beginning to put on, you
look as if you had a mind to attack it.'

'So far from it,' said I, 'that I know nothing more splendid in the
whole mass of our poetry. And I feel almost guilty of high treason
against the majesty of the sublimer muses in the remark I am going to
hazard on the celebrated lines which follow. The poet's object, through
this and the two following pages, is to establish the infinite superiority
of mind over unconscious matter, even in its fairest forms. The idea is
as just as the execution is beautiful ; so also is his supreme elevation of
intellect over

> Greatness of bulk, or symmetry of parts.

Nothing, again, can be finer than his subsequent preference of

> The powers of genius and design,

over even the stupendous range

> Of planets, suns, and adamantine spheres.

He proceeds to ransack the stores of the mental and the moral world,
as he had done the world of matter, and, with a pen dipped in Hippo-
crene, opposes to the latter

" The charms of virtuous friendship," etc.
" The candid blush
Of him who strives with fortune to be just."
" All the mild majesty of private life."
" The graceful tear that streams from others' woes." '

' Why, Charles,' said Sir John, ' I am glad to find you the enthusiastic eulogist of the passage of which I suspected you were about to be
the saucy censurer.'

' Censure,' replied I, 'is perhaps too strong a term for any part,
especially the most admired part, of this fine poem. I need not repeat
the lines on which I was going to risk a slight observation ; they live in
the mind and memory of every lover of the muses.'

' I will read the next passage, however,' said Sir John, ' that I may
be better able to controvert your criticism :

Look then abroad through nature to the range
Of planets, suns, and adamantine spheres,
Wheeling unshaken through the void immense,
And speak, oh man ! does this capacious scene,
With half that kindling majesty dilate
Thy strong conception, as when Brutus rose
Refulgent from the stroke of Cæsar's fate
Amid the crowd of patriots, and his arm
Aloft extending, like eternal Jove
When guilt brings down the thunder, call'd aloud
On Tully's name, and shook his crimson steel,
And bade the father of his country hail ;
For, lo ! the tyrant prostrate in the dust,
And Rome again is free !

What a grand and powerful passage !' said Sir John.

' I acknowledge it,' said I ; ' but is it as just as it is grand ? *Le vrai
est le seul beau.* Is it a fair and direct opposition between mind and
matter ? The poet could not have expressed the image more nobly,
but might he not, out of the abundant treasures of his opulent mind,
have chosen it with more felicity ? Is an act of murder, even of a
usurper, as happily contrasted with the organisation of matter as the
other beautiful instances I named, and which he goes on to select ?
The superiority of mental beauty is the point he is establishing, and
his elaborate preparation leads you to expect all his other instances to
be drawn from pure mental excellence. His other exemplifications are
general, this is particular ; they are a class, this is only a variety. I
question if Milton, who was at least as ardent a champion for liberty,
and as much of a party-man as Akenside, would have used this illustration. Milton, though he often insinuates a political stroke in his
great poem, always, I think, generalises. Whatever had been his principles, or at whatever period he had written, I question, when he wanted
to describe the overthrow of authority by the rebel angels, if he would
have illustrated it by Cromwell's seizing the mace, or the decapitation
of Charles ; much less, if he would have selected those two instances as
the triumph of mind over matter.'

' But,' said Sir John, ' you forget that Akenside professedly adopts
the language of Cicero in his second Philippic.' He then read the note
beginning with, ' Cæsare interfecto,' etc.

' True,' said I, ' I am not arguing the matter as a point of fact, but as
a point of just application.   I pass over the comparison of Brutus with
Jove, which, by the way, would have become Tully better than Akenside, but which Tully would have perhaps thought too bold.   Cicero
adorns his oration with this magnificent description. He relates it as
an event ; the other uses it as an illustration of that to which, I humbly
conceive, it does not exactly apply.   The orator paints the violent death
of a hero ; the poet adopts the description of this violent death, or
rather of the stroke which caused it, to illustrate the perfection of intellectual grandeur.   After all, it is as much a party question as a poetical
one, on which the critic will be apt to be guided in his decision by his
politics rather than by his taste.   The splendour of the passage, however, will inevitably dazzle the feeling reader, till it produce the common
effect of excessive brightness, that of somewhat blinding the beholder.'

Chapter IX.

HILE we were thus pleasantly engaged, the servant announced
Mrs. Fentham ; and a fashionable-looking woman, about the
middle of her life, rather youthfully dressed, and not far from
handsome, made her appearance.   Instead of breaking forth
into the usual modish jargon, she politely entered into the subject in
which she found us engaged ; envied Lady Belfield the happiness of
elegant quiet, which she herself might have been equally enjoying at
her own house, and professed herself a warm admirer of poetry.   She
would probably have professed an equal fondness of metaphysics,
geometry, military tactics, or the Arabic language, if she had happened
to have found us employed in the study of either.

From poetry, the transition to painting was easy and natural.   Mrs.
Fentham possessed all the phraseology of connoisseurship, and asked
me if I was fond of pictures.   I professed the delight I took in them in
strong, that is, in true terms.   She politely said that Mr. Fentham had
a very tolerable collection of the best masters, and particularly a Titian,
which she would be happy to have the honour of showing me next
morning.   I bowed my thankful assent ; she appointed the hour, and
soon after, looking at her watch, said she was afraid she must leave the
delights of such a select and interesting society for a far less agreeable
party.

When she was gone, I expressed my obligations to her politeness,
and anticipated the pleasure I should have in seeing her pictures.
' She is much more anxious that you should see her *originals*,' said
Lady Belfield, smiling. ' The kindness is not *quite* disinterested ; take
care of your heart.'   Sir John rather gravely said, ' It is with reluctance
that I ever say anything to the prejudice of anybody that I receive in
my house ; but, as the son of my valued friend, I think it fair to tell
you that this vigilant matron keeps a keen look-out after all young men
of fortune.   This is not the first time that that Titian has been made
the bait to catch a promising acquaintance.   Indeed, it is now grown

so stale that, had you not been a new man, she would hardly have risked it. If you had happened not to like painting, some book would have been offered to you. The return of a book naturally brings on a visit. But all these devices have not yet answered. The damsels still remain, like Shakspeare's plaintive maid, " in single blessedness." They do not however, like her, spend gloomy nights

> Chanting cold hymns to the pale, lifeless moon ;

but in singing sprightlier roundelays to lively auditors.'

I punctually attended the invitation, effectually shielded from danger by the friendly intimation, and a still more infallible ægis, the charge of my father never to embark in any engagement till I had made my visit to Mr. Stanley. My veneration for his memory operated as a complete defence.

I saw and admired the pictures. The pictures brought on an invitation to dinner. I found Mrs. Fentham to be, in her conversation, a sensible, correct, knowing woman. Her daughters were elegant in their figures, well instructed in the usual accomplishments, well bred, and apparently well tempered. Mr. Fentham was a man of business, and of·the world. He had a great income from a place under Government, out of which the expenses of his family permitted him to save nothing. Private fortune he had little or none. His employment engaged him almost entirely, so that he interfered but little with domestic affairs. A general air of elegance, almost amounting to magnificence, pervaded the whole establishment.

I at first saw but little to excite any suspicion of the artificial character of the lady of the house. The first gleam of light which let in the truth was the expressions most frequent in Mrs. Fentham's mouth —'What will the world say ?' 'What will people think ?' 'How will such a thing appear ?' 'Will it have a good look ?' 'The world is of opinion,' 'Won't such a thing be censured ?' On a little acquaintance, I discovered that human applause was the motive of all she said, and reputation her great object in all she did. Opinion was the idol to which she sacrificed. Decorum was the inspirer of her duties, and praise the reward of them. The standard of the world was the standard by which she weighed actions ; she had no higher principle of conduct. She adopted the forms of religion because she saw that, carried to a certain degree, they rather produced credit than censure. While her husband adjusted his accounts on the Sunday morning, she regularly carried her daughters to church, except a headache had been caught at the Saturday's opera ; and as regularly exhibited herself and them afterwards in Hyde Park. As she said it was Mr. Fentham's leisure day, she complimented him with always having a great dinner on Sundays, but alleged her piety as a reason for not having cards in the evening at home, though she had no scruple to make one at a private party at a friend's house ; soberly conditioning, however, that there should not be more than *three tables ;* the right or wrong, the decorum or impropriety, the gaiety or gravity, always being made specifically to depend on the number of tables.

She was, in general, extremely severe against women who had lost their reputation, though she had no hesitation in visiting a few of the most dishonourable, if they were of high rank or belonged to a certain set.   In that case she excused herself by saying, 'that, as fashionable people continued to countenance them, it was not for her to be scrupulous.   One must sail with the stream ; I can't set my face against the world.'   But if an unhappy girl had been drawn aside, or one who had not rank to bear her out had erred, that altered the case, and she then expressed the most virtuous indignation.   When modesty happened to be in repute, not the necks of Queen Elizabeth and her courtly virgins were more entrenched in ruffs and shrouded in tuckers than those of Mrs. Fentham and her daughters ; but when *display* became the order of the day, the Grecian Venus was scarcely more unconscious of a veil.

With a very good understanding, she never allowed herself one original thought, or one spontaneous action.   Her ideas, her language, and her conduct were entirely regulated by the ideas, language, and conduct of those who stood well with the world.   Vanity in her was a steady, inward, but powerfully pervading principle.   It did not evaporate in levity or indiscretion, but was the hidden, though forcible spring of her whole course of action.   She had all the gratification which vanity affords in secret, and all the credit which its prudent operation procures in public.   She was apparently guilty of no excess of any kind.   She had a sober scale of creditable vices, and never allowed herself to exceed a few stated degrees in any of them.   She reprobated gaming, but could not exist without cards.   Masquerades she censured as highly extravagant and dangerous, but when given by ladies of high quality, at their own houses, she thought them an elegant and proper amusement.   Though she sometimes went to the play, she did not care for what passed on the stage, for she confessed the chief pleasure the theatre afforded, was to reckon up, when she came home, how many duchesses and countesses had bowed to her across the house.

A complete despot at home, her arbitrariness is so veiled by correctness of manner, and studied good breeding, that she obtains the credit of great mildness and moderation.   She is said not to love her daughters, who come too near her in age, and go too much beyond her in beauty, to be forgiven ; yet, like a consummate politician, she is ever labouring for their advancement.   She has generally several schemes in hand, and always one scheme under another, the underplot ready to be brought forward if the principal one fails.   Though she encourages pretenders, yet she is afraid to accept of a tolerable proposal, lest a better should present itself : but if the loftier hope fails, she then contrives to lure back the inferior offer.   She can balance to a nicety, in the calculation of chances, the advantages or disadvantages of a higher possibility against a lower probability.

Though she neither wants reading nor taste, her mind is never sufficiently disengaged to make her an agreeable companion.   Her head is always at work, conjecturing the event of every fresh ball and every new acquaintance.   She cannot even

Take her tea without a stratagem.

She set out in life with a very slender acquaintance, and clung for a while to one or two damaged peeresses, who were not received by women of their own rank. But I am told it was curious to see with what adroitness she could extricate herself from a disreputable acquaintance, when a more honourable one stept in to fill the niche. She made her way rapidly, by insinuating to one person of note how intimate she was with another, and to both what handsome things each said of the other. By constant attentions, petty offices, and measured flattery, she has got footing into almost every house of distinction. Her decorum is invariable. She boasts that she was never guilty of the indecency of violent passion. Poor woman! she fancies there is no violent passion but that of anger. Little does she think that ambition, vanity, the hunger of applause, a rage for being universally known, are all violent passions, however modified by discretion or varnished by art. She suffers, too, all that 'vexation of spirit' which treads on the heels of 'vanity.' Disappointment and jealousy poison the days devoted to pleasure. The party does not answer. The wrong people never stay away, and the right ones never come. The guest for whom the fête is made is sure to fail. Her party is thin, while that of her competitor overflows; or there is a plenty of dowagers, and a paucity of young men. When the costly and elaborate supper is on the table, excuses arrive : even if the supper is crowded, the daughters remain upon hands. How strikingly does she exemplify the strong expression of—'labouring in the fire for very vanity'—' Of giving her money for that which is not bread, and her labour for that which satisfieth not !'

After spending the day at Mrs. Fentham's, I went to sup with my friends in Cavendish Square. Lady Belfield was impatient for my history of the dinner. But Sir John said, laughing, ' You shall not say a word, Charles—I can tell you how it was, as exactly as if I had been there.—Charlotte, who has the best voice, was brought out to sing, but was placed a little behind, as her person is not quite perfect ; Maria, who is the most picturesque figure, was put *to attitudinize* at the harp, arrayed in the costume, and assuming the fascinating graces, of Marmion's Lady Heron :

> Fair was her rounded arm, as o'er
> The strings her fingers flew.

Then, Charles, was the moment of peril! then, according to your favourite Milton's most incongruous image :

> You took in sounds that might create a soul
> Under the ribs of death.

For fear, however, that your heart of adamant should hold out against all these perilous assaults, its vulnerability was tried in other quarters. The Titian would naturally lead to Lavinia's drawings. A beautiful sketch of the Lakes would be produced, with a gentle intimation, what a sweet place Westmoreland must be to live in ! When you had exhausted all proper raptures on the art and on the artist, it would be recollected, that as Westmoreland was so near Scotland, you would naturally be fond of a reel—the reel of course succeeded.' Then, putting himself into an attitude, and speaking theatrically, he continued :

> ' Then universal Pan,
> Knit with the Graces and the Hours in dance.

Oh ! no, I forget, universal Pan could not join—but he could admire. Then all the perfections of all the nymphs burst on you in full blaze.—Such a concentration of attractions you never could resist ! You are *but* a man, and now, doubtless, a lost man.'—Here he stopped to finish his laugh, and I was driven reluctantly to acknowledge that his picture, though a caricature, was, notwithstanding, a resemblance.

' And so,' said Sir John, 'you were brought under no power of incantation by this dangerous visit. You will not be driven, like the tempted Ithacan, to tie yourself to a mast, or to flee for safety from the enchantment of these syrens.'

While we were at supper, with more gravity, he said, ' Among the various objects of ambition, there are few in life which bring less accession to its comfort, than an unceasing struggle to rise to an elevation in society very much above the level of our own condition, without being aided by any stronger ascending power than mere vanity. Great talents, of whatever kind, have a natural tendency to rise, and to lift their possessor. The flame, in mounting, does but obey its impulse. But when there is no energy more powerful than the passion to be great, destitute of the gifts which confer greatness, the painful efforts of ambition are like water forced above its level by mechanical powers. It requires constant exertions of art, to keep up what was first set a-going. Poor Mrs. Fentham's head is perpetually at work, to maintain the elevation she has reached. And how little, after all, is she considered by those on whose caresses her happiness depends ! She has lost the esteem of her original circle, where she might have been respected, without gaining that of her high associates, who, though they receive her, still refuse her claims of equality. She is not considered as of their *establishment*, it is but *toleration* at best.'

At Mrs. Fentham's I encountered Lady Bab Lawless, a renowned modish dowager, famous for laying siege to the heart of every distinguished man, with the united artillery of her own wit and her daughters' beauty. How many ways there are of being wrong ! She was of a character diametrically opposite to that of Mrs. Fentham. She had the same end in view, but the means she used to accomplish it were of a bolder strain. Lady Bab affected no delicacy, she laughed at reserve, she had shaken hands with decorum.

> She held the *noisy* tenor of her way]

with no assumed refinement ; and, so far from shielding her designs behind the mask of decency, she disdained the obsolete expedient. Her plans succeeded the more infallibly, because her frankness defeated all suspicion. A man could never divine that such gay and open assaults could have their foundation in design, and he gave her full credit for artless simplicity, at the moment she was catching him in her toils. If she now and then had gone too far, and by a momentary oversight, or excessive levity, had betrayed too much, with infinite address she would make a crane-neck turn, and fall to discussing, not without ability, some moral or theological topic. Thus she affected to establish the character of a woman, thoughtless through wit, indiscreet through simplicity, but religious on principle.

As there is no part of the appendage to a wife which I have ever more dreaded than a Machiavellian mother, I should have been deaf to wit, and blind to beauty, and dead to advances, had their united batteries been directed against me. But I had not the ambition to aspire to that honour. I was much too low a mark for her lofty aim. She had a natural antipathy to every name that could not be found in the red book. She equally shrunk from untitled opulence and indigent nobility. She knew by instinct if a younger son was in the room, and by a petrifying look checked his most distant approaches ; while, with her powerful spells, she never failed to draw within her magic circle the splendid heir, and charm him to her purpose.

Highly born herself, she had early been married to a rich man of inferior rank, for the sake of a large settlement. Her plan was, that her daughters (who, by the way, are modest and estimable), should find in the man they married still higher birth than their own, and more riches than her husband's.

It was a curious speculation to compare these two friends, and to observe how much less the refined manœuvres of Mrs. Fentham answered, than the open assaults of the intrepid Lady Bab. All the intricacies and labyrinths which the former has been so skilful and so patient in weaving, have not yet enthralled one captive, while the composed effrontery, the affecting to take for granted the offer which was never meant to be made, and treating that as concluded which was never so much as intended, drew the unconscious victim of the other into the trap, before he knew it was set. The depth of her plot consisted in not appearing to have any. It was a novelty in intrigue ; an originality which defied all competition, and in which no imitator has any chance of success.

Chapter X.

SIR JOHN carried me one morning to call on Lady Denham, a dowager of fashion, who had grown old in the trammels of the world. Though she seems resolved to die in the harness, yet she piques herself on being very religious, and no one inveighs against infidelity or impiety with more pointed censure. 'She has a granddaughter,' said Sir John, ' who lives with her, and whom she has trained to walk precisely in her own steps, and which, she thinks, is the way she should go. The girl,' added he, smiling, ' is well looking, and will have a handsome fortune, and I am persuaded that, as my friend, I could procure you a good reception.'

We were shown into her dressing-room, where we found her with a book lying open before her. From a glance which I caught of the large black letter, I saw it was a 'Week's Preparation.' This book, it seems, constantly lay open before her from breakfast till dinner, at this season. It was Passion week. But as this is the room in which she sees all her morning visitors, to none of whom is she ever denied, even at this period of retreat, she could only pick up momentary snatches of reading in the short intervals between one person bowing out, and another courtesying in. Miss Denham sat by, painting flowers.

Sir John asked her ladyship, if she would go and dine in a family way with Lady Belfield. She drew up, looked grave, and said, with much solemnity, that she should never think of dining abroad at this holy season. Sir John said, 'As we have neither cards nor company, I thought you might as well have eaten your chicken in my house as in your own.' But though she thought it a sin to dine with a sober family, she made herself amends for the sacrifice, by letting us see that her heart was brimful of the world, pressed down and running over. She indemnified herself for her abstinence from its diversions, by indulging in the only pleasures which she thought compatible with the sanctity of the season—uncharitable gossip, and unbounded calumny. She would not touch a card for the world, but she played over to Sir John the whole game of the preceding Saturday night ; told him by what a shameful inattention her partner had lost the odd trick ; and that she should not have been beaten, after all, had not her adversary, she verily believed, contrived to look over her hand.

Sir John seized the only minute in which we were alone, to ask her to add a guinea to a little sum he was collecting for a poor tradesman with a large family, who had been burnt out a few nights ago. ' His wife,' added he, ' was your favourite maid Dixon, and both are deserving people.' ' Ah, poor Dixon ! she was always unlucky,' replied the lady. ' How could they be so careless ! surely they might have put the fire out sooner. They should not have let it get ahead. I wonder people are not more active.' ' It is too late to inquire about that,' said Sir John ; ' the question now is, not how their loss might have been prevented, but how it may be repaired.' ' I am really quite sorry,' said she, ' that I can give you nothing. I have had so many calls lately, that my charity purse is completely exhausted, and that abominable property-tax makes me quite a beggar.'

While she was speaking, I glanced on the open leaf at ' Charge them that are rich in this world, that they be ready to give ;' and, directing my eye further, it fell on, ' Be not deceived. God is not mocked.' These were the awful passages which formed a part of her ' Preparation,' and this was the practical use she made of them !

A dozen persons, of both sexes, ' had their exits and their entrances ' during our stay ; for the scene was so strange and the character so new to me, that I felt unwilling to stir. Among other visitors, was Signor Squallini, a favourite opera singer, whom she patronized. Her face was lighted up with joy at the sight of him. He brought her an admired new air, in which he was preparing himself, and sung a few notes, that she might say she had heard it the first. She felt all the dignity of the privilege, and extolled the air with all the phrases, cant, and rapture of *dilettanteism.*

After this, she drew a paper from between the leaves of her still open book, which she showed him. It contained a list of all the company she had engaged to attend his benefit. ' I will call on some others,' said she, ' to-morrow after prayers. I am sorry this is a week in which I cannot see my friends at their assemblies, but on Sunday you know it will be over, and I shall have my house full in the evening. Next Monday will be Easter, and I shall be at our dear duchess's private masquerade, and then I hope to see and engage the whole world. Here are ten guineas,' said she in a half whisper to the obsequious signor. ' You may mention what I gave for *my* ticket ; it may set the fashion going.' She then pressed a ticket on Sir John, and another on me. He declined, saying, with great *sang froid,* ' You know we are *Handelians.*' What excuse I made I do not well know ; I only know that I saved my ten guineas with a very bad grace, but felt bound in conscience to add them to what I had before subscribed to poor Dixon.

Hitherto I had never seen the gnat-strainer and the camel-swallower so strikingly exemplified. And it is observable how forcibly the truth of Scripture is often illustrated by those who live in the boldest opposition to it. If you have any doubt while you are reading, go into the world, and your belief will be confirmed.

As we took our leave, she followed us to the door. I hoped it was with the guinea for the fire ; but she only whispered Sir John, though he did not go himself, to prevail on such and such ladies to go to Squallini's benefit. ' Pray do,' said she ; 'it will be a charity. Poor fellow ! he is sadly out at elbows ; he has a fine liberal spirit, and can hardly make his large income do.'

When we got into the street, we admired the splendid chariot and laced liveries of this *indigent* professor, for whom our charity had been just solicited, and whose ' liberal spirit,' my friend assured me, consisted in sumptuous living, and the indulgence of every fashionable vice.

I could not restrain my exclamations as soon as we got out of hearing. To Sir John the scene was amusing, but to him it had lost the interest of novelty. ' I have known her ladyship about twelve years,' said he, ' and of course have witnessed a dozen of these annual paroxysms of devotion. I am persuaded that she is a gainer by them on her own principle—that is, in the article of pleasure. This short periodical abstinence whets her appetite to a keener relish for suspended enjoyment ; and while she fasts from amusements, her blinded conscience enjoys a feast of self-gratulation. She feeds on the remembrance of her self-denial, even after she has returned to those delights which she thinks her retreat has fairly purchased. She considers religion as a system of pains and penalties, by the voluntary enduring of which for a short time she shall compound for all the indulgences of the year. She is persuaded that something must be annually forborne, in order to make her peace. After these periodical atonements, the Almighty, being in her debt, will be obliged at last to pay her with heaven. This composition, which rather brings her in on the creditor side, not only quiets her conscience for the past, but enables her joyfully to enter on a new score.'

I asked Sir John how Lady Belfield *could* associate with a woman of a character so opposite to her own. ' What can we do ?' said he. ' We cannot be singular ; we must conform *a little* to the world in which we live.' Trusting to his extreme good-nature, and fired at the scene to which I had been a witness, I ventured to observe that nonconformity to such a world as that of which this lady was a specimen was the very criterion of the religion taught by Him who had declared, by way of pre-eminent distinction, that ' His kingdom was not of this world.'

' You are a young man,' answered he mildly, 'and this delicacy and these prejudices would soon wear off if you were to live some time in the world.' ' My dear Sir John,' said I warmly, 'by the grace of God, I never *will* live in the world—at least, I will never associate with that part of it whose society would be sure to wear off that delicacy and remove those prejudices. Why, this is retaining all the worst part of popery. Here is the abstinence, without the devotion ; the outward observance, without the interior humiliation ; the suspending of sin, not only without any design of forsaking it, but with a fixed resolution of returning to it, and of increasing the gust by the forbearance. Nay, the sins she retains in order to mitigate the horrors of forbearance are as bad as those she lays down. A postponed sin, which is fully intended to be resumed, is as much worse than a sin persisted in as deliberate hypocrisy is worse than the impulse of passion. I desire not a more explicit comment on a text, which I was once almost tempted to think unjust ; I mean, the greater facility of the entrance of gross and notorious offenders into heaven than of these formalists. No ! if Miss Denham were sole heiress to Crœsus, and joined the beauty of Cleopatra to the wit of Sappho, I never would connect myself with a disciple of that school.'

' How many ways there are of being unhappy !' said Sir John, as we returned one day from a ride we had taken some miles out of town, to call on a friend of his. ' Mr. Stanhope, whom we have just quitted, is a man of great elegance of mind. His early life was passed in liberal studies, and in the best company. But his fair prospects were blasted by a disproportionate marriage. He was drawn in by a vanity too natural to young men—that of fancying himself preferred by a woman, who had no one recommendation but beauty. To be admired by her whom all his acquaintance admired gratified his *amour propre*. He was overcome by her marked attentions so far as to declare himself, without knowing her real disposition. It was some time before his prepossession allowed him to discover that she was weak and ill-informed, selfish and bad-tempered. What she wanted in understanding, she made up in spirit. The more she exacted, the more he submitted ; and her demands grew in proportion to his sacrifices. My friend, with patient affection, struggled for a long time to raise her character, and to enlighten her mind ; but finding that she pouted whenever he took up a book, and that she even hid the newspaper before he had read it, complaining that he preferred anything to her company, the softness of his temper and his habitual indolence at length prevailed. His better judgment sank in the hopeless contest. For a quiet life he has submitted to a disgraceful life. The compromise has not answered. He has incurred the degradation which, by a more spirited conduct, he might have avoided, and has missed the quiet which he sacrificed his dignity to purchase. He compassionates her folly, and continues to translate her wearisome interruptions into the flattering language of affection.

'In compliment to her, no less than in justification of his own choice, he has persuaded himself that all women are pretty much alike ; that in point of capacity, disposition, and knowledge, he has but drawn the common lot, with the balance in his favour of strong affection and un-sullied virtue. He hardly ever sees his fine library, which is the object of her supreme aversion, but wastes his days in listless idleness and his evenings at cards, the only thing in which she takes a lively interest. His fine mind is, I fear, growing mean and disingenuous. The gentle-ness of his temper leads him not only to sacrifice his peace, but to infringe on his veracity in order to keep her quiet.

'All the entertainment he finds at dinner is a recapitulation of the faults of her maids, or the impertinence of her footmen, or the negli-gence of her gardener. If, to please her, he joins in the censure, she turns suddenly about, and defends them. If he vindicates them, she insists on their immediate dismission ; and no sooner are they irre-vocably discharged than she is continually dwelling on their perfections, and then it is only their successors who have any faults.

'He is now so afraid of her driving out his few remaining old servants, if she sees his partiality for them, that, in order to conceal it, he affects to reprimand them, as the only means for them to secure her favour. Thus the integrity of his heart is giving way to a petty duplicity, and the openness of his temper to shabby artifices. He could submit to the loss of his comfort, but sensibly feels the diminution of his credit. The loss of his usefulness, too, is a constant source of regret. She will not even suffer him to act as a magistrate, lest her doors should be beset with vagabonds, and her house dirtied by men of business. If he chance to commend a dish he has tasted at a friend's house—yes, everybody's things are good but hers ; she can never please ; he had better always dine abroad if nothing is fit to be eaten at home.

'Though poor Stanhope's conduct is so correct, and his attachment to his wife so notorious, he never ventures to commend anything that is said or done by another woman. She has, indeed, no definite object of jealousy, but feels an uneasy, vague sensation of envy at any thing or person he admires. I believe she would be jealous of a fine day if her husband praised it.

'If a tale reaches her ears of a wife who has failed of her duty, or if the public papers record a divorce, then she awakens her husband to a sense of his superior happiness, and her own irreproachable virtue. Oh, Charles, the woman who, reposing on the laurels of her boasted virtue, allows herself to be a disobliging, a peevish, a gloomy, a discon-tented companion, defeats one great end of the institution, which is happiness. The wife who violates the marriage vow is indeed more criminal, but the very magnitude of her crime emancipates her hus-band ; while she who makes him, not dishonourable, but wretched, fastens on him a misery for life, from which no laws can free him, and under which religion alone can support him.'

We continued talking till we reached home on the multitude of marriages in which the parties are 'joined, not matched,' and where the term *union* is a miserable misnomer. I endeavoured to turn all these new acquaintances to account, and considered myself, at every visit I made, as taking a lesson for my own conduct. I beheld the miscarriages of others not only with concern for the individual, but as beacons to light me on my way. It was no breach of charity to use the aberrarations of my acquaintance for the purpose of making my own course more direct. I took care, however, never to lose sight of the humbling consideration that my own deviations were equally liable to become the object of their animadversion, if the same motive had led them to the same scrutiny.

I remained some weeks longer in town, indulging myself in all its safe sights and all its sober pleasures. I examined whatever was new in art, or curious in science. I found out the best pictures, saw the best statues, explored the best museums, heard the best speakers in the courts of law, the best preachers in the Church, and the best orators in Parliament ; attended the best lectures, and visited the best company, in the most correct, though not always the most fashionable, sense of the term. I associated with many learned, sensible, and some pious men, commodities with which London, with all its faults, abounds, perhaps, more than any other place on the habitable globe. I became acquainted with many agreeable, well-informed, valuable women, with a few who even seemed in a good measure to live above the world while they were living in it.

There is a large class of excellent female characters, who, on account of that very excellence, are little known, because to be known is not their object. Their ambition has a better taste. They pass through life honoured and respected in their own small but not unimportant sphere, and approved by Him 'whose they are, and whom they serve,' though their faces are hardly known in promiscuous society. If they occasion little sensation abroad, they produce much happiness at home. And when once a woman, who has 'all appliances and means to get it,' *can* withstand the intoxication of the flatterer and the adoration of the fashionable, *can* conquer the fondness for public distinction, *can* resist the temptations of that magic circle to which she is courted, and in which she is qualified to shine—this is indeed a trial of firmness, a trial in which those who have never been called to resist themselves can hardly judge of the merit of resistance in others.

These are the women. who bless, dignify, and truly adorn society. The painter indeed does not make his fortune by their sitting to him ; the jeweller is neither brought into vogue by furnishing their diamonds, nor undone by not being paid for them ; the prosperity of the milliner does not depend on affixing their name to a cap or a colour ; the poet does not celebrate them ; the novelist does not dedicate to them ; but they possess the affection of their husbands, the attachment of their children, the esteem of the wise and good, and, above all, they possess *His* favour, 'whom to know is life eternal.' Among these I doubt not I might have found objects highly deserving of my heart, but the injunction of my father was a sort of panoply which guarded it.

I am persuaded that such women compose a larger portion of the sex than is generally allowed. It is not the number, but the noise which makes a sensation ; and a set of fair dependent young creatures who are every night forced, some of them reluctantly, upon the public eye, and a bevy of faded matrons rouged and repaired for an ungrateful public, dead to their blandishments, do not compose the whole female world. I repeat it—a hundred amiable women, who are living in the quiet practice of their duties and the modest exertion of their talents, do not fill the public eye, or reach the public ear, like one aspiring leader who, hungering for observation, and disdaining censure, dreads not abuse, but oblivion ; who thinks it more glorious to head a little phalanx of fashionable followers, than to hold out, as from her commanding eminence and imposing talents she might have done, a shining example of all that is great, and good, and dignified in woman. These self-appointed queens maintain an absolute but ephemeral empire over that little *fantastic aristocracy* which they call the world. Admiration besets them, crowds attend them, conquests follow them, inferiors imitate them, rivals envy them, newspapers extol them, sonnets deify them. A few ostentatious charities are opposed as a large atonement for a *few amiable weaknesses*, while the unpaid tradesman is exposed to ruin by their vengeance if he refuse to trust them, and to a gaol if he continue to do it.

Chapter II.

THE three days previous to my leaving London were passed with Sir John and Lady Belfield. Knowing I was on the wing for Hampshire, they promised to make their long-intended visit to Stanley Grove during my stay there.

On the first of these days, we were agreeably surprised at the appearance of Dr. Barlow, an old friend of Sir John, and the excellent rector of Mr. Stanley's parish. Being obliged to come to town on urgent business for a couple of days, he was charged to assure me of the cordial welcome which awaited me at the Grove. I was glad to make this early acquaintance with this highly respectable divine. I made a thousand inquiries about his neighbours, and expressed my impatience to know more of a family, in whose characters I already felt a more than common interest.

'Sir,' said he, 'if you set me talking of Mr. Stanley, you must abide by the consequences of your indiscretion, and bear with the loquacity of which that subject never fails to make me guilty. He is a greater blessing to me as a friend, and to my parish as an example and a benefactor, than I can describe.' I assured him that he could not be too minute in speaking of a man whom I had been early taught to admire, by that exact judge of merit, my late father.

'Mr. Stanley,' said the worthy doctor, 'is about six-and-forty ; his admirable wife is six or seven years younger. He passed the early part of his life in London, in the best society. His commerce with the world was, to a mind like his, all pure gain ; for he brought away from

4

it all the good it had to give, without exchanging for it one particle of his own integrity. He acquired the air, manners, and sentiments of a gentleman, without any sacrifice of his sincerity. Indeed, he may be said to have turned his knowledge of the world to a religious account, for it has enabled him to recommend religion to those who do not like it well enough to forgive, for its sake, the least awkwardness of gesture or inelegance of manner.

'When I became acquainted with the family,' continued he, 'I told Mrs. Stanley, that I was afraid her husband hurt religion in one sense, as much as he recommended it in another ; for, that some men who would forgive him his piety for the sake of his agreeableness, would be led to dislike religion more than ever in other men, in whom the jewel was not so well set. "We should like your religious men well enough," will they say, "if they all resembled Stanley." Whereas the truth is, they do not so much *like* Mr. Stanley's religion, as *bear* with it for the pleasure which his other qualities afford them. She assured me, that this was not altogether the case, for that his other qualities having pioneered his way, and hewed down the prejudices which the reputation to piety naturally raises, his endeavours to be useful to them were much facilitated, and he not only kept the ground he had gained, but was often able to turn this influence over his friends to a better account than they had intended. He converted their admiration of him into arms against their own errors.

'He possesses in perfection,' continued Dr. Barlow, 'that sure criterion of abilities, a great power over the minds of his acquaintance, and has in a high degree that rare talent, the art of conciliation without the aid of flattery. I have seen more men brought over to his opinion by a management derived from his knowledge of mankind, and by a principle which forbade his ever using this knowledge but for good purposes, than I ever observed in any other instance ; and this without the slightest deviation from his scrupulous probity.

'He is master of one great advantage in conversation, that of not only knowing *what* to say that may be useful, but exactly *when* to say it ; in knowing when to press a point, and when to forbear ; in his sparing the self-love of a vain man, whom he wishes to reclaim, by contriving to make him feel himself wrong, without making him appear ridiculous. The former he knows is easily pardoned, the latter never. He has studied the human heart long enough to know, that to wound pride is not the way to cure, but to inflame it ; and that exasperating self-conceit will never subdue it. He seldom, I believe, goes into company without an earnest desire to be useful to some one in it ; but if circumstances are adverse, if the *mollia tempora fandi* does not present itself, he knows he should lose more than they would gain, by trying to make the occasion where he does not find it. And I have often heard him say, that when he cannot benefit others, or be benefited by them, he endeavours to benefit himself by the disappointment, which does his own mind as much good, by humbling him with the sense of his own uselessness, as the subject he wished to have introduced might have done them.

'The death of his only son about six years ago, who had just entered

his eighth year, is the only interruption his family have had to a felicity
so unbroken, that I told Mr. Stanley, some such calamity was necessary
to convince him that he was not to be put off with so poor a portion as
this world has to give. I added, that I should have been tempted to
doubt his being in the favour of God, if he had totally escaped chas-
tisement. A circumstance which, to many parents, would have greatly
aggravated the blow, rather lightened it to him : the boy, had he lived
to be of age, was to have had a large independent fortune from a
distant relation, which will now go to a remote branch, unless there
should be another son. " This wealth," said he to me, " might have
proved the boy's snare, and this independence his destruction. He
who does all things well has afflicted the parents, but He has saved
the child." The loss of an only son, however, sat heavy on his heart,
but it was the means of enabling him to glorify God by his submission,
I should rather say, by his acquiescence. Submission is only yielding
to what we cannot help : acquiescence is a more sublime kind of
resignation ; it is a conviction that the Divine will is holy, just, and
good. He one day said to me, " We were too fond of the mercy, but
not sufficiently grateful for it. We loved him so passionately, that we
might have forgotten who bestowed him. To preserve us from this
temptation, God in great mercy withdrew him. Let us turn our eyes
from the one blessing we have lost, to the countless mercies which are
continued to us, and especially to the hand which confers them ; to the
hand which, if we continue to murmur, may strip us of our remaining
blessings."

' I cannot,' continued Dr. Barlow, ' make a higher eulogium of
Mrs. Stanley than to say, that she is every way worthy of the husband
whose happiness she makes. They have a large family of lovely
daughters, of all ages. Lucilla, the eldest, is near nineteen ; you
would think me too poetical were I to say she adorns every virtue with
every grace ; and yet I should only speak the simple truth. Phœbe,
who is just turned of fifteen, has not less vivacity and sweetness than
her sister, but, from her extreme naïveté and warm-heartedness, she
has somewhat less discretion ; and her father says, that her education
has afforded him not less pleasure, but more trouble, for the branches
shot so fast as to call for more pruning.'

Before I had time to thank the good doctor for his interesting little
narrative, a loud rap announced company. It was Lady Bab Lawless.
With her usual versatility she plunged at once into every subject with
everybody. She talked to Lady Belfield of the news and her nursery,
of poetry with Sir John, of politics with me, and of religion with Dr.
Barlow. She talked well upon most of these points, and not ill upon
any of them : for she had the talent of embellishing subjects of which
she knew but little, and a kind of conjectural sagacity and rash dexterity,
which prevented her from appearing ignorant, even when she knew
nothing. She thought that a full confidence in her own powers was
the sure way to raise them in the estimation of others, and it generally
succeeded.

Turning suddenly to Lady Belfield, she said, ' Pray, my dear, look
at my flowers.' ' They are beautiful roses, indeed,' said Lady Belfield,

'and as exquisitely exact as if they were artificial.'—'Which in truth they are,' replied Lady Bab. 'Your mistake is a high compliment to them, but not higher than they deserve. Look especially at these roses in my cap. You positively shall go and get some at the same place.' 'Indeed,' said Lady Belfield, 'I am thinking of laying aside flowers, though my children are hardly old enough to take them.' 'What affectation!' replied Lady Bab, 'why, you are not above two or three and thirty ; I am almost as old again, and yet I don't think of giving up flowers to my children, or my grandchildren, who will be soon wanting them. Indeed, I only now wear *white* roses.' I discovered by this, that white roses made the same approximation to sobriety in dress, that three tables made to it in cards. 'Seriously, though,' continued Lady Bab, 'you must and shall go and buy some of Fanny's flowers. I need only tell you, it will be the greatest charity you ever did, and then I know you won't rest till you have been. A beautiful girl maintains her dying mother by making and selling flowers. Here is her direction,' throwing a card on the table. 'Oh no, this is not it. I have forgot the name, but it is within two doors of your hair-dresser, in what d'ye call the lane, just out of Oxford Street. It is a poor miserable hole, but her roses are as bright as if they grew in the gardens of Armida.' She now rung the bell violently, saying she had overstayed her time, though she had not been in the house ten minutes.

Next morning I attended Lady Belfield to the exhibition. In driving home through one of the narrow passages near Oxford Street, I observed that we were in the street where the poor flower-maker lived. Lady Belfield directed her footman to inquire for the house. We went into it, and in a small but clean room, up three pair of stairs, we found a very pretty and very genteel young girl at work on her gay manufacture. The young woman presented her elegant performances with an air of uncommon grace and modesty.

She was the more interesting, because the delicacy of her appearance seemed to proceed from ill health, and a tear stood in her eye while she exhibited her works. 'You do not seem well, my dear,' said Lady Belfield, with a kindness which was natural to her. 'I never care about my own health, madam,' replied she, 'but I fear my dear mother is dying.' She stopped, and the tears which she had endeavoured to restrain, now flowed plentifully down her cheeks. 'Where is your mother, child?' said Lady Belfield. 'In the next room, madam.' 'Let us see her,' said her ladyship, 'if it won't too much disturb her.' So saying, she led the way, and I followed her.

We found the sick woman lying on a little poor, but clean bed, pale and emaciated, but she did not seem so near her end as Fanny's affection had made her apprehend. After some kind expressions of concern, Lady Belfield inquired into their circumstances, which she found were deplorable. 'But for that dear girl, madam, I should have perished with want,' said the good woman ; 'since our misfortunes, I have had nothing to support me but what she earns by making these flowers. She has ruined her own health, by sitting up the greatest part of the night to procure me necessaries, while she herself lives on a crust.'

I was so affected with this scene, that I drew Lady Belfield into the next room : 'If we cannot preserve the mother, at least let us save the daughter from destruction,' said I ; 'you may command my purse.' 'I was thinking of the same thing,' she replied. 'Pray, my good girl, what sort of education have you had?' 'Oh, madam,' said she, 'one much too high for my situation. But my parents, intending to qualify me for a governess, as the safest way of providing for me, have had me taught everything necessary for that employment. I have had the best masters, and I hope I have not misemployed my time.' 'How comes it, then,' said I, 'that you were not placed out in some family?' 'What, sir! and leave my dear mother helpless and forlorn? I had rather live only on my tea and dry bread, which indeed I have done for many months, and supply her little wants, than enjoy all the luxuries in the world at a distance from her.'

'What were your misfortunes occasioned by?' said I, while Lady Belfield was talking with the mother. 'One trouble followed another, sir,' said she, 'but what most completely ruined us, and sent my father to prison, and brought a paralytic stroke on my mother, was his being arrested for a debt of seven hundred pounds. This sum, which he had promised to pay, was long due to him for laces, and to my mother for millinery and fancy dresses, from a lady who has not paid it to this moment ; and my father is dead, and my mother dying! this sum would have saved them both!'

She was turning away to conceal the excess of her grief, when a venerable clergyman entered the room. It was the rector of the parish, who came frequently to administer spiritual consolation to the poor woman. Lady Belfield knew him slightly, and highly respected his character. She took him aside, and questioned him as to the disposition and conduct of these people, especially the young woman. His testimony was highly satisfactory. The girl, he said, had not only had an excellent education, but her understanding and principles were equally good. He added, that he reckoned her beauty among her misfortunes. It made good people afraid to take her into the house, and exposed her to danger from those of the opposite description.

I put my purse into Lady Belfield's hands, declining to make any present myself, lest, after the remark he had just made, I should incur the suspicions of the worthy clergyman.

We promised to call again the next day, and took our leave, but not till we had possessed ourselves of as many flowers as she could spare. I begged that we might stop and send some medical assistance to the sick woman, for though it was evident that all relief was hopeless, yet it would be a comfort to the affectionate girl's heart to know that nothing was omitted which might restore her mother.

Chapter XII.

N the evening we talked over our little adventure with Sir John, who entered warmly into the distresses of Fanny, and was inclined to adopt our opinion, that if her character and attainments stood the test of a strict inquiry, she might hereafter probably be transplanted into their family as governess. We were interrupted in the formation of this plan by a visit from Lady Melbury, the acknowledged queen of beauty and of ton. I had long been acquainted with her character, for her charms and her accomplishments were the theme of every man of fashion, and the envy of every modish woman.

She is one of those admired but pitiable characters, who, sent by Providence as an example to their sex, degrade themselves into a warning. Warm-hearted, feeling, liberal, on the one hand ; on the other, vain, sentimental, romantic, extravagantly addicted to dissipation and expense, and, with that union of contrarieties which distinguishes her, equally devoted to poetry and gaming, to liberality and injustice. She is too handsome to be envious, and too generous to have any relish for detraction, but she gives to excess into the opposite fault. As Lady Denham can detect blemishes in the most perfect, Lady Melbury finds perfections in the most depraved. From a judgment which cannot discriminate, a temper which will not censure, and a hunger for popularity which can feed on the coarsest applause, she flatters egregiously and universally, on the principle of being paid back usuriously in the same coin. Prodigal of her beauty, she exists but on the homage paid to it from the drawing-room at St. James's, to the mob at the opera house door. Candour in her is as mischievous as calumny in others, for it buoys up characters which ought to sink. Not content with being blind to the bad qualities of her favourites, she invents good ones for them, and you would suppose her corrupt 'little senate' was a choir of seraphims.

A recent circumstance related by Sir John was quite characteristical. Her favourite maid was dangerously ill, and earnestly begged to see her lady, who always had loaded her with favours. To all company she talked of the virtues of the poor Toinette, for whom she not only expressed but felt real compassion. Instead of one apothecary, who would have sufficed, two physicians were sent for ; and she herself resolved to go up and visit her as soon as she had finished setting to music an elegy on the death of her Java sparrow. Just as she had completed it she received a fresh entreaty to see her maid, and was actually got to the door in order to go upstairs, when the milliner came in with such a distracting variety of beautiful new things, that there was no possibility of letting them go till she had tried everything on, one after the other. This took up no little time. To determine which she should keep and which return, where all was so attractive, took up still more. After numberless vicissitudes and fluctuations of racking thought, it was at length decided she should take the whole. The milliner withdrew ; the lady went up—Toinette had just expired. I found her manners no less fascinating than her person. With all her modish graces, there was a tincture of romance and an appearance of softness and sensibility which gave her the variety of two characters. She was the enchanting woman of fashion, and the elegiac muse.

Lady Belfield had taken care to cover her work-table with Fanny's flowers, with a view to attract any chance visitor. Lady Melbury admired them excessively. ' You must do more than admire them,' said Lady Belfield ; ' you must buy and recommend.' She then told her the affecting scene we had witnessed, and described the amiable girl who supported the dying mother by making these flowers. ' It is quite enchanting,' continued she, resolving to attack Lady Melbury in her own sentimental way, ' to see this sweet girl twisting rose-buds, and forming hyacinths into bouquets.' ' Dear, how charming !' exclaimed Lady Melbury ; ' it is really quite touching. I will make a subscription for her, and write at the head of the list a melting description of her case. She shall bring me all her flowers, and as many more as she can make. But no ; we will make a party, and go and see her ; you shall carry me. How interesting to see a beautiful creature making roses and hyacinths ! Her delicate hands and fair complexion must be amazingly set off by the contrast of the bright flowers. If it were a coarse-looking girl spinning hemp, to be sure one should pity her, but it would not be half so moving. It will be delightful. I will call on you to-morrow, exactly at two, and carry you all. Perhaps,' whispered she to Lady Belfield, ' I may work up the circumstance into a sonnet. Do think of a striking title for it. On second thoughts, the sonnet shall be sent about with the subscription, and I'll get a pretty vignette to suit it.'

' That fine creature,' said Sir John, in an accent of compassion, as she went out, ' was made for nobler purposes. How grievously does she fall short of the high expectations her early youth had raised ! Oh ! what a sad return does she make to Providence for his rich and varied bounties ! Vain of her beauty, lavish of her money, careless of her reputation ; associating with the worst company, yet formed for the best ; living on the adulation of parasites, whose understanding she despises ! I grieve to compare what she is with what she might have been had she married a man of spirit, who would prudently have guided and tenderly have restrained her. He has ruined her and himself by his indifference and easiness of temper. Satisfied with knowing how much she is admired and he envied, he never thought of reproving or restricting her. He is proud of her, but has no particular delight in her company, and, trusting to her honour, lets her follow her own devices, while he follows his. She is a striking instance of the eccentricity of that bounty which springs from mere sympathy and feeling. Her charity requires stage effect—objects that have novelty, and circumstances which, as Mr. Bayes says, "elevate and surprise." She lost, when an infant, her mother, a woman of sense and piety, who, had she lived, would have formed the ductile mind of the daughter, turned her various talents into other channels, and raised her character to the elevation it was meant to reach. Had she a child, I verily think her sweet nature would quite domesticate her.'

'How melancholy,' said I, 'that so superior a woman should live so much below her high destination! She is, doubtless, destitute of any thought of religion.'

'You are much mistaken,' replied Sir John. 'I will not say, indeed, that she entertains much *thought* about it, but she by no means denies its truth, nor neglects occasionally to exhibit its outward and visible signs. She has not yet completely forgotten

All that the nurse and all the priest have taught.

I did not think that, like Lady Denham, she considers it as a commutation, but she preserves it as a habit. A religious exercise, however, never interferes with a worldly one. They are taken up in succession, but with this distinction—the worldly business is to be done, the religious one is not altogether to be left undone. She has a moral chemistry which excels in the amalgamation of contradictory ingredients. On a Sunday at Melbury Castle, if by any strange accident she and her lord happen to be there together, she first reads him a sermon, and plays at cribbage with him the rest of the evening. In town, one Sunday, when she had a cold, she wrote a very pleasing hymn, and then sat up all night at deep play. She declared, if she had been successful, she would have given her winnings to charity ; but as she lost some hundreds, she said she could now with a safe conscience borrow that sum from her charity purse, which she had hoped to add to it, to pay her debt of honour.'

Next day, within two hours of her appointed time, she came, and was complimented by Sir John on her punctuality. 'Indeed,' said she, 'I *am* rather late, but I met with such a fascinating German novel that it positively chained me to my bed till past three. I assure you I never lose time by not rising. In the course of a few winters I have exhausted half Hookham's catalogue before some of my acquaintance are awake, or I myself out of bed.'

We soon stopped at the humble door of which we were in search. Sir John conducted Lady Melbury up the little winding stairs. I assisted Lady Belfield. We reached the room, where Fanny was just finishing a beautiful bunch of jonquils. 'How picturesque !' whispered Lady Melbury to me. 'Do lend me your pencil ; I must take a sketch of that sweet girl with the jonquils in her hand. My dear creature,' continued she, 'you must not only let me have these, but you must make me twelve dozen more flowers as fast as possible, and be sure let me have a great many sprigs of jessamine and myrtle.' Then snatching up a wreath of various-coloured geraniums, 'I must try this on my head by the glass.' So saying, she ran into an adjoining room, the door of which was open ; Lady Belfield having before stolen into it, to speak to the poor invalid.

As soon as Lady Melbury got into the room, she uttered a loud shriek. Sir John and I ran in, and were shocked to find her near fainting. 'Oh, Belfield,' said she, 'this is a trick, and a most cruel one ! Why did you not tell me where you were bringing me ? Why did you not tell me the people's name ?'—'I have never heard it myself,' said Sir John ; 'on my honour, I do not understand you.'—'You know as much of the woman as I know,' said Lady Belfield. 'Alas! much more,' cried she, as fast as her tears would give her leave to speak. She retired to the window for air, wringing her hands, and called for a glass of water to keep her from fainting. I turned to the sick woman for an explanation ; I saw her countenance much changed.

'This, sir,' said she, 'is the lady whose debt of seven hundred pounds ruined me, and was the death of my husband.' I was thunderstruck, but went to assist Lady Melbury, who implored Sir John to go home with her instantly, saying her coach should come back for us. 'But, dear Lady Belfield, do lend me twenty guineas ; I have not a shilling about me.'—'Then, my dear Lady Melbury,' said Lady Belfield, 'how *could* you order twelve dozen expensive flowers ?'—'Oh,' said she, 'I did not mean to have paid for them till next year.'—'And how,' replied Lady Belfield, 'could the debt which was not to have been paid for a twelvemonth have relieved the pressing wants of a creature who must pay ready money for her materials ? However, as you are so distressed, we will contrive to do without your money.'—'I would pawn my diamond necklace directly,' returned she, 'but,' speaking lower, 'to own the truth, it is already in the jeweller's hands, and I wear a paste necklace of the same form.'

Sir John, knowing I had been at my banker's that morning, gave me such a significant look as restrained my hand, which was already on my pocket-book. In great seeming anguish she gave Sir John her hand, who conducted her to her coach. As he was leading her downstairs, she solemnly declared she would never again run in debt, never order more things than she wanted, and, above all, would never play while she lived. She was miserable, because she durst not ask Lord Melbury to pay this woman, he having already given her money three times for the purpose, which she had lost at faro. Then, retracting, she protested, if ever she *did* touch a card again, it should be for the sole purpose of getting something to discharge this debt. Sir John earnestly conjured her not to lay 'that flattering unction to her soul,' but to convert the present vexation into an occasion of felicity, by making it the memorable and happy era of abandoning a practice which injured her fortune, her fame, her principles, and her peace. 'Poor thing,' said Sir John, when he repeated this to us,

> Ease will recant
> Vows made in pain, as violent and void.

In an interval of weeping, she told me,' added he, 'that she was to be at the opera to-night. To the opera, faro will succeed, and to-morrow probably the diamond earrings will go to Grey's in pursuit of the necklace.'

Lady Belfield inquired of Fanny how it happened that Lady Melbury, who talked with *her* without surprise or emotion, discovered so much of both at the bare sight of her mother. The girl explained this by saying that she had never been in the way while they lived in Bond Street, when her ladyship used to come, having been always employed in an upper room, or attending her masters.

Before we parted, effectual measures were taken for the comfortable subsistence of the sick mother, and for alleviating the sorrows and lightening the labours of the daughter ; and next morning I set out on my journey for Stanley Grove, Sir John and Lady Belfield promising to follow me in a few weeks.

As soon as I got into my postchaise, and fairly turned my back on London, I fell into a variety of reflections on the persons with whom I had been living. In this soliloquy I was particularly struck with that discrepancy of characters, all of which are yet included under the broad, comprehensive appellation of *Christians.* I found that, though all differed widely from each other, they differed still more widely from that rule by which they professed to walk. Yet not one of these characters was considered as disreputable. There was not one that was profane or profligate ; not one who would not in conversation have defended Christianity, if its truth had been attacked ; not one who derided or even neglected its forms, and who in her own class would not have passed for religious. Yet how little had any one of them adorned the profession she adopted ! Of Mrs. Ranby, Mrs. Fentham, Lady Bab Lawless, Lady Denham, Lady Melbury, which of them would not have been startled had her Christianity been called in question ? Yet how merely speculative was the religion of even the most serious among them ! How superficial, or inconsistent, or mistaken, or hollow, or hypocritical, or self-deceiving, was that of all the others ! Had either of them been asked from what source she drew her religion, she would indignantly have answered, ‘From the Bible.’ Yet if we compare the copy with the model, the Christian with Christianity, how little can we trace the resemblance ! In what particular did their lives imitate the life of Him *who pleased not Himself;* who *did the will of His Father ;* who *went about doing good ?* How irreconcilable is their faith with the principles which He taught ! How dissimilar their practice with the precepts He delivered ! How inconsistent their lives with the example He bequeathed ! How unfounded their hope of heaven, if an entrance into heaven be restricted to those who are *like-minded with Christ !*

Chapter XIII.

M Y father had been early in life intimately connected with the family of Mr. Stanley. Though this gentleman was his junior by several years, yet there subsisted between them such a similarity of tastes, sentiments, views, and principles, that they lived in the closest friendship ; and both their families having in the early part of their lives resided in London, the occasions of that thorough mutual knowledge that grows out of familiar intercourse were much facilitated. I remembered Mr. Stanley, when I was a very little boy, paying an annual visit to my father at the Priory, and I had retained an imperfect but pleasing impression of his countenance and engaging manners.

Having had a large estate left him in Hampshire, he settled there on his marriage ; and intercourse of letters had kept up the mutual attach-

ment between him and my father. On the death of each parent I had
received a cordial invitation to come and soothe my sorrows in his
society. My father enjoined me that one of my first visits after his
death should be to the Grove ; and, in truth, I now considered my
Hampshire engagement as the *bonne bouche* of my southern excursion.

I reached Stanley Grove before dinner. I found a spacious mansion,
suited to the ample fortune and liberal spirit of its possessor. I was
highly gratified with the fine forest scenery in the approach to the park.
The house had a noble appearance without, and within it was at once
commodious and elegant. It stood on the south side of a hill, nearer
the bottom than the summit, and was sheltered on the north-east by a
fine old wood. The park, though it was not very extensive, was striking
from the beautiful inequality of the ground, which was richly clothed
with the most picturesque oaks I ever saw, interspersed with stately
beeches. The grounds were laid out in good taste ; but though the
hand of modern improvement was visible, the owner had in one instance
spared

> The obsolete prolixity of shade,

for which the most interesting of poets so pathetically pleads. The
poet's plea had saved the avenue.

I was cordially welcomed by Mr. and Mrs. Stanley ; and by that
powerful and instantaneous impression which fine sense and good
breeding, joined to high previous veneration of character, produce on
the feelings of the guest, I at once felt myself at home. All the preliminaries of gradual acquaintance were in a manner superseded, and I
soon experienced that warm and affectionate esteem which seemed
scarcely to require intercourse to strengthen, or time to confirm it. Mr.
Stanley had only a few minutes to present me to his lady and two
lovely daughters before we were summoned to dinner, to which a considerable party had been invited ; for the neighbourhood was populous,
and rather polished.

The conversation after dinner was rational, animated, and instructive.
I observed that Mr. Stanley lost no opportunity which fairly offered for
suggesting useful reflections. But what chiefly struck me in his manner
of conversing was that, without ever pressing religion unseasonably
into the service, he had the talent of making the most ordinary topics
subservient to instruction, and of extracting some profitable hint, or
striking out some important light, from subjects which in ordinary
hands would have been unproductive of improvement. It was evident
that piety was the predominating principle of his mind, and that he
was consulting its interests as carefully when prudence made him forbear to press it, as when propriety allowed him to introduce it. This
piety was rather visible in the sentiment than the phrase. He was of
opinion that bad taste could never advance the interests of Christianity.
And he gave less offence to worldly men than most religious people I
have known, because, though he would on no human consideration
abate one atom of zeal, nor lower any doctrine, nor disguise any truth,
nor palliate, nor trim, nor compromise, yet he never contended for
words or trifling distinctions. He thought it detracted from no man's

piety to bring all his elegance of expression, his correctness of taste,
and his accuracy of reasoning, to the service of that cause which lies
the nearest to the heart of every Christian, and demands the best exertion of his best faculties.

He was also forward to promote subjects of practical use in the
affairs of common life, suited to the several circumstances and pursuits
of his guests. But he particularly rejoiced that there was so broad,
and safe, and unenclosed a field as general literature. This, he observed, always supplies men of education with an ample refuge from all
vulgar and dangerous and unproductive topics. ' If we cannot,' said
he, ' by friendly intercourse always raise our principles, we may always
keep our understandings in exercise ; and those authors who supply so
peccable a creature as man with subjects of elegant and innocent discussion I do not reckon among the lowest benefactors of mankind.'

In my farther acquaintance with Mr. Stanley, I have sometimes observed with what address he has converted a merely moral passage to
a religious purpose. I have known him, when conversing with a man
who would not have relished a more sacred authority, seize on a sentiment in ' Tully's Offices' for the lowest degree in his scale of morals,
and then, gradually ascending, trace and exalt the same thought through
Paley, or Johnson, or Addison, or Bacon, till he has unsuspectedly
landed his opponent in the pure ethics of the Gospel, and surprised
him into the adoption of a Christian principle.

As I had heard there was a fine little flock of children, I was surprised and almost disappointed, every time the door opened, not to see
them appear, for I already began to take an interest in all that related
to this most engaging family. The ladies having, to our great gratification, sat longer than is usual at most tables, at length obeyed the signal
of the mistress of the house. They withdrew, followed by the Miss
Stanleys,
                    With grace
            Which won who saw to wish their stay.

After their departure the conversation was not changed. There was
no occasion ; it could not become more rational, and we did not desire
that it should become less pure. Mrs. Stanley and her fair friends had
taken their share in it with a good sense and delicacy which raised the
tone of our society ; and we did not give them to understand, by a loud
laugh before they were out of hearing, that we rejoiced in being eman-
cipated from the restraint of their presence.

Mrs. Stanley is a graceful and elegant woman. Among a thousand
other excellencies, she is distinguished for her judgment in adapting
her discourse to the character of her guests, and for being singularly
skilful in selecting her topics of conversation. I never saw a lady who
possessed the talent of diffusing at her table so much pleasure to those
around her without the smallest deviation from her own dignified purity.
She asks such questions as strangers may be likely to gain, at least not
to lose, credit by answering ; and she suits her interrogations to the
kind of knowledge they may be supposed likely to possess. By this,
two ends are answered : while she gives her guest an occasion of appearing to advantage, she puts herself in the way of gaining some in-

formation. From want of this discernment, I have known ladies ask a gentleman just arrived from the East Indies questions about America ; and others, from the absence of that true delicacy which, where it exists, shows itself even on the smallest occasions, who have inquired of a person how he liked such a book, though she knew that, in the nature of things, there was no probability of his ever having heard of it—thus assuming an ungenerous superiority herself, and mortifying another by a sense of his own comparative ignorance. If there is any one at table who from his station has least claim to attention, he is sure to be treated with particular kindness by Mrs. Stanley ; and the diffident never fail to be encouraged, and the modest to be brought forward, by the kindness and refinement of her attentions.

When we were summoned to the drawing-room, I was delighted to see four beautiful children, fresh as health and gay as youth could make them, busily engaged with the ladies. One was romping, another singing ; a third was showing some drawings of birds, the natural history of which she seemed to understand ; a fourth had spread a dissected map on the carpet, and had pulled down her eldest sister on the floor to show her Copenhagen. It was an animating scene. I could have devoured the sweet creatures. I got credit with the little singer by helping her to a line which she had forgotten, and with the geographer by my superior acquaintance with the shores of the Baltic.

In the evening, when the company had left us, I asked Mrs. Stanley how she came so far to deviate from established custom as not to produce her children immediately after dinner. ' You must ask me,' said Mr. Stanley, smiling, ' for it was I who first ventured to suggest this bold innovation. I love my children fondly, but my children I have always at home. I have my friends but seldom, and I do not choose that any portion of the time that I wish to dedicate to intellectual and social enjoyment should be broken in upon by another and an interfering pleasure, which I have always within my reach. At the same time, I like my children to see my friends ; company amuses, improves and polishes them. I therefore consulted with Mrs. Stanley how we could so manage as to enjoy our friends without locking up our children. She recommended this expedient. The time, she said, spent by the ladies from their leaving the dining-room till the gentlemen came in to tea was often a little heavy—it was rather an interval of anticipation than of enjoyment. Those ladies who had not much *mind* had soon exhausted their admiration of each other's worked muslins and lace sleeves ; and those who *had* would be glad to rest it so agreeably. She therefore proposed to enliven that dull period by introducing the children.

' This little change has not only succeeded in our own family, but has been adopted by many of our neighbours. For ourselves it has answered a double purpose : it not only delights the little things, but it delights them with less injury than the usual season of their appearance. Our children have always as much fruit as they like after their own dinner ; they do not, therefore, want or desire the fruits, the sweetmeats, the cakes, and the wine with which the guests, in order to please mamma, are too apt to cram them. Besides, poor little dears, it mixes too much selfishness with the natural delight they have in seeing company, by connecting with it the idea of the good things they shall get. But by this alteration we do all in our power to infuse a little disinterestedness into the pleasure they have in coming to us. We love them too tenderly to crib their little enjoyments, so we give them two pleasures instead of one ; for they have their dessert and our company in succession.'

Though I do not approve of too great familiarity with servants, yet I think that to an old and faithful domestic superior consideration is due. My attendant on my present tour had lived in our family from his youth, and had the care of me before I can remember. His fidelity and good sense, and, I may add, his piety, had obtained for him the privilege of free speaking. 'Oh, sir,' said he, when he came to attend me next morning, 'we are got into the right house at last. Such a family ! So godly ! so sober ! so charitable ! 'Tis all of a piece here, sir. Mrs. Comfit, the housekeeper, tells me that her master and mistress are the example of all the rich, and the refuge of all the poor in the neighbourhood ; and as to Miss Lucilla, if the blessing of them that are ready to perish can send anybody to heaven, she will go there sure enough.'

This rhapsody of honest Edwards warmed my heart, and put me in mind that I had neglected to inquire after this worthy housekeeper, who had lived with my grandfather, and was at his death transplanted into the family of Mr. Stanley. I paid a visit the first opportunity to the good woman in her room, eager to learn more of a family who so much resembled my own parents, and for whom I had already conceived something more tender than mere respect.

I congratulated Mrs. Comfit on the happiness of living in so valuable a family. In return, she was even eloquent in their praises. 'Her mistress,' she said, 'was a pattern for ladies—so strict, and yet so kind ; but now, indeed, Miss Lucilla had taken almost all the family cares from her mamma. The day she was sixteen, sir (that is about two years and a half ago), she began to inspect the household affairs a little, and as her knowledge increased she took more and more upon her. Miss Phœbe will very soon be old enough to relieve her sister ; but my mistress won't let her daughters have anything to do with family affairs till they are almost women grown, both for fear it should take them off from their learning, and also give them a low turn about eating and caring for niceties, and lead them into vulgar gossip and familiarity with servants. It is time enough, she says, when their characters are a little formed ; they will then gain all the good, and escape all the danger.'

Seeing me listen with the most eager and delighted attention, the worthy woman proceeded : 'In summer, sir, Miss Stanley rises at six, and spends two hours in her closet, which is stored with the best books. At eight she consults me on the state of provisions and other family matters, and gives me a bill of fare, subject to the inspection of her mamma. The cook has great pleasure in acting under her direction, because she allows that miss understands when things are well done, and never finds fault in the wrong place, which, she says, is a great mortification in serving ignorant ladies, who praise or find fault by chance—not according to the cook's performance, but their own humour. She looks over my accounts every week, which, being kept so short, give her but little trouble ; and once a month she settles everything with her mother.

' 'Tis a pleasure, sir, to see how skilful she is in accounts ! One can't impose upon her a farthing, if one would ; and yet she is so mild and so reasonable, and so quick at distinguishing what are mistakes and what are wilful faults ! Then she is so compassionate ! It will be a heart-breaking day at the Grove, sir, whenever miss marries. When my master is sick, she writes his letters, reads to him, and assists her mamma in nursing him.

' After her morning's work, sir, does she come into company tired and cross, as ladies do who have done nothing, or are ·but just up ? No ; she comes in to make breakfast for her parents, as fresh as a rose, and as gay as a lark. An hour after breakfast she and my master read some learned books together. She then assists in teaching her little sisters, and never were children better instructed. One day in a week she sets aside both for them and herself to work for the poor, whom she also regularly visits at their own cottages two evenings in the week ; for she says it would be troublesome and look ostentatious to have her father's doors crowded with poor people, neither could she get at their wants and their characters half so well as by going herself to their own houses. My dear mistress has given her a small room as a storehouse for clothing and books for her indigent neighbours. In this room, each of the younger daughters, the day she is seven years old, has her own drawer, with her name written on it ; and almost the only competition among them is whose shall be soonest filled with caps, aprons, and handkerchiefs. The working-day is commonly concluded by one of these charitable visits. The dear creatures are loaded with their little work-baskets crammed with necessaries. This, sir, is the day, and it is always looked forward to with pleasure by them all. Even little Celia, the youngest, who is but just turned of five, will come to me and beg for something good to put in her basket for poor Mary or Betty such-a-one. I wonder I do not see anything of the little darlings ; it is about the time they used to pay me a visit.

' On Sundays before church they attend the village school, when the week's pocket-money, which has been carefully hoarded for the purpose, is produced for rewards to the most deserving scholars. And yet, sir, with all this, you may be in the house a month without hearing a word of the matter, it is all done so quietly ; and when they meet at their meals, they are more cheerful and gay than if they had been ever so idle.'

Here Mrs. Comfit stopped, for just then two sweet little cherry-cheeked figures presented themselves at the door, swinging a straw basket between them, and crying out, in a little begging voice, ' Pray, Mrs. Comfit, bestow your charity,—we want something coarse for the hungry, and something nice for the sick,—poor Dame Alice and her little granddaughter !' They were going on, but, spying me, they coloured up to the ears, and ran away as fast as they could, though I did all in my power to detain them.

Chapter IIV.

HEN Miss Stanley came in to make breakfast, she beautifully exemplified the worthy housekeeper's description. I have sometimes seen young women whose simplicity was destitute of elegance, and others in whom a too elaborate polish had nearly effaced their native graces : Lucilla appeared to unite the simplicity of nature to the refinement of good breeding. It was thus she struck me at first sight. I forebore to form a decided opinion, till I had leisure to observe whether her mind fulfilled all that her looks promised.

Lucilla Stanley is rather perfectly elegant than perfectly beautiful. I have seen women as striking, but I never saw one so interesting. Her beauty is countenance : it is the stamp of mind intelligibly printed on the face. It is not so much the symmetry of features, as the joint triumph of intellect and sweet temper. A fine old poet has well described her :

> Her pure and eloquent blood
> Spoke in her cheeks, and so distinctly wrought,
> That one could almost say her body thought.

Her conversation, like her countenance, is compounded of liveliness, sensibility, and delicacy. She does not say things to be quoted, but the effect of her conversation is, that it leaves an impression of pleasure on the mind, and a love of goodness on the heart. She enlivens without dazzling, and entertains without overpowering. Contented to please, she has no ambition to shine. There is nothing like effort in her expression, or vanity in her manner. She has rather a playful gaiety than a pointed wit. Of repartee she has little, and dislikes it in others ; yet I have seldom met with a truer taste for inoffensive wit. Taste is indeed the predominating quality of her mind ; and she may rather be said to be a nice judge of the genius of others than to be a genius herself. She has a quick perception of whatever is beautiful or defective in composition or in character. The same true taste pervades her writing, her conversation, her dress, her domestic arrangements, and her gardening, for which last she has both a passion and a talent. Though she has a correct ear, she neither sings nor plays ; and her taste is so exact in drawing, that she really seems to have *le compas dans l'œil ;* yet I never saw a pencil in her fingers, except to sketch a seat or a bower for the pleasure-ground. Her notions are too just to allow her to be satisfied with mediocrity in anything ; and for perfection in many things, she thinks that life is too short, and its duties too various and important. Having five younger sisters to assist, has induced her to neglect some acquisitions which she would have liked. Had she been an only daughter, she owns that she would have indulged a little more in the garnish and decoration of life.

At her early age, the soundness of her judgment on persons and things cannot be derived from experience ; she owes it to a *tact* so fine as enables her to seize on the strong feature, the prominent circumstance, the leading point, instead of confusing her mind and dissipating her attention on inferior parts of a character, a book, or a business. This justness of thinking teaches her to rate things according to their worth, and to arrange them according to their place. Her manner of speaking adds to the effect of her words ; and the tone of her voice expresses, with singular felicity, gaiety or kindness, as her feelings direct, and the occasion demands. This manner is so natural, and her sentiments spring so spontaneously from the occasion, that it is obvious that display is never in her head, nor an eagerness for praise in her heart. I never heard her utter a word which I could have wished unsaid, or a sentiment I would have wished unthought.

As to her dress, it reminds me of what Dr. Johnson once said to an acquaintance of mine, of a lady who was celebrated for dressing well. ' The best evidence that I can give you of her perfection in this respect is, that one can never remember what she had on.' The dress of Lucilla is not neglected, and it is not studied. She is as neat as the strictest delicacy demands, and as fashionable as the strictest delicacy permits ; and her nymph-like form does not appear to less advantage for being veiled with scrupulous modesty.

Oh ! if women in general knew what was their real interest ! if they could guess with what a charm even the *appearance* of modesty invests its possessor, they would dress decorously from mere self-love, if not from principle. The designing would assume modesty as an artifice, the coquet would adopt it as an allurement, the pure as her appropriate attraction, and the voluptuous as the most infallible art of seduction.

What I admired in Miss Stanley, and what I have sometimes regretted the want of in some other women, is, that I am told she is so lively, so playful, so desirous of amusing her father and mother when alone, that they are seldom so gay as in their family party. It is then that her talents are all unfolded, and that her liveliness is without restraint. She was rather silent the two or three first days after my arrival, yet it was evidently not the silence of reserve or inattention, but of delicate propriety. Her gentle frankness and undesigning temper gradually got the better of this little shyness, and she soon began to treat me as the son of her father's friend. I very early found, that though a stranger might behold her without admiration, it was impossible to converse with her with indifference. Before I had been a week at the Grove, my precautions vanished, my panoply was gone, and yet I had not consulted Mr. Stanley.

In contemplating the captivating figure and the delicate mind of this charming girl, I felt that imagination, which misleads so many youthful hearts, had preserved mine. The image my fancy had framed, and which had been suggested by Milton's heroine, had been refined indeed, but it had not been romantic. I had early formed an ideal standard in my mind ; too high, perhaps, but its very elevation had rescued me from the common dangers attending the society of the sex. I was continually comparing the women with whom I conversed, with the fair conception which filled my mind. The comparison might be unfair to them ; I am sure it was not unfavourable to myself, for it preserved me from the fascination of mere personal beauty, the allure-ments of factitious character, and the attractions of ordinary merit.

I am aware that love is apt to throw a radiance around the being it prefers, till it becomes dazzled, less perhaps with the brightness of the object itself, than with the beams with which imagination has invested it. But religion, though it had not subdued my imagination, had chas-tised it. It had sobered the splendours of fancy, without obscuring them. It had not extinguished the passions, but it had taught me to regulate them.——I now seemed to have found the being of whom I had been in search. My mind felt her excellences, my heart acknow-ledged its conqueror. I struggled, however, not to abandon myself to its impulses. I endeavoured to keep my own feelings in order, till I had time to appreciate a character, which appeared as artless as it was correct. And I did not allow myself to make this slight sketch of Lucilla, and of the effect she produced on my heart, till more intimate acquaintance had justified my prepossession.

But let me not forget that Mr. Stanley had another daughter. If Lucilla's character is more elevated, Phœbe's is not less amiable. Her face is equally handsome, but her figure is somewhat less delicate. She has a fine temper, and strong virtues. The little faults she has, seem to flow from the excess of her good qualities. Her susceptibility is extreme, and to guide and guard it, finds employment for her mother's fondness and her father's prudence. Her heart overflows with gratitude for the smallest service. This warmth of her tenderness keeps her affections in more lively exercise than her judgment; it leads her to overrate the merit of those she loves, and to estimate their excellences less by their own worth than by their kindness to her. She soon behaved to me with the most engaging frankness, and her innocent vivacity encouraged, in return, that affectionate freedom with which one treats a beloved sister.

The other children are gay, lovely, interesting, and sweet-tempered. Their several acquisitions, for I detest the term *accomplishments*, since it has been warped from the true meaning in which Milton used it, seem to be so many individual contributions brought in to enrich the common stock of domestic delight. Their talents are never put into exercise by artificial excitements. Habitual industry, quiet exertion, successive employments, affectionate intercourse, and gay and animated relaxation, make up the round of their cheerful day.

I could not forbear admiring in this happy family the graceful union of piety with cheerfulness ; strictness of principle embellished, but never relaxed, by gaiety of manners ; a gaiety, not such as requires turbulent pleasures to stimulate it, but evidently the serene yet animated result of well-regulated minds ;—of minds actuated by a tenderness of conscience, habitually alive to the perception of the smallest sin, and kindling into holy gratitude at the smallest mercy.

I often called to mind that my father, in order to prevent my being deceived and run away with by the persons who appeared lively at first sight, had early accustomed me to discriminate carefully, whether it was not the *animal* only that was lively, and the man dull. I have found this caution of no small use in my observations on the other sex. I had frequently remarked, that the musical and the dancing ladies, and those who were most admired for modish attainments, had little *intellectual* gaiety. In numerous instances I found that the mind was the only part which was not kept in action ; and no wonder, for it was the only part which had received no previous forming, no preparatory moulding.

When I mentioned this to Mr. Stanley, 'The education,' replied he, ' which now prevails, is a Mahometan education. It consists entirely in making woman an object of attraction. There are, however, a few reasonable people left, who, while they retain the object, improve upon the plan. They, too, would make woman attractive ; but it is by sedulously labouring to make the understanding, the temper, the mind, and the manners of their daughters, as engaging as these Circassian parents endeavour to make the person.'

Chapter XV.

THE friendly rector frequently visited at Stanley Grove, and, for my father's sake, honoured me with his particular kindness. Dr. Barlow filled up all my ideas of a country clergyman of the higher class. There is a uniform consistency runs through his whole life and character, which often brings to my mind, allowing for the revolution in habits that almost two hundred years have necessarily produced, the incomparable *country parson* of the ingenious Mr. George Herbert.*

' I never saw *zeal without innovation*,' said Mr. Stanley, 'more exemplified than in Dr. Barlow. His piety is as enlightened as it is sincere. No errors in religion escape him through ignorance of their existence, or through carelessness in their detection, or through in·activity in opposing them. He is too honest not to attack the prevailing evil, whatever shape it may assume ; too correct to excite in the wise any fears that his zeal may mislead his judgment, and too upright to be afraid of the censures which active piety must ever have to encounter from the worldly and the indifferent, from cold hearts and unfurnished heads.

' From his affectionate warmth, however, and his unremitting application, arising from the vast importance he attaches to the worth of souls, the man of the world might honour him with the title of enthusiast ; while his prudence, sober-mindedness, and regularity, would

---

* See Herbert's ' Country Parson,' under the heads of the parson in his house, the parson praying, the parson preaching, the parson comforting, the parson's church, the parson catechising, the parson in mirth, etc., etc. The term parson has now indeed a vulgar and disrespectful sound, but in Herbert's time it was used in its true sense, *persona ecclesiæ.* I would recommend to those who have not seen it, this sketch of the ancient clerical life. As Mr. Herbert was a man of quality, he knew what became the more opulent of his function ; as he was eminently pious, he practised all that he recommended.—' This appellation of parson,' says Judge Blackstone, ' however depreciated by clownish and familiar use, is the most legal, most beneficial, and most honourable title, which a parish priest can enjoy.'—*Vide Blackstone's Commentaries.*

draw on him from the fanatic, the appellation of formalist.   Though he is far from being " content to *dwell* in decencies," he is careful never to neglect them.   He is a clergyman all the week, as well as on Sunday ; for he says, if he did not spend much of the intermediate time in pastoral visits, there could not be kept up that mutual inter-course of kindness which so much facilitates his own labours, and his people's improvement.   They listen to him because they love him, and they understand him because he has familiarized them by private dis-course to the great truths which he delivers from the pulpit.

' Dr. Barlow has greatly diminished the growth of innovation in his parishes, by attacking the innovator with his own weapons.   Not indeed by stooping to the same disorderly practices, but by opposing an enlightened earnestness to an eccentric earnestness ; a zeal *with* knowledge to a zeal *without* it.   He is of opinion that activity does more good than invective, and that the latter is too often resorted to because it is the cheaper substitute.

' His charity, however, is large, and his spirit truly catholic.   He honours all his truly pious brethren, who are earnest in doing good, though they may differ from him as to the manner of doing it.   Yet his candour never intrenches on his firmness ; and while he will not dispute with others about shades of difference, he maintains his own opinions with the steadiness of one who embraced them on the fullest con-viction.

' He is a "scholar, and being a good and a ripe one," it sets him above aiming at the paltry reputation to be acquired by those false embellishments of style, those difficult and uncommon words, and that laboured inversion of sentences, by which some injudicious clergymen make themselves unacceptable to the higher, and unintelligible to the lower, and, of course, the larger part of their audience.   He always bears in mind that the common people are not foolish, they are only ignorant.   To meet the one, he preaches good sense ; to suit the other, plain language.   But while he seldom shoots over the heads of the un-informed, he never offends the judicious.   He considers the advice of Polonius to his son to be as applicable to preachers as to travellers—

> Be thou familiar, but by no means vulgar.

In his pulpit he is no wrangling polemic, but a genuine Bible Christian, deeply impressed himself with the momentous truths he so earnestly presses upon others.   His mind is so imbued, so saturated, if I may hazard the expression, with scriptural knowledge, that from that rich storehouse, he is ever ready to bring forth *treasures new and old*, and to apply them wisely, temperately, and seasonably.

' Though he carefully inculcates universal holiness in all his dis-courses, yet his practical instructions are constantly deduced from those fundamental principles of Christianity which are the root and life and spirit of all goodness.   Next to a solid piety, and a deep acquaintance with the Bible, he considers it of prime importance to a clergyman to be thoroughly acquainted with human nature in general, and with the state of his own parish in particular.   The knowledge of both will alone preserve him from preaching too personally so as to hurt, or too generally so as not to touch.

'He is careful not to hurry over the prayers in so cold, inattentive, and careless a manner, as to make the audience suspect he is saving himself, that he may make a greater figure in delivering the sermon. Instead of this, the devout, reverential, and impressive manner in which he pronounces the various parts of the Liturgy, best prepares his own heart, and the hearts of his people, to receive benefit from his discourse. His petitions are delivered with such sober fervour, his exhortations with such humble dignity, his thanksgivings with such holy animation, as carry the soul of the hearer along with him. When he ascends the pulpit, he never throws the liturgical service into the background by a long elaborate composition of his own, delivered with superior force and emphasis. And he pronounces the Lord's prayer with a solemnity which shows that he recollects its importance and its Author.

'In preaching, he is careful to be distinctly heard, even by his remotest auditors ; and by constant attention to this important article, he has brought his voice, which was not strong, to be particularly audible. He affixes so much importance to a distinct delivery, that he smilingly told me, he suspected the grammatical definition of a substantive was originally meant for a clergyman, whose great object it was, if possible, *to be seen,* but indispensably to be *heard, felt, and understood.*

'His whole performance is distinguished by a grave and majestic simplicity, as far removed from the careless reader of a common story, as from the declamation of an actor. His hearers leave the church, not so much in raptures with the preacher, as affected with the truths he has delivered. He says, he always finds he has done most good when he has been least praised, and that he feels most humbled when he receives the warmest commendation, because men generally extol most the sermons which have probed them least ; whereas those which really do good, being often such as make them most uneasy, are consequently the least likely to attract panegyric. " *They* only bear true testimony to the excellence of a discourse," added he, " not who commend the composition or the delivery, but who are led by it to examine their own hearts, to search out its corruptions, and to reform their lives. Reformation is the flattery I covet."

'He is aware that the generality of hearers like to retire from a sermon with the comfortable belief that little is to be done on *their* parts. Such hearers he always disappoints by leaving on their minds at the close some impressive precept deduced from, and growing out of, the preparatory doctrine. He does not press any one truth to the exclusion of all others. He proposes no subtleties, but labours to excite seriousness, to alarm the careless, to quicken the supine, to confirm the doubting. He presses eternal things as things near at hand ; as things in which every living man has an equal interest.'

Mr. Stanley says, that 'though Dr. Barlow was considered at Cambridge as a correct young man, who carefully avoided vice and even irregularity, yet, being cheerful and addicted to good society, he had a disposition to innocent conviviality which might, unsuspectedly, have

led him into the errors he abhorred. He was struck with a passage in
a letter from Dr. Johnson to a young man who had just taken orders,
in which, among other wholesome counsel, he advises him " to acquire
the courage to refuse *sometimes* invitations to dinner." It is inconceivable what a degree of force and independence his mind acquired by
the occasional adoption of this single hint. He is not only,' continued
Mr. Stanley, ' the spiritual director, but the father, the counsellor, the
arbitrator, and the friend of those whom Providence has placed under
his instruction.

' He is happy in an excellent wife, who, by bringing him a considerable fortune, has greatly enlarged his power of doing good. But still
more essentially has she increased his happiness, and raised his
character, by her piety and prudence. By the large part she takes in
his affairs, he is enabled to give himself wholly up to the duties of his
profession. She is as attentive to the bodies as her husband is to the
souls of his people, and educates her own family as sedulously as he
instructs his parish.

' One day, when I had been congratulating Dr. Barlow on the
excellence of his wife's character, the conversation fell, by a sudden
transition, on the celibacy of the Romish clergy. He smiled and said,
" Let us ministers of the Reformation be careful never to provoke the
people to wish for the restoration of that part of popery. I often reflect
how peculiarly incumbent it is on us to select such partners as shall
never cause our emancipation from the old restrictions to be regretted.
And we ourselves ought, by improving the character of our wives, to
repay the debt we owe to the ecclesiastical laws of Protestantism for
the privilege of possessing them."

' Will it be thought too trifling to add how carefully this valuable pair
carry their consistency into the most minute details of their family
arrangements ? Their daughters are no less patterns of decorum and
modesty in their dress and appearance, than in the more important
parts of their conduct. The doctor says, " that the most distant and
inconsiderable appendages to the temple of God should have something
of purity and decency. Besides," added he, " with what face could I
censure improprieties from the pulpit if the appearance of my own family
in the pew below were to set my precepts at defiance by giving an
example of extravagance and vanity to the parish, and thus, by making
the preacher ridiculous, make his expostulations worse than ineffectual."

' So conscientious a rector,' added Mr. Stanley, ' could not fail to be
particularly careful in the choice of a curate ; and a more humble, pious,
diligent assistant than Mr. Jackson could not easily be found. He is
always a welcome guest at my table. But this valuable man, who was
about as good a judge of the world as the great Hooker, made just such
another indiscreet marriage. He was drawn in to choose his wife, the
daughter of a poor tradesman in the next town, because he concluded
that a woman bred in humble and active life would necessarily be humble
and active herself. *Her* reason for accepting *him* was because she
thought that as every clergyman was a *gentleman*, she, of course, as his
wife, should be a *gentlewoman*, and fit company for anybody.'

' He instructs my parish admirably,' said Dr. Barlow, ' but his own little family he cannot manage. His wife is continually reproaching him, that though he may know the way to heaven, he does not know how to push his way in the world. His daughter is the finest lady in the parish, and outdoes them all, not only in the extremity, but the immodesty of the fashion. It is her mother's great ambition that she should excel the Miss Stanleys and my daughters in music, while her good father's linen betrays sad marks of negligence. I once ventured to tell Mrs. Jackson that there was only one reason which could excuse the education she had given her daughter, which was, that I presumed she intended to qualify her for getting her bread ; and that if she would correct the improprieties of the girl's dress, and get her instructed in useful knowledge, I would look out for a good situation for her. This roused her indignation. She refused my offer with scorn, saying, that when she asked my charity she would take my advice, and desired I would remember that one clergyman's daughter was as good as another. I told her that there was indeed a sense in which one clergyman was as good as another, because the profession dignified the lowest of the order, if, like her husband, he was a credit to that order. Yet still there were gradations in the church as well as in the state. But between the *wives* and *daughters* of the higher and lower clergy, there was the same distinction which riches and poverty have established between those of the higher and lower orders of the laity, and that rank and independence in the one case, confer the same outward superiority as rank and independence in the other.'

Chapter XVI.

AMONG the visitors at Stanley Grove, there was a family of ladies, who, though not particularly brilliant, were singularly engaging from their modesty, gentleness, and good sense. One day, when they had just left us, Mr. Stanley obliged me with the following little relation : Mrs. Stanley and Lucilla only being present.

' Lady Aston has been a widow almost seven years. On the death of Sir George, she retired into this neighbourhood with her daughters, the eldest of whom is about the age of Lucilla. She herself had had a pious but a very narrow education. Her excessive grief for the loss of her husband augmented her natural love of retirement, which she cultivated, not to the purpose of improvement, but to the indulgence of melancholy. Soon after she settled here, we heard how much good she did, and in how exemplary a manner she lived, before we saw her. She was not very easy of access, even to us ; and after we had made our way to her, we were the only visitors she admitted for a long time. We soon learnt to admire her deadness to the world, and her unaffected humility. Our esteem for her increased with our closer intercourse, which, however, enabled us also to observe some considerable mistakes in her judgment, especially in the mode in which she was training up her daughters. These errors we regretted, and with all possible tenderness ventured to point out to her. The girls were the prettiest demure little nuns you ever saw—mute and timid, cheerless and in-active, but kind, good, and gentle.

' Their pious mother, who was naturally of a fearful and doubting mind, had had this pensive turn increased by several early domestic losses, which, even previous to Sir George's death, had contributed to fix something of a too tender and hopeless melancholy on her whole character. There are two refuges for the afflicted ; two diametrically opposite ways of getting out of sorrow—religion, and the world. Lady Aston had wisely chosen the former. But her scrupulous spirit had made the narrow way narrower than religion required. She read the Scriptures diligently, and she prayed over them devoutly ; but she had no judicious friend to direct her in these important studies. As your Mrs. Ranby attended only to the doctrines, and our friend Lady Belfield trusted indefinitely to the promises, so poor Lady Aston's broken spirit was too exclusively carried to dwell on the threatenings ; together with the rigid performance of those duties which she earnestly hoped might enable her to escape them. This round of duty, of watch-fulness, and prayer, she invariably performed with almost the sanctity of an apostle, but with a little too much of the scrupulosity of an ascetic. While too many are rejoicing with unfounded confidence in those animating passages of Scripture which the whole tenor of their lives demonstrates not to belong to them, she trembled at those denuncia-tions which she could not fairly apply to herself. And the promises from which she might have derived reasonable consolation, she over-looked as designed for others.

' Her piety, though sincere, was a little tinctured with superstition. If any petty strictness was omitted, she tormented herself with cause-less remorse. If any little rule was broken, she repaired the failure with treble diligence the following day ; and laboured to retrieve her perplexed accounts with the comfortless anxiety of a person who is working out a heavy debt. I endeavoured to convince her, that an inferior duty which clashed with one of a higher order, might be safely postponed at least, if not omitted.

' A diary has been found useful to many pious Christians, as a record of their sins, and of their mercies. But this poor lady spent so much time in weighing the offences of one day against those of another, that before the scruple was settled, the time for action was past. She brought herself into so much perplexity by reading over this journal of her infirmities, that her difficulties were augmented by the very means she had employed to remove them ; and her conscience was disturbed by the method she had taken to quiet it. This plan, however, though distressing to a troubled mind, is wholesome to one of a contrary cast.

' *My* family, as you have seen, are rather exact in the distribution of their time, but we do not distress ourselves at interruptions which are unavoidable : but *her* arrangements were carried on with a rigour which made her consider the smallest deviation as a sin that required severe repentance. Her alms were expiations, her self-denials penances. She was rather a disciple of the mortified Baptist, than of the merciful Redeemer. Her devotions were sincere, but discouraging. They con-sisted much in contrition, but little in praise ; much in sorrow for sin, but little in hope of its pardon. She did not sufficiently cast her care and confidence on the great propitiation. She firmly believed all that her Saviour had done and suffered, but she had not the comfort of practically appropriating the sacrifice. While she was painfully working out her salvation with fear and trembling, she indulged the most unfounded apprehensions of the Divine displeasure. At Aston Hall the Almighty was literally feared, but he was not glorified. It was the obedience of a slave, not the reverential affection of a child.

'When I saw her denying herself and her daughters the most innocent enjoyments, and suspecting sin in the most lawful indulgences, I took the liberty to tell her how little acceptable uncommanded austerities and arbitrary impositions were to the God of mercies. I observed to her, that the world, that human life, that our own sins and weaknesses, found us daily and hourly occasions of exercising patience and self-denial ; that life is not entirely made up of great evils or heavy trials, but that the perpetual recurrence of petty evils and small trials is the ordinary and appointed exercise of the Christian graces. To bear with the failings of those about us, with their infirmities, their bad judgment, their ill-breeding, their perverse tempers ; to endure neglect where we feel we have deserved attention, and ingratitude where we expected thanks ; to bear with the company of disagreeable people, whom Providence has placed in our way, and whom He has perhaps provided on purpose for the trial of our virtue ; these are the best exercises ; and the better because not chosen by ourselves. To bear with vexations in business, with disappointments in our expectations, with interruptions of our retirement, with folly, intrusion, disturbance, in short, with whatever opposes our will, and contradicts our humour ; this habitual acquiescence appears to be more of the essence of self-denial that any little rigours or inflictions of our own imposing. These constant, inevitable, but inferior evils, properly improved, furnish a good moral discipline, and might well in the days of ignorance have superseded pilgrimage and penance. It has this advantage, too, over the other, that it sweetens the temper and promotes humility, while the former gives rigidness instead of strength, and inflexibility instead of firmness.'

' I have often thought,' said I, when Mr. Stanley made a pause, 'that we are apt to mistake our vocation by looking out of the way for occasions to exercise great and rare virtues, and by stepping over those ordinary ones which lie directly in the road before us. When we read, we fancy we could be martyrs, and when we come to act, we cannot even bear a provoking word.'

Miss Stanley looked pleased at my remark, and in a modest tone observed, that ' in no one instance did we deceive ourselves more than in fancying we could do great things well, which we were never likely to be called to do at all ; while, if we were honest, we could not avoid owning how negligently we performed our own little appointed duties, and how sedulously we avoided the petty inconveniences which these duties involved.'

' By kindness,' resumed Mr. Stanley, ' we gradually gained Lady Aston's confidence, and of that confidence we have availed ourselves to give something of a new face to the family. Her daughters, good as they were dutiful, by living in a solitude unenlivened by books and unvaried by improving company, had acquired a manner rather resembling fearfulness than delicacy. Religious they were, but they had contracted gloomy views of religion. They considered it as something that must be endured in order to avoid punishment, rather than as a principle of peace, and trust, and comfort ; as a task to be gone through, rather than as a privilege to be enjoyed. They were tempted to consider the Almighty as a hard master, whom, however, they were resolved to serve, rather than as a gracious father who was not only loving, but *love* in the abstract. Their mother was afraid to encourage a cheerful look, lest it might lead to levity ; or a sprightly thought, for fear it might have a wrong tendency. She forgot, or rather she did not know, that young women were not formed for contemplative life. She forgot that in all our plans and operations we should still bear in mind that there are two worlds. As it is the fault of too many to leave the *next* out of their calculation, it was the error of Lady Aston, in forming the minds of her children, to leave out *this.* She justly considered heaven as their great aim and end ; but neglected to qualify them for the present temporal life, on the due use and employment of which so obviously depends the happiness of that which is eternal.

' Her charities were very extensive, but of these charities her sweet daughters were not made the active dispensers, because an old servant, who governed not only the family, but her lady also, chose that office herself. Thus the bounty being made to flow in partial channels, the woman's relations and favourites almost entirely engrossing it, it did little comparative good.

' With fair understandings, the Miss Astons had acquired very little knowledge ; their mother's scrupulous mind found something dangerous in every author who did not professedly write on religious subjects. If there were one exceptionable page in a book, otherwise valuable, instead of suppressing the page, she suppressed the book. And indeed, my dear Charles, grieved am I to think how few authors of the more entertaining kind we *can* consider as perfectly pure, and put, without caution, restriction, or mutilation, into the hands of our daughters. I am, however, of opinion, that as they will not always have their parents for tasters, and as they will everywhere, even in the most select libraries, meet with these mixed works, in which, though there is much to admire, yet there is something to expunge, it is the safest way to accustom them early to hear read the most unexceptionable parts of these books. Read them yourself to them without any air of mystery ; tell them that what you omit is not worth reading, and then the omissions will not excite but stifle curiosity. The books to which I allude are those where the principle is sound and the tendency blameless, and where the few faults consist rather in coarseness than in corruption.

' But to return : she fancied that these inexperienced creatures, who had never tried the world, and whose young imaginations had perhaps painted it in all the brilliant colours with which erring fancy gilds the scenes it has never beheld, and the pleasures it has never tried, could renounce it as completely as herself, who had exhausted what it has to give, and was weary of it. She thought they could live contendedly in their closets, without considering that she had neglected to furnish their minds with that knowledge which may make the closet a place of enjoyment, by supplying the intervals of devotional with entertaining reading.

'We carried Lucilla and Phœbe to visit them : I believe she was a little afraid of their gay countenances. I talked to her of the necessity of literature to inform her daughters, and of pleasures to enliven them. The term pleasure alarmed her still more than that of literature. "What pleasures were allowed to religious people? She would make her daughters as happy as she dared, without offending her Maker." I quoted the devout but liberal Hooker, who exhorts us not to regard the Almighty as a captious sophist, but as a merciful Father.

'During this conversation we were sitting under the fine-spreading oak on my lawn, in front of that rich bank of flowers which you so much admire. It was a lovely evening in the end of June, the setting sun was all mild radiance, the sky all azure, the air all fragrance. The birds were in full song. The children, sitting on the grass before us, were weaving chaplets of wild flowers :

It looked like nature in the world's first spring.'

'My heart was touched with joy and gratitude. "Look, madam," said I, "at the bountiful provision which a beneficent Father makes, not only for the necessities, but for the pleasures of his children :

——— not content
With every food of life to nourish man,
He makes all nature beauty to his eye
And music to his ear.

' " These flowers are of so little apparent use, that it might be thought profuseness in any economy short of that which is divine, to gratify us at once with such forms, and such hues, and such fragrance. It is a gratification not necessary, yet exquisite, which lies somewhere between the pleasures of sense and intellect, and in a measure partakes of both. It elevates while it exhilarates, and lifts the soul from the gift to the giver. God has not left his goodness to be *inferred* from abstract speculation, from the conclusions of reason, from deduction and argument ; we not only collect it from observation, but we have palpable evidences of His bounty, we feel it with our senses. Were God a hard master, might He not withhold these superfluities of goodness? Do you think He makes such rich provision for us, that we should shut our eyes and close our ears to them? Does He present such gifts with one hand, and hold in the other a stern interdict of ' touch not, taste not, handle not ?' And can you believe He is less munificent in the economy of grace, than in that of nature ? Do you imagine that He provides such abundant supplies for our appetites and senses here, without providing more substantial pleasures for our future enjoyment ? Is not what we see a prelude to what we hope for, a pledge of what we may expect ? a specimen of larger, higher, richer bounty, an encouraging cluster from the land of promise? If from His works we turn to His Word, we shall find the same inexhaustible goodness exercised to still nobler purposes. Must we not hope then, even by analogy, that He has in store blessings exalted in their nature, and eternal in their duration, for all those who love and serve him in the Gospel of His Son?"

'We now got on fast. She was delighted with my wife, and grew less and less afraid of my girls. I believe, however, that we should have made a quicker progress in gaining her confidence if we had looked less happy. I suggested to her to endeavour to raise the tone of her daughters' piety, to make their habits less monastic, their tempers more cheerful, their virtues more active ; to render their lives more useful by making them the immediate instruments of her charity ; to take them out of themselves, and teach them to compare their factitious distresses with real substantial misery, and to make them feel grateful for the power and the privilege of relieving it.

'As Dr. Barlow has two parishes which join, and we had preoccupied the ground in our own, I advised them to found a school in the next, for the instruction of the young, and a friendly society for the aged, of their own sex. We prevailed on them to be themselves not the nominal but the active patronesses, to take the measure of all the wants and all the merit of their immediate neighbourhood, to do everything under the advice and superintendence of Dr. Barlow, and to make him their " guide, philosopher, and friend." By adopting this plan, they now see poverty of which they only used to hear, and know personally the dependents whom they protect.

'Dr. Barlow took infinite pains to correct Lady Aston's views of religion. " Let your notions of God," said he, " be founded, not on your own gloomy apprehensions and visionary imaginations, but on what is revealed in His Word, else the very intenseness of your feelings, the very sincerity of your devotion, may betray you into enthusiasm, into error, into superstition, into despair. Spiritual notions which are not grounded on scriptural truth, and directed and guarded by a close adherence to it, mislead tender hearts and warm imaginations. But while you rest on the sure, unperverted foundation of the Word of God, and pray for His Spirit to assist you in the use of His Word, you will have little cause to dread that you shall fear Him too much, or serve Him too well. I earnestly exhort you," continued he, " not to take the measure of your spiritual state from circumstances which have nothing to do with it. Be not dismayed at an incidental depression which may depend on the state of your health, or your spirits, or your affairs. Look not for sensible communications. Do not consider rapturous feelings as any criterion of the favour of your Maker, nor the absence of them as any indication of His displeasure. An increasing desire to know Him more and serve Him better, an increasing desire to do and to suffer His whole will, a growing resignation to His providential dispensations, is a much surer, a much more unequivocal test."

'I next,' continued Mr. Stanley, 'carried our worthy curate, Mr. Jackson, to visit her, and proposed that she should engage him to spend a few hours every week with the young ladies. I recommended that after he had read with them a portion of Scripture, of which he would give them a sound and plain exposition, he should convince them he had not the worse taste for being religious by reading with them some books of general instruction, history, travels, and polite literature. This would imbue their minds with useful knowledge, form their taste, and fill up profitably and pleasantly that time which now lay heavy on their hands, and, without intrenching on any of their duties, would qualify them to discharge them more cheerfully.

' I next suggested that they should study gardening, and that they should put themselves under the tuition of Lucilla, who is become the little Repton of the valley. To add to the interest, I requested that a fresh piece of ground might be given them, that they might not only exercise their taste, but be animated with seeing the complete effect of their own exertions ; as a creation of their own would be likely to afford them more amusement than improving on the labours of another.

' I had soon the gratification of seeing my little Carmelites, who used, when they walked in the garden, to look as if they came to dig a daily portion of their own graves, now enjoying it, embellishing it, and delighted by watching its progress ; and their excellent mother, who, like Spenser's Despair, used to look ' as if she never dined,' now enjoying the company of her select friends. The mother is become almost cheerful, and the daughters almost gay. Their dormant faculties are awakened. Time is no longer a burden, but a blessing ; the day is too short for their duties, which are performed with alacrity, since they have been converted into pleasures. You will believe I did not hazard all these terrible innovations as rapidly as I recount them, but gradually, as they were able to bear it.

' This happy change in themselves has had the happiest consequences. Their friends had conceived the strongest prejudices against religion from the gloomy garb in which they had seen it arrayed at Aston Hall. The uncle, who was also the guardian, had threatened to remove the girls before they were quite moped to death : the young baronet was actually forbidden to come home at the holidays ; but now the uncle is quite reconciled to *them,* and almost to *religion.* He has resumed his fondness for the daughters ; and their brother, a fine youth at Cambridge, is happy in spending his vacations with his family, to whom he is become tenderly attached. He has had his own principles and character much raised by the conversation and example of Dr. Barlow, who contrives to be at Aston Hall as much as possible when Sir George is there. He is daily expected to make his mother a visit, when I shall recommend him to your particular notice and acquaintance.'

Lucilla, blushing, said she thought her father had too exclusively recommended the brother to my friendship ; she would venture to say the sisters were equally worthy of my regard, adding, in an affectionate tone, ' They are everything that is amiable and kind. The more you know them, sir, the more you will admire them ; for their good qualities are kept back by the best quality of all, their modesty.' This candid and liberal praise did not sink the fair eulogist herself in my esteem.

Chapter XVII.

HAD now been near three weeks at the Grove. Ever since my arrival I had contracted the habit of pouring out my heart to Mr. and Mrs. Stanley, with grateful affection and filial confidence. I still continued to do it on all subjects except one.

The more I saw of Lucilla, the more difficult I found it to resist her numberless attractions. I could not persuade myself that either prudence or duty demanded that I should guard my heart against such a combination of amiable virtues and gentle graces—virtues and graces which, as I observed before, my mind had long been combining as a delightful idea, and which I now saw realised in a form more engaging than even my own imagination had allowed itself to picture.

I did not feel courage sufficient to risk the happiness I actually enjoyed by aspiring too suddenly to a happiness more perfect. I dared not yet avow to the parents or the daughter feelings which my fears told me might possibly be discouraged, and which, if discouraged, would at once dash to the ground a fabric of felicity that my heart, not my fancy, had erected, and which my taste, my judgment, and my principles equally approved, and delighted to contemplate.

The great critic of antiquity, in his treatise on the drama, observes that the introduction of a new person is of the next importance to a new incident. Whether the introduction of two interlocutors is equal in importance to two incidents, Aristotle has forgotten to establish. This dramatic rule was illustrated by the arrival of Sir John and Lady Belfield, who, though not new to the reader or the writer, were new at Stanley Grove.

This early friendship of the two gentlemen had suffered little diminution from absence, though their intercourse had been much interrupted ; Sir John, who was a few years younger than his friend, since his marriage, having lived as entirely in the town as Mr. Stanley had done in the country. Mrs. Stanley had, indeed, seen Lady Belfield a few times in Cavendish Square, but her ladyship had never before been introduced to the other inhabitants of the Grove.

The guests were received with cordial affection, and easily fell into the family habits, which they did not wish to interrupt, but from the observation of which they hoped to improve their own. They were charmed with the interesting variety of characters in the lovely young family, who, in return, were delighted with the politeness, kindness, and cheerfulness of their father's guests.

Shall I avow my own meanness ? Cordially as I loved the Belfields, I am afraid I saw them arrive with a slight tincture of jealousy. They would, I thought, by enlarging the family circle, throw me at a farther distance from the being whom I wished to contemplate nearly. They would, by dividing her attention, diminish my proportion. I had been hitherto the sole guest ; I was now to be one of several. This was the first discovery I made that love is a narrower of the heart. I tried to subdue the ungenerous feeling, and to meet my valuable friends with a warmth adequate to that which they so kindly manifested. I found that a wrong feeling, at which one has virtue enough left to blush, is seldom lasting, and shame soon expelled it.

The first day was passed in mutual inquiries and mutual communications. Lady Belfield told me that the amiable Fanny, after having wept over the grave of her mother, was removed to the house of the benevolent clergyman, who had kindly promised her an asylum till Lady Belfield's return to town, when it was intended she should be received into her family, that worthy man and his wife having taken on themselves a full responsibility for her character and disposition, and generously promised that they would exert themselves to advance her progress in knowledge during the interval. Lady Belfield added that every inquiry respecting Fanny, whom we must now call Miss Stokes, had been attended with the most satisfactory result, her principles being as unquestionable as her talents.

After dinner, I observed that whenever the door opened, Lady Belfield's eye was always turned towards it, in expectation of seeing the children. Her affectionate heart felt disappointment on finding that they did not appear, and she could not forbear whispering me, who sat next her, ' that she was afraid the piety of our good friends was a little tinctured with severity. For her part, she saw no reason why religion should diminish one's affection for one's children, and rob them of their innocent pleasures.' I assured her gravely I thought so too, but forbore telling her how totally inapposite her application was to Mr. and Mrs. Stanley. She seemed glad to find me of her opinion, and gave up all hope of seeing the ' little melancholy recluses,' as she called them, ' unless,' she said, laughing, ' she might be permitted to look at them through the grate of their cells.' I smiled, but did not undeceive her, and affected to join in her compassion. When we went to attend the ladies in the drawing-room, I was delighted to find Lady Belfield sitting on a low stool, the whole gay group at play around her. A blush mixed itself with her good-natured smile as we interchanged a significant look. She was questioning one of the elder ones, while the youngest sat on her lap singing. Sir John entered, with that kindness and good humour so natural to him, into the sports of the others, who, though wild with health and spirits, were always gentle and docile. He had a thousand pleasant things to entertain them with. He too, it seems, had not been without his misgivings.

' Are not these poor, miserable recluses ?' whispered I maliciously to her ladyship ; ' and are not these rueful looks proof positive that religion diminishes our innocent pleasures, to give them their full range in a fresh, airy apartment, instead of cramming them into an eating-room, of which the air is made almost fœtid by the fumes of the dinner and a crowded table ? And is it not better that they should spoil the pleasure of the company, though the mischief they do is bought by the sacrifice of their own liberty ?'—' I make my *amende*,' said she. ' I never will be so forward again to suspect piety of ill-nature.'—' So far from it, Caroline,' said Sir John, ' that we will adopt the practice we were so forward to blame ; and I shall not do it,' said he, 'more from regard to the company than to the children, who I am sure will be gainers in point of enjoyment. Liberty, I perceive, is to them positive pleasure, and paramount to any which our false epicurism can contrive for them.'

'Well, Charles,' said Sir John, as soon as he saw me alone, 'now tell us about this Lucilla, this paragon, this nonpareil of Dr. Barlow's. Tell me, what is she ? or rather, what is she not ?'

'First,' replied I, ' I will, as you desire, define her by negatives. She is *not* a professed beauty, she is *not* a professed genius, she is *not* a professed philosopher, she is *not* a professed wit, she is *not* a professed anything ; and I thank my stars she is *not* an artist !'—' Bravo, Charles ! Now as to what she is.'—'She is,' replied I, 'from nature, a woman, gentle, feeling, animated, modest ; she is, by education, elegant, informed, enlightened ; she is, from religion, pious, humble, candid, charitable.'

'What a refreshment will it be,' said Sir John, 'to see a girl of fine sense, more cultivated than accomplished—the creature, not of fiddlers and dancing-masters, but of nature, of books, and of good company ! If there is the same mixture of spirit and delicacy in her character that there is of softness and animation in her countenance, she is a dangerous girl, Charles.'

'She certainly does,' said I, 'possess the essential charm of beauty where it exists, and the most effectual substitute for it where it does not—the power of prepossessing the beholder by her look and manner, in favour of her understanding and temper.'

This prepossession I afterwards found confirmed, not only by her own share in the conversation, but by its effect on myself ; I always feel that our intercourse unfolds not only her powers but my own. In conversing with such a woman I am apt to fancy that I have more understanding, because her animating presence brings it more into exercise.

After breakfast next day, the conversation happened to turn on the indispensable importance of unbounded confidence to the happiness of married persons. Mr. Stanley expressed his regret, that though it was one of the grand ingredients of domestic comfort, yet it was sometimes unavoidably prevented by an unhappy inequality of mind between the parties, by violence, or imprudence, or imbecility on one side, which almost compelled the other to a degree of reserve, as incompatible with the design of the union, as with the frankness of the individual.

'We have had an instance among our own friends,' replied Sir John, ' of this evil being produced, not by any of the faults to which you have adverted, but by an excess of misapplied sensibility in two persons of near equality as to merit, and in both of whom the utmost purity of mind and exactness of conduct rendered all concealment superfluous. Our worthy friends Mr. and Mrs. Hamilton married from motives of affection, and with a high opinion of each other's merit, which their long and intimate connection has rather contributed to exalt than to lower ; and yet, now, at the end of seven years, they are only beginning to be happy. They contrived to make each other and themselves as uncomfortable by an excess of tenderness, as some married pairs are rendered by the want of it. A mistaken sensibility has intrenched not only on their comfort, but on their sincerity. Their resolution never to give each other pain, has led them to live in a constant state of petty concealment. They are neither of them remarkably healthy, and to hide from each other every little indisposition, has kept up a continual vigilance to conceal illness on the one part, and to detect it on the other, till it became a trial of skill which could make the other most unhappy ; each suffering much more by suspicion when there was no occasion for it, than they could have done by the acknowledgment of slight complaints, when they actually existed.

'This valuable pair, after seven years' apprenticeship to a petty martyrdom, have at last found out that it is better to submit to the inevitable ills of life cheerfully and in concert, and to comfort each other under them cordially, than alternately to suffer and inflict the pain of perpetual disingenuousness. They have at last discovered that uninterrupted prosperity is not the lot of man. Each is happier now with knowing that the other is sometimes sick, than they used to be with suspecting they were always so. The physician is now no longer secretly sent for to one, when the other is known to be from home. The apothecary is at last allowed to walk boldly up the public staircase, fearless of detection.

'These amiable persons have at length attained all that was wanting to their felicity, that of each believing the other to be well when they *say* they are so. They have found out that unreserved communication is the lawful commerce of conjugal affection, and that all concealment is contraband.'

'Surely,' said I, when Sir John had done speaking, 'it is a false compliment to the objects of our affection, if, for the sake of sparing them a transient uneasiness, we rob them of the comfort to which they are entitled, of mitigating our suffering by partaking it. All dissimulation is disloyalty to love. Besides, it appears to me to be an introduction to wider evils, and I should fear both for the woman I loved, and for myself, that if once we allowed ourselves concealment in one point where we thought the motive excused us, we might learn to adopt it in others where the principle was more evidently wrong.'

'Besides,' replied Mr. Stanley, 'it argues a lamentable ignorance of human life, to set out with an expectation of health without interruption, and of happiness without alloy. When young persons marry with the fairest prospects, they should never forget that infirmity is inseparably bound up with their very nature, and that in bearing one another's burdens, they fulfil one of the highest duties of the union.'

Chapter XVIII.

FTER supper, when only the family party were present, the conversation turned on the unhappy effects of misguided passion. Mrs. Stanley lamented that novels, with a very few admirable exceptions, had done infinite mischief by so completely establishing the omnipotence of love, that the young reader was almost systematically taught an unresisting submission to a feeling, because the feeling was commonly represented as irresistible.

'Young ladies,' said Sir John, smiling, 'in their blind submission to this imaginary omnipotence, are apt to be necessarians. When they *fall* in love, as it is so justly called, they then obey their *fate;* but in their stout opposition to prudence and duty, they most manfully exert their *free will;* so that they want nothing but the *knowledge absolute* of the miseries attendant on an indiscreet attachment, completely to exemplify the occupation assigned by Milton to a class of beings to whom it would not be gallant to resemble young ladies.'

Mrs. Stanley continued to assert that ill-placed affection only became invincible because its supposed invincibility had been first erected into a principle. She then adverted to the power of religion in subduing the passions, that of love among the rest.

I ventured to ask Lucilla, who was sitting next me (a happiness which by some means or other I generally contrived to enjoy), what were her sentiments on this point? With a little confusion she said, 'to conquer an ill-placed attachment, I conceive may be effected by motives inferior to religion. Reason, the humbling conviction of having made an unworthy choice, for I will not resort to so bad a motive as pride, may easily accomplish it. But to conquer a well-founded affection, a justifiable attachment, I should imagine, requires the powerful principle of Christian piety; and what cannot that effect?' She stopped and blushed, as fearing she had said too much.

Lady Belfield observed, that she believed a virtuous attachment might possibly be subdued by the principle Miss Stanley had mentioned; yet she doubted if it were in the power of religion itself to enable the heart to conquer aversion, much less to establish affection for an object for whom dislike had been entertained.

'I believe,' said Mr. Stanley, 'the example is rare, and the exertion difficult; but that which is difficult to us is not impossible to Him who has the hearts of all men in His hand. And I am happy to resolve Lady Belfield's doubt by a case in point. You cannot, Sir John, have forgotten our old London acquaintance Carlton?'

'No,' replied he, 'nor can I ever forget what I have since heard of his ungenerous treatment of that most amiable woman, his wife. I suppose he has long ago broken her heart?'

'You know,' resumed Mr. Stanley, 'they married not only without any inclination on either side, but on her part with something more than indifference, with a preference for another person. *She* married through an implicit obedience to her mother's will, which she had never in any instance opposed. *He*, because his father had threatened to disinherit him if he married any other woman ; for as they were distant relations, there was no other way of securing the estate in the family.'

'What a motive for a union so sacred and so indissoluble !' exclaimed I, with an ardour which raised a smile in the whole party. I asked pardon for my involuntary interruption, and Mr. Stanley proceeded.

' She had long entertained a partiality for a most deserving young clergyman, much her inferior in rank and fortune. But though her high sense of filial duty led her to sacrifice this innocent inclination, and though she resolved never to see him again, and had even prevailed on him to quit the country and settle in a distant place, yet Carlton was ungenerous and inconsistent enough to be jealous of her without loving her. He was guilty of great irregularities, while Mrs. Carlton set about acquitting herself of the duties of a wife with the most meek and humble patience, burying her sorrows in her own bosom, and not allowing herself even the consolation of complaining.

' Among the many reasons for his dislike, her piety was the principal. He said religion was of no use but to disqualify people for the business of life ; that it taught them to make a merit of despising their duties, and hating their relations ; and that pride, ill-humour, opposition, and contempt for the rest of the world, were the meat and drink of all those who pretended to religion.

' At first she nearly sunk under his unkindness ; her health declined, and her spirits failed. In this distress she applied to the only sure refuge of the unhappy, and took comfort in the consideration that her trials were appointed by a merciful Father, to detach her from a world which she might have loved too fondly, had it not been thus stripped of its delights.

' When Mrs. Stanley, who was her confidential friend, expressed the tenderest sympathy in her sufferings, she meekly replied, " Remember who are they whose robes are washed white in the kingdom of glory ; *it is they who come out of great tribulation.* I endeavour to strengthen my faith with a view of what the best Christians have suffered, and my hope with meditating on the shortness of all suffering. I will confess my weakness," added she ; "of the various motives to patience under the ills of life which the Bible presents, though my reason and religion acknowledge them all, there is not one which comes home so powerfully to my feelings as this—*the time is short.*"

'Another time Mrs. Stanley, who had heard of some recent irregularities of Carlton, called upon her, and, lamenting the solitude to which she was often left for days together, advised her to have a female friend in the house, that her mind might not be left to prey upon itself by living so much alone. She thanked her for the kind suggestion, but said she felt it was wiser and better not to have a confidential friend always at hand ; "for of what subject should we talk," said she, "but of my husband's faults ? Ought I to allow myself in such a practice ? It would lead me to indulge a habit of complaint which I am labouring to subdue. The compassion of my friend would only sharpen my feelings, which I wish to blunt. Giving vent to a flame only makes it rage the more ; if suppressing cannot subdue it, at least the consciousness that I am doing my duty will enable me to support it. When we feel," added she, " that we are *doing* wrong, the opening our heart may strengthen our virtue ; but when we are *suffering* wrong, the mind demands another sort of strength—it wants higher support than friendship has to impart. It pours out its sorrows in prayer with fuller confidence, knowing that He who sees can sustain, that He who hears will recompense ; that He will judge, not our weakness, but our efforts to conquer it ; not our success, but our endeavours ; with Him, endeavour is victory.

' " The grace I most want," added she, " is humility. A partial friend, in order to support my spirits, would flatter my conduct ; gratified with her soothing, I should, perhaps, not so entirely cast myself for comfort on God. Contented with human praise, I might rest in it. Besides, having endured the smart, I would not willingly endure it in vain. We know Who has said, ' If you suffer with me, you shall also reign with me.' It is not, however, to mere suffering that the promise is addressed, but to suffering for His sake, and in His Spirit." Then, turning to the Bible which lay before her, and pointing to the sublime passage of St. Paul, which she had just been reading, " Our light affliction, which is but for a moment, worketh for us a far more exceeding and eternal weight of glory," " Pray," said she, " read this in connection with the next verse, which is not always done. *When* is it that it works for us this weight of glory ? *Only* ' while we are looking at the things which are not seen.' Do admire the beauty of this position, and how the good is weighed against the evil, like two scales differently filled : the affliction is light, and but for a moment ; the glory is a *weight*, and it is for *ever*. 'Tis a feather against lead, a grain of sand against the universe, a moment against eternity. Oh, how the scale which contains this world's light trouble kicks the beam when weighèd against the glory which shall be revealed."

' At the end of two years she had a little girl. This opened to her a new scene of duties, and a fresh source of consolation. Her religion proves itself to be of the right stamp, by making her temper still more sweet, and diffusing the happiest effects through her whole character and conversation. When her husband had stayed out late, or even all night, she never reproached him. When he was at home, she received his friends with as much civility as if she had liked them. He found that his house was conducted with the utmost prudence, and that, while she maintained his credit at his table, her personal expenses were almost nothing—indeed, self seemed nearly annihilated in her. He sometimes felt disappointed because he had no cause of complaint, and was angry that he had nothing to condemn.

' As he has a very fine understanding, he was the more provoked, because he could not help seeing that her blameless conduct put him continually in the wrong. All this puzzled him. He never suspected there was a principle out of which such consequences could grow, and was ready to attribute to insensibility that patience which nothing short of Christian piety could have inspired. He had conceived of religion as a visionary system of words and phrases, and concluded that from so unsubstantial a theory it would be a folly to look for practical effects.

'Sometimes, when he saw her nursing his child, of whom he was very fond, he was almost tempted to admire the mother, who is a most pleasing figure ; and now and then, when his heart was thus softened for a moment, he would ask himself what reasonable ground of objection there was either to her mind or person.

'Mrs. Carlton, knowing that his affairs must necessarily be embarrassed by the extraordinary expenses he had incurred, when the steward brought her usual year's allowance, she refused to take more than half, and ordered him to employ the remainder on his master's account. The faithful old man was ready to weep, and could not forbear saying, "Madam, you could not do more for a kind husband. Besides, it is but a drop of water in the ocean."—"That drop," said she, "it is my duty to contribute." When the steward communicated this to Carlton, he was deeply affected, refused to take the money, and again was driven to resort to the wonderful principle from which such right but difficult actions could proceed.'

Here I interrupted Mr. Stanley. ' I am quite of the steward's opinion,' said I. ' That a woman should do this and much more for the man who loved her, and whom she loved, is quite intelligible to every being who has a heart ; but for a cruel, unfeeling tyrant, I do not comprehend it. What say you, Miss Stanley ?'

' Under the circumstances you suppose,' said she, blushing, ' I think the woman would have no shadow of merit ; her conduct would be a mere gratification, an entire indulgence of her own feelings. The triumph of affection would have been cheap ; Mrs. Carlton's was the triumph of religion—of a principle which could subdue an attachment to a worthy object, and act with such generosity towards an unworthy one.'

Mr. Stanley went on. ' Mrs. Carlton frequently sat up late, reading such books as might qualify her for the education of her child, but always retired before she had reason to expect Mr. Carlton, lest he might construe it into upbraiding. One night, as he was not expected to come home at all, she sat later than usual, and had indulged herself with taking her child to pass the night in her bed. With her usual earnestness, she knelt down, and offered up her devotions by her bedside, and, in a manner particularly solemn and affecting, prayed for her husband. Her heart was deeply touched, and she dwelt on these petitions in a strain peculiarly fervent. She prayed for his welfare in both worlds, and earnestly implored that she might be made the humble instrument of his happiness. She meekly acknowledged her own many offences ; of his she said nothing.

' Thinking herself secure from interruption, her petitions were uttered aloud, her voice often faltering, and her eyes streaming with tears. Little did she suspect that the object of her prayers was within hearing of them. He had returned home unexpectedly, and, coming softly into the room, heard her pious aspirations. He was inexpressibly affected. He wept and sighed bitterly. The light from the candles on the table fell on the blooming face of his sleeping infant, and on that of his weeping wife. It was too much for him. But he had not the virtuous courage to give way to his feelings ; he had not the generosity to come forward and express the admiration he felt. He withdrew unperceived, and passed the remainder of the night in great perturbation of spirit. Shame, remorse, and confusion raised such a conflict in his mind as prevented him from closing his eyes ; while she slept in quiet, and awoke in peace.

'The next morning, during a very short interview, he behaved to her with a kindness which she had never before experienced. He had not resolution to breakfast with her, but promised, with affection in his words and manner, to return to dinner. The truth was, he never quitted home, but wandered about his woods to compose and strengthen his mind. This self-examination was the first he had practised ; its effects were salutary.

'A day or two previous to this they had dined at our house. He had always been much addicted to the pleasures of the table. He expressed high approbation of a particular dish, and mentioned again when he got home how much he liked it. The next morning Mrs. Carlton wrote to Lucilla, to beg the receipt for making this ragout : and this day, when he returned from his solitary ramble and "compunctious visitings," the favourite dish, most exquisitely dressed, was produced at his dinner. He thanked her for this obliging attention, and, turning to the butler, directed him to tell the cook that no dish was ever so well dressed. Mrs. Carlton blushed when the honest butler said, " Sir, it was my mistress dressed it with her own hands, because she knew your honour was fond of it."

'Tears of gratitude rushed into Carlton's eyes, and tears of joy over-flowed those of the old domestic, when his master, rising from the table, tenderly embraced his wife, and declared he was unworthy of such a treasure. " I have been guilty of a public wrong, Johnson," said he to his servant, " and my reparation shall be as public. I can never deserve her, but my life shall be spent in endeavouring to do so."

'The little girl was brought in, and her presence seemed to cement this new-formed union. An augmented cheerfulness on the part of Mrs. Carlton invited an increased tenderness on that of her husband. He began every day to discover new excellencies in his wife, which he readily acknowledged to herself and to the world. The conviction of her worth had gradually been producing esteem, esteem now ripened into affection, and his affection for his wife was mingled with a blind sort of admiration of that piety which had produced such effects. He now began to think home the pleasantest place, and his wife the pleasantest companion.

'A gentle censure from him on the excessive frugality of her dress, mixed with admiration of the purity of its motive, was an intimation to her to be more elegant. He happened to admire a gown worn by a lady whom they had visited. She not only sent for the same materials, but had it made by the same pattern—a little attention of which he felt the delicacy.

'He not only saw, but in no long time acknowledged, that a religion which produced such admirable effects could not be so mischievous a principle as he had supposed, nor could it be an inert principle. Her prudence has accomplished what her piety began. She always watched the turn of his eye, to see how far she might venture, and changed the discourse when the look was not encouraging. She never tired him with lectures, never obtruded serious discourse unseasonably, nor pro-, longed it improperly. His early love of reading, which had for some years given way to more turbulent pleasures, he has resumed, and frequently insists that the books he reads to her shall be of her own chusing. In this choice she exercises the nicest discretion, selecting such as may gently lead his mind to higher pursuits, but which, at the same time, are so elegantly written as not to disgust his taste. In all this Mrs. Stanley is her friend and counsellor.

'While Mrs. Carlton is advancing her husband's relish for books of piety, he is forming hers to polite literature. She herself often proposes an amusing book, that he may not suspect her of a wish to abridge his innocent gratifications ; and by this complaisance she gains more than she loses, for, not to be outdone in generosity, he often proposes some pious one in return. Thus their mutual sacrifices are mutual benefits. She has found out that he has a highly cultivated understanding, and he has discovered that she has a mind remarkably susceptible of cultivation. He has by degrees dropped most of his former associates, and has entirely renounced the diversions into which they led him. He is become a frequent and welcome visitor here. His conduct is uniformly respectable, and I look forward with hope to his becoming even a shining character. There is, however, a pertinacity, I may say a sincerity, in his temper, which somewhat keeps him back. He will never adopt any principle without the most complete conviction of his own mind ; nor profess any truth of which he himself does not actually feel the force.'

Lady Belfield, after thanking Mr. Stanley for his interesting little narrative, earnestly requested that Sir John would renew his acquaintance with Mr. Carlton, that she herself might be enabled to profit by such an affecting example of the power of genuine religion as his wife exhibited ; confessing that one such living instance would weigh more with her than a hundred arguments. Mrs. Stanley obligingly promised to invite them to dinner the first leisure day.

Mr. Stanley now informed us that Sir George Aston was arrived from Cambridge, on a visit to his mother and sisters ; that he was a youth of great promise, whom he begged to introduce to us as a young man in whose welfare he took a lively concern, and on the right formation of whose character much would depend, as he had a large estate, and the family interest in the county would give him a very considerable influence. To this influence it was, therefore, of great importance to give a right direction. We next morning took a ride to Aston Hall, and I commenced an acquaintance with the engaging young baronet, which I doubt not, from what I saw and heard, will hereafter ripen into friendship.

Chapter XIX.

HE good rector joined the party at dinner. The conversation afterwards happened to turn on the value of human opinion ; and Sir John Belfield made the hackneyed observation, that the desire of obtaining it should never be discouraged, it being highly useful as a motive of action.

'Yes,' said Dr. Barlow, ' it certainly has its uses in a world, the affairs of which must be chiefly carried on by worldly men ; a world which is itself governed by low motives. But human applause is not a Christian principle of action ; nay, it is so adverse to Christianity, that our Saviour Himself assigns it as a powerful cause of men's not believing, or at least not confessing Him, *because they loved the praise of men.* The eager desire of fame is a sort of separation line between Paganism and Christianity. The ancient philosophers have left us many shining examples of moderation in earthly things, and of the contempt for riches. So far the light of reason and a noble self-denial carried them ; and many a Christian may blush at these instances of their superiority ; but of an indifference to fame, of a deadness to human applause, except as founded on loftiness of spirit, disdain of their judges, and self-sufficient pride, I do not recollect any instance.'

'And yet,' said Sir John, ' I remember Seneca says in one of his epistles, that no man expresses such a respect and devotion to virtue, as he who forfeits the *repute* of being a good man, that he may not forfeit the *conscience* of being such.'

'They might,' replied Mr. Stanley, 'incidentally express some such sentiment, in a well-turned period, to give antithesis to an expression, or weight to an apophthegm ; they might declaim against it in a fit of disappointment, in the burst of indignation excited by a recent loss of popularity ; but I question if they ever once acted upon it. I question if Marius himself, sitting amidst the ruins of Carthage, actually felt it. Seldom, if ever, does it seem to have been inculcated as a principle, or enforced as a rule of action : nor could it, it was " against the canon law of their foundation."'

Sir John. 'Yet a good man struggling with adversity is, I think represented by one of their authors as an object worthy the attention of the gods.'

Stanley. 'Yes—but the Divine approbation alone was never proposed as the standard of right, or the reward of actions, except by Divine revelation.'

'Nothing seems more difficult,' said I, ' to settle than the standard of right. Every man has a standard of his own, which he considers as of universal application. One makes his own tastes, desires, and appetites, his rule of right ; another, the example of certain individuals, fallible like himself ; a third, and indeed the generality, the maxims, habits, and manners of the fashionable part of the world.'

Sir John. ' But since it is so difficult to discriminate between allowable indulgence and criminal conformity, the life of a conscientious man, if he be not constitutionally temperate, or habitually firm, must be poisoned with solicitude, and perpetually rankled with the fear of exceeding his limits.'

Stanley. ' My dear Belfield, the peace and security of a Christian, we well know, are not left to depend on constitutional temperance, or habitual firmness. These are, as the young Numidian says :

Perfections that are placed in bones and nerves.

There is a higher and surer way to prevent the solicitude, which is, by correcting the principle ; to get the heart set right ; to be jealous over ourselves, to be careful never to venture to the edge of our lawful limits ; in short, and that is the only infallible standard, to live in the conscientious practice of measuring all we say, and do, and think, by the unerring rule of God's Word.'

Sir John. ' The impossibility of reaching the perfection which that rule requires, sometimes discourages well-meaning men, as if the attempt were hopeless.'

Dr. Barlow. ' That is, sir, because they take up with a kind of hearsay Christianity. Its reputed pains and penalties drive them off from inquiring for themselves. They rest on the surface. If they would go deeper, they would see that the Spirit which dictated the Scripture is a Spirit of power, as well as a Spirit of promise. All that He requires us to do, He enables us to perform. He does not prescribe " rules " without furnishing us with " arms." '

In answer to some further remarks of Sir John, who spoke with due abhorrence of any instance of actual vice, but who seemed to have no just idea of its root and principle, Dr. Barlow observed : ' While every one agrees in reprobating wicked actions, few, comparatively, are aware of the natural and habitual evil which lurks in the heart. To this the Bible particularly directs our attention. In describing a bad character, it does not say that his *actions* are flagitious, but that " God is not in all his *thoughts.*" This is the description of a thoroughly worldly man. Those who are given up completely to the world, to its maxims, its principles, its cares, or its pleasures, cannot entertain thoughts of God. And to be unmindful of His providence, to be regardless of His presence, to be insensible to His mercies, must be nearly as offensive to Him as to deny His existence. Excessive dissipation, a supreme love of money, or an entire devotedness to ambition, drinks up that spirit, swallows up that affection, exhausts that vigour, starves that zeal, with which a Christian should devote himself to serve his Maker.

' Pray observe,' continued Dr. Barlow, 'that I am not speaking of avowed profligates, but of decent characters ; men who, while they are pursuing with keen intenseness the great objects of their attachment, do not deride or even totally neglect religious observances ; yet think they do much and well, by affording some old scraps of refuse time to a few weary prayers, and sleepy thoughts, from a mind worn down with engagements of pleasure, or projects of accumulation, or schemes of ambition. In all these several pursuits, there may be nothing which, to the gross perceptions of the world, would appear to be moral turpitude. The pleasure may not be profligacy, the wealth so cherished may not have been fraudulently obtained, the ambition, in human estimation, may not be dishonourable ; but an alienation from God, an indifference to eternal things, a spirit incompatible with the spirit of the Gospel, will be found at the bottom of all these restless pursuits.'

' I am entirely of your opinion, doctor,' said Mr. Stanley ; 'it is taking up with something short of real Christianity ; it is an apostacy from the doctrines of the Bible ; it is the substitution of a spurious and popular religion, for that which was revealed from heaven ; it is a departure from the faith once delivered to the saints,—that has so fatally sunk our morality, and given countenance to that low standard of practical virtue which prevails. If we lower the principle, if we obscure the light, if we reject the influence, if we sully the purity, if we abridge the strictness of the Divine law, there will remain no ascending power in the soul, no stirring spirit, no quickening aspiration after perfection, or stretching forward after that holiness to which the beatific vision is specifically promised. It is vain to expect that the practice will rise higher than the principle which inspires it, that the habits will be superior to the motives which govern them.'

Dr. Barlow. ' Selfishness, security, and sensuality are predicted by our Saviour, as the character of the last times. In alluding to the antediluvian world, and the cause of its destruction, eating, drinking, and marrying could not be named in the Gospel as things censurable in themselves, they being necessary to the very existence of that world, which the abuse of them was tending to destroy. Our Saviour does not describe criminality by the excess, but by the spirit of the act. He speaks of eating, not gluttony ; of drinking, not intoxication ; of marriage, not licentious intercourse. This seems a plain intimation, that carrying on the transactions of the world in the spirit of the world, and that habitual deadness to the concerns of eternity, in beings so alive to the pleasures or the interests of the present moment, do not indicate a state of safety, even where gross acts of vice may be rare.'

Mr. Stanley. ' It is not by a few, or even by many instances of excessive wickedness, that the moral state of a country is to be judged, but by a general averseness and indifference to *real* religion. A few examples of glaring impiety may furnish more subject for declamation, but are not near so deadly a symptom. It is no new remark, that more men are undone by an excessive indulgence in things permitted, than by the commission of avowed sins.'

Sir John. ' How happy are those who, by their faith and piety, are delivered from these difficulties !'

Stanley. ' My dear Belfield, where are those privileged beings? It is one sad proof of human infirmity, that the best men have continually these things to struggle with. What makes the difference is, that those whom we call good men struggle on to the end, while the others, not seeing the danger, do not struggle at all.'

' Christians,' said Dr. Barlow, ' who would strictly keep within the bounds prescribed by their religion, should imitate the ancient Romans, who carefully watched that their god Terminus, who defined their limits, should never recede ; the first step of his retreat, they said, would be the destruction of their security.'

Sir John. 'But, doctor, pray what remedy do you recommend against this natural, I had almost said this invincible, propensity to overvalue the world ? I did not mean a propensity merely to overrate its pleasures and its honours, but a disposition to yield to its dominion over the mind, to indulge a too earnest desire of standing well with it, to cherish a too anxious regard for its good opinion ?'

Dr. Barlow. 'The knowledge of the disease should precede the application of the remedy. Human applause is by a worldly man reckoned not only among the luxuries of life, but among articles of the first necessity. An undue desire to obtain it has certainly its foundation in vanity ; and it is one of our grand errors to reckon vanity a trivial fault. An over-estimation of character, and an anxious wish to conciliate all suffrages, is an infirmity from which even worthy men are not exempt ; nay, it is a weakness from which, if they are not governed by a strict religious principle, worthy men are in most danger. Reputation being in itself so very desirable a good, those who actually possess it and in some sense deserve to possess it, are apt to make it their standard, and to rest in it as their supreme aim and end.'

Sir John. 'You have exposed the latent principle, it remains that you suggest its cure.'

Dr. Barlow. ' I believe the most effectual remedy would be, to excite in his mind frequent thoughts of our divine Redeemer, and of *His* estimate of that world on which we so fondly set our affections, and whose approbation we are too apt to make the chief object of our ambition.

Sir John. ' I allow it to have been necessary, that Christ, in the great end which He had to accomplish, should have been poor, and neglected, and contemned, and that He should have trampled on the great things of this world, human applause among the rest ; but I do not conceive that this obligation extends to his followers, nor that we are called upon to partake the poverty which he preferred, or to renounce the wealth and grandeur which He set at nought, or to imitate Him in making himself of no reputation.'

Dr. Barlow. 'We are not called to resemble Him in His external circumstances. It is not our bounden duty to be necessarily exposed to the same contempt ; nor are we obliged to embrace the same ignominy. Yet it seems a natural consequence of our Christian profession, that the things which He despised, we should not venerate ; the vanities He trampled on, we should not admire ; the world which He censured, we ought not to idolize ; the ease which He renounced, we should not rate too highly ; the fame which He set at nought, we ought not anxiously to covet. Surely the followers of Him who was "despised and rejected of men" should not seek their highest gratification from the flattery and applause of men. The truth is, in all discourses on this subject, we are compelled continually to revert to the observation, that Christianity is a religion of the *heart.* And though we are not called upon to partake the poverty and meanness of His situation, yet the precept is clear and direct, respecting the temper by which we should be governed : " Let the same *mind* be in you which was also in Christ Jesus." If, therefore, we happen to possess that wealth and grandeur which He disdained, we should *possess them as though we possessed them not.* We have a fair and liberal permission to use them as His gift, and to His glory, but not to erect them into the supreme objects of our attachment. In the same manner, in every other point, it is still the spirit of the act, the temper of the mind, to which we are to look. For instance, I do not think that I am obliged to show my faith by sacrificing my son, nor my obedience by selling all that I have to give to the poor ; but I think I am bound by the spirit of these two powerful commands to practise a cheerful acquiescence in the whole will of God, in suffering and renouncing, as well as in doing, when I know what is really His will.'

Chapter XX.

HE pleasant reflections excited by the interesting conversation of the evening, were cruelly interrupted by my faithful Edwards. ' Sir,' said he, when he came to attend me, ' do you know that all the talk of the Hall to-night at supper was, that Miss Stanley is going to be married to young Lord Staunton. He is a cousin of Mrs. Carlton's, and Mr. Stanley's coachman brought home the news from thence yesterday. I could not get at the very truth, because Mrs. Comfit was out of the way ; but all the servants agree, that though he is a lord, and rich, and handsome, he is not half good enough for her. Indeed, sir, they say he is no better than he should be.'

I was thunderstruck at this intelligence. It was a trial I had not suspected. ' Does he visit here then, Edwards ?' said I, ' for I have neither seen nor heard of him.' ' No, sir,' said he, ' but miss meets him at Mr. Carlton's.' This shocked me beyond expression. Lucilla meet a man at another house ! Lucilla carry on a clandestine engagement ! Can Mrs. Carlton be capable of conniving at it ! Yet if it were not clandestine, why should he not visit at the Grove ?

These tormenting reflections kept me awake the whole night. To acquit Lucilla, Edwards' story made difficult ; to condemn her, my heart found impossible. One moment I blamed my own foolish timidity, which had kept me back from making any proposal ; and the next, I was glad that the delay would enable me to sift the truth, and to probe her character. ' If I do not find consistency here,' said I, ' I shall renounce all confidence in human virtue.' I arose early, and went to indulge my meditations in the garden. I saw Mr. Stanley sitting under the favourite oak. I was instantly tempted to go and open my heart to him, but seeing a book in his hand, I feared to interrupt him ; and was turning into another walk, till I had acquired more composure. He called after me, and invited me to sit down.

How violent were my fluctuations ! How inconsistent were my feelings ! How much at variance was my reason with my heart ! The man on earth with whom I wished to confer invited me to a conference. With a mind under the dominion of a passion which I was eager to declare, yet agitated with an uncertainty which I had as much reason to fear might be painfully as pleasantly removed, I stood doubtful whether to seize or decline the occasion which thus presented itself to me. A moment's reflection, however, convinced me that the opportunity was too inviting to be neglected. My impatience for an *éclaircissement* on Lord Staunton's subject was too powerful to be any longer resisted.

At length, with the most unfeigned diffidence, and a hesitation which I feared would render my words unintelligible, I ventured to express my tender admiration of Miss Stanley, and implored permission to address her.

My application did not seem to surprise him. He only gravely said, ' We will talk of this some future day.' This cold and laconic reply instantly sunk my spirits. I was shocked, and visibly confused. ' It is too late,' said I to myself. ' Happy Lord Staunton !' He saw my distress, and, taking my hand with the utmost kindness of voice and manner, said, ' My dear young friend, content yourself for the present with the assurance of my entire esteem and affection. This is a very early declaration. You are scarcely acquainted with Lucilla ; you do not yet know,' added he, smiling, ' half her faults.'

' Only tell me, my dear sir,' said I, a little reassured, and grasping his hand, ' that when you know all mine, you will not reject me. Only tell me that you feel no repugnance—that you have no other views— that Miss Stanley has no other——' here I stopped, my voice failed— the excess of my emotion prevented me from finishing my sentence. He encouragingly said, ' I know not that Lucilla has any attachment. For myself, I have no views hostile to your wishes. You have a double interest in my heart. You are endeared to me by your personal merit, and by my tender friendship for your beloved father. But be not im- petuous. Form no sudden resolution. Try to assure yourself of my daughter's affection before you ask it of her. Remain here another month as my welcome guest, as the son of my friend. Take that month to examine your own heart, and to endeavour to obtain an interest in her's ; we will then resume the subject.'

' But, my dear sir,' said I, ' is not Lord Staunton——' ' Set your heart entirely at rest,' said he. ' Though we are both a little aristo- cratic in our political principles, yet when the competition is for the happiness of life, and the interests of virtue, both Lucilla and her father think, with Dumont, that :

> ' A lord
> Opposed against a man, is but a man.'

So saying, he quitted me ; but with a benignity in his countenance and manner that infused not only consolation, but joy into my heart. My spirits were at once elated. To be allowed to think of Lucilla ! To be permitted to attach myself to her ! To be sure her heart was not engaged ! To be invited to remain a month longer under the same roof with her—to see her—to hear her—to talk to her—all this was a happiness so great that I did not allow myself to repine because it was not all I had wished to obtain.

I met Mrs. Stanley soon after. I perceived by her illuminated countenance that my proposal had been already communicated to her. I ventured to take her hand, and with the most respectful earnestness intreated her friendship—her good offices. ' I dare not trust myself with you just now,' said she, with an affectionate smile ; ' Mr. Stanley will think I abet rebellion, if through my encouragement you should violate your engagements with him.   But,' added she, kindly pressing my hand, ' you need not be much afraid of *me*.   Mr. Stanley's sentiments on this point, as on all others, are exactly my own.   We have but one heart and one mind, and that heart and mind are not unfavourable to your wishes.'   With a tear in her eyes, and affection in her looks, she tore herself away, evidently afraid of giving way to her feelings.

I did not think myself bound by any point of honour to conceal the state of my heart from Sir John Belfield, who, with his lady, joined me soon after in the garden.   I was astonished to find that my passion for Miss Stanley was no secret to either of them.   Their penetration had left me nothing to disclose.   Sir John, however, looked serious, and affected an air of mystery which a little alarmed me.   ' I own,' said he, ' there is some danger of your success.'   I eagerly inquired what he thought I had to fear ?   ' You have everything to fear,' replied he, in a tone of grave irony, ' which a man not four-and-twenty, of an honourable family, with a clear estate of four thousand a year, a person that all the ladies admire, a mind which all the men esteem, and a temper which endears you to men, women, and children, *can* fear from a little country girl, whose heart is as free as a bird, and who, if I may judge by her smiles and blushes whenever you are talking to her, would have no mortal objection to sing in the same cage with you.'

' It will be a sad, dull novel, however,' said Lady Belfield—' all is likely to go on so smoothly that we shall flag for want of incident.   No difficulties nor adventures to heighten the interest.   No cruel stepdame, no tyrant father, no capricious mistress, no moated castle, no intriguing confidante, no treacherous spy, no formidable rival, not so much as a duel, or even a challenge, I fear, to give variety to the monotonous scene.'

I mentioned Edward's report respecting Lord Staunton, and owned how much it had disturbed me.   ' That he admires her,' said Lady Belfield, ' is notorious.   That his addresses have not been encouraged, I have also heard, but not from the family.   As to Lucilla, she is the last girl that would ever insinuate, even to me, to whom she is so unreserved, that she had rejected so great an offer.   I have heard her express herself, with an indignation foreign to her general mildness, against women who are guilty of this fashionable, this dishonourable indelicacy.'

' Well, but Charles,' said Sir John, ' you must positively assume a little dejection to diversify the business.   It will give interest to your countenance, and pathos to your manner, and tenderness to your accent.   And you must forget all attentions, and neglect all civilities.   And you must appear absent, and *distrait* and *rêveur ;* especially while your fate hangs in some suspense.   And you must read Petrarch, and repeat Tibullus, and write sonnets.   And when you are spoken to you must not listen.   And you must wander in the grove by moonshine, and talk to the Oreads, and the Dryads, and the Naiads—oh no, unfortunately, I am afraid there are no Naiads within hearing.   You must make the woods vocal with the name of Lucilla ; luckily 'tis such a poetical name, that Echo won't be ashamed to repeat it. I have gone through it all, Charles, and know every high-way and by-way in the map of love. I will, however, be serious for one moment, and tell you, for your comfort, that though at your age I was full as much in for it as you are now, yet, after ten years' union, Lady Belfield has enabled me to declare :

How much the wife is dearer than the bride.'

A tear glistened in her soft eyes at this tender compliment.

Just at that moment Lucilla happened to cross the lawn at a distance. At sight of her, I could not, as I pointed to her, forbear exclaiming, in the words of Sir John's favourite poet :

' There doth beauty dwell,
There most conspicuous, ev'n in outward shape,
Where dawns the high expression of a MIND.'

' This is very fine,' said Sir John, sarcastically. ' I admire all you young enthusiastic philosophers, with your intellectual refinement. You pretend to be captivated only with *mind;* I observe, however, that, previous to your raptures, you always take care to get this mind lodged in a fair and youthful form. This mental beauty is always prudently enshrined in some elegant corporeal frame before it is worshipped. I should be glad to see some of these intellectual adorers in love with the mind of an old or ugly woman. I never heard any of you fall into ecstasies in descanting on the mind of your grandmother.' After some further irony, they left me to indulge my meditations, in the nature of which a single hour had made so pleasant a revolution.

Chapter XXI.

THE conversation of two men bred at the same school or college, when they happen to meet afterwards, is commonly uninteresting, not to say tiresome, to a third person, as involving local circumstances in which he has no concern. But this was not always the case since the meeting of my two friends. Something was generally to be gained by their communications, even on these unpromising topics.

At breakfast Mr. Stanley said : ' Sir John, you will see here at dinner to-morrow our old college acquaintance, Ned Tyrrel. Though he does not commonly live at the family house in this neighbourhood, but at a little place he has in Buckinghamshire, he comes among us periodically, to receive his rents. He always invites himself, for his society is not the most engaging.'

' I heard,' replied Sir John, ' that he became a notorious profligate after he left Cambridge, though I have lost sight of him ever since we parted there. But I was glad to learn lately that he is become quite a reformed man.'

' He is so far reformed,' replied Mr. Stanley, ' that he is no longer grossly licentious ; but in laying down the vices of youth, he has taken up successively those which he thought better suited to the successive stages of his progress. As he withdrew himself from his loose habits and connexions, ambition became his governing passion. He courted public favour, thirsted for place and distinction, and laboured, by certain obliquities, and some little sacrifices of principle, to obtain promotion. Finding it did not answer, and all his hopes failing, he now rails at ambition, wonders men will wound their consciences and renounce their peace for vain applause and " the bubble reputation." His sole delight at present, I hear, is in amassing money, and reading contro-versial divinity Avarice has supplanted ambition, just as ambition expelled profligacy.

' In the interval in which he was passing from one of these stages to the other, in a very uneasy state of mind, he dropped in by accident where a famous irregular preacher was disseminating his antinomian doctrines. Caught by his vehement but coarse eloquence, and capti-vated by an alluring doctrine which promised much while it required little, he adopted the soothing but fallacious tenet. It is true, I hear he is become a more respectable man in his conduct, but I doubt, though I have not lately seen him, if his present state may not be rather worse than his former one.

' In the two previous stages he was disturbed and dissatisfied ; here he has taken up his rest. Out of this stronghold it is not probable that any subsequent vice will ever drive him, or true religion draw him. He sometimes attends public worship, but, as he thinks no part of it but the sermon of much value, it is only when he likes the preacher. He has little notion of the respect due to established institutions, and does not heartily like any precomposed forms of prayer, not even our incom-parable Liturgy. He reads such religious books only as tend to estab-lish his own opinions, and talks and disputes loudly on certain doctrinal points. But an accumulating Christian, and a Christian who, for the purpose of accumulation, is said to be uncharitable, and even somewhat oppressive, is a paradox which I cannot solve, and an anomaly which I cannot comprehend. Covetousness is, as I said, a more creditable vice than Ned's former ones, but for that very reason more dangerous.'

' From this sober vice,' said I, ' proceeded the blackest crime ever per-petrated by human wickedness ; for it does not appear that Judas, in his direful treason, was instigated by malice. It is observable that, when our Saviour names this sin, it is with an emphatical warning, as know-ing its mischief to be greater because its scandal was less. Not con-tented with a single caution, he doubles his exhortation : " *Take heed* and *beware* of covetousness." '

After some remarks of Sir John which I do not recollect, Mr. Stanley said : ' I did not intend making a philippic against covetousness, a sin to which I believe no one here is addicted. Let us not, however, plume ourselves in not being guilty of a vice to which, as we have no natural bias, so in not committing it we resist no temptation. What I meant to insist on was that exchanging a turbulent for a quiet sin, or a scan-dalous for an orderly one, is not reformation—or, if you will allow me the strong word, is not conversion.'

Mr. Tyrrel, according to his appointment, came to dinner, and brought with him his nephew, Mr. Edward Tyrrel, whom he had lately entered at the university, with a design to prepare him for holy orders. He was a well-disposed young man, but his previous education was said to have been very much neglected, and he was rather deficient in the necessary learning. Mr. Stanley had heard that Tyrrel had two reasons for breeding him to the Church : in the first place, he fancied it was the cheapest profession, and in the next he had laboured to infuse into him some particular opinions of his own which he wished to disseminate through his nephew. Sir George Aston having accidentally called, he was prevailed on to stay ; and Dr. Barlow was of the party.

Mr. Tyrrel, by his observations, soon enabled us to discover that his religion had altered nothing but his language. He seemed evidently more fond of controversy than of truth, and the whole turn of his conversation indicated that he derived his religious security rather from the adoption of a party than from the implantation of a new principle.

' His discourse is altered,' said Mr. Stanley to me afterwards, ' but I greatly fear his heart and affections remain unchanged.'

Mr. Stanley contrived, for the sake of his two academical guests, particularly young Tyrrel, to divert the conversation to the subject of learning, more especially clerical learning.

In answer to a remark of mine on the satisfaction I had felt in seeing such a happy union of learning and piety in two clergymen who had lately dined at the Grove, Mr. Stanley said : ' Literature is an excellent thing when it is not the best thing a man has. It can surely be no offence to our Maker to cultivate carefully his highest natural gift, our reason. In pious men it is peculiarly important, as the neglect of such cultivation in certain individuals has led to much error in religion, and given much just offence to the irreligious, who are very sharp-sighted to the faults of pious characters. I therefore truly rejoice to see a higher tone of literature now prevailing, especially in so many of our pious young divines ; the deficiency of learning in some of their well-meaning predecessors having served to bring not only themselves but religion also into contempt, especially with men who have only learning.'

Tyrrel. ' I say nothing against the necessity of learning in a lawyer, because it may help him to lead a judge, and to mislead a jury ; nor in a physician, because it may advance his credit by enabling him to conceal the deficiencies of his art ; nor in a private gentleman, because it may keep him out of worse mischief. But I see no use of learning in the clergy. There is my friend Dr. Barlow. I would willingly give up all his learning if he would go a little deeper into the doctrines he professes to preach.'

Mr. Stanley. ' I should indeed think Dr. Barlow's various knowledge of little value, did he exhibit the smallest deficiency in the great points to which you allude. But when I am persuaded that his learning is so far from detracting from his piety that it enables him to render it more extensively useful, I cannot wish him dispossessed of that knowledge which adorns his religion without diminishing its good effects.'

7

Tyrrel. 'You will allow that those first great publishers of Christianity, the apostles, had none of this vain learning.'

Stanley. 'It is frequently pleaded by the despisers of learning that the apostles were illiterate. The fact is too notorious, and the answer too obvious, to require to be dwelt upon. But it is unfortunately adduced to illustrate a position to which it can never apply, the vindication of an unlettered clergy. It is a hackneyed remark, but not the less true for being old, that the wisdom of God chose to accomplish the first promulgation of the Gospel by illiterate men, to prove that the work was His own, and that its success depended not on the instruments employed, but on the divinity of the truth itself. But if the Almighty chose to establish His religion by miracles, He chooses to carry it on by means. And He no more sends an ignorant peasant or fisherman to instruct men in Christianity now, than He appointed a Socrates or a Plato to be its publishers at first. As, however, there is a great difference in the situations, so there may be a proportionable difference allowed in the attainments of the clergy. I do not say it is necessary for every village curate to be a profound scholar, but as he may not always remain in obscurity, there is no necessity for his being a contemptible one.'

Sir John. 'What has been said of those who affect to despise birth has been applied also to those who decry learning : neither is ever undervalued except by men who are destitute of them. And it is worthy of observation that, as literature and religion both sunk together in the dark ages, so both emerged at the same auspicious era.'

Mr. Stanley, finding that Dr. Barlow was not forward to embark in a subject which he considered as rather personal, said : 'Is it presumptuous to observe that, though the apostles were unlettered men, yet those instruments who were to be employed in services singularly difficult the Almighty condescended partly to fit for their peculiar work by great human attainments ? The Apostle of the Gentiles was brought up at the feet of Gamaliel ; and Moses, who was destined to the high office of a great legislator, was instructed in all the wisdom of the most learned nation then existing. The Jewish lawgiver, though under the guidance of inspiration itself, did not fill his station the worse for this preparatory institution. To how important a use the apostle converted *his* erudition we may infer from his conduct in the most learned and polished assembly in the world. He did not unnecessarily exasperate the polite Athenians by coarse upbraiding or illiterate clamour, but he attacked them on their own ground. With what discriminating wisdom, with what powerful reasoning, did he unfold to them that God whom they ignorantly worshipped ! With what temper, with what elegance, did he expose their shallow theology ! Had he been as unacquainted with *their* religion as they were with *his*, he had wanted the appropriate ground on which to build his instruction. He seized on the inscription of their own Pagan altar as a text from which to preach the doctrines of Christianity. From his knowledge of their errors, he was enabled to advance the cause of truth. He made their poetry, which he quoted, and their mythology, which he would not have been able to explode if he had not understood it, a thesis from which to deduce the doctrine of the resurrection. Thus softening their prejudices, and letting them see the infinite superiority of that Christianity which he enforced to the mere learning and mental cultivation on which they so highly valued themselves. By the same sober discretion, accurate reasoning, and graceful elegance, he afterwards obtained a patient hearing and a favourable judgment from King Agrippa.'

Dr. Barlow. 'It has always appeared to me that a strong reason why the younger part of a clergyman's life should be in a good measure devoted to learning is, that he may afterwards discover its comparative vanity. It would have been a less difficult sacrifice for St. Paul to profess that he renounced all things for religion if he had had nothing to renounce ; and to count all things as dross in the comparison, if he had had no gold to put in the empty scale. Gregory Nazianzen, one of the most accomplished masters of Greek literature, declared that the chief value which he set upon it was that, in possessing it, he had something of worth in itself to esteem as nothing in comparison of Christian truth. And it is delightful to hear Selden and Grotius, and Pascal and Salmasius, whom I may be allowed to quote without being suspected of professional prejudice, as none of them were clergymen, while they warmly recommended to others that learning of which they themselves were the most astonishing examples, at the same time dedicating their lives to the advancement of religion. It is delightful, I say, to hear them acknowledge that their learning was only valuable as it put it in their power to promote Christianity, and to have something to sacrifice for its sake.'

Tyrrel. 'I can willingly allow that a poet, a dramatic poet especially, may study the works of the great critics of antiquity with some profit ; but that a Christian writer of sermons can have any just ground for studying a Pagan critic, is to me quite inconceivable.'

Stanley. 'And yet, Mr. Tyrrel, the sermon is a work which demands regularity of plan, as well as a poem. It requires, too, something of the same unity, arrangement, divisions, and lucid order as a tragedy ; something of the exordium and the peroration which belong to the composition of the orator. I do not mean that he is constantly to exhibit all this, but he should always understand it. And a discreet clergyman, especially one who is to preach before auditors of the higher rank, and who, in order to obtain respect from them, wishes to excel in the art of composition, will scarcely be less attentive to form his judgment by some acquaintance with Longinus and Quintilian than a dramatic poet. A writer of verse, it is true, may please to a certain degree by the force of mere genius, and a writer of sermons will instruct by the mere power of his piety ; but neither the one nor the other will ever write well if they do not possess the principles of good writing, and form themselves on the models of good writers.'

'Writing,' said Sir John, 'to a certain degree is an art, or, if you please, a trade. And as no man is allowed to set up in an ordinary trade till he has served a long apprenticeship to its *mysteries* (the word, I think, used in indentures), so no man should set up for a writer till he knows somewhat of the mysteries of the art he is about to practise. He may, after all, if he wants talents, produce a vapid and inefficient book ;

but, possess what talents he may, he will, without knowledge, produce a crude and indigested one.'

Tyrrel. ' Still I insist upon it, that in a Christian minister the lustre of learning is tinsel, and human wisdom folly.'

Stanley. ' I am entirely of your opinion, if he rest in his learning as an *end*, instead of using it as a *means ;* if the fame, or the pleasure, or even the human profit of learning be his ultimate object. Learning in a clergyman, without religion, is dross—is nothing : not so religion without learning. I am persuaded that much good is done by men who, though deficient in this respect, are abundant in zeal and piety ; but the good they do arises from the exertion of their piety, and not from the deficiency of their learning. Their labours are beneficial from the talent they exercise, and not from their want of another talent. The Spirit of God can work, and often does work, by feeble instruments, and divine truth by its own omnipotent energy can effect its own purposes. But particular instances do not go to prove that the instrument ought not to be fitted and polished, and sharpened for its allotted work. Every student should be emulously watchful that he do not diminish the stock of professional credit by his idleness ; he should be stimulated to individual exertion, by bearing in mind that the English clergy have always been allowed by foreigners to be the most learned body in the world.'

Dr. Barlow. ' What Mr. Stanley has said of the value of knowledge does not at all militate against such fundamental prime truths as— " This is eternal life, to *know* God, and Jesus Christ whom he has sent ;" " I desire to *know* nothing, save Jesus Christ ;" " The natural man cannot *know* the things of the Spirit of God ;" " The world by wisdom *knew* not God :" and a hundred other such passages.'

Tyrrel. ' Ay, Doctor, now you talk a little more like a Christian minister. But from the greater part of what has been asserted, you are all of you such advocates for human reason and human learning, as to give an air of paganism to your sentiments.'

Stanley. ' It does not diminish the utility, though it abases the pride of learning, that Christianity did not come into the world by human discovery, or the disquisitions of reason, but by immediate revelation. Those who adopt your way of thinking, Mr. Tyrrel, should bear in mind that the work of God, in changing the heart, is not intended to supply the place of the human faculties. God expects, in His most highly favoured servants, the diligent exercise of their natural powers ; and if any human being has a stronger call for the exercise of wisdom and judgment than another, it is a religious clergyman. Christianity does not supersede the use of natural gifts, but turns them into their proper channel.

' One distinction has often struck me : the enemy of mankind seizes on the soul through the medium of the passions and senses ; the Divine friend of man addresses him through his rational powers—*the eyes of your understanding being enlightened*, says the apostle.'

Here I ventured to observe, that ' the highest panegyric bestowed on one of the brightest luminaries of our church, is, that his name is seldom mentioned without the epithet *judicious* being prefixed to it.'

Yet does Hooker want fervour? Does Hooker want zeal? Does Hooker want courage in declaring the whole counsel of God ?'

Sir John. ' I hope we have now no clergymen to whom we may apply the biting sarcasm of Dr. South on some of the popular but illiterate preachers of the opposite party in his day, " that there was all the confusion of Babel, without the gift of tongues." '

Stanley. ' And yet that party produced some great scholars, and many eminently pious men. But look back to that day, and especially to the period a little antecedent to it, at those prodigies of erudition, the old bishops and other divines of our church. They were, perhaps, somewhat too profuse of their learning in their discourses, or rather, they were so brimful that they involuntarily overflowed. A juster taste, in our time, avoids that lavish display, which then not only crowded the margin, but forced itself into every part of the body of the work. The display of erudition might be wrong, but one thing is clear—it proved they had it ; and, as Dryden said, when he was accused of having too much wit, " after all, it is a good crime." '

' We may justly,' said Dr. Barlow, ' in the refinement of modern taste, censure their prolixity, and ridicule their redundancies ; we may smile at their divisions, which are numberless, and at their subdivisions, which were endless ; we may allow that this labour for perspicuity sometimes produced perplexity : but let us confess they always went to the bottom of whatever they embarked in. They ransacked the stores of ancient learning, and the treasures of modern science, not to indulge their vanity by obtruding their acquirements, but to prove, to adorn, and to illustrate the doctrine they delivered. How incredible must their industry have been, when the bare transcript of their voluminous folios seems alone sufficient to have occupied a long life !'

' The method,' said I, ' which they adopted, of saying everything that could be said on all topics and exhausting them to the very dregs, though it may and does tire the patience of the reader, yet it never leaves him ignorant ; and, of two evils, had not an author better be tedious than superficial ? From an overflowing vessel you may gather more indeed than you want, but from an empty one you can gather nothing.'

Tyrrel. ' It appears to me that you wish to make a clergyman everything but a Christian, and to bestow upon him every requisite except faith.'

Stanley. ' God forbid that I should make any comparison between human learning and Christian principle ; the one is indeed lighter than the dust of the balance, when weighed against the other. All I contend for is, that they are not incompatible, and that human knowledge, used only in subserviency to that of the Scriptures, may advance the interests of religion. For the better elucidation of those Scriptures, a clergyman should know not a little of ancient languages. Without some insight into remote history and antiquities, especially the Jewish, he will be unable to explain many of the manners and customs recorded in the sacred volume. Ignorance in some of these points has drawn many attacks on our religion from sceptical writers. As to a thorough knowledge of ecclesiastical history, it would be superfluous to recommend that, it being the history of his own immediate profession. It is therefore requisite, not only for the general purposes of instruction, but that he may be enabled to guard against modern innovation, by knowing the origin and progress of the various heresies with which the Church in all ages has been infested.'

Tyrrel. 'But he may be thoroughly acquainted with all this, and not have one spark of light.'

Dr. Barlow. 'He may, indeed ; with deep concern I allow it. I will go further. The pride of learning, when not subdued by religion, may help to extinguish that spark. Reason has been too much decried by one party, and too much deified by the other. The difference between reason and revelation seems to be the same as between the eye and the light ; the one is the organ of vision, the other the source of illumination.'

Tyrrel. ' Take notice, Stanley, that, if I can help it, I'll never attend your accomplished clergyman.'

Stanley (smiling). ' I have not yet completed the circle of his accomplishments. Besides what we call book-learning, there is another species of knowledge in which some truly good men are sadly deficient —I mean an acquaintance with human nature. The knowledge of the world, and of Him who made it, the study of the heart of man, and of Him who has the hearts of all men in his hand, enable a minister to excel in the art of instruction ; one kind of knowledge reflecting light upon the other. The knowledge of mankind, then, I may venture to assert, is, next to religion, one of the first requisites of a preacher ; and I cannot help ascribing the little success which has sometimes attended the ministry of even worthy men, to their want of this grand ingredient. It will diminish the use they might make of the great doctrines of our religion, if they are ignorant of the various modifications of the human character to which those doctrines are to be addressed.

' As no man ever made a true poet without this talent, one may venture to say, that few without it have ever made eminent preachers. Destitute of this, the most elaborate addresses will be only random shot, which if they hit, it will be more owing to chance than to skill. Without this knowledge, warmed by Christian affection, guided by Christian judgment, tempered by Christian meekness, a clergyman will not be able in the pulpit to accommodate himself to the various wants of his hearers. Without this knowledge, in his private spiritual visits, he will resemble those empirics in medicine who have but one method of treatment for all diseases, and who apply indiscriminately the same pill and the same drop to the various distempers of all ages, sexes, and constitutions. This spirit of accommodation does not consist in falsifying, or abridging, or softening, or disguising any truth ; but in applying truth in every form, communicating it in every direction, and diverting it into every channel. Some good men seem sadly to forget that precept—*making a difference*—for they act as if all characters were exactly alike.'

Tyrrel. 'You talk as if you would wish clergymen to depart from the singleness of truth, and preach two gospels.'

Stanley. 'Far from it. But though truth is single, the human character is multiplied almost to infinity, and cannot be addressed with advantage if it be not well understood. I am ashamed of having said so much on such a subject in presence of Dr. Barlow, who is silent through delicacy. I will only add that a learned young clergyman is not driven for necessary relaxation to improper amusements. His mind will be too highly set to be satisfied with those light diversions which purloin time without affording the necessary renovation to the body and spirits, which is the true and lawful end of all amusement. In all circumstances, learning confers dignity on his character. It enables him to raise the tone of general conversation, and is a safe kind of medium with persons of a higher class who are not religious ; and it will always put it in his power to keep the standard of intercourse above the degrading topics of diversions, sports, and vulgar gossip.'

Dr. Barlow. 'You see, Mr. Tyrrel, that a prudent combatant thinks only of defending himself on that side where he is assaulted. If Mr. Stanley's antagonist had been a vehement advocate for clerical learning as the great essential of his profession, he would have been the first to caution him against the pride and inflation which often attend learning when not governed by religion. Learning not so governed might injure Christian humility, and thus become a far more formidable enemy to religion than that which it was called in to oppose.'

Sir John said, smiling, ' I will not apply to the clergy what Rasselas says to Imlac, after he had been enumerating the numberless qualities necessary to the perfection of the poetic art—" Thou hast convinced me that no man can be a poet ;"—but if all Stanley says be just, I will venture to assert, that no common share of industry and zeal will qualify a young student for that sacred profession. I have indeed no experience on the subject, as it relates to the clerical order, but I conceive, in general, that learning is the best human preservative of virtue ; that it safely fills up leisure, and honourably adorns life, even where it does not form the business of it.'

' Learning, too,' said I, ' has this strong recommendation, that it is the offspring of a most valuable virtue, I mean industry ; a quality on which I am ashamed to see pagans frequently set a higher value than we seem to do.'

' I believe, indeed,' replied Sir John, ' that the ancients had a higher idea of industry and severe application than we have. Tully calls them the *imperatoriæ virtutes*, and Alexander said that slaves might indulge in sloth, but that it was a most royal thing to labour.'

Stanley. ' It has been the error of sensible men of the world, to erect talents and learning into idols, which they would have universally and exclusively worshipped. This has perhaps driven some religious men into such a fear of over-cultivating learning, that they do not cultivate it at all. Hence the intervals between their religious employments, and intervals there must be while we are invested with these frail bodies, are languid and insipid, wasted in trifling and sauntering. Nay, it is well if this disoccupation of the intellect do not lead from sloth to improper indulgences.'

' You are perfectly right,' said Sir John, ' our friend Thompson is a living illustration of your remark. He was at college with us ; he brought from thence a competent share of knowledge ; has a fair understanding, and the manners of a gentleman. For several years past, he has not only adopted a religious character, but is truly pious. As he is much in earnest, he very properly assigns a considerable portion of his time to religious-reading. But as he is of no profession, the intermediate hours often hang heavy on his hands. He continues to live, in some measure, in the world, without the inconsistency of entering into its pursuits ; but, having renounced the study of human learning, and yet accustoming himself to mix occasionally with general society, he has few subjects in common with his company, but is dull and silent in all rational conversation of which religion is not the professed object. He takes so little interest in any literary or political discussion, however useful, that it is evident nothing but his good breeding prevents his falling asleep. At the same time, he scruples not to violate consistency in another respect, for his table is so elaborately luxurious, that it seems as if he were willing to add to the pleasures of sense what he deducts from those of intellect.'

' I have often thought,' said Mr. Stanley, ' of sending him Dr. Barlow's *three sermons on industry in our calling as Christians—industry as gentlemen—and industry as scholars ;* which sermons, by the way, I intended to have made my son read at least once a year, had he lived, that he might see the consistency, the compatibility, nay, the analogy of the two latter with the former. I wish the spirit of these three discourses was infused into every gentleman, every scholar, and every Christian through the land. For my own part, I should have sedulously laboured to make my son a sound scholar ; while I should have laboured still more sedulously to convince him that the value of learning depends solely on the purposes to which it is devoted. I would have a Christian gentleman able to beat the world at its own weapons, and convince it, that it is not from penury of mind, or inability to distinguish himself in other matters, that he applies himself to seek that wisdom which is from above ; that he does not fly to religion as a shelter from the ignominy of ignorance, but from a deep conviction of the comparative vanity of that very learning, which he yet is so assiduous to acquire.'

During this conversation, it was amusing to observe the different impressions made on the minds of our two college guests. Young Tyrrel, who, with moderate parts and slender application, had been taught to adopt some of his uncle's dogmas, as the cheapest way of being wise, greedily swallowed his eulogium of clerical ignorance, which the young man seemed to feel as a vindication of his own neglected studies, and an encouragement to his own mediocrity of intellect : while the interesting young baronet, though silent through modesty, discovered in his intelligent eyes evident marks of satisfaction, in hearing that literature, for which he was every day acquiring a higher relish, warmly recommended as the best pursuit of a gentleman, by the two men in the world for whose judgment he entertained the highest reverence. At the same time it raised his veneration for Christian piety, when he saw it so sedulously practised by these advocates for human learning.

Chapter XXII.

URING these conversations, I remarked that Lucilla, though she commonly observed the most profound silence, had her attention always riveted on the speaker. If that speaker was Dr. Barlow, or her father, or any one whom she thought entitled to particular respect, she gently laid down her work, and as quietly resumed it when they had done speaking.

I observed to Sir John Belfield, afterwards, as we were walking together, how modestly flattering her manner was when any of us were reading! How intelligent her silence! How well bred her attention!

'I have often contrasted it,' replied he, 'with the manner of some other ladies of my acquaintance, who are sometimes of our quiet evening party. When one is reading history, or any ordinary book, aloud to them, I am always pleased that they should pursue their little employments. It amuses themselves, and gives ease and familiarity to the social circle. But while I have been reading, as has sometimes happened, a passage of the highest sublimity or most tender interest, I own I feel a little indignant to see the shuttle plied with as eager assiduity as if the Destinies themselves were weaving the thread. I have known a lady take up the candle-stick to search for her netting-pin, in the midst of Cato's soliloquy ; or stoop to pick up her scissors, while Hamlet says to the ghost, "I'll go no further." I remember another who would whisper across the table to borrow silk, while Lear has been raving in the storm, or Macbeth starting at the spirit of Banquo ; and make signs for a thread-paper, while Cardinal Beaufort "dies, and makes no sign." Nay, once I remember, when I was with much agitation hurrying through the gazette of the battle of Trafalgar, while I pronounced, almost agonized, the last memorable words of the immortal Nelson, I heard one lady whisper to another that she had broken her needle.'

'It would be difficult to determine,' replied I, 'whether this inattention most betrays want of sense, of feeling, or of good breeding. The habit of attention should be carefully formed in early life, and then the mere force of custom would teach these ill-bred women "to assume the virtue if they have it not."'

The family at the Grove was with us an inexhaustible topic whenever we met. I remarked to Sir John, 'that I had sometimes observed in charitable families a display, a bustle, a kind of animal restlessness, a sort of mechanical *besoin* to be charitably busy. · That though they fulfilled conscientiously one part of the apostolic injunction, that of 'giving,' yet they failed in the other clause, that of doing it 'with simplicity.' 'Yes,' replied he, 'I visit a charitable lady in town, who almost puts me out of love with benevolence. Her own bounties form the entire subject of her conversation. As soon as the breakfast is removed, the table is always regularly covered with plans, and proposals, and subscription papers. This display conveniently performs the threefold office of publishing her own charities, furnishing subjects of altercation, and raising contributions on the visitor. Her narratives really cost me more than my subscription. She is so full of debate, and detail, and opposition ; she makes you read so many papers of her own drawing up, and so many answers to the schemes of other people, and she has so many objections to every other person's mode of doing good, and so many arguments to prove that her own is the best, that she appears less like a benevolent lady than a chicaning attorney.'

'Nothing,' said I, 'corrects this bustling bounty so completely, as when it is mixed up with religion, I should rather say, as when it flows from religion. This motive, so far from diminishing the energy, augments it ; but it cures the display, and converts the irritation into a principle. It transfers the activity from the tongue to the heart. It is the only sort of charity which "blesses twice." All charity, indeed, blesses the receiver ; but the blessing promised to the giver, I have sometimes trembled to think, may be forfeited even by a generous mind, from ostentation and parade in the manner, and want of purity in the motive.'

'In Stanley's family,' replied he, in a more serious tone, 'I have met with a complete refutation of that favourite maxim of the world, that religion is a dull thing itself, and makes its professors gloomy and morose. Charles ! I have often frequented houses where pleasure was the avowed object of idolatry. But to see the votaries of the "reeling goddess," after successive nights passed in her temples ! to see the languor, the listlessness, the discontent—you would rather have taken them for her victims than her worshippers. So little mental vivacity, so little gaiety of heart ! In short, after no careless observation, I am compelled to declare, that I never saw two forms less alike than those of Pleasure and Happiness.'

'Your testimony, Sir John,' said I, 'is of great weight in a case of which you are so experienced a judge. What a different scene do we now contemplate ! Mr. Stanley seems to have diffused his own spirit through the whole family. What makes his example of such efficacy is, that he considers the Christian *temper* as so considerable a part of Christianity. This temper seems to imbue his whole soul, pervade his whole conduct, and influence his whole conversation. I see every day some fresh occasion to admire his candour, his humility, his constant reference, not as a topic of discourse, but as a principle of conduct, to the Gospel, as the standard by which actions are to be weighed. His conscientious strictness of speech, his serious reproof of calumnies, his charitable construction of every case which has two sides ; "his simplicity and godly sincerity ;" his rule of referring all events to providential direction, and his invariable habit of vindicating the Divine goodness under dispensations apparently the most unfavourable.'

Here Sir John left me, and I could not forbear pursuing the subject in soliloquy as I proceeded in my walk.—I reflected with admiration that Mr. Stanley, in his religious conversation, rendered himself so useful, because instead of the uniform nostrum of *the drop and the pill*, he applied a different class of arguments as the case required, to

.objectors to the different parts of Christianity ; to ill-formed persons who adopted a partial Gospel, without understanding it as a scheme, or embracing it as a whole.—To those who allow its truth merely on the same ground of evidence that establishes the truth of any other well authenticated history, and who, satisfied with this external evidence, not only do not feel its power on their own heart, but deny that it has any such influence on the hearts of others ;—to those who believe the Gospel to be a mere code of ethics ;—to their antipodes, who assert that Christ has lowered the requisitions of the law ;—to Lady Belfield, who rests on her charities, Sir John on his correctness, Lady Aston on her austerities ;—to this man, who values himself solely on the stoutness of his orthodoxy, to another on the firmness of his integrity, to a third on the peculiarities of his party :—to all these he addresses himself with a particular view to their individual errors. This he does with such a discriminating application to the case, as might lead the ill-informed to suspect that he was not equally earnest in those other points, which, not being attacked, he does not feel himself called on to defend, but which, had they been attacked, he would then have defended with equal zeal, as relative to the discussion. To crown all, I contemplated that affectionate warmth of heart, that sympathizing kindness, that tenderness of feeling, of which the gay and the thoughtless fancy that they themselves possess the monopoly, while they make over harshness, austerity, and want of charity to religious men, as their inseparable characteristics.

These qualities excite in my heart a feeling compounded of veneration and of love. And, oh ! how impossible it is, even in religion itself, to be disinterested ! All these excellencies I contemplate with a more heartfelt delight, from the presumptuous hope that I may one day have the felicity of connecting myself still more intimately with them.

Chapter XXIII.

SOME days after, while we were conversing over our tea, we heard the noise of a carriage ; and Mr. Stanley, looking out from a bow window in which he and I were sitting, said it was Lady and Miss Rattle driving up the avenue. He had just time to add, ' These are our *fine* neighbours. They always make us a visit as soon as they come down, while all the gloss and lustre of London is fresh upon them. We have always our regular routine of conversation. While her ladyship is pouring the fashions into Mrs. Stanley's ear, Miss Rattle, who is about Phœbe's age, entertains my daughters and me with the history of her own talents and acquirements.'

Here they entered. After a few compliments, Lady Rattle seated herself between Lady Belfield and Mrs. Stanley, at the upper end of the room ; while the fine, sprightly, boisterous girl of fifteen or sixteen threw herself back on the sofa at nearly her full length, between Mr.

Stanley and me, the Miss Stanleys and Sir John sitting near us, within hearing of her lively loquacity.

'Well, Miss Amelia,' said Mr. Stanley, 'I dare say you have made good use of your time this winter ; I suppose you have ere now completed the whole circle of the arts. Now let me hear what you have been doing, and tell me your whole achievements, as frankly as you used to do when you was a little girl.' 'Indeed,' replied she, 'I have not been idle, if I must speak the truth. One has so many things to learn, you know. I have gone on with my French and Italian, of course, and I am beginning German. Then comes my drawing master ; he teaches me to paint flowers and shells, and to draw ruins and buildings, and to take views. He is a good soul, and is finishing a set of pictures, and half-a-dozen fire-screens which I began for mamma. He *does* help me, to be sure, but indeed I do some of it myself, don't I, mamma ?' calling out to her mother, who was too much absorbed in her own narratives to attend to her daughter.

'And then,' pursued the young prattler, 'I learn varnishing, and gilding, and japanning. And next winter I shall learn modelling, and etching, and engraving in mezzotinto and aquatinta, for Lady Di. Dash learns etching, and mamma says, as I shall have a better fortune than Lady Di., she vows I shall learn everything she does. Then I have a dancing master, who teaches me the Scotch and Irish steps ; and another who teaches me attitudes ; and I shall soon learn the waltz, and I can stand longer on one leg already than Lady Di. Then I have a singing master, and another who teaches me the harp, and another for the piano-forte. And what little time I can spare from these *principal* things, I give by odd minutes to ancient and modern history, and geography, and astronomy, and grammar, and botany. Then I attend lectures on chemistry, and experimental philosophy, for as I am not yet come out, I have not much to do in the evenings ; and mamma says, there is nothing in the world that money can pay for, but what I shall learn. And I run so delightfully fast from one thing to another, that I am never tired. What makes it so pleasant is, as soon as I am fairly set in with one master, another arrives. I should hate to be long at the same thing. But I shan't have a great while to work so hard, for as soon as I come out I shall give it all up, except music and dancing.'

All this time Lucilla sat listening with a smile, behind the complacency of which she tried to conceal her astonishment. Phœbe, who had less self-control, was on the very verge of a broad laugh. Sir John, who had long lived in a soil where this species is indigenous, had been too long accustomed to all its varieties, to feel much astonishment at this specimen, which, however, he sat contemplating with philosophical but discriminating coolness.

For my own part, my mind was wholly absorbed in contrasting the coarse manners of this voluble, and intrepid, but good-humoured girl, with the quiet, cheerful, and unassuming elegance of Lucilla.

'I should be afraid, Miss Rattle,' said Mr. Stanley, 'if you did not look in such blooming health, that, with all these incessant labours, you did not allow yourself time for rest. Surely you never sleep ?'

'Oh yes, that I do, and eat too,' said she ; 'my life is not quite so hard and moping as you fancy. What between shopping and morning visitings with mamma, and seeing sights, and the park, and the gardens, (which, by the way, I hate, except on a Sunday, when they are crowded,) and our young balls, which are four or five in a week after Easter, and mamma's music parties at home, I contrive to enjoy myself tolerably, though after I have been presented I shall be a thousand times better off, for then I shan't have a moment to myself. Won't that be delightful ?' said she, twitching my arm rather roughly, by way of recalling my attention, which, however, had seldom wandered.

As she had now run out her London materials, the news of the neighbourhood next furnished a subject for her volubility. After she had mentioned in detail one or two stories of low village gossip ; while I was wondering how she could come at them, she struck me dumb by quoting the coachman as her authority. This enigma was soon explained. The mother and daughter having exhausted their different topics of discourse nearly at the same time, they took their leave, in order to enrich every family in the neighbourhood, on whom they were going to call, with the same valuable knowledge which they had imparted to us.

Mr. Stanley conducted Lady Rattle, and I led her daughter ; but as I offered to hand her into the carriage, she started back with a sprightly motion, and screamed out, 'Oh no, not in the inside, pray help me up to the *Dickey ;* I always protest I never *will* ride with anybody but the coachman, if we go ever so far.' So saying, with a spring which showed how much she despised my assistance, the little hoyden was seated in a moment, nodding familiarly at me, as if I had been an old friend.

Then with a voice emulating that which, when passing by Charing Cross, I have heard issue from an over-stuffed stage vehicle, when a robust sailor has thrust his body out at the window, the fair creature vociferated, 'Drive on, coachman !' He obeyed, and she, turning round her whole person, continued nodding at me till they were out of sight.

'Here is a mass of accomplishments,' said I, 'without one particle of mind, one ray of common sense, or one shade of delicacy ! Surely somewhat less time and less money might have sufficed to qualify a companion for the coachman !'

'What poor creatures are we men,' said I to Mr. Stanley, as soon as he came in. 'We think it very well, if after much labour and long application we can attain to one or two of the innumerable acquirements of this gay little girl. Nor is this, I find, the rare achievement of one happy genius—there is a whole class of these miraculous females. Miss Rattle

Is knight o' th' shire, and represents them all.'

'It is only young ladies,' replied he, 'whose vast abilities, whose mighty grasp of mind, can take in everything. Among men, learned men, talents are commonly directed into some one channel, and fortunate is he who in that one attains to excellence. The linguist is rarely a painter, nor is the mathematician often a poet. Even in one profession there are divisions and subdivisions. The same lawyer never thinks of presiding both in the King's Bench and in the Court of Chancery. The science of healing is not only divided into its three distinct branches, but in the profession of surgery only, how many are the sub-divisions! One professor undertakes the eye, another the ear, and a third the teeth. But woman, ambitious, aspiring, universal, triumphant, glorious woman, even at the age of a schoolboy, encounters the whole range of the arts, attacks the whole circle of the sciences!'

'A mighty maze, and *quite* without a plan,' replied Sir John, laughing. ' But the truth is, the misfortune does not so much consist in their learning everything, as in their knowing nothing ; I mean nothing well. When gold is beaten out so wide, the lamina must needs be very thin. And you may observe, the more valuable attainments, though they are not to be left out of the modish plan, are kept in the background ; and are to be picked up out of the odd remnants of that time, the sum of which is devoted to frivolous accomplishments. All this gay confusion of acquirements, these holiday splendours, this superfluity of enterprise, enumerated in the first part of her catalogue, is the *real business* of education ; the latter part is incidental, and if taught is not learnt.

' As to the lectures so boastfully mentioned, they may be doubtless made very useful subsidiaries to instruction. They most happily illustrate book-knowledge ; but if the pupil's instructions in private do not pre-cede and keep pace with these useful public exhibitions, her knowledge will be only presumptuous ignorance. She may learn to talk of oxygen and hydrogen, and deflagration and trituration, but she will know nothing of the science except the terms. It is not knowing the names of his tools that makes an artist ; and I should be afraid of the vanity which such superficial information would communicate to a mind not previously prepared, nor exercised at home in corresponding studies. But, as Miss Rattle honestly confessed, as soon as she *comes out,* all these things will die away of themselves, and dancing and music will be almost all which will survive of her multifarious pursuits.'

' I look upon the great predominance of music in female education,' said Mr. Stanley, ' to be the source of more mischief than is suspected ; not from any evil in the thing itself, but from its being such a gulf of time, as really to leave little room for solid acquisitions. I love music, and, were it only cultivated as an amusement, should commend it. But the monstrous proportion, or rather disproportion, of life which it swallows up, even in many religious families (and this is the chief subject of my regret), has converted an innocent diversion into a positive sin. I question if many gay men devote more hours in a day to idle purposes, than the daughters of many pious parents spend in this amusement. All these hours the mind lies fallow, improvement is at a stand, if even it does not retrograde. Nor is it the shreds and scraps of time stolen in the intervals of better things that is so devoted ; but it is the morning, the prime, the profitable, the active hours, when the mind is vigorous, the spirits light, the intellect awake and fresh, and the whole being wound up by the refreshment of sleep, and animated by the return of light and life, for nobler services.'

'If,' said Sir John, 'music were cultivated to embellish retirement, to be practised where pleasures are scarce, and good performers are not to be had, it would quite alter the case. But the truth is, these highly-taught ladies are not only living in public, where they constantly hear the most exquisite professors, but they have them also at their own houses. Now one of these two things must happen. Either the performance of the lady will be so inferior as not to be worth hearing on the comparison, or so good that she will fancy herself the rival, instead of the admirer of the performer, whom she had better pay and praise than fruitlessly emulate.'

'This anxious struggle to reach the unattainable excellence of the professor,' said Mr. Stanley, 'often brings to my mind the contest for victory between the ambitious nightingale and the angry lutanist in the beautiful prolusion of Strada.'

'It is to the predominance of this talent,' replied I, 'that I ascribe that want of companionableness of which I complain. The excellence of musical performance is a decorated screen, behind which all defects in domestic knowledge, in taste, judgment, and literature, and the talents which make an elegant companion are creditably concealed.'

'I have made,' said Sir John, 'another remark. Young ladies, who from apparent shyness do not join in the conversation of a small select party, are always ready enough to entertain them with music on the slightest hint. Surely it is equally modest to *say* as to *sing*, especially to sing those melting strains we sometimes hear sung, and which we should be ashamed to hear said. After all, how few hours are there in a week, which a man engaged in the pursuits of life, and a woman in the duties of a family, wish to employ in music. I am fond of it myself, and Lady Belfield plays admirably ; but with the cares inseparable from the conscientious discharge of her duty with so many children, how little time has she to play, or I to listen ! But there is no day, no hour, no meal in which I do not enjoy in her the ever-ready pleasure of an elegant and interesting companion. A man of sense, when all goes smoothly, wants to be entertained ; under vexation, to be soothed ; in difficulties, to be counselled ; in sorrow, to be comforted. In a mere artist, can he reasonably look for these resources ?'

'Only figure to yourself,' replied Mr. Stanley, 'my six girls daily playing their four hours apiece, which is now a moderate allowance ! As we have but one instrument, they must be at it in succession, day and night, to keep pace with their neighbours. If I may compare light things with serious ones, it would resemble,' added he, smiling, 'the perpetual psalmody of good Mr. Nicholas Ferrar, who had relays of musicians every six hours, to sing the whole Psalter through every day and night ! I mean not to ridicule that holy man ; but my girls thus keeping their useless vigils in turn, we should only have the melody without any of the piety. No, my friend ! I will have but two or three singing birds to cheer my little grove. If all the world are performers, there will soon be no hearers. Now, as I am resolved in my own family that some shall listen, I will have but few to perform.'

' It must be confessed,' said Sir John, 'that Miss Rattle is no servile imitator of the vapid tribe of the superficially accomplished. Her violent animal spirits prevent her from growing smooth by attrition. She is as rough and angular as rusticity itself could have made her. Where strength of character, however, is only marked by the worst concomitant of strength, which is coarseness, I should almost prefer inanity itself.'

' I should a little fear,' said I, 'that I lay too much stress on companionableness, on the *positive duty of being agreeable at home*, had I not early learnt the doctrine from my father, and seen it exemplified so happily in the practice of my mother.'

' I entirely agree with you, Charles,' said Mr. Stanley, 'as to the absolute *morality* of being agreeable and even entertaining in one's own family circle. Nothing so soon and so certainly wears out the happiness of married persons, as that too common bad effect of familiarity, the sinking down into dulness and insipidity ; neglecting to keep alive the flame by the delicacy which first kindled it ; want of vigilance in keeping the temper cheerful by Christian discipline, and the faculties bright by constant use. Mutual affection decays of itself, even where there is no great moral turpitude, without mutual endeavours, not only to improve, but to amuse.'

' This,' continued he, 'is one of the great arts of *home enjoyment*. That it is so little practised, accounts in a good measure for the undomestic turn of too many married persons. The man meets abroad with amusement, and the woman with attentions, to which they are not accustomed at home. Whereas a capacity to please on the one part, and a disposition to be pleased on the other, in their own house, would make most visits appear dull. But then the disposition and the capacity must be cultivated antecedently to marriage. A woman, whose whole education has been rehearsal, will always be dull, except she lives on the stage, constantly displaying what she has been sedulously acquiring. Books, on the contrary, well-chosen books, do not lead to exhibition. The knowledge a woman acquires in private desires no witnesses ; the possession is the pleasure. It improves herself, it embellishes her family society, it entertains her husband, it informs her children. The gratification is cheap, is safe, is always to be had at home.'

' It is superfluous,' said Sir John, ' to decorate women so highly ; for early youth is itself a decoration. We mistakingly adorn most that part of life which least requires it, and neglect to provide for that which will want it most. It is for that sober period when life has lost its freshness, the passions their intenseness, and the spirits their hilarity, that we should be preparing. Our wisdom would be to anticipate the wants of middle life, to lay in a store of notions, ideas, principles, and habits, which may preserve, or transfer to the mind that affection, which was at first partly attracted by the person. But to add a vacant mind to a form which has ceased to please ; to provide no subsidiary aid to beauty while it lasts, and especially no substitute when it is departed, is to render life comfortless and marriage dreary.'

'The reading of a cultivated woman,' said Mr. Stanley, 'commonly occupies less time than the music of a musical woman, or the idleness of an indolent woman, or the dress of a vain woman, or the dissipation of a fluttering woman ; she is therefore likely to have more leisure for her duties, as well as more inclination, and a sounder judgment for performing them. But pray observe that I assume my reading woman to be a religious woman ; and I will not answer for the effect of a literary vanity, more than for that of any other vanity, in a mind not habitually disciplined by Christian principle, the only safe and infallible antidote for knowledge of every kind.'

Before we had finished our conversation, we were interrupted by the arrival of the post. Sir John eagerly opened the newspaper ; but instead of gratifying our impatience with the intelligence for which we panted from the glorious Spaniards, he read a paragraph which stated 'that Miss Denham had eloped with Signor Squallini, that they were on their way to Scotland, and that Lady Denham had been in fits ever since.'

Lady Belfield with her usual kindness was beginning to express how much she pitied her old acquaintance. 'My dear Caroline,' said Sir John, 'there is too much substantial and inevitable misery in the world, for you to waste much compassion on this foolish woman. Lady Denham has little reason to be surprised at an event which all reasonable people must have anticipated. Provoking and disgraceful as it is, what has she to blame but her own infatuation ? This Italian was the associate of all her pleasures ; the constant theme of her admiration. He was admitted when her friends were excluded. The girl was continually hearing that music was the best gift, and that Signor Squallini was the best gifted. Miss Denham,' added he, laughing, 'had more wit than your Strada's nightingale. Instead of dropping down dead on the lute for envy, she thought it better to run away with the lutanist for love. I pity the poor girl, however, who has furnished such a commentary to our text, and who is rather the victim of a wretched education than of her own bad propensities.'

Chapter XXIV.

HAD generally found that a Sunday passed in a visit was so heavy a day, that I had been accustomed so to arrange my engagements, as commonly to exclude this from the days spent from home. I had often found that even where the week had been pleasantly occupied, the necessity of passing several hours of a season peculiarly designed for religious purposes, with people whose habits have little similarity with our own, either draws one into their relaxed mode of getting rid of the day, or drives one to a retirement, which having an unsociable appearance, is liable to the reproach of austerity and gloom.

The case was quite different at Stanley Grove. The seriousness was without severity, and the cheerfulness had no mixture of levity. The family seemed more than usually animated, and there was a variety in the religious pursuits of the young people, enlivened by intervals of cheerful and improving conversation, which particularly struck Lady Belfield. She observed to me, that the difficulty of getting through the Sunday, without any mixture of worldly occupations or amusements on the one hand, or of disgust and weariness on the other, was among the many right things which she had never been able to accomplish in her own family.

As we walked from church one Sunday, Miss Stanley told me that her father does not approve the habit of criticising the sermon. He says that the custom of pointing out the faults cannot be maintained, without the custom of watching for them—that it gives the attention a wrong turn, and leads the hearer only to treasure up such passages as may serve for animadversion, and a display, not of Christian temper, but of critical skill ; and if the general tenor and principle be right, that is the main point they are to look to, and not to hunt for philological errors—that the hearer would do well to observe whether it is not 'he that sleeps,' as often at least as 'Homer nods :' a remark exemplified at church, as often as on the occasion which suggested it—that a critical spirit is the worst that can be brought out of church, being a symptom of an unhumbled mind, and an evidence, that whatever the sermon may have done for others, it has not benefited the caviller.

Here Mr. Stanley joined us. I found he did not encourage his family to take down the sermon. 'It is no disparagement,' said he, 'to the discourse preached, to presume that there may be as good already printed. Why, therefore, not read the printed sermon at home in the evening, instead of that by which you ought to have been improving while it was delivering ! If it be true that *faith cometh by hearing*, an inferior sermon, "coming warm and instant from the heart," assisted by all the surrounding solemnities, which make a sermon *heard* so different from one *read*, may strike more forcibly than an abler discourse coolly perused at home. In writing, the mechanical act must necessarily lessen the effect to the writer, and to the spectator it diminishes the dignity of the scene, and seems like shorthand writers taking down a trial.

'But that my daughters may not plead this as an excuse for inatten‐ tion,' continued he, 'I make it a part of their evening duty to repeat what they retain, separately to me in my library. The consciousness that this repetition will be required of them, stimulates their diligence ; and the exercise itself not only strengthens the memory, but habituates to serious reflection.'

At tea, Phœbe, a charming warm-hearted creature, but who, now and then, carried away by the impulse of the moment, forgets habits and prohibitions, said, 'I think, papa, Dr. Barlow was rather dull to-day. There was nothing new in the sermon.' 'My dear,' replied her father, 'we do not go to church to hear news. Christianity is no novelty ; and though it is true that we go to be instructed, yet we require to be reminded full as much as to be taught. General truths are what we all acknowledge, and all forget. We acknowledge them, because a general assent of the understanding costs but little ; and we forget them, because the remembrance would force upon the conscience a great deal of practical labour. To believe, and remember, and act upon, common, undisputed general truths, is the most important part of religion. This, though in fact very difficult, is overlooked, on account of its being supposed very easy. To keep up in the heart a lively impression of a few plain momentous truths, is of more use than the ablest discussion of a hundred controverted points.

' Now tell me, Phœbe, do you really think that you have remembered and practised all the instructions that you have received from Dr. Barlow's sermons last year ? If you have, though you will have a better right to be critical, you will be less disposed to be so. If you have not, do not complain that the sermon is not new, till you have made all possible use of the old ones ; which, if you had done, you would have acquired so much humility, that you would meekly listen even to what you already know. But however the discourse may have been superfluous to such deep divines as Miss Phœbe Stanley, it will be very useful to me, and to other hearers who are not so wise.'

Poor Phœbe coloured up to her ears ; tears rushed into her eyes. She was so overcome with shame, that, regardless of the company, she flew into her father's arms, and softly whispered that if he would forgive her foolish vanity, she would never again be above being taught. The fond, but not blind father, withdrew with her. Lucilla followed, with looks of anxious love.

During their short absence, Mrs. Stanley said, ' Lucilla is so practically aware of the truth of her father's observation, that she often says she finds as much advantage as pleasure in teaching the children at her school. This elementary instruction obliges her continually to recur to first principles, and to keep constantly uppermost in her mind those great truths contained in the articles of our belief, the commandments, and the prayer taught by our Redeemer. This perpetual simplifying of religion, she assures me, keeps her more humble, fixes her attention on fundamental truths, and makes her more indifferent to controverted points.'

In a few minutes Mr. Stanley and his daughters returned cheerful and happy ; Lucilla smiling like the angel of peace and love.

' If I were not afraid,' said Lady Belfield, ' of falling under the same censure with my friend Phœbe,' smiling on the sweet girl, ' I should venture to say, that I thought the sermon rather too severe.'

' Do not be afraid, madam,' replied Mr. Stanley ; ' though I disapprove that cheap and cruel criticism which makes a man *an offender for a word*, yet discussion does not necessarily involve censoriousness ; so far from it, it is fair to discuss whatever seems to be doubtful, and I shall be glad to hear your ladyship's objections.'

' Well then,' replied she, in the most modest tone and accent, ' with all my reverence for Dr. Barlow, I thought him a little unreasonable in seeming to expect universal goodness from creatures whom he yet insisted were fallen creatures.'

' Perhaps, madam,' said Mr. Stanley, ' you mistook his meaning, for he appeared to me perfectly consistent, not only with himself, but with his invariable rule and guide, the Scriptures. Sanctification, will you allow me to use so serious a word, however imperfect, must be universal. It is not the improvement of any one faculty, or quality, or temper, which divines mean, when they say we are renewed in part, so much as that the change is not perfect, the holiness is not complete in *any* part, or power, or faculty, though progressive in all. He who earnestly desires a universal victory over sin, knows which of his evil dispositions or affections it is that is yet unsubdued. This rebellious enemy he vigilantly sets himself to watch against, to struggle with, and, through divine grace, to conquer. The test of his sincerity does not so much consist in avoiding many faults to which he has no temptation, as in conquering that one to which his natural bent and bias forcibly impel him.'

Lady Belfield said, ' But is it not impossible to bring every part of our nature under this absolute dominion? Suppose a man is very passionate, and yet very charitable ; would you look upon that person to be in a dangerous state ?'

' It is not my province, madam, to decide,' replied Mr. Stanley. ' " God," as Bishop Sanderson says, " reserves this *royalty* to himself, of being the searcher of hearts." I cannot judge how far he resists anger, nor what are his secret struggles against it. God, who expects not perfection, expects sincerity. Though complete, unmixed goodness is not to be attained in this imperfect state, yet the earnest desire after it is the only sure criterion of the sincerity we profess. If the man you allude to does not watch and pray, and strive against the passion of anger, which is his natural infirmity, I should doubt whether any of his affections were really renewed ; and I should fear that his charity was rather a mere habitual feeling, though a most amiable one, than a Christian grace. He indulges in charity, because it is a constitutional bias, and costs him nothing. He indulges in passion, because it is a natural bias also ; and to set about a victory over it would cost him a great deal. This should put him on a strict self-examination ; when he would probably find that, while he gives the uncontrolled reins to any one wrong inclination, his religion, even when he does right things, is questionable. True religion is seated in the heart : that is the centre from which all the lines of right practice must diverge. It is the great duty and chief business of a Christian to labour to make all his affections, with all their motives, tendencies, and operations, subservient to the word and will of God. His irregular passions, which are still apt to start out into disorder, will require vigilance to the end. He must not think all is safe, because the more tractable ones are not rebellious ; but he may entertain a cheerful hope, when those which were once rebellious are become tractable.'

' I feel the importance of what you say,' returned Lady Belfield ; ' but I feel also my utter inability to set about it.'

' My dear madam,' said Mr. Stanley, ' this is the best and most salutary feeling you can have. That very consciousness of insufficiency will, I trust, drive you to the fountain of all strength and power : it will quicken your faith, and animate your prayer ; faith, which is the habitual principle of confidence in God ; and prayer. which is the exercise of that principle toward Him who is the object of it.'

'But Dr. Barlow,' said Lady Belfield, 'was so discouraging! He seemed to intimate as if the conflict of a Christian with sin must be as lasting as his life; whereas I had hoped, that victory once obtained was obtained for ever.'

' The *strait gate*,' replied Mr. Stanley, 'is only the entrance of religion; the *narrow way* is a continued course. The Christian life, my dear Lady Belfield, is not a point, but a progress. It is precisely in the race of Christianity as in the race of human glory. Julius Cæsar and St. Paul describe their respective warfares in nearly the same terms. "We should count nothing done, while anything remains undone,"* says the warrior. " Not counting myself to have attained—forgetting the things which are behind, and pressing forward to those which are before," says the apostle. And it is worth remarking, that they both made the disqualifying observation after attainments almost incredible. As there was no being a hero by any idler way, so there is no being a Christian by any easier road. The necessity of pursuit is the same in both cases, though the objects pursued differ as widely as the vanities of time from the riches of eternity.

' Do not think, my dear madam,' added Mr. Stanley, 'that I am erecting myself into a censor, much less into a model. The corruptions which I lament, I participate. The deficiencies which I deplore, I feel. Not only when I look abroad, am I persuaded of the general prevalence of evil by what I see, but when I look into my own heart, my conviction is confirmed by what I experience. I am conscious, not merely of frailties, but of sins. I will not hypocritically accuse myself of gross offences which I have no temptation to commit, and from the commission of which, motives inferior to religion would preserve me. But I am continually humbled in detecting mixed motives in almost all I do. Such strugglings of pride with my endeavours after humility! Such irresolution in my firmest purposes! So much imperfection in my best actions! So much want of simplicity in my purest designs! Such fresh shoots of selfishness where I had hoped the plant itself had been eradicated! Such frequent deadness in duty! Such coldness in my affections! Such infirmity of will! Such proneness to earth in my highest aspirations after heaven! All these you see would hardly make, in the eyes of those who want Christian discernment, very gross sins; yet they prove demonstrably the root of sin in the heart, and the infection of nature tainting my best resolves.'

' The true Christian,' said I, when Mr. Stanley had done speaking, 'extracts humility from the very circumstance which raises pride in the irreligious. The sight of any enormity in another makes the mere moralist proud that he is exempt from it, while the religious man is humbled from a view of the sinfulness of that nature he partakes, a nature which admits of such excesses, and from which excesses he knows that he himself is preserved by Divine grace alone. I have often observed, that comparison is the aliment of pride in the worldly man, and of self-abasement in the Christian.'

Poor Lady Belfield looked comforted on finding that her friend Mr. Stanley was not quite so perfect as she had feared. 'Happy are those,'

* Nil actum reputans dum quod superesset agendum.—LUCAN.

exclaimed she, looking at Lucilla, 'the innocence of whose lives recommends them to the Divine favour.'

'Innocence,' replied Mr. Stanley, 'can never be pleaded as a ground
of acceptance, because the thing does not exist. Innocence excludes
the necessity of repentance, and where there is no sin there can be no
need of a Saviour. Whatever, therefore, we may be in comparison
with others, innocence can afford no plea for our acceptance, without
annulling the great plan of our redemption.'

'One thing puzzles me,' said Lady Belfield; 'the most worthless
people I converse with deny the doctrine of human corruption, a
doctrine, the truth of which one should suppose their own feelings
must confirm; while those few excellent persons, who almost seem to
have escaped it, insist the most peremptorily on its reality. But if it
be really true, surely the mercies of God are so great, that he will
overlook the frailties of such weak and erring mortals. So gracious a
Saviour will not exact such rigorous obedience from creatures so
infirm.'

'Let not what I am going to say, my dear Lady Belfield,' replied
Mr. Stanley, 'offend you; the correctness of your conduct exempts
you from any particular application. But there are too many Christians, who while they speak with reverence of Christ as the Saviour of
sinners, do not enough consider him as a deliverer from sin. They
regard him rather as having lowered the requisitions of the law, and
exonerated his followers from the necessity of that strictness of life
which they view as a burdensome part of religion. From this burden
they flatter themselves it was the chief object of the Gospel to deliver
them; and from this supposed deliverance it is, that they chiefly consider it as a merciful dispensation. A cheap Christianity, of which we
can acquit ourselves by a general recognition and a few stated observances, which require no sacrifices of the will, nor rectification of the
life, is, I assure you, the prevailing system; the religion of that
numerous class who like to save appearances, and to decline realities;
who expect everything hereafter, while they resolve to give up nothing
here; but who keep heaven in view as a snug reversion after they
shall have squeezed out of this world, to the very last dregs and drop-
pings, all it has to give.'

Lady Belfield with great modesty replied, 'Indeed I am ashamed
to have said so much upon a topic on which I am unable and unused
to debate. Sir John only smiles, and looks resolved not to help me
out. Believe me, however, my dear sir, that what I have said proceeds
not from presumption, but from an earnest desire of being set right.
I will only venture to offer one more observation on the afternoon's
sermon. Dr. Barlow, to my great surprise, spoke of the death of
Christ as exhibiting *practical* lessons. Now, though I have always
considered it in a general way as the cause of our salvation, yet its
preceptive and moral benefits, I must confess, do not appear to me at
all obvious.'

'I conceive,' replied Mr. Stanley, 'our deliverance from the punishment incurred by sin, to be one great end and object of the death of
our Redeemer; but I am very far from considering this as the only

benefit attending it. I conceive it to be most abundant in instruction, and the strongest possible incentive to practical goodness, and that in a great variety of ways. The death of our Redeemer shows us the infinite value of our souls, by showing the inestimable price paid for them, and thus leads us to more diligence in securing their eternal felicity. It is calculated to inspire us with an unfeigned hatred of sin, and more especially to convince us of God's hatred to that, for the pardon of which such a sacrifice was deemed necessary. Now if it actually produce such an effect, it consequently stimulates us to repentance, and to an increasing dread of violating those engagements which we have so often made, to lead a better life. Then the contemplation of this stupendous circumstance will tend to fill our hearts with such a sense of gratitude and obedience, as will be likely to preserve us from relapsing into fresh offences. Again—can any motive operate so powerfully on us towards producing universal charity and forgiveness? Whatever promotes our love to God will dispose us to an increased love for our fellow-creatures. We cannot converse with any man, we cannot receive a kindness from any man, nay, we cannot receive an injury from any man, for whom the Redeemer has not died. The remembrance of the sufferings which procured pardon for the greatest offences, has a natural tendency to lead us to forgive small ones.'

Lady Belfield said, 'I had not indeed imagined there were any practical uses in an event to which I had been, however, accustomed to look with reverence as an atonement for sin.'

'Of these practical effects,' replied Mr. Stanley, 'I will only farther observe, that all human considerations put together cannot so powerfully inspire us with an indifference to the vanities of life, and the allurements of unhallowed pleasures. No human motive can be so efficacious in sustaining the heart under trials, and reconciling it to afflictions. For what trials and afflictions do not sink into nothing in comparison with the sufferings attending that august event, from which we derive this support? The contemplation of this sacrifice also degrades wealth, debases power, annihilates ambition. We rise from this contemplation with a mind prepared to bear with the infirmities, to relieve the wants, to forgive the unkindnesses of men. We extract from it a more humbling sense of ourselves, a more subdued spirit, a more sober contempt of whatever the world calls great, than all the lectures of ancient philosophy or the teachers of modern morals ever inspired.'

During this little debate, Sir John maintained the most invincible silence. His countenance bore not the least mark of ill-humour, or impatience, but it was serious and thoughtful, except when his wife got into any little difficulty ; he then encouraged her by an affectionate smile, but listened like a man who has not quite made up his mind, yet thinks the subject too important to be dismissed without a fair and candid hearing.

Chapter XXV.

HILE we were at breakfast next morning, a sweet little gay girl flew into the room almost breathless with joy ; and running to her mother, presented her with a beautiful nosegay.

'Oh, I see you were the industrious girl last week, Kate,' said Mrs. Stanley, embracing her, and admiring the flowers. Lady Belfield looked inquisitively. 'It is an invention of Lucilla's,' said the mother, 'that the little one who performs best in the school-room, instead of having any reward which may excite vanity or sensuality, shall be taught to gratify a better feeling, by being allowed to present her mother with a nosegay of the finest flowers, which it is reward enough to see worn at dinner, to which she is always admitted when there is no company.'

'Oh, pray do not consider us as company ; pray let Kate dine with us to-day,' said Lady Belfield. Mrs. Stanley bowed her assent and went on. 'But this is not all. The flowers they present they also raise. I went rather too far, when I said that no vanity was excited ; they are vain enough of their carnations, and each is eager to produce the largest. In this competition, however, the vanity is not personal Lucilla has some skill in raising flowers, each girl has a subordinate post under her. Their father often treats them with half a day's work, and then they all treat me with tea and cakes in the honey-suckle arbour of their own planting, which is called Lucilla's bower. It would be hard to say whether parents or children most enjoy these happy holidays.'

At dinner, Mrs. Stanley appeared with her nosegay in a large knot of ribbons, which was eyed with no small complacency by little Kate. I observed that Lucilla, who used to manifest much pleasure in the conversation after dinner, was beckoned out of the room by Phœbe as soon as it was over. I felt uneasy at an absence to which I had not been accustomed ; but the cause was explained, when at six o'clock, Kate, who was the queen of the day, was sent to invite us to drink tea in Lucilla's bower ; we instantly obeyed the summons.

'I knew nothing of this,' said the delighted mother, while we were admiring the elegant arrangements of this little fête. The purple clematis twisting its flexile branches with those of the pale woodbine, formed a sweet and fragrant canopy to the arched bower, while the flowery tendrils hung down on all sides. Large bunches of roses, intermixed with the silver stars of the jessamine, were stuck into the moss on the inside, as a temporary decoration only. The finest plants had been brought from the greenhouse for the occasion. It was a delicious evening, and the little fairy festivity, together with the flitting about of the airy spirits which had prepared it, was absolutely enchanting. Sir John, always poetical, exclaimed in rapture :

'Hesperian fables true,
If true, here only.'

I needed not this quotation to bring the garden of Eden to my mind, for Lucilla presided. Phœbe was all alive. The other little ones had decorated Kate's flaxen hair with a wreath of woodbines. They sung two or three baby stanzas, which they had composed among themselves, in which Kate was complimented as queen of the fête. The youngest daughter of Lady Aston, who was about Kate's age, and two little girls of Dr. Barlow's, were of the children's party on the green. The elder sisters of both families made part of the company within.

When we were all seated in our enchanting bower, and drinking our tea, at which we had no other attendants than the little Hebes themselves, I asked Kate how it happened that she seemed to be distinguished on this occasion from her little sisters. ' Oh, sir,' said she, ' it is because it is my birthday. I am eight years old to-day. I gave up all my gilt books, with pictures, this day twelvemonth, and to-day I give up all my little story-books, and I am now going to read such books as men and women read.'

She then ran to her companions, who ranged themselves round a turf seat at a little distance before us, to which was transferred a profusion of cakes and fruit from the bower. While they were devouring them, I turned to Mr. Stanley, and desired an explanation of Kate's speech.

' I make,' said he, ' the renouncing their baby books a kind of epocha, and by thus distinctly marking the period, they never think of returning back to them. We have in our domestic plan several of these artificial divisions of life. These little celebrations are eras, that we use as marking-posts, from which we set out on some new course.'

' But as to Kate's books ?' said Lady Belfield. ' We have,' replied Mr. Stanley, ' too many elementary books. They are read too much, and too long. The youthful mind, which was formerly sick from inanition, is now in danger from a plethora.

' Much, however, will depend on capacity and disposition. A child of slower parts may be indulged till nine years old with books which a lively genius will look down upon at seven. A girl of talents *will* read. To *her* no excitement is wanting. The natural appetite is a sufficient incentive. The less brilliant child requires the allurement of lighter books. She wants encouragement, as much as the other requires restraint.'

' But don't you think,' said Lady Belfield, ' that they are of great use in attracting children to love reading ?' ' Doubtless they are,' said Mr. Stanley. ' The misfortune is, that the stimulants used to attract at first, must be not only continued but heightened, to keep up the attraction. These books are novels in miniature, and the excess of them will lead to the want of novels at full length. The early use of savoury dishes is not usually followed by an appetite for plain food. To the taste thus pampered history becomes dry, grammar laborious, and religion dull.

' My wife, who was left to travel through the wide expanse of universal history, and the dreary deserts of Rapin and Mezerai, is, I will venture to assert, more competently skilled in ancient French and English history, than any of the girls who have been fed, or rather starved, on extracts and abridgments. I mean not to recommend the two last-named authors for very young people. They are dry and tedious, and children in our days have opportunities of acquiring the same knowledge with less labour. We have brighter, I wish I could say safer, lights. Still, fact, and not wit, is the leading object of history.

'Mrs. Stanley says, that the very tediousness of her historians had a good effect ; they were a ballast to her levity, a discipline to her mind, of which she has felt the benefit in her subsequent life.

'But to return to the mass of children's books. The too great profusion of them protracts the imbecility of childhood. They arrest the understanding instead of advancing it. They give forwardness without strength. They hinder the mind from making vigorous shoots, teach it to stoop when it should soar, and to contract when it should expand. Yet I allow that many of them are delightfully amusing, and to a certain degree instructive. But they must not be used as the basis of instruction, and but sparingly used at all as refreshment from labour.'

'They inculcate morality and good actions, surely,' said Lady Belfield. 'It is true,' replied Mr. Stanley, 'but they often inculcate them on a worldly principle, and rather teach the pride of virtue, and the profit of virtue, than point out the motive of virtue and the principle of sin. They reprobate bad actions as evil and injurious to others, but not as an offence against the Almighty. Whereas the Bible comes with a plain, straightforward, simple, but powerful principle, " How shall I do this great wickedness and sin against God ?" " Against THEE, THEE only have I sinned, and done this evil in THY sight."

' Even children should be taught that when a man has committed the greatest possible crime against his fellow-creature, still the offence against God is what will strike a true penitent with the deepest remorse. All morality which is not drawn from this scriptural source is weak, defective, and hollow. These entertaining authors seldom ground their stories on any intimation that human nature is corrupt ; that the young reader is helpless, and wants assistance ; that he is guilty, and wants pardon.'

' Surely, my dear Mr. Stanley,' said Lady Belfield, ' though I do not object to the truth and reasonableness of anything you have said, I cannot think that these things can possibly be made intelligible to children.'

'The framers of our catechism, madam, thought otherwise,' replied Mr. Stanley. 'The catechism was written for children, and contains all the seeds and principles of Christianity for men. It evidently requires much explanation, much development ; still it furnishes a wide and important field for colloquial instruction, without which young persons can by no means understand a composition so admirable, but so condensed. The catechism speaks expressly of " a death unto sin " —of " a new birth unto righteousness "—of " being born in sin "—of being " the children of wrath "—of becoming " the children of grace "— of " forsaking sin by repentance "—of " believing the promises of God by faith." Now, while children are studying these great truths in the catechism, they are probably at the same time almost constantly reading some of those entertaining stories which are grounded and built on a quite opposite principle, and do not even imply the existence of any such fundamental truths.'

'Surely,' interrupted Lady Belfield, 'you would not have these serious doctrines brought forward in story-books !'

'By no means, madam,' replied Mr. Stanley ; 'but I will venture to assert, that even story-books should not be founded on a principle directly *contradictory* to them, nay, totally *subversive* of them. The " Arabian Nights," and other Oriental books of fable, though loose and faulty in many respects, yet have always a reference to the religion of the country. Nothing is introduced against the law of Mahomet ; nothing subversive of the opinions of a Mussulman. I do not quarrel with books for having *no* religion, but for having a *false* religion. A book which in nothing opposes the principles of the Bible, I would be far from calling a bad book, though the Bible was never named in it.'

Lady Belfield observed, 'That she was sorry to say her children found religious studies very dry and tiresome ; though she took great pains, and made them learn by heart a multitude of questions and answers, a variety of catechisms and explanations, and the best abridgments of the Bible.'

'My dear Lady Belfield,' replied Mr. Stanley, 'you have fully accounted for the dryness and dulness of which you complain. Give them the *Bible itself.* I never yet knew a child who did not delight in the Bible histories, and who would not desire to hear them again and again. From the histories, Mrs. Stanley and I proceed with them to the parables ; and from them to the miracles, and a few of the most striking prophecies. When they have acquired a good deal of this desultory knowledge, we begin to weave the parts into a whole. The little girl who had the honour of dining with you to-day, has begun this morning to read the Scriptures with her mother systematically. We shall soon open to her something of the *scheme* of Christianity, and explain how those miracles and prophecies confirm the truth of that religion in which she is to be more fully instructed.

'Upon their historical knowledge, which they acquire by picking out the most interesting stories, we endeavour to ground principles to enlighten their minds, and precepts to influence their conduct. With the genuine language of Scripture I have taken particular care they shall be well acquainted, by digging for the ore in its native bed. While they have been studying the stories, their minds have at the same time been imbued with the impressive phraseology of Scripture. I make a great point of this, having often seen this useful impression effectually prevented by a multitude of subsidiary histories, and explanations, which too much supersede the use of the original text.

'Only observe,' continued he, 'what divine sentiments, what holy precepts, what devout ejaculations, what strokes of self-abasement, what flights of gratitude, what transports of praise, what touches of penitential sorrow, are found comprised in some one short sentence woven into almost every part of the historical Scriptures ! Observe this, and then confess what a pity it is that children should be commonly set to read the history in a meagre abridgment, stripped of those gems with which the original is so richly inlaid ! These histories and expositions become very useful afterwards to young people who are thoroughly conversant with the Bible itself.'

Sir John observed, that he had been struck with the remarkable *disinterestedness* of Mr. Stanley's daughters, and their indifference to things about which most children were so eager. 'Selfishness,' said Mr. Stanley, 'is the hydra we are perpetually combating ; but the monster has so much vitality, that new heads spring up as fast as the old ones are cut off. *To counteract selfishness, that inborn, inbred mischief, I hold to be the great art of education.* Education, therefore, cannot be adequately carried on, except by those who are deeply convinced of the doctrine of human corruption. This evil principle, as it shows itself early, must be early lopped, or the rapid shoots it makes will, as your favourite Eve observes,

> 'Soon mock our scant manuring.'

'This counteraction,' continued Mr. Stanley, 'is not like an art or a science which is to be taken up at set times, and laid aside till the allotted period of instruction returns ; but as the evil shows itself at all times, and in all shapes, the *whole force* of instruction is to be bent against it. Mrs. Stanley and I endeavour that not one reward we bestow, not one gratification we afford, shall be calculated to promote it. Gratifications children ought to have. The appetites and inclinations should be reasonably indulged. We only are cautious not to employ them as the *instruments of recompense*, which would look as if we valued them highly, and thought them a fit remuneration for merit ; I would rather show a little indulgence to sensuality *as* sensuality, than make it the reward of goodness, which seems to be the common way. While I indulged the appetite of a child, I would never hold out that indulgence which I granted to the lowest, the animal part of his nature, as a payment for the exertion of his mental or moral faculties.'

'You have one great advantage,' said Sir John, 'and I thank God it is the same in Cavendish-square, that you and Mrs. Stanley draw evenly together. Nothing impedes domestic regulations so effectually as where parents, from difference of sentiment, ill-humour or bad judgment, obstruct each other's plans, or where one parent makes the other insignificant in the eyes of their children.'

'Mr. Reynolds,' replied Mr. Stanley, 'a friend of mine in this neighbourhood, is in this very predicament. To the mother's weakness the father's temperate discipline seems cruelty. She is perpetually blaming him before the children for setting them to their books. Her attentions are divided between their health, which is perfect, and their pleasure, which is obstructed by her foolish zeal to promote it, far more than by his prudent restrictions. Whatever the father helps them to at table, the mother takes from them, lest it should make them sick. What he forbids is always the very thing which is good for them. She is much more afraid, however, of overloading their memories than their stomachs. Reading, she says, will spoil the girls' eyes, stooping to write will ruin their chests, and working will make them round-shouldered. If the boys run, they will have fevers ; if they jump they will sprain their ankles ; if they play at cricket, a blow may kill them ; if they swim, they will be drowned—the shallowness of the stream is no argument of safety.

' Poor Reynolds' life is one continued struggle between his sense of duty to his children, and his complaisance to his wife. If he carries his point, it is at the expense of his peace ; if he relaxes, as he commonly does, his children are the victims. He is at length brought to submit his excellent judgment to her feeble mind, lest his opposition should hurt her health ; and he has the mortification of seeing his children trained as if they had nothing but bodies.

' To the wretched education of Mrs. Reynolds herself, all this mischief may be attributed ; for she is not a bad, though an ignorant woman ; and having been harshly treated by her own parents, she fell into the vulgar error of vulgar minds, that of supposing the opposite of wrong must necessarily be right. As she found that being perpetually contradicted had made herself miserable, she concluded that never being contradicted at all would make her children happy ; the event has answered, as might have been foreseen. Never was a more discontented, disagreeing, troublesome family. The gratification of one want instantly creates a new one. And it is only when they are quite worn out with having done nothing, that they take refuge in their books, as less wearisome than idleness.'

Sir John, turning to Lady Belfield, said in a very tender tone, ' My dear Caroline, this story, in its principal feature, does not apply to us. We concur completely, it is true, but I fear we concur by being both wrong ; we both err by excessive indulgence. As to the case in point, while children are young, they may perhaps lean to the parent who spoils them, but I have never yet seen an instance of young persons, where the parents differed, who did not afterwards discover a much stronger affection for the one who had reasonably restrained them, than for the other, whose blind indulgence had at once diminished her importance and their own reverence.'

I observed to Mr. Stanley, that as he had so noble a library, and wished to inspire his children with the love of literature, I was surprised to see their apartment so slenderly provided with books.

' This is the age of excess in everything,' replied he ; ' nothing is a gratification, of which the want has not been previously felt. The wishes of children are all so anticipated, that they never experience the pleasure excited by wanting and waiting. Of their initiatory books they *must* have a pretty copious supply. But as to books of entertainment or instruction of a higher kind, I never allow them to possess one of their own, till they have attentively read and improved by it ; this gives them a kind of title to it ; and that desire of property so natural to human creatures, I think stimulates them in despatching books which are in themselves a little dry. Expectation with them, as with men, quickens desire, while possession deadens it.'

By this time the children had exhausted all the refreshments set before them, and had retreated to a little farther distance, where, without disturbing us, they freely enjoyed their innocent gambols—playing, singing, laughing, dancing, reciting verses, trying which could puzzle the other in the names of plants, of which they pulled single leaves to increase the difficulty; all succeeded each other. Lady Belfield, looking consciously at me, said, 'These are the creatures whom I foolishly suspected of being made miserable by restraint, and gloomy through want of indulgence.'

'After long experience,' said Mr. Stanley, 'I will venture to pronounce, that not all the anxious cutting out of pleasure, not all the costly indulgences which wealth can procure, not all the contrivances of inventive man for his darling youthful offspring, can find out an amusement so pure, so natural, so cheap, so rational, so healthful, I had almost said so religious, as that unbought pleasure connected with a garden.'

Kate and Celia, who had for some time been peeping into the bower, in order to catch an interval in the conversation, as soon as they found our attention disengaged, stole in among us : each took the fond father by a hand, and led him to the turf seat. Phœbe presented him with a book, which he opened, and out of it read, with infinite humour, grace, and gaiety, 'The Diverting History of John Gilpin.' This, it seems, was a pleasure to which they had been led to look forward for some time, but which, in honour of Kate, had been purposely withheld till this memorable day. His little auditors, who grouped themselves around him on the grass, were nearly convulsed with laughter, nor were the tenants of the bower much less delighted.

As we walked into the house, Mr. Stanley said, 'Whenever I read to my children a light and gay composition, which I often do, I generally take care it shall be the work of some valuable author, to whose writings this shall be a pleasant and a tempting prelude. What child of spirit who hears John Gilpin, will not long to be thought old and wise enough to read the 'Task?' The remembrance of the infant rapture will give a predilection for the poet. Desiring to keep their standard high, I accustom them to none but good writers, in every sense of the word ; by this means they will be less likely to stoop to ordinary ones when they shall hereafter come to choose for themselves.'

Lady Belfield regretted to me that she had not brought some of her children to the Grove. 'To confess a disgraceful truth,' said she, 'I was afraid they would have been moped to death ; and, to confess another truth, still more disgraceful to my own authority, my indulgence has been so injudicious, and I have maintained so little control, that I durst not bring some of them, for fear of putting the rest out of humour : I am now in a school, where I trust I may learn to acquire firmness, without any diminution of fondness.'

Chapter XXV.

THE next morning, Mr. Stanley proposed that we should pay a visit to some of his neighbours. He and Sir John Belfield rode on horseback, and I had the honour of attending the ladies in the sociable. Lady Belfield, who has now become desirous of improving her own too relaxed domestic system by the experience of Mrs. Stanley, told her how much she admired the cheerful obedience of her children. She said, 'she did not so much wonder to see them so good, but she owned she was surprised to see them so happy.'

'I know not,' replied Mrs. Stanley, 'whether the increased insubordination of children is owing to the new school of philosophy and politics, but it seems to me to make part of the system. When I go sometimes to stay with a friend in town to do business, she is always making apologies that she cannot go out with me—"her daughters want the coach." If I ask leave to see the friends who call on me in such a room, "her daughters have company there," or "they want the room for their music," or "it is preparing for the children's ball in the evening." If a messenger is required, "her daughters want the footmen." There certainly prevails a spirit of independence, a revolutionary spirit, a separation from the parent state. *It is the children's world.*'

'You remind me, madam,' said I, 'of an old courtier, who, being asked by Louis XV. which age he preferred, (his own, or the present?) replied, "Sire, I passed my youth in respecting old age, and I find I must now pass my old age in respecting children."'

'In some other houses,' said Mrs. Stanley, 'where we visit, besides that of poor Mr. Reynolds, the children seem to have all the accommodations ; and I have observed that the convenience and comfort of the father is but a subordinate consideration. The respectful terms of address are nearly banished from the vocabulary of children, and the somewhat too orderly manner which once prevailed is superseded by an incivility, a roughness, a want of attention, which is surely not better than the harmless formality which it has driven out.'

Just as she had said this, we stopped at Mr. Reynolds' gate ; neither he nor his lady were at home. Mr. Stanley, who wished to show us a fine reach of the river from the drawing-room window, desired the servant to show us into it. There we beheld a curious illustration of what we had heard. In the ample bow-window lay a confused heap of the glittering spoils of the most expensive toys. Before the rich silk chairs knelt two of the children, in the act of rapidly demolishing their fine painted playthings ; 'others apart sat on *the floor* retired,' and more deliberately employed in picking to pieces their little gaudy works of art. A pretty girl, who had a beautiful wax doll on her lap, almost, as big as herself, was pulling out its eyes, that she might see how they were put in. Another, weary of this costly baby, was making a little doll of rags. A turbulent-looking boy was tearing out the parchment from a handsome new drum, that he might see, as he told us, where the noise came from. These I forgave, as they had meaning in their mischief.

Another, having kicked about a whole little gilt library, was sitting, with the decorated pages torn asunder at his feet, reading a little dirty penny book, which the kitchen-maid had bought of a hawker at the door. The Persian carpet was strewed with the broken limbs of a painted horse, almost as large as a pony, while the discontented little master was riding astride on a long rough stick. A bigger boy, after having broken the panels of a fine gilt coach, we saw afterwards, in the court-yard, nailing together a few dirty bits of ragged elm boards, to make himself a wheelbarrow.

'Not only the disciple of the fastidious Jean Jacques,' exclaimed I, 'but the sound votary of truth and reason, must triumph at such an instance of the satiety of riches, and the weariness of ignorance and idleness. One such practical instance of the insufficiency of affluence to *bestow* the pleasures which industry must *buy;* one such actual exemplification of the folly of supposing that injudicious profusion and mistaken fondness can supply that pleasure which must be worked out before it can be enjoyed, is worth a whole folio of argument or exhortation.'—The ill-bred little stock paid no attention to us, and only returned a rude " n—o " or " ye—s " to our questions.'

'Caroline,' said Sir John, 'these painted ruins afford a good lesson for us. We must desire our rich uncles and our generous godmothers to make an alteration in their presents, if they cannot be prevailed upon to withhold them.'

'It is a sad mistake,' said Mr. Stanley, 'to suppose that youth wants to be so incessantly amused. They want not pleasures to be chalked out for them. Lay a few cheap and coarse materials in their way, and let their own busy inventions be suffered to work. They have abundant pleasure in the mere freshness and novelty of life, its unbroken health, its elastic spirit, its versatile temper, and its ever-new resources.'

'So it appears, Stanley,' said Sir John, 'when I look at your little group of girls, recluses as they are called. How many cheap, yet lively pleasures do they seem to enjoy !—their successive occupations, their books, their animating exercise, their charitable rounds, their ardent friendships, the social table, at which the elder ones are companions, not mutes ; the ever-varying pleasures of their garden,

Increasing virtue, and approving heaven.

While we were sitting with Lady Aston, on whom we next called, Mr. Stanley suddenly exclaimed, 'The Miss Flams are coming up the gravel walk !' Lady Aston looked vexed, but correcting herself said, ' Mr. Stanley, we owe this visit to you, or rather to your friend,' bowing to me ; 'they saw your carriage stop here, or they would not have done so dull a thing as to have called on me.'

These new guests presented a new scene, very uncongenial to the timid and tranquil spirit of the amiable hostess. There seemed to be a contest between the sisters, who should be most eloquent, most loud, or most inquisitive. They eagerly attacked me all at once, as supposing me to be overflowing with intelligence from the metropolis, a place which they not only believed to contain exclusively all that was worth seeing, but all that was worth hearing. The rest of the world they considered as a barren wilderness, of which the hungry inhabitants could only be kept from starving, by such meagre aliment as the occasional reports of its pleasures, fashions, and anecdotes, which might now and then be conveyed by some stray traveller, might furnish.

'It is so strange to us,' said Miss Bell, ' and so monstrously dull and vulgar, to be in the country at this time of the year, that we don't know what to do with ourselves.'

'As to the time of year, madam,' said I, 'if ever one would wish to be in the country at all, surely this month is the point of perfection. The only immoral thing with which I could ever charge our excellent Sovereign is, that he was born in June, and has thus furnished his fashionable subjects with a loyal pretence for encountering "the sin and sea-coal of London," to borrow Will Honeycomb's phrase, in the finest month of the twelve. But where that is the real motive with one, it is the pretence of a thousand.'

'How can you be so shocking?' said she, 'but papa is really grown so cross and so stingy, as to prevent our going to town at all these last two or three years; and for so mean a reason, that I am ashamed to tell you.' Out of politeness I did not press to know; I needed not, for she was resolved I should not 'burst in ignorance.'

She went on—'Do you know, he pretends that times are hard, and public difficulties increasing; and he declares that whatever privations we endure, government must be supported: so that he says, it is right to draw in, in the only way in which he can do it honestly; I am sure it is not doing it creditably. Did you ever hear anything so shabby?' 'Shabby, madam,' replied I; 'I honour a gentleman who has integrity enough to do a right thing, and good sense enough not to be ashamed to own it.'

'Yes, but papa need not. The steward declares, if he would only raise his tenants a very little, he would have more than enough; but papa is inflexible. He says my brother must do as he pleases when he comes to the estate, but that he himself promised, when he came into possession, that he would never raise the rents, and that he will never be worse than his word.' As I could not find in my heart to join in abusing a gentleman for resolving never to be worse than his word, I was silent.

She then inquired with more seriousness, if there were any prospect of peace. I was better pleased with this question, as it implied more anxiety for the lives of her fellow-creatures, than I had given her credit for. 'I am anxiously looking into all the papers,' continued she, without giving me time to speak, 'because as soon as there is peace, papa has promised we shall go to town again. If it was not for that, I should not care if there was war till doomsday, for what with marching regiments, and militia, and volunteers, nothing can be pleasanter than it makes the country, I mean as far as the country *can* be pleasant.' They then ran over the names and respective merits of every opera singer, every dancer, and every actor, with incredible volubility; and I believe they were not a little shocked at my slender acquaintance with the nomenclature, and the little interest I took in the criticisms they built upon it.

Poor Lady Aston looked oppressed and fatigued, but inwardly rejoiced, as she afterwards owned to me, that her daughters were not within hearing. I was of a different opinion, upon the Spartan principle of making their children sober by the spectacle of the intoxicated Helots. Miss Bell's eloquence seemed to make but little impression on Sir George; or rather, it produced an effect directly contrary to admiration. His good taste seemed to revolt at her flippancy. Every time I see this young man, he rises in my esteem. His ingenuous temper and engaging modesty set off to advantage a very fair understanding.

In our way home, we were accosted by Mr. Flam. After a rough but hearty salutation, and a cordial invitation to come and dine with him, he galloped off, being engaged on business. 'This is an honest country squire of the old cut,' said Mr. Stanley afterwards. 'He has a very good estate, which he has so much delight in managing, that he has no pleasure in anything else. He was prevailed on by his father to marry his present wife, for no other reason than because her estate joined to his, and broke in a little on the *arrondissement;* but it was judged that both being united, all might be brought within a ring fence. This was thought a reason sufficiently powerful for the union of two immortal beings, whose happiness here and hereafter might be impeded or promoted by it ! The felicity of the connection has been in exact proportion to the purity of the motive.'

I could not forbear interrupting Mr. Stanley, by observing that nothing had surprised or hurt me more in the little observation I had made on the subject of marriage, than the frequent indifference of parents to the moral, and especially to the religious character of the man who proposed himself. 'That family, fortune, and connections should have their full share in the business, I readily admit,' added I, 'but that it should ever form the chief, often the only ground of acceptance, has, I confess, lowered mankind in my esteem more completely than almost any other instance of ambition, avarice, or worldliness. That a very young girl, who has not been carefully educated, should be captivated by personal advantages, and even infatuated by splendour, is less surprising, than that parents, who having themselves experienced the insufficiency of riches to happiness—that they should be eagerly impatient to part from a beloved daughter, reared with fondness at least, if not with wisdom, to a man of whose principles they have any doubt, and of whose mind they have a mean opinion, is a thing I cannot understand. And yet what proposal almost is rejected on this ground?' Lucilla's eyes at this moment shone with such expressive brightness, that I exultingly said to myself, 'Lord Staunton ! I defy thee !'

'The mischief of this lax principle is of wide extent,' replied Mr. Stanley. 'When girls are continually hearing what an advantageous, what a desirable marriage such a young friend has made, with a man so rich, so splendid, so great ; though they have been accustomed to hear this very man condemned for his profligacy perhaps, at least they know him to be destitute of piety—when they hear that these things are not considered as any great objection to the union, what opinion must these girls form, not only of the maxims by which the world is governed, but of the truth of that religion which those persons profess ?

'But to return to Mr. Flam. He passed through the usual course of education, but has profited so little by it, that though he has a certain natural shrewdness in his understanding, I believe he has scarcely read a book these twenty years, except " Burns' Justice," and " The Agricultural Reports." Yet, when he wants to make a figure, he now and then lards his discourse with a scrap of threadbare Latin, which he used to steal in his schoolboy exercises. He values himself on his integrity, and is not destitute of benevolence. These, he says, are the sum and substance of religion ; and though I combat this mistaken notion as often as he puts it in my power, yet I must say that some who make more profession would do well to be as careful in these points. He often contrasts himself with his old friend Ned Tyrrel, and is proud of showing how much better a man he is without religion, than Ned is with all his pretensions to it. It is by thus comparing ourselves with worse men that we grow vain, and with more fortunate men, that we become discontented.

' All the concern he gives himself about his wife and daughter is, that they shall not run him in debt ; and indeed he is so liberal, that he does not drive them to the necessity. In everything else they follow their own devices. They teased him, however, to let them spend two or three winters in town, the mother hinting *that it would answer.* He was prevailed on to try it as a speculation, but the experiment failed. He now insists that they shall go no more till the times mend to any of the advertising places, such as London, Brighton, or Bath ; he says, that attending so many fairs and markets is very expensive, especially as the girls don't go off. He will now see what can be done by private contract at home, without the cost of journeys, with fresh keep and trimming, and docking into the bargain. They must now take their chance among country dealers ; and provided they will give him a son-in-law whose estate is free from incumbrances, who pays his debts, lives within his income, does not rack his tenants, never drinks claret, hates the French, and loves field sports, he will ask no more questions.'

I could not but observe, how preferable the father's conduct, with all its faults, was to that of the rest of the family. ' I had imagined,' said I, ' that this coarse character was quite out of print. Though it is religiously bad, and of course morally defective, yet it is so politically valuable, that I should not be sorry to see a new edition of these obsolete squires, somewhat corrected, and better lettered.'

' All his good qualities,' said Mr. Stanley, ' for want of religion, have a flaw in them. His good nature is so little directed by judgment, that while it serves the individual, it injures the public. As a brother magistrate, I am obliged to act in almost constant opposition to him, and his indiscretions do more mischief by being of a nature to increase his popularity. He is fully persuaded that occasional intoxication is the best reward for habitual industry ; and insists that it is a good old English kindness, to make the church-ringers periodically tipsy at the holidays, though their families starve for it the whole week. He and I have a regular contest at the annual village fairs, because he insists that my refusing to let them begin on a Sunday is abridging their few rights, and robbing them of a day which they might add to their pleasure, without injury to their profit. He allows all the strolling players, mountebanks, and jugglers to exhibit, because, he says, it is a charity. His charity however, is so short-sighted, that he does not see, that while these vagabonds are supplying the wants of the day, their improvident habits suffer them to look no farther. That his own workmen are spending their hard-earned money in these illegal diversions, while the expense is the least mischief which their daughters incur.'

Our next visit was to Mr. Carlton, whom I had found in one or two previous interviews to be a man of excellent sense, and a perfect gentleman. Sir John renewed with pleasure his acquaintance with the husband, while Lady Belfield was charmed to be introduced to the wife, with whose character she was so enamoured, and whose gentle manners were calculated to confirm the affection which her little history had inspired.

Chapter XXVII.

N the morning, Mr. Stanley, Sir John Belfield, and I, took a walk, to call on our valuable rector. On our return home, amidst that sort of desultory conversation which a walk often produces—' Since we left the parsonage, sir,' said I, addressing myself to Mr. Stanley, ' I have been thinking how little justice has been done to the clerical character in those popular works of imagination which are intended to exhibit a picture of living manners. There are, indeed, a very few happy exceptions. Yet I cannot but regret that so many fair occasions have been lost of advancing the interests of religion by personifying her amiable graces in the character of her ministers. I allude not to the attack of the open infidel, nor the sly insinuation of the concealed sceptic, nor do I advert to the broad assault of the enemy of good government, who, falling foul of every established institution, would naturally be expected to show little favour to the ministers of the Church. But I advert to those less prejudiced and less hostile writers, who having, as I would hope, no political nor moral motive for undermining the order, would rather desire to be considered as among its friends and advocates.'

' I understand you,' replied Mr. Stanley ; ' I believe that this is often done, not from any disrespect to the sacred function, nor from any wish to depreciate an order which even common sense and common prudence, without the intervention of religion, tell us cannot be set in too respectable a light. I believe it commonly arises from a different cause. The writer himself having but a low idea of the requirements of Christianity, is consequently neither able nor willing to affix a very elevated standard for the character of its ministers. Some of these writers, however, describe a clergyman, in general terms, as a paragon of piety, but they seldom make him act up to the description with which he sets out. He is represented, in the gross, as adorned with all the attributes of perfection, but when he comes to be drawn out in detail, he is found to exhibit little of that superiority which had been ascribed to him in the lump. You are told how religious he is ; but when you come to hear him converse, you are not always quite certain whether he professes the religion of the Shaster or the Bible. You hear of his moral excellence, but you find him adopting the maxims of the world,

and living in the pursuits of ordinary men. In short, you will find that
he has little of a clergyman, except the name.'

' A sensible little work of fiction,' replied I, ' lately fell in my way.
Among its characters was that of a grave divine. From the strain of
panegyric bestowed on him, I expected to have met with a rival to the
fathers of the primitive church. He is presented as a model; and,
indeed, he counsels, he exhorts, he reproves, he instructs—but he goes
to a masquerade.'

' This assimilation of general piety,' said Mr. Stanley, 'with occasional
conformity to the practice of the gay world, I should fear, would produce
two ill effects. It will lower the professional standard to the young
reader while he is perusing the ideal character, and the comparison
will dispose him to accuse of forbidding strictness the pious clergyman
of real life. After having been entertained with the mixture of religion
and laxity in the imaginary divine whom he has been following from
the serious lecture to the scene of revelry, will he not be naturally disposed to accuse of moroseness the existing divine, who blends no such
contradictions?

' But the evil of which I more particularly complain,' continued he,
' because it exists in works universally read, and written, indeed, with
a life and spirit which make them both admired and remembered, is
found in the ingenious and popular novels of the witty class. In some
of these, even where the author intends to give a favourable representation of a clergyman, he more frequently exhibits him for the purpose of
merriment than for that of instruction.'

' I confess with shame,' said Sir John, ' that the spirit, fire, and
knowledge of mankind, of the writers to whom you allude, have made
me too generally indulgent to their gross pictures of life, and to the loose
morals of their good men.'

' *Good men!*' said Mr. Stanley. ' After reading some of those works
in the early part of my life, I amused myself with the idea that I should
like to interweave the character of a *Christian* among the heroes of
Fielding and Smollet, as the shortest way of proving their *good men* to
be worthless fellows ; and to show how little their admired characters
rise, in point of morals, above the heroes of the Beggar's Opera.

' Knowledge of the world,' continued he, ' should always be used to
mend the world. A writer employs this knowledge honestly, when he
points out the snares and pitfalls of vice. But when he covers those
snares and pitfalls with flowers, when he fascinates in order that he
may corrupt, when he engages the affections by polluting them, I know
not how a man can do a deeper injury to society, or more fatally inflame
his own future reckoning.'

' But to return to our more immediate subject,' said I, ' I cannot
relish their singling out of the person of a pious clergyman as a peculiarly
proper vehicle for the display of humour. Why qualities which excite
ridicule should be necessarily blended with such as command esteem,
is what I have never been able to comprehend.'

' Even where the characters,' replied Mr. Stanley, ' have been so
pleasingly delineated as to attract affection by their worth and benevolence, there is always a drawback from their respectability by some

trait that is ludicrous, some situation that is unclerical, some incident that is absurd. There is a contrivance to expose them to some awkward distress ; there is some palpable weakness to undo the effect of their general example, some impropriety of conduct, some gross error in judgment, some excess of simplicity, which, by infallibly diminishing the dignity, weakens the influence of the character, and of course lessens the veneration of the reader.'

'I have often,' replied I, 'felt that though we may love the man we laugh at, we shall never reverence him. We may like him as a companion, but we shall never look up to him as an instructor.'

'I know no reason,' observed Mr. Stanley, 'why a pious divine may not have as much wit and humour as any other man. And we have it on the word of the wittiest of the whole body, Dr. South, that "piety does not necessarily involve dulness." An author may lawfully make his churchman as witty as he pleases, or rather as witty as he can : but he should never make him the butt of the wit of other men, which is, in fact, making him the butt of his own wit. What is meant to be a *comical parson* is no respectable or prudent exhibition ; nor, with the utmost stretch of candour, can I believe that the motive of the exhibitor is always of the purest kind.

'How far,' continued Mr. Stanley, 'authors have found it necessary to add these diverting appendages in order to qualify piety, how far they have been obliged to dilute religion, so as to make it palatable and pardonable, I will not pretend to decide. But whether such a mixture be not calculated to leave a lasting effect on the mind, unfavourable to the clerical character ; whether these associations are not injurious even to religion itself, let those declare, if they would speak honestly, who have been accustomed to be excessively delighted with such combinations.'

'I am a little afraid,' returned Sir John, 'that I have formerly in some degree fallen under this censure. But, surely, Stanley, you would not think it right to lavish *undue* praise even on characters of a better stamp ; you would not commend ordinary merit highly, and, above all, you would not, I presume, screen the faults of the worthless ?'

'I am as far from insisting,' replied he, 'on the universal piety of the clergy, as from bespeaking reverence for the unworthy individual ; all I contend for is, that no arts should ever be employed to discredit the *order*. The abettors of revolutionary principles, a few years ago, had the acuteness to perceive, that so to discredit it was one of their most powerful engines. Had not that spirit been providentially extinguished, they would have done more mischief to religion by their artful mode of introducing degrading pictures of our national instructors, in their popular tracts, than the Hobbes's and the Bolingbrokes' had done by blending irreligion with their philosophy, or the Voltaires and the Gibbons by interweaving it into their history. Whatever is mixed up with our amusements is swallowed with more danger, because with more pleasure and less suspicion, than anything which comes under a graver name and more serious shape.'

'I presume,' said Sir John, 'you do not mean to involve in your censure the exquisitely keen satires of Erasmus on the ecclesiastics of his day : and I remember that you yourself could never read without delight the pointed wit of Boileau against the spiritual voluptuaries of his time, in his admirable *Lutrin.* Perhaps you are not disposed to give the same quarter to the pleasant ridicule of Le Sage ?'

' We justify ourselves as good Protestants,' rejoined Mr. Stanley, ' for pardoning the severe but just attacks of the reformer and the poet on the vices of a corrupt church. Though, to speak the truth, I am not quite certain that even these two discriminating and virtuous authors did not, especially Erasmus, now and then indulge themselves in a sharpness which seemed to bear upon religion itself, and not merely on the luxury and idleness of its degenerate ministers. As to Le Sage, who, with all his wit, I should never have thought of bringing into such good company, he was certainly withheld by no restraints either moral or religious. And it is obvious to me, that he seems rather gratified that he had the faults to expose, than actuated by an honest zeal, by exposing to correct them.'

' I wish I could say,' replied Sir John, ' that the Spanish friar of Dryden, and the witty Opera of the living Dryden, did not fall under the same suspicion. I have often observed, that as Lucian dashes with equal wit and equal virulence at every religion, of every name and every nation, so Dryden, with the same diffusive zeal, attacks the ministers of every religion. In ransacking muftis, monks, and prelates, to confirm his favourite position,

That priests of all religions are the same,

he betrays a secret wish to intimate that not only the priests of all religions, but the religions of all priests, are pretty much alike.'

' He has, however,' said Mr. Stanley, ' made a sort of palinode, by his consummately beautiful poem of the *good parson.* Yet even this lovely picture he could not allow himself to complete without a fling at the order, which he declares, at the conclusion, he only spares for the sake of one exception.'

' Rousseau,' said Sir John, ' seems to be the only sceptic who has not, in this respect, acted unfairly. His Savoyard vicar is represented as a grave, consistent, and exemplary character.'

' True,' replied Mr. Stanley. ' But don't you perceive why he is so represented ? He is exhibited as a model of goodness, in order to exalt the scanty faith and unsound doctrines of which he is made the teacher.'

' I would not,' continued he, ' call that man an enemy to the church who should reprobate characters who are a dishonour to it. But the just though indignant biographer of a real Sterne, or a real Churchill, exhibits a very different spirit, and produces a very different effect, from the painter of any imaginary *Thwackum* or *Supple.* In the historian, concealment would be blameable and palliation mischievous. He fairly exposes the individual without wishing to bring any reproach on the profession. What I blame is, employing the vehicle of fiction for the purpose of blackening, or in any degree discrediting, a body of men who depend much for the success of their labours on public opinion, and on the success of whose labours depends so large a portion of the public virtue.'

' I have sometimes,' said I, ' heard my father express his surprise that the most engaging of all writers—Mr. Addison—a man so devout himself, so forward to do honour to religion on all occasions, should have let slip so fair an opportunity for exalting the value of a country clergyman as the description of Sir Roger de Coverley's chaplain naturally put into his hands.'*

' You must allow,' said Sir John, ' that he has made him worthy, and that he has not made him absurd.'

' I grant it,' replied I, ' but he has made him dull and acquiescent. He has made him anything rather than a pattern.'

' But what I most regret,' said Mr. Stanley, ' is, that the use he has made of this character is to give the stamp of his own high authority to a practice, which though it is characteristically recommended by the whimsical knight, whose original vein of humour leaves every other far behind it, yet should never have had the sanction of the author of Saturday pieces in the *Spectator*—I mean, the practice of the minister of a little country parish preaching to farmers and peasants the most learned, logical, and profound discourses in the English language.'

' It has, I believe,' replied Sir John, ' excited general wonder, that so consummate a judge of propriety should have commended as suitable instruction for illiterate villagers, the sermons of those incomparable scholars, Fleetwood, South, Tillotson, Barrow, Calamy, and Sanderson.'

' But this is not the worst,' said Mr. Stanley, ' for Mr. Addison not only clearly approves it in the individual instance, but takes occasion from it to establish a general rule, and indefinitely to advise the country clergy to adopt the custom of preaching these same discourses "*instead of wasting their spirits in laborious compositions of their own.*" '

' Surely,' replied I, ' an enemy of religion could not easily have devised a more effectual method for thinning the village church, or lessening the edification of the unlettered auditor, than this eminent advocate for Christianity has here incautiously suggested.'

' I am sorry,' said Mr. Stanley, ' that such a man has given such a sanction for reducing religious instruction to little more than a form, and for seeming to consider the mere act of attending public worship as the sole end of its institution, without sufficiently taking into the account the nature and the importance of the instruction itself ; and without considering that nothing can be edifying which is not intelligible. Besides, it is not only preventing the improvement of the people, but checking that of the preacher. It not only puts a bar to his own advancement in the art of teaching, but retards that growth in piety which might have been promoted in himself while he was preparing in secret to promote that of his hearers.'

' And yet,' replied Sir John, ' to speak honestly, I am afraid, had I been the patron, I should have been so gratified myself with hearing those fine compositions, that I could not heartily have blamed my chaplain for preaching no other.'

* See *Spectator*, Vol. ii., No, 107.

'My dear Sir John,' said Mr. Stanley, 'neither your good sense nor your good nature would, I am persuaded, allow you to purchase your own gratification at the expense of a whole congregation. You, a man of learning and of leisure, can easily supply any deficiency of ability in plain but useful sermons. But how would the tenants, the workmen and the servants (for of such at least was Sir Roger's congregation composed), how would those who have little other means of edification indemnify themselves for the loss of that single opportunity which the whole week affords them? Is not that a most inequitable way of proportioning instruction, which, while it pleases or profits the well-informed individual, cuts off the instruction of the multitude? If we may twist a text from its natural import, is it "rightly dividing the word of truth," to feast the patron, and starve the parish?'

Chapter XXVIII.

THOUGH Mr. Stanley had checked my impetuosity on my application to him, and did not encourage my addresses with a promptitude suited to the ardour of my affection, yet as the warmth of my attachment, notwithstanding I made it a duty to restrain its outward expression, could not escape either his penetration or that of his admirable wife, they began a little to relax in the strictness with which they had avoided speaking of their daughter. They never indeed introduced the subject themselves, yet it somehow or other never failed to find its way into all conversation in which I was one of the interlocutors.

Sitting one day in Lucilla's bower with Mrs. Stanley, and speaking, though in general terms, on the subject nearest my heart, with a tenderness and admiration as sincere as it was fervent, I dwelt particularly on some instances which I had recently heard from Edwards of her tender attention to the sick poor, and her zeal in often visiting them without regard to weather, or the accommodation of a carriage.

'I assure you,' said Mrs. Stanley, 'you over-rate her. Lucilla is no prodigy dropped down from the clouds. Ten thousand other young women, with natural good sense, and good temper, might with the same education, the same neglect of what is useless, and the same attention to what is necessary, acquire the same habits and the same principles. Her being no prodigy, however, perhaps makes her example, as far as it goes, more important. She may be more useful because she carries not that discouraging superiority, which others might be deterred from imitating through hopelessness to reach. If she is not a miracle whom others might despair to emulate, she is a Christian whom every girl of a fair understanding and good disposition may equal, and whom I hope and believe, many girls excel.'

I asked Mrs. Stanley's permission to attend the young ladies in one of their benevolent rounds. 'When I have leisure to be of the party,' replied she, smiling, 'you shall accompany us. I am afraid to trust your warm feelings. Your good nature would perhaps lead you to commend as a merit, what in fact deserves no praise at all, the duty being so obvious and so indispensable. I have often heard it regretted that ladies have no stated employment, no profession. It is a mistake. *Charity is the calling of a lady ; the care of the poor is her profession.* Men have little time or taste for details. Women of fortune have abundant leisure, which can in no way be so properly or so pleasantly filled up, as in making themselves intimately acquainted with the worth and the wants of all within their reach. With their wants, because it is their bounden duty to administer to them ; with their worth, because without this knowledge they cannot administer prudently and appropriately.'

I expressed to Mrs. Stanley the delight with which I had heard of the admirable regulations of her family in the management of the poor, and how much their power of doing good was said to be enlarged by the judgment and discrimination with which it was done.

'We are far from thinking,' replied she, 'that our charity should be limited to our own immediate neighbourhood. We are of opinion, that it should not be left undone anywhere, but that *there* it should be done indispensably. We consider our own parish as our more appropriate field of action, where Providence, by "fixing the bounds of our habitation," seems to have made us peculiarly responsible for the comfort of those whom he has doubtless placed around us for that purpose. It is thus that the Almighty vindicates his justice, or rather calls on us to vindicate it. It is thus he explains why he admits natural evil into the world, by making the wants of one part of the community an exercise for the compassion of the other.

' Surely,' added Mrs. Stanley, 'the reason is particularly obvious, why the bounty of the affluent ought to be most liberally, though not exclusively, extended to the spot whence they derive their revenues. There seems indeed to be a double motive for it. The same act Involves a duty both to God and to man. The largest bounty to the necessitous on our estates, is rather justice than charity. 'Tis but a kind of peppercorn acknowledgment to the great Lord and Proprietor of all, from whom we hold them. And to assist their own labouring poor is a kind of natural debt, which persons who possess great landed property owe to those from the sweat of whose brow they derive their comforts, and even their riches. 'Tis a commutation, in which, as the advantage is greatly on our side, so is our duty to diminish the difference, of paramount obligation.'

I then repeated my request, that I might be allowed to take a practical lesson in the next periodical visit to the cottages.

Mrs. Stanley replied, 'As to my girls, the elder ones, I trust, are such veterans in their trade, that your approbation can do them no harm, nor do they stand in need of it as an incentive. But should the little ones find that their charity procures them praise, they might perhaps be charitable for the sake of praise, their benevolence might be set at work by their vanity, and they might be led to do that from the love of applause, which can only please God when the principle is pure. *The iniquity of our holy things*, my good friend, requires much Christian vigilance. Next to not giving at all, the greatest fault is to give from ostentation. The contest is only between two sins. The motive robs the act of the very name of virtue, while the good work that is paid in praise, is stripped of the hope of higher retribution.'

On my assuring Mrs. Stanley, that I thought such an introduction to their systematic schemes of charity might inform my own mind and improve my habits, she consented, and I have since been a frequent witness of their admirable method; and have been studying plans, which involve the good both of body and soul. Oh! if I am ever blest with a coadjutress, a directress let me rather say, formed under such auspices, with what delight shall I transplant the principles and practices of Stanley Grove to the Priory! Nor indeed would I ever marry but with the animating hope that not only myself, but all around me, would be the better and the happier for the presiding genius I shall place there.

Sir John Belfield had joined us while we were on this topic. I had observed sometimes that though he was earnest on the general principle of benevolence, which he considered as a most imperious duty, or, as he said in his warm way, as so lively a pleasure, that he was almost ready to suspect if it *were* a duty; yet I was sorry to find that his generous mind had not viewed this large subject under all its aspects. He had not hitherto regarded it as a matter demanding anything but money; while time, inquiry, discrimination, system, he confessed he had not much taken into the account. He did a great deal of good, but had not allowed himself time or thought for the best way of doing it. Charity, as opposed to hardheartedness and covetousness, he warmly exercised; but when with a willing liberality he had cleared himself from the suspicion of those detestable vices, he was indolent in the proper distribution of money, and somewhat negligent of its just application. Nor had he ever considered, as every man should do, because every man's means are limited, how the greatest quantity of good could be done with any given sum.

But the worst of all was, he had imbibed certain popular prejudices respecting the more *religious* charities; prejudices altogether unworthy of his enlightened mind. He too much limited his ideas of bounty to bodily wants. This distinction was not with him, as it is with many, invented as an argument for saving his money, which he most willingly bestowed for feeding and clothing the necessitous. But as to the propriety of affording them religious instruction, he owned he had not made up his mind. He had some doubts whether it were a duty. Whether it were a benefit, he had still stronger doubts; adding, that he should begin to consider the subject more attentively than he had yet done.

Mrs. Stanley in reply said, 'I am but a poor casuist, Sir John, and I must refer you to Mr. Stanley for abler arguments than I can use. I will venture, however, to say, that even on your own ground it appears to be a pressing duty. If sin be the cause of so large a portion of the miseries of human life, must not that be the noblest charity which cures, or lessens, or prevents sin? And are not they the truest benefactors even to the bodies of men, who by the religious exertions to prevent the corruption of vice, prevent also, in some measure, that poverty and disease which are the natural concomitants of vice? If in endeavouring to make men better, by the infusion of a religious principle which shall check idleness, drinking, and extravagance, we put them in the way to become healthier, and richer, and happier, it will furnish a practical argument which I am sure will satisfy your benevolent heart.'

Chapter XXIX.

M R. TYRREL and his nephew called on us in the evening, and interrupted a pleasant and useful conversation on which we were just entering.

'Do you know, Stanley,' said Mr. Tyrrel, 'that you have absolutely corrupted my nephew, by what passed at your house the other day in favour of reading. He has ever since been ransacking the shelves for idle books.'

'I should be seriously concerned,' replied Mr. Stanley, 'if anything I had said should have drawn Mr. Edward off from more valuable studies, or diverted him from the important pursuit of religious knowledge.'

'Why, to do him justice, and you too,' resumed Mr. Tyrrel, 'he has since that conversation begun assiduously to devote his mornings to serious reading, and it is only an hour's leisure in the evening, which he used to trifle away, that he gives to books of taste; but I had rather he would let them all alone. The best of them will only fill his heart with cold morality, and stuff his head with romance and fiction. I would not have a religious man ever look into a book of your *belles lettres* nonsense; and if he be really religious, he will make a general bonfire of the poets.'

'That is rather too sweeping a sentence,' said Mr. Stanley. 'It would, I grant you, have been a benefit to mankind, if the entire works of some celebrated poets, and a considerable portion of the works of many not quite so exceptionable, were to assist the conflagration of your pile.'

'And if fuel failed,' said Sir John Belfield, 'we might not only rob Belinda's altar of her

> Twelve tomes of French romances neatly gilt,

but feed the flame with countless marble-covered octavos for the modern school. But having made this concession, allow me to observe, that because there has been a voluptuous Petronius, a profane Lucretius, and a licentious Ovid, to say nothing of the numberless modern poets, or rather individual poems, that are immoral and corrupt—shall we therefore exclude all works of imagination from the library of a young man? Surely we should not indiscriminately banish the Muses, as infallible corrupters of the youthful mind; I would rather consider a blameless poet as the auxiliar of virtue. Whatever talent enables a writer to possess an empire over the heart, and to lead the passions at his command, puts it in his power to be of no small service to mankind. It is no new remark, that the abuse of any good thing is no argument against its legitimate use. Intoxication affords no just reason against the use of wine, nor prodigality against the possession of wealth. In the instance in dispute, I should rather infer that a talent capable of diffusing so much mischief, was susceptible of no small benefit. That it has been so often abused by its misapplication, is one of the highest instances of the ingratitude of man for one of the highest gifts of God.'

'I cannot think,' said I, 'that the Almighty conferred such a faculty with a wish to have it extinguished. Works of imagination have in many countries been a chief instrument of civilization. Poetry has not only preceded science in the history of human progress, but it has in many countries preceded the knowledge of the mechanical arts; and I have somewhere read, that in Scotland they could write elegant Latin verse before they could make a wheel-barrow. For my own part, in my late visit to London, I thought the decline of poetry no favourable symptom.'

'I rejoice to hear it *is* declining,' said Tyrrel. 'I hope that what is decaying, may in time be extinguished.'

'Mr. Tyrrel would have been delighted with what I was displeased with,' replied I. 'I met with philosophers, who were like Plato in nothing but in his abhorrence of the Muses; with politicians, who resembled Burleigh only in his enmity to Spenser; and with warriors, who, however they might emulate Alexander in his conquests, would never have imitated him in sparing "the house of Pindarus."'

'The *art* of poetry,' said Mr. Stanley, 'is to touch the passions, and its *duty* to lead them on the side of virtue. To raise and to purify the amusements of mankind; to multiply and to exalt pleasures, which, being purely intellectual, may help to exclude such as are gross, in beings so addicted to sensuality, is surely not only to give pleasure, but to render service. It is allowable to seize every avenue to the heart of a being so prone to evil; to rescue him by every fair means not only from the degradation of vice, but from the dominion of idleness. I do not now speak of gentlemen of the sacred function to which Mr. Edward Tyrrel aspires, but of those who, having no profession, have no stated employment; and who, having more leisure, will be in danger of exceeding the due bounds in the article of amusement. Let us then endeavour to allure our youth of fashion from the low pleasures of the dissolute; to snatch them not only from the destruction of the gaming-table, but from the excesses of the dining-table, by inviting them to an elegant delight that is safe, and especially by enlarging the range of pure mental pleasure.

'In order to this, let us do all we can to cultivate their taste, and innocently indulge their fancy. Let us contend with impure writers, those deadliest enemies to the youthful mind, by exposing to them, in the chaster author, images more attractive, wit more acute, learning more various; in all of which excellencies our first-rate poets certainly excel their vicious competitors.'

'Would you, Mr. Tyrrel,' said Sir John, 'throw into the enemy's camp all the light arms, which often successfully annoy where the heavy artillery cannot reach?'

'Let us,' replied Mr. Stanley, 'rescue from the hands of the profane and the impure the monopoly of wit which they affect to possess, and which they would possess, if no good men had written works of elegant literature, and if all good men totally despised them.'

'For my own part,' said Mr. Tyrrel, 'I believe that a good man, in my sense of the word, will neither write works of imagination, nor read them.'

'At your age and mine, and better employed as we certainly may be,' said Mr. Stanley, 'we want not such resources. I myself, though I strongly retain the relish, have little leisure for the indulgence, which yet I would allow, though with great discrimination, to the young and the unoccupied. What is to whet the genius of the champions of virtue, so as to enable them successfully to combat the leaders of vice and infidelity, if we refuse to let them be occasionally sharpened and polished by such studies? That model of brilliant composition, Bishop Jeremy Taylor, was of this opinion, when he said, "by whatever instrument piety is advantaged, use that, though thou grindest thy spears and arrows at the forges of the Philistines."'

'I know,' continued Mr. Stanley, 'that a Christian need not borrow weapons of attack or defence from the classic armoury ; but, to drop all metaphor, if he be called upon to defend truth and virtue against men whose minds are adorned with all that is elegant, strengthened with all that is persuasive, and enriched with all that is persuasive, from the writers in question, is he likely to engage with due advantage, if his own mind be destitute of the embellishments with which theirs abound? While wit and imagination are *their* favourite instruments, shall we consider the aid of either as useless, much less as sinful, in their opponents?'

'While young men *will* be amused,' said Sir John, 'it is surely of importance that they should be *safely* amused. We should not, therefore, wish to obliterate in authors such faculties as wit and fancy, nor to extinguish a taste for them in readers.'

'Show me any one instance of good that ever was effected by any one poet,' said Mr. Tyrrel, 'and I will give up the point ; while, on the other hand, a thousand instances of mischief might doubtless be produced.'

'The latter part of your assertion, sir,' said I, 'I fear is too true : but to what evil has elevation of fancy led Milton, or Milton his readers? In what labyrinths of guilt did it involve Spenser or Cowley? Has Thomson or has Young added to the crimes or the calamities of mankind? Into what immoralities did it plunge Gay or Goldsmith? Has it tainted the purity of Beattie in his "Minstrel," or that of the living minstrel of the "Lay !" What reader has Mason corrupted, or what reader has Cowper not benefited? Milton was an enthusiast, both in religion and politics. Many enthusiasts with whom he was connected doubtless condemned the exercise of his imagination in his immortal poem as a crime ; but his genius was too mighty to be restrained by opposition, and his imagination too vast and powerful to be kept down by a party. Had he confined himself to his prose writings, weighty and elaborate as some of them are, how little service would he have done the world, and how little would he now be read or quoted ! In his lifetime, politics might blind his enemies, and fanaticism his friends. But now, who, comparatively, reads the Iconoclastes? who does not read Comus ?'

' What, then,' said Mr. Tyrrel, ' you would have our young men spend their time in reading idle verses, and our girls, I suppose, in reading loose romances ?'

' It is to preserve both from evils which I deprecate,' said Mr. Stanley, ' that I would consign the most engaging subjects to the best hands, and raise the taste of our youth, by allowing a little of their leisure, and of their leisure only, to such amusements, and that chiefly with a view to disengage them from worse pursuits. It is not romance, but indolence ; it is not poetry, but sensuality, which are the prevailing evils of the day—evils far more fatal in themselves, far more durable in their effects, than the perusal of works of wit and genius. Imagination will cool of itself ; the effervescence of fancy will soon subside ; but absorbing dissipation, but paralyzing idleness, but degrading self-love :

' " Grows with their growth, and strengthens with their strength." '

' A judicious reformer,' said Sir John, ' will accommodate his remedy to an existing and not an imaginary evil. When the old romances, the grand Cyrus's, the Celias, the Cassandras, the Pharamonds, and the Amadi's, had turned all the young heads in Europe ; or when the fury of knight-errantry demanded the powerful reign of Cervantes to check it—it was a duty to attempt to lower the public delirium. When, in our own age and country, Sterne wrote his corrupt, but too popular lesser work, he became the mischievous founder of the school of sentiment. A hundred writers communicated, a hundred thousand readers caught the infection. Sentimentality was the disease which then required to be expelled. The reign of Sterne is past. Sensibility is discarded, and with it the softness which it must be confessed belonged to it. Romance is vanished, and with it the heroic though somewhat unnatural elevation which accompanied it. We have little to regret in the loss of either ; nor have we much cause to rejoice in what we have gained by the exchange. A pervading and substantial selfishness, the striking characteristic of our day, is no great improvement on the wildness of the old romance, or the vapid puling of the sentimental school.'

' Surely,' said I (L'Almanac des Gourmands at that instant darting across my mind), ' it is as honourable for a gentleman to excel in critical as in culinary skill. It is as noble to cultivate the intellectual taste, as that of the palate. It is at least as creditable to discuss the comparative merits of Sophocles and Shakespeare, as the rival ingredients of a soup or a sauce. I will even venture to affirm that it is as dignified an amusement to run a tilt in favour of Virgil or Tasso against their assailants, as to run a barouche against a score of rival barouches ; and though I own that, in Gulliver's " land of the Houyhnhnms," the keeping up the breed of horses might have been the nobler patriotism, yet in Great Britain it is hitherto at least become no contemptible exertion of skill and industry to keep up the breed of gentlemen.'

Chapter XXX.

STROLLED out alone, intending to call at the rectory, but was prevented by meeting the worthy Doctor Barlow, who was coming to the Grove. I could not lose so fair an opportunity of introducing a subject that was seldom absent from my thoughts. I found it was a subject on which I had no new discoveries to impart. He told me he had seen and rejoiced in the election my heart had made. I was surprised at his penetration. He smiled, and said, he 'took no great credit for his sagacity, in perceiving what was obvious to spectators far more indifferent than himself ; that I resembled those animals who, by hiding their heads in the earth, fancied nobody could see them.'

I asked him a thousand questions about Lucilla, whose fine mind I knew he had in some measure contributed to form. I inquired, with an eagerness which he called jealousy, who were her admirers ? 'As many men as have seen her,' replied he, 'I know no man who has so many rivals as yourself. To relieve your apprehensions, however, I will tell you, that though there have been several competitors for her favour, not one has been accepted. There has, indeed, this summer been a very formidable candidate, young Lord Staunton, who has a large estate in the county, and whom she met on a visit.' At these words I felt my fears revive. A young and handsome peer seemed so redoubtable a rival, that for a moment I only remembered she was a woman, and forgot that she was Lucilla.

'You may set your heart at rest,' said Dr. Barlow, who saw my emotion. 'She heard he had seduced the innocent daughter of one of his tenants, under the most specious pretence of honourable love. This, together with the looseness of his religious principles, led her to give his lordship a positive refusal, though he is neither destitute of talents, nor personal accomplishments.'

How ashamed was I of my jealousy ! How I felt my admiration increase ! Yet I thought it was too great before, to admit of augmentation. 'Another proposal,' said Dr. Barlow, 'was made to her father by a man every way unexceptionable. But she desired him to be informed that it was her earnest request that he would proceed no farther, but spare her the pain of refusing a gentleman, for whose character she entertained a sincere respect ; but being persuaded she could never be able to feel more than respect, she positively declined receiving his addresses, assuring him, at the same time, that she sincerely desired to retain as a friend, him whom she felt herself obliged to refuse as a husband. She is as far from the vanity of seeking to make conquests, as from the ungenerous insolence of using ill those whom her merit has captivated, and whom her judgment cannot accept.'

After admiring, in the warmest terms, the purity and generosity of her heart, I pressed Dr. Barlow still farther, as to the interior of her mind. I questioned him as to her early habits, and particularly as to her religious attainments, telling him that nothing was indifferent to me which related to Lucilla.

'Miss Stanley,' replied he, 'is governed by a simple, practical end in all her religious pursuits. She reads her Bible, not from habit, that she may acquit herself of a customary form ; not to exercise her ingenuity by allegorizing literal passages, or spiritualizing plain ones, but that she may improve in knowledge. and grow in grace. She accustoms herself to meditation, in order to get her mind more deeply imbued with a sense of eternal things. She practises self-examination, that she may learn to watch against the first rising of bad dispositions, and to detect every latent evil in her heart. She lives in the regular habit of prayer ; not only that she may implore pardon for sin, but that she may obtain strength against it. She told me one day, when she was ill, that if she did not constantly examine the actual state of her mind, she should pray at random, without any certainty what particular sins she should pray against, or what were her particular wants. She has read much Scripture and little controversy. There are some doctrines that she does not pretend to define, which she yet practically adopts. She cannot, perhaps, give you a disquisition on the mysteries of the Holy Spirit, but she can and does fervently implore His guidance and instruction ; she believes in His efficacy, and depends on His support. She is sensible that those truths, which, from their deep importance, are most obvious, have more of the vitality of religion, and influence practice more than those abstruse points, which unhappily split the religious world into so many parties.

'If I were to name what are her predominant virtues, I should say sincerity and humility. Conscious of her own imperfections, she never justifies her faults, and seldom extenuates them. She receives reproof with meekness, and advice with gratitude. Her own conscience is always so ready to condemn her, that she never wonders nor takes offence at the censures of others.

'That softness of manner which you admire in her is not the varnish of good breeding, nor is it merely the effect of good temper, though in both she excels, but it is the result of humility. She appears humble, not because a mild exterior is graceful, but because she has inward conviction of unworthiness which prevents an assuming manner. Yet her humility has no cant ; she never disburdens her conscience by a few disparaging phrases, nor lays a trap for praise by indiscriminately condemning herself. Her humility never impairs her cheerfulness ; for the sense of her wants directs her to seek, and her faith enables her to find, the sure foundation of a better hope than any which can be derived from delusive confidence in her own goodness.

'One day,' continued Dr. Barlow, 'when I blamed her gently for her backwardness in expressing her opinion on some serious points, she said, "I always feel diffident in speaking on these subjects, not only lest I should be *thought* to assume, but lest I really *should* assume a degree of piety which may not belong to me. My great advantages make me jealous of myself. My dear father has so carefully instructed me, and I live so much in the habit of hearing his pious sentiments, that I am often afraid of appearing better than I am, and of pretend-

10

ing to feel in my heart what perhaps I only approve in my judgment. When my beloved mother was ill," continued she, "I often caught myself saying, mechanically, God's will be done! when, I blush to own, how little I felt in my heart of that resignation of which my lips were so lavish."'

I hung with inexpressible delight on every word Doctor Barlow uttered, and expressed my fears that such a prize was too much above my deserts, to allow me to encourage very sanguine hopes. 'You have my cordial wishes for your success,' said he, 'though I shall lament the day when you snatch so fair a flower from our fields, to transplant it into your northern gardens.'

We had now reached the park-gate, where Sir John and Lady Belfield joined us. As it was very hot, Dr. Barlow proposed to conduct us a nearer way. He carried us through a small nursery of fruit trees, which I had not before observed, though it was adjoining the ladies' flower-garden, from which it was separated and concealed by a row of tall trees. I expressed my surprise that the delicate Lucilla would allow so coarse an inclosure to be so near her ornamented ground. 'You see she does all she can to shut it out,' replied he. 'I will tell you how it happens, for I cannot vindicate the taste of my fair friend without exposing a better quality in her. But if I betray her, you must not betray me.

'It is a rule when any servant who has lived seven years at the Grove marries, provided they have conducted themselves well, and make prudent choice, for Mr. Stanley to give them a piece of ground on the waste to build a cottage ; he also allows them to take stones from his quarry, and lime from his kiln ; to this he adds a bit of ground for a garden. Mrs. Stanley presents some kitchen furniture, and gives a wedding dinner ; and the rector refuses his fee for performing the ceremony.'

'Caroline,' said Sir John, 'this is not the first time since we have been at the Grove that I have been struck with observing how many benefits naturally result to the poor, from the rich living on their own estates. Their dependents have a thousand petty local advantages, which cost almost nothing to the giver, which are yet valuable to the receiver, and of which the absent never think.'

'You have heard,' said Dr. Barlow, 'that Miss Stanley, from her childhood, has been passionately fond of cultivating a garden. When she was hardly fourteen she began to reflect that the delight she took in this employment was attended neither with pleasure nor profit to any one but herself, and she became jealous of a gratification which was so entirely selfish. She begged this piece of waste ground of her father, and stocked it with a number of fine young fruit trees of the common sort—apples, pears, plums, and the smaller fruits. When there is a wedding among the older servants, or when any good girl out of her school marries, she presents their little empty garden with a dozen young apple trees, and a few trees of the other sorts, never forgetting to embellish their little court with roses and honeysuckles. These last she transplants from the shrubbery, not to fill up the *village-garden*, as it is called, with anything that is of no positive use. She employs a poor lame man in the village a day in the week to look after this nursery ; and by cuttings and grafts a good stock is raised on a small space. It is done at her own expense, Mr. Stanley making this a condition when he gave her the ground ; "Otherwise," said he, "trifling as it is, it would be my charity and not hers, and she would get thanked for a kindness which would cost her nothing." The warm-hearted little Phœbe co-operates in this, and in all her sister's labours of love.

'Some such union of charity with every personal indulgence she generally imposes on herself ; and from this association she has acquired another virtue, for she tells me, smiling, that she is sometimes obliged to content herself with practising frugality instead of charity. When she finds she cannot afford both her own gratification, and the charitable act which she wanted to associate with it, and is therefore compelled to give up the charity, she compels herself to give up the indulgence also. By this self-denial she gets a little money in hand for the next demand, and thus is enabled to afford both next time.'

As he finished speaking, we spied the lame gardener pruning and clearing the trees. 'Well, James,' said the Doctor, 'how does your nursery thrive ?' 'Why, sir,' said the poor man, 'we are rather thin of stout trees at present. You know we had three weddings at Christmas, which took thirty-six of my best apple-trees at a blow, besides half a dozen tall pear-trees, and as many plums. But we shall soon fetch it up, for Miss Lucilla makes me plant two for every one that is removed, so that we are always provided for a wedding, come when it will.'

I now recollected that I had been pleased with observing so many young orchards and flourishing cottage-gardens in the village ; little did I suspect the fair hand which could thus in a very few years diffuse an air of smiling comfort around these humble habitations, and embellish poverty itself. She makes, they told me, her periodical visits of inspection, to see that neatness and order do not degenerate.

Not to appear too eager, I asked the poor man some questions about his health, which seemed infirm. 'I am but weak, sir,' said he, 'for matter of that, but I should have been dead long ago, but for the squire's family. He gives me the run of his kitchen, and Miss Lucilla allows me half-a-crown a week, for one day's work and any odd hour I can spare ; but she don't let me earn it, for she is always watching for fear it should be too hot, or too cold, or too wet for me ; and she brings me my dose of bark herself into this tool-house, that she may be sure I take it ; for she says servants and poor people like to have medicines provided for them, but don't care to take them. Then she watches that I don't throw my coat on the wet grass, which, she says, gives labouring men so much rheumatism ; and she made me this nice flannel waistcoat, sir, with her own hands. At Christmas they give me a new suit from top to toe, so that I want for nothing but a more thankful heart, for I never can be grateful enough to God and my benefactors.'

I asked some further questions, only to have the pleasure of hearing him talk longer about Lucilla. 'But, sir,' said he, interrupting me, 'I hear bad news, very bad news. Pray, your honour, forgive me.' 'What do you mean, James,' said I, seeing his eyes fill. 'Why, sir, all the servants at the Grove will have it that you are come to carry off Miss Lucilla. God bless her, whenever she goes. Your Mr. Edwards, sir, says you are one of the best of gentlemen ; but indeed, indeed, I don't know who can deserve her. She will carry a blessing whenever she goes.' The honest fellow put up the sleeve of his coat to brush away his tears, nor was I ashamed of those with which his honest affection filled my own. While we were talking, a poor little girl, who, I knew by her neat uniform, belonged to Miss Stanley's school, passed us, with a little basket in her hand. James called to her, and said, 'Make haste, Rachel, you are after your time.'

' What, this is market-day, James, is it,' said Dr. Barlow, 'and Rachel is come for her nosegays?' ' Yes, sir,' said James ; ' I forgot to tell their honours, that every Saturday, as soon as the school is over, the younger misses give Rachel leave to come and fetch some flowers out of their garden, which she carries to the town to sell ; she commonlʸ gets a shilling, half of which they make her lay out to bring home a little tea for her poor sick mother, and the other half she saves up to buy shoes and stockings for herself and her crippled sister. Every little is a help where there is nothing, sir.'

Sir John said nothing, but looked at Lady Belfield, whose eyes glistened while she softly said, ' Oh, how little do the rich ever think what the aggregate even of their own squandered shillings would do in the way of charity, were they systematically applied to it.'

James now unlocked a little private door, which opened into the pleasure-ground. There, at a distance, sitting in a circle on the new-mown grass, under a tree, we beheld all the little Stanleys, with a basket of flowers between them, out of which they were earnestly employed in sorting and tying up nosegays. We stood some time admiring their little busy faces and active fingers, without their perceiving us, and got up to them just as they were putting their prettily-formed bouquets in Rachel's basket, with which she marched off, with many charges from the children to waste no time by the way, and to be sure to leave the nosegay that had the myrtle in it at Mrs. Williams's.

' How many nosegays have you given to Rachel to-day, Louisa ?' said Dr. Barlow to the eldest of the four. ' Only three apiece, sir,' replied she. ' We think it a bad day when we can't make up our dozen. They are all our own ; we seldom touch mamma's flowers, and we never suffer James to take ours, because Phœbe says it might be tempting him.' Little Jane lamented that Lucilla had given them nothing to-day, except two or three sprigs of her best flowering myrtle, which, added she, ' we make Rachel give into the bargain to a poor sick lady, who loves flowers, and used to have good ones of her own, but who has now no money to spare, and could not afford to give more than the common price for a nosegay for her sick-room ! So we always slip a nice flower or two out of the green-house into her little bunch, and say nothing. When we walk that way, we often leave her some flowers ourselves, and would do it oftener, if it did not hurt poor Rachel's trade.'

As we walked away from the sweet prattlers, Dr. Barlow said, ' These little creatures already emulate their sisters in associating some petty kindness with their own pleasures. The act is trifling, but the habit is good ; as is every habit which helps to take us out of self ; which teaches us to transfer our attention from our own gratification, to the wants or the pleasures of another.'

' I confess,' said Lady Belfield, as we entered the house, ' that it never occurred to me that it was any part of charity to train my children to the habit of sacrificing their time or their pleasure for the benefit of others, though, to do them justice, they are very feeling and very liberal with their money.'

' My dear Caroline,' said Sir John, ' it is our money, not theirs. It is, I fear, a cheap liberality, and abridges not themselves of one enjoyment. They well know we are so pleased to see them charitable, that we shall instantly repay them with interest whatever they give away ; so that we have hitherto afforded them no opportunity to show their actual dispositions. Nay, I begin to fear they become charitable through covetousness, if they find out that the more they give the more they shall get. We must correct this artificial liberality as soon as we go home.',

---

Chapter XXXI.

FEW days after, Sir John Belfield and I agreed to take a ride to Mr. Carlton's, where we breakfasted. Nothing could be more rational than the whole turn of his mind, nor more agreeable and unreserved than his conversation. His behaviour to his amiable wife was affectionately attentive ; and Sir John, who is a most critical observer, remarked that it was quite natural and unaffected. It appeared to be the result of esteem inspired by her merit, and quickened by a sense of his own former unworthiness, which made him feel as if he could never do enough to efface the memory of past unkindness. He manifested evident symptoms of a mind earnestly intent on the discovery and pursuit of moral and religious truth ; and from the natural ardour of his character, and the sincerity of his remorse, his attainments seemed likely to be rapid and considerable.

The sweet benignity of Mrs. Carlton's countenance was lighted up at our entrance with a smile of satisfaction. We had been informed with what pleasure she observed every accession of right-minded acquaintance which her husband made. Though her natural modesty prevented her from introducing any subject herself, yet when anything useful was brought forward by others, she promoted it by a look compounded of pleasure and intelligence.

After a variety of topics had been despatched, the conversation fell on the prejudices which were commonly entertained by men of the world against religion. ' For my own part,' said Mr. Carlton, ' I must confess that no man had ever more and stronger prejudices to combat than myself. I mean not my own exculpation, when I add, that the imprudence, the want of judgment, and, above all, the incongruous mixtures and inconsistencies in many characters who are reckoned religious, are ill-calculated to do away the unfavourable opinions of men of an opposite way of thinking. As I presume that you, gentlemen, are not ignorant of the errors of my early life—error, indeed, is an appellation far too mild—I shall not scruple to own to you the source of those prejudices which retarded my progress, even after I became ashamed of my deviations from virtue. I had felt the turpitude of my bad habits long before I had courage to renounce them ; and I renounced them long before I had courage to avow my abhorrence of them.'

Sir John and I expressed ourselves extremely obliged by the candour of his declaration, and assured him that his further communications would not only gratify but benefit us.

' Educated as I had been,' said Mr. Carlton, ' in an almost entire ignorance of religion, mine was rather an habitual indifference than a systematic unbelief. My thoughtless course of life, though it led me to hope that Christianity might not be true, yet had by no means been able to convince me that it was false. As I had not been taught to search for truth at the fountain, for I was unacquainted with the Bible, I had no readier means for forming my judgment, than by observing, though with a careless and casual eye, what effect religion produced in those who professed to be influenced by it. My observations augmented my prejudices. What I saw of the professors increased my dislike of the profession. All the charges brought by their enemies, for I had been accustomed to weigh the validity of testimony, had not riveted my dislike so much, as the difference between their own avowed principles and their obvious practice. Religious men should be the more cautious of giving occasion for reproach, as they know the world is always on the watch, and is more glad to have its prejudices confirmed than removed.

' I seize the moment of Mrs. Carlton's absence' (who was just then called out of the room, but returned almost immediately) ' to observe, that what rooted my disgust was, the eagerness with which the mother of my inestimable wife, who made a great parade of religion, pressed the marriage of her only child with a man whose conduct she knew to be irregular, and of whose principles she entertained a just, that is, an unfavourable opinion. To see, I repeat, the religious mother of Mrs. Carlton obviously governed in her zeal for promoting our union by motives as worldly as those of my poor father, who pretended to no religion at all, would have extremely lowered any respect which I might have previously been induced to entertain for characters of that description. Nor was this disgust diminished by my acquaintance with Mr. Tyrrel. I had known him while a professed man of the world, and had at that time, I fear, disliked his violent temper, his narrow mind, and his coarse manners, more than his vices.

' I had heard of the power of religion to change the heart, and I ridiculed the wild chimera. My contempt for this notion was confirmed by the conduct of Mr. Tyrrel in his new character. I found it had produced little change in him, except furnishing him with a new subject of discussion. I saw that he had only laid down one set of opinions, and taken up another, with no addition whatever to his virtues, and with the addition to his vices of spiritual pride and self-confidence ; for with hypocrisy I have no right to charge any man. I observed that Tyrrel and one or two of his new friends rather courted attack than avoided it. They considered discretion as the infirmity of a worldly mind, and every attempt at kindness or conciliation as an abandonment of faith. They eagerly ascribed to their piety, the dislike which was often excited by their peculiarities. I found them apt to dignify the disapprobation which their singularity occasioned, with the name of persecution. I have seen them take comfort in the belief that it was their religion which was disliked, when perhaps it was chiefly their oddities.

'At Tyrrel's I became acquainted with your friends Mr. and Mrs. Ranby. I leave you to judge whether their characters, that of the lady especially, were calculated to do away my prejudices. I had learnt from my favourite Roman poet a precept in composition, of never making a god appear, except on occasions worthy of a god. I have since had reason to think this rule as justly theological as it is classical. So thought not the Ranbys.

'It will indeed readily be allowed by every reflecting mind, as God is to be viewed in all his works, so his "never-failing providence ordereth all things both in heaven and on earth." But surely there is something very offensive in the indecent familiarity with which the name of God and Providence is brought in on every trivial occasion, as was the constant practice of Mr. and Mrs. Ranby. I was not even then so illogical a reasoner as to allow a general and deny a particular providence. If the one were true, I inferred that the other could not be false. But I felt that the religion of these people was of a slight texture and a bad taste. I was disgusted with littleness in some instances, and with inconsistency in others. Still their absurdity gave me no right to suspect their sincerity.

'Whenever Mrs. Ranby had a petty inclination to gratify, she had always recourse to what she called the *leadings of Providence.* In matters of no more moment than whether she should drink tea with one neighbour instead of another, she was *impelled,* or *directed,* or *over-ruled.* I observed that she always took care to interpret these *leadings* to her own taste, and, under their sanction, she always did what her fancy led her to do. She professed to follow this guidance on such minute occasions, that I had almost said, her piety seemed a little impious. To the actual dispensations of Providence, especially when they came in a trying or adverse shape, I did not observe more submission than I had seen in persons who could not be suspected of religion. I must own to you also, that as I am rather fastidious, I began to fancy that vulgar language, quaint phrases, and false grammar, were necessarily connected with religion. The sacrifice of taste and elegance seemed indispensable, and I was inclined to fear that if *they* were right, it would be impossible to get to heaven with good English.'

'Though I grant there is some truth in your remarks, sir,' said I, 'you must allow that when men are determined at all events to hunt down religious characters, they are never at a loss to find plausible objections to justify their dislike ; and while they conceal, even from themselves, the real motive of their aversion, the vigilance with which they pry into the characters of men who are reckoned pious, is exercised with the secret hope of finding faults enough to confirm their prejudices.'

'As a general truth, you are perfectly right,' said Mr. Carlton ; 'but at the period to which I allude, I had now got to that stage of my progress, as to be rather searching for instances to invite than to repel me in my inquiry.'

'You will grant, however,' said I, 'that it is a common effect of prejudice to transfer the faults of a religious man to religion itself. Such a man happens to have an uncouth manner, an awkward gesture, an unmodulated voice ; his allusions may be coarse, his phraseology quaint, his language slovenly. The solid virtues which may lie disguised under these incumbrances go for nothing. The man is absurd, and therefore Christianity is ridiculous. Its truth, however, though it may be eclipsed, cannot be extinguished. Like its divine Author, it is the same yesterday, to-day, and for ever.'

'There was another repulsive circumstance,' replied Mr. Carlton : 'the scanty charities both of Tyrrel and his new friends, so inferior to the liberality of my father and of Mr. Flam, who never professed to be governed by any higher motive than mere feeling, strengthened my dislike. The calculations of mere reason taught me that the religious man who does not greatly exceed the man of the world in his liberalities, falls short of him ; because the worldly man who gives liberally, acts above his principle, while the Christian who does no more, falls short of his. And though I by no means insist that liberality is a certain indication of piety, yet I will venture to assert that the want of the one is no doubtful symptom of the absence of the other.

'I next resolved to watch carefully the conduct of another description of Christians, who come under the class of the formal and the decent. They were considered as more creditable, but I did not perceive them to be more exemplary. They were more absorbed in the world, and more governed by its opinion. I found them clamorous in defence of the church in words, but neither adorning it by their lives, or embracing its doctrines in their hearts. Rigid in the observance o some of its external rites, but little influenced by its liberal principles and charitable spirit. They venerated the establishment merely as a political institution, but of her outward forms they conceived, as comprehending the whole of her excellence. Of her spiritual beauty and superiority, they seemed to have no conception. I observed in them less warmth of affection for those with whom they agreed in external profession, than of rancour for those who differed from them, though but a single shade, and in points of no importance. They were cordial haters, and frigid lovers. Had they lived in the early ages, when the church was split into parties by paltry disputes, they would have thought the controversy about the time of keeping Easter, of more consequence than the event itself which that festival celebrates.'

'My dear sir,' said I, as soon as he had done speaking, 'you have accounted very naturally for your prejudices. Your chief error seems to have consisted in the selection of the persons you adopted as

standards. They all differed as much from the right as they differed
from each other : and the truth is, their vehement desire to differ from
each other, was a chief cause why they departed so much from the
right. But your instances were so unhappily chosen, that they prove
nothing against Christianity. The two opposite descriptions of persons
who deterred you from religion, and who passed muster in their
respective corps, under the generic term of religious, would, I believe,
be scarcely acknowledged as such by the soberly and soundly pious.'

'My own subsequent experience,' resumed Mr. Carlton, 'has confirmed the justness of your remark. When I began, through the
gradual change wrought in my views and actions, by the silent but
powerful preaching of Mrs. Carlton's example, to have less interest in
believing that Christianity was false, I then applied myself to search
for reasons to believe that it was true. But plain, abstract reasoning,
though it might catch hold on beings who are all pure intellect, and
though it might have given a right bias even to *my* opinions, would
probably never have determined my conduct, unless I saw it clothed,
as it were, with a body. I wanted examples which should influence
me to act, as well as proofs which should incline me to believe ; something which would teach me what to do, as well as what to think. I
wanted exemplifications as well as precepts. I doubted of all merely
speculative truth. I wanted, from beholding the effect, to refer back
to the principle. I wanted arguments more palpable and less theoretic.
Surely, said I to myself, if religion be a real principle, it must be an
operative one, and I would rationally infer that Christianity were true,
if the tone of Christian practice were high.

'I began to look clandestinely into Henrietta's Bible. There I
indeed found that the spirit of religion was invested with just such a
body as I had wished to see ; that it exhibited actions as well as sentiments, characters as well as doctrines ; the life portrayed evidently
governed by the principle inculcated ; the conduct and the doctrine in
just correspondence. But if the Bible be true, thought I, may we not
reasonably expect that the principles which once produced the exalted
practice which that Bible records, will produce similar effects now?

'I put, rashly perhaps, the truth of Christianity on this issue, and
sought society of a higher stamp. Fortunately, the increasing external
decorum of my conduct began to make my reception less difficult
among good men than it had been. Hitherto, and that for the sake
of my wife, my visits had rather been endured than encouraged ; nor
was I myself forward to seek the society which shunned me. Even of
those superior characters, with whom I did occasionally associate, I
had not come near enough to form an exact estimate.

'DISINTERESTEDNESS and CONSISTENCY had become with me a
sort of touchstone, by which to try the characters I was investigating.
My experiment was favourable. I had for some time observed my
wife's conduct with a mixture of admiration as to the act, and in-
credulity as to the motive. I had seen her foregoing her own indulgences, that she might augment those of a husband whom she had so
little reason to love. Here were the two qualities I required, with a
renunciation of self without parade or profession. Still this was a

solitary instance. When, on a nearer survey, I beheld Dr. Barlow exhibiting by his exemplary conduct during the week, the best commentary on his Sunday's sermon; when I saw him refuse a living of nearly twice the value of that he possessed, because the change would diminish his usefulness—I was *staggered*.

'When I saw Mr. and Mrs. Stanley spending their time and fortune as entirely in acts of beneficence, as if they had built their eternal hope on charity alone, and yet utterly renouncing any such confidence, and trusting entirely to another foundation; when I saw Lucilla, a girl of eighteen, refuse a young nobleman of a clear estate, and neither disagreeable in his person or manner, on the single avowed ground of his loose principles; when the noble rejection of the daughter was supported by the parents, whose principles no arguments drawn from rank or fortune could subvert or shake—I was *convinced*.

'These, and some other instances of the same nature, were exactly the test I had been seeking. Here was *disinterestedness* upon full proof. Here was consistency between practice and profession. By such examples, and by cordially adopting those principles which produced them, together with a daily increasing sense of my past enormities, I hope to become in time less unworthy of the wife to whom I owe my peace on earth, and my hope in heaven.'

The tears which had been collecting in Mrs. Carlton's eyes for some time, now silently stole down her cheeks. Sir John and myself were deeply affected with the frank and honest narrative to which we had been listening. It raised in us an esteem and affection for the narrator which has since been continually augmenting. I do not think the worse of his state for the difficulties which impeded it, nor that his advancement will be less sure, because it has been gradual. His fear of delusion has been a salutary guard. The apparent slowness of his progress has arisen from his dread of self-deception, and the diligence of his search is an indication of his sincerity.

'But did you not find,' said I, 'that the piety of these more correct Christians drew upon them nearly as much censure and suspicion as the indiscretion of the enthusiasts? And that the formal class, who were nearly as far removed from effective piety as from wild fanaticism, ran away with all the credit of religion?'

'With those,' replied Mr. Carlton, 'who are on the watch to discredit Christianity, no consistency can stand their determined opposition; but the fair and candid inquirer will not reject the truth, when it forces itself on the mind with a clear and convincing evidence.'

Though I had been joining in the general subject, yet my thoughts had wandered from it to Lucilla, ever since her noble rejection of Lord Staunton had been named by Mr. Carlton as one of the causes which had strengthened his unsteady faith. And while he and Sir John were talking over their youthful connections, I resumed with Mrs. Carlton, who sat next me, the interesting topic.

'Lord Staunton,' said she, 'is a relation, and not a very distant one, of ours. He used to take more delight in Mr. Carlton's society when it was less improving, than he does now that it has become really valuable ; yet he often visits us. Miss Stanley now and then indulges me with her company for a day or two. In these visits Lord Staunton happened to meet her two or three times. He was enchanted with her person and manners, and exerted every art and faculty of pleasing, which it must be owned he possesses. Though we should both have rejoiced in an alliance with the excellent family at the Grove, through this sweet girl, I thought it my duty not to conceal from her the irregularity of my cousin's conduct in one particular instance, as well as the general looseness of his religious principles. The caution was the more necessary, as he had so much prudence and good breeding, as to behave with general propriety while under our roof ; and he allowed me to speak to him more freely than any other person. When I talked seriously, he sometimes laughed, always opposed, but was never angry.

'One day he arrived quite unexpectedly when Miss Stanley was with me. He found us in my dressing-room reading together a *Dissertation on the power of religion to change the heart.* Dreading some levity, I strove to hide the book, but he took it out of my hand, and glancing his eye on the title, he said, laughing, " This is a foolish subject enough ; a *good heart* does not want changing, and with a *bad* one none of *us three* have anything to do." Lucilla spoke not a syllable. All the light things he uttered, and which he meant for wit, so far from raising a smile, increased her gravity. She listened, but with some uneasiness, to a desultory conversation between us, in which I attempted to assert the power of the Almighty to rectify the mind, and alter the character. Lord Staunton treated my assertion as a wild chimera, and said he was sure I had more understanding than to adopt such a methodical notion ; professing at the same time a vague admiration for virtue and goodness, which, he said, bowing to Miss Stanley, were *natural* where they existed at all ; that a good heart did not want mending, and a bad one could not be mended, with other similar expressions, all implying contempt of my position, and exclusive compliment to her.

'After dinner, Lucilla stole away from a conversation, which was not very interesting to her, and carried her book to the summer-house, knowing that Lord Staunton liked to sit long at table. But his lordship missing her for whom the visit was meant, soon broke up the party, and hearing which way she took, pursued her to the summer-house. After a profusion of compliments, expressive of his high admiration, he declared his passion in very strong and explicit terms, and requested her permission to make proposals to her father, to which he conceived she could have no possible objection.

'She thanked him with great politeness for his favourable opinion, but frankly told him that, though extremely sensible of the honour he intended her, thanks were all she had to offer in return ; she earnestly desired the business might go no further, and that he would spare himself the trouble of an application to her father, who always kindly allowed her to decide for herself, in a concern of so much importance.

'Disappointed, shocked, and irritated at a rejection so wholly unexpected, he insisted on knowing the cause. Was it his person ? Was
it his fortune ? Was it his understanding to which she objected ? She
honestly assured him it was neither. His rank and fortune were above
her expectations. To his natural advantages there could be no reasonable objection. He still vehemently insisted on her assigning the
true cause. She was then driven to the necessity of confessing, that
she feared his principles were not those of a man, with whom she could
venture to trust her own.

' He bore this reproof with more patience than she had expected.
As she had made no exception to his person and understanding, both
of which he rated very highly, he could better bear with the charge
brought against his principles, on which he did not set so great a
value. She had indeed wounded his pride, but not in the part where
it was most vulnerable. " If that be all," said he, gaily, " the objection is at an end ; your charming society will reform me, your influence will raise my principles, and your example will change my
character."

' " What, my lord," said she, her courage increasing with her indignation, " this from *you !* From you, who declared only this morning, that
the work of changing the heart was too great for the Almighty Himself ?
You do not now scruple to declare that it is in my power ! That work
which is too hard for Omnipotence, your flattery would make me believe
a weak girl can accomplish. No, my lord, I will never add to the
number of those rash women who have risked their eternal happiness
on this vain hope. It would be too late to repent of my folly after my
presumption had incurred its just punishment."

' So saying, she left the summer-house with a polite dignity, which, as
he afterwards told me, increased his passion, while it inflamed his pride
almost to madness. Finding she refused to appear, he quitted the
house, but not his design. His applications have since been repeated,
but though he has met with the firmest repulses, both from the parents
and the daughter, he cannot be prevailed upon to relinquish his hope.
It is so far a misfortune to us, as Lucilla now never comes near us,
except he is known not to be in the country. Had the objection been
to his person or fortune, he says, as it would have been substantial, it
might have been insuperable ; but where the only ground of difference
is mere matter of opinion, he is sure that time and perseverance will
conquer such a chimerical objection.'

I returned to the Grove, not only cured of every jealous feeling, but
transported with such a decisive proof of the dignity and purity of Miss
Stanley's mind.

Chapter XXXII.

ISS SPARKES, a neighbouring lady, whom the reputation of being a wit and an Amazon had kept single at the age of five and forty, though her person was not disagreeable, and her fortune was considerable, called in one morning while we were at breakfast. She is remarkable for her pretension to odd and opposite qualities. She is something of a scholar, and a huntress—a politician, and a farrier. She outrides Mr. Flam, and outargues Mr. Tyrrel ; excels in driving four-in-hand, and in canvassing at an election. She is always anxious about the party, but never about the candidate, in whom she requires no other merit but his being in the opposition, which she accepts as a pledge for all other merit. In her adoption of any talent, or her exercise of any quality, it is always sufficient recommendation to her that it is not feminine.

From the window we saw her descend from her lofty phaeton, and when she came in :

The cap, the whip, the masculine attire,

the loud voice, the intrepid look, the independent air, the whole deportment, indicated a disposition rather to confer protection than to accept it.

She made an apology for her intrusion, by saying that her visit was rather to the stable than the breakfast-room. One of the horses was a little lame, and she wanted to consult Mr. Stanley's groom, who it seems was her oracle in that science, in which she herself is a professed adept.

During her short visit, she laboured so sedulously not to diminish by her conversation the character she was so desirous to establish, that her efforts defeated the end they aimed to secure. She was witty with all her might, and her sarcastic turn, for wit it was not, made little amends for her want of simplicity. I perceived that she was fond of the bold, the marvellous, and the incredible. She ventured to tell a story or two, so little within the verge of ordinary probability, that she risked her credit for veracity, without perhaps really violating truth. The credit acquired by such relations seldom pays the relater for the hazard run by the communication.

As we fell into conversation, I observed the peculiarities of her character. She never sees any difficulties in any question. Whatever topic is started, while the rest of the company are hesitating as to the propriety of their determination, she alone is never at a loss. Her answer always follows the proposition, without a moment's interval for examination herself, or for allowing any other person a chance of delivering an opinion.

Mr. Stanley, who always sets an example of strict punctuality to his family, had to-day come in to perform his family devotions somewhat later than usual. I could perceive that he had been a little moved. His countenance wanted something of its placid serenity, though it seemed to be a seriousness untinctured with anger. He confessed while we were at breakfast, that he had been spending above an hour, in bringing one of his younger children to a sense of a fault she had committed. ' She has not,' said he, 'told an absolute falsehood, but in what she said there was prevarication, there was pride, there was passion. Her perverseness has at length given way. Tears of resentment are changed into tears of contrition. But she is not to appear in the drawing-room to-day. She is to be deprived of the honour of carrying food to the poor in the evening. Nor is she to furnish her contingent of nosegays to Rachel's basket. This is a mode of punishment we prefer to that of curtailing any personal indulgences ; the importance we should assign to the privation would be setting too much value on the enjoyment.'

' You should be careful, Mr. Stanley,' said Miss Sparkes, ' not to break the child's spirit. Too tight a rein will check her generous ardour, and curb her genius. I would not subdue the independence of her mind, and make a tame, dull animal, of a creature whose very faults give indications of a soaring nature.' Even Lady Belfield, to whose soft and tender heart the very sound of punishment, or even privation, carried a sort of terror, asked Mr. Stanley, ' if he did not think that he had taken up a trifling offence too seriously, and punished it too severely.'

' The thing is a trifle in itself,' replied he, 'but infant prevarication unnoticed, and unchecked, is the prolific seed of subterfuge, of expediency, of deceit, of falsehood, of hypocrisy.'

' But the dear little creature,' said Lady Belfield, ' is not addicted to equivocation. I have always admired her correctness in her pleasant prattle.'

' It is for that very reason,' replied Mr. Stanley, ' that I am so careful to check the first indication of the contrary tendency. As the fault is a solitary one, I trust the punishment will be so too. For which reason I have marked it in a way, to which her memory will easily recur. Mr. Brandon, an amiable friend of mine, but of an indolent temper, through a negligence in watching over an early propensity to deceit, suffered his only son to run on from one stage of falsehood to another, till he settled down into a most consummate hypocrite. His plausible manners enabled him to keep his more turbulent vices out of sight. Impatient when a youth of that contradiction to which he had never been accustomed when a boy, he became notoriously profligate. His dissimulation was at length too thin to conceal from his mistaken father his more palpable vices. His artifices finally involved him in a duel, and his premature death broke the heart of my poor friend.

' This sad example led me in my own family to watch this evil in the bud. Divines often say, that unbelief lies at the root of all sin. This seems strikingly true in our conniving at the faults of our children. If we really believed the denunciations of Scripture, could we, for the sake of momentary gratification, not so much to our child, as to ourselves (which is the case in all blameable indulgence), overlook that fault which may be the germ of unspeakable miseries ? In my view of things, deceit is no slight offence. I feel myself answerable in no small degree for the eternal happiness of these beloved creatures whom Providence has especially committed to my trust.'

'But it is such a severe trial,' said Lady Belfield, 'to a fond parent to inflict voluntary pain !'

'Shall we feel for their pain, and not for their danger ?' replied Mr. Stanley. 'I wonder how parents who love their children as I love mine, can put in competition a temporary indulgence, which may foster one evil temper, or fasten one bad habit, with the eternal welfare of that child's soul. A soul of such inconceivable worth, whether we consider its nature, its duration, or the price which was paid for its redemption ! What parent, I say, can by his own rash negligence, or false indulgence, risk the happiness of such a soul, not for a few days or years, but for a period compared with which the whole duration of time is but a point? A soul of such infinite faculties, which has a capacity for improving in holiness and happiness through all the countless ages of eternity ?'

Observing Sir John listen with some amusement, Mr. Stanley went on : 'What remorse, my dear friend, can equal the pangs of him, who has reason to believe that his child has not only lost this eternity of glory, but incurred an eternity of misery, through the carelessness of that parent who assigned his very fondness as a reason for his neglect? Think of the state of such a father, when he figures to himself the thousands and ten thousands of glorified spirits that stand before the throne and his darling excluded !—excluded, perhaps, by his own ill-judging fondness. Oh, my friends, disguise it as we may, and deceive ourselves as we will, want of faith is as much at the bottom of this sin as of all others. Notwithstanding an indefinite, indistinct notion which men call faith, they do not actually *believe* in this eternity ; they believe it in a general way, but they do not believe in it practically, personally, influentially.'

While Mr. Stanley was speaking with an energy which evinced how much his own heart was affected, Miss Sparkes, by the impatience of her looks, evidently manifested that she wished to interrupt him. Good breeding, however, kept her silent till he had done speaking : she then said : 'though she allowed that absolute falsehood, and falsehood used for mischievous purposes, was really criminal, yet there was a danger on the other hand of laying too severe restrictions on freedom of speech ; that there might be such a thing as tacit hypocrisy ;—that people might be guilty of as much deceit by suppressing their sentiments, if just, as by expressing such as were not quite correct. That a repulsive treatment was calculated to extinguish the fire of invention. She thought also that there were occasions where a harmless falsehood might not only be pardonable, but laudable. But then she admitted, that a falsehood, to be allowed, must be inoffensive.'

Mr. Stanley said, ' that an inoffensive falsehood was a perfect anomaly. But allowing it possible, that an individual instance of deceit might be passed over, which, however, he never could allow, yet one successful falsehood, on the plea of doing good, would necessarily make way for another, till the limits which divide right and wrong would be completely broken down, and every distinction between truth and falsehood be utterly confounded. If such latitude were allowed, even to obtain some good purpose, it would gradually debauch all human intercourse. The smallest deviation would naturally induce a pernicious habit, endanger the security of society, and violate an express law of God.'

'There is no tendency,' said Sir John Belfield, 'more to be guarded against among young persons of warm hearts and lively imaginations. The feeling will think falsehood good if it is meant to *do* good, and the fanciful will think it justifiable if it is ingenious.'

Phœbe, in presenting her father with a dish of coffee, said in a half whisper, ' Surely, papa, there can be no harm in speaking falsely on a subject, where I am ignorant of the truth.'

'There are occasions, my dear Phœbe,' replied her father, 'in which ignorance itself is a fault. Inconsiderateness is always one. It is your duty to deliberate before you speak. It is your duty not to deceive by your negligence in getting at the truth ; or by publishing false information as truth, though you have reason to suspect it may be false. You well know who it is that associates him that *loveth* a lie, with him that *maketh* it.'

' But, sir,' said Miss Sparkes, ' if by a falsehood I could preserve a life, or save my country, falsehood would then be meritorious, and I should glory in deceiving.'

' Persons, madam,' said Mr. Stanley, ' who, in debate, have a favourite point to carry, are apt to suppose extreme cases, which *can* and *do* very rarely, if ever, occur. This they do in order to compel the acquiescence of an opponent to what ought never to be allowed. It is a proud and fruitless speculation. The infinite power of God can never stand in need of the aid of a weak mortal to help Him out in His difficulties. If He sees fit to preserve the life, or save the country, He not driven to such shifts. Omnipotence can extricate Himself, and is accomplish His own purposes, without endangering an immortal soul.'

Miss Sparkes took her leave soon after, in order, as she said, to go to the stable and take the groom's opinion. Mr. Stanley insisted that her carriage should be brought round to the door, to which we all attended her. He inquired which was the lame horse. Instead of answering, she went directly up to the animal, and, after patting him with some technical jockey phrases, she fearlessly took up his hind leg, carefully examined the foot, and while she continued standing in what appeared to the ladies a perilous, and to me a disgusting, situation, she ran over all the terms of the veterinary art with the groom ; and when Miss Stanley expressed some fear of her danger, and some dislike of her coarseness, she burst into a loud laugh, and, slapping her on the shoulder, asked her if it was not better to understand the properties and diseases of so noble an animal, than to waste her time in studying confectionary with old Goody Comfit, or in teaching the Catechism to little ragged beggar-brats ?

As soon as she was gone, the lively Phœbe, who, her father says, has narrowly escaped being a wit herself, cried out, ' Well, papa, I must say that I think Miss Sparkes, with all her faults, is rather an agreeable woman.' ' I grant that she is amusing,' returned he, ' but I do not allow her to be quite agreeable. Between these, Phœbe, there is a wide distinction. To a correct mind no one can be agreeable who is incorrect. Propriety is so indispensable to agreeableness, that when a lady allows herself to make any, even the smallest, sacrifice of veracity, religion, modesty, candour, or the decorums of her sex, she may be shining, she may be showy, she may be amusing, but she cannot, properly speaking, be agreeable. Miss Sparkes, I very reluctantly confess, does sometimes make these sacrifices, in a degree to make her friends look about them, though not in a degree to alarm her own principles. She would not tell a direct falsehood for the world : she does not indeed invent, but she embellishes, she enlarges, she exaggerates, she discolours. In her moral grammar there is no positive or comparative degree. Pink with her is scarlet. The noise of a popgun is a cannon. A shower is a tempest. A person of small fortune is a beggar. One in easy circumstances, a Crœsus. A girl, if not perfectly well made, is deformity personified ; if tolerable, a Grecian Venus. Her favourites are angels ; her enemies dæmons.

'She would be thought very religious, and I hope that she will one day become so. Yet she sometimes treats serious things with no small levity, and, though she would not originally say a very bad word, yet she makes no scruple of repeating, with great glee, profane stories told by others. Besides, she possesses the dangerous art of exciting an improper idea, without using an improper word. Gross indecency would shock her, but she often verges so far towards indelicacy as to make Mrs. Stanley uneasy. Then she is too much of a genius to be tied down by any considerations of prudence. If a good thing occurs, out it comes, without regard to time or circumstance. She would tell the same story to a bishop as to her chambermaid. If she says a right thing, which she often does, it is seldom in the right place. She makes her way in society, without attaching many friends. Her bon-mots are admired and repeated ; yet I never met with a man of sense, who, though he may join in flattering her, did not declare, as soon as she was out of the room, that he would not for the world that she should be his wife or daughter. It is irksome to her to converse with her own sex, while she little suspects that ours is not properly grateful for the preference with which she honours us.

'She is,' continued Mr. Stanley, 'charitable with her purse, but not with her tongue ; she relieves her poor neighbours, and indemnifies herself by slandering her rich ones. She has, however, many good qualities, is generous, and compassionate, and I would on no account speak so freely of a lady whom I receive at my house were it not that, if I were quite silent after Phœbe's expressed admiration, she might conclude that I saw nothing to condemn in Miss Sparkes, and might be copying her faults under the notion that being entertaining made amends for everything.'

Chapter XXXIII.

NE morning Sir John, coming in from his ride, gaily called out to me, as I was reading, 'Oh, Charles, such a nice piece of news! The Miss Flams are converted. They have put on tuckers—they were at church twice on Sunday—Blair's Sermons are sent for, and *you* are the reformer.' This ludicrous address reminded Mr. Stanley that Mr. Flam had told him we were all in disgrace for not having called on the ladies, and it was proposed to repair this neglect.

'Now take notice,' said Sir John, 'if you do not see a new character assumed. Thinking Charles to be a fine man of the town, the modish racket, which indeed is their natural state, was played off, but it did not answer. As they probably, by this time, suspect your character to be somewhat between the Strephon and the Hermit, we shall now, in return, see something between the wood-nymph and the nun; I shall not wonder if the extravagantly modish Miss Bell

> Is now Pastora by a fountain's side.'

Though I would not attribute the change to the cause assigned by Sir John, yet I confess we found, when we made our visit, no small revolution in Miss Bell Flam. The parts of the Arcadian nymph, the reading lady, the lover of retirement, the sentimental admirer of domestic life, the censurer of thoughtless dissipation, were each acted in succession, but so skilfully touched, that the shades of each melted in the other, without any of those violent transitions which a less experienced actress would have exhibited; Sir John slyly, yet with affected gravity, assisting her to sustain this newly adopted character, which, however, he was sure would last no longer than the visit.

When we returned home, we met the Miss Stanleys in the garden, and joined them. 'Don't you admire,' said Sir John, 'the versatility of Miss Bell's genius? You, Charles, are not the first man on whom an assumed fondness for rural delights has been practised. A friend of mine was drawn in to marry, rather suddenly, a thorough-paced town-bred lady, by her repeated declarations of her passionate fondness for the country, and the rapture she expressed when rural scenery was the subject. All she knew of the country was, that she had now and then been on a party of pleasure at Richmond, in the fine summer months; a great dinner at the Star and Garter, gay company, a bright day, lovely scenery, a dance on the green, a partner to her taste, French horns on the water, altogether constituted a feeling of pleasure, from which she had really persuaded herself that she was fond of the country. But when all these concomitants were withdrawn, when she had lost the gay partner, the dance, the horns, the flattery, and the frolic, and nothing was left but her books, her own dull mansion, her domestic employments and the sober society of her husband, the pastoral vision vanished. She discovered, or rather he discovered, but too late, that the country had

not only no charms for her, but that it was a scene of constant *ennui*
and vapid dulness. She languished for the pleasures she had quitted,
and he for the comforts he had lost. Opposite inclinations led to
opposite pursuits ; difference of taste, however, needed not to have led
to a total disunion, had there been on the part of the lady such a degree
of attachment as might have induced a spirit of accommodation, or such
a fund of principle as might have taught her the necessity of making
those sacrifices, which affection, had it existed, would have rendered
pleasant, or duty would have made light, had she been early taught
self-government.'

Miss Stanley, smiling, said, 'she hoped Sir John had a little over-
charged the picture.' He defended himself by declaring he drew from
the life, and that from his long observation he could present us with a
whole gallery of such portraits. He left me to continue my walk with
the two Miss Stanleys.

The more I conversed with Lucilla, the more I saw that good breeding in her was only the outward expression of humility, and not an art
employed for the purpose of enabling her to do without it. We continued to converse on the subject of Miss Flam's fondness for the gay
world. This introduced a natural expression of my admiration of Miss
Stanley's choice of pleasures and pursuits, so different from those of
most other women of her age.

With the most graceful modesty she said, ' Nothing humbles me more
than compliments ; for when I compare what I hear, with what I feel,
I find the picture of myself drawn by a flattering friend, so utterly
unlike the original in my own heart, that I am more sunk by my own consciousness of the want of resemblance, than elated that another has not
discovered it. It makes me feel like an impostor. If I contradict this
favourable opinion, I am afraid of being accused of affectation ; and if
I silently swallow it, I am contributing to the deceit of passing for what
I am not.' This ingenuous mode of disclaiming flattery only raised her
in my esteem, and the more, as I told her such humble renunciation of
praise could only proceed from that inward principle of genuine piety,
and devout feeling, which made so amiable a part of her character.

' How little,' said she, 'is the human heart known except to Him who
made it ! While a fellow-creature may admire our apparent devotion,
He who appears to be its object, witnesses the wandering of the heart
which seems to be lifted up to Him. He sees it roving to the ends of
the earth, busied about anything rather than Himself ; running after
trifles which not only dishonour a Christian, but would disgrace a
child. As to my very virtues, if I dare apply such a word to myself,
they sometimes lose their character by not keeping their proper place.
They become sins by infringing on higher duties. If I mean to perform an act of devotion, some crude plan of charity forces itself on my
mind ; and what with trying to drive out one, and to establish the other,
I rise dissatisfied and unimproved, and resting my sole hope, not on
the duty which I have been performing, but on the mercy which I have
been offending.'

I assured her, with all the simplicity of truth, and all the sincerity of
affection, that this confession only served to raise my opinion of the

piety she disclaimed ; that such deep consciousness of imperfection, so quick a discernment of the slightest deviation, and such constant vigilance to prevent it, were the truest indications of an humble spirit ; and those who thus carefully guarded themselves against small errors, were in little danger of being betrayed into great ones.

She replied, smiling, that ' she should not be so angry with vanity, if it would be contented to keep its proper place among the vices ; but her quarrel with it was, that it would mix itself with our virtues, and rob us of their reward.'

'Vanity, indeed,' replied I, 'differs from the other vices in this : *they* commonly are only opposite to the one contrary virtue, while this vice has a kind of ubiquity, is on the watch to intrude everywhere, and weakens all the virtues which it cannot destroy. I believe vanity was the harpy of the ancient poets, which they tell us tainted whatever it touched.'

'Self-deception is so easy,' replied Miss Stanley, 'that I am even afraid of highly extolling any good quality, lest I should sit down satisfied with having borne my testimony in its favour, and so rest contented with the praise instead of the practice. Commending a right thing is a cheap substitute for doing it, with which we are too apt to satisfy ourselves.'

'There is no mark,' I replied, 'which more clearly distinguishes that humility which has the love of God for its principle, from its counterfeit, a false and superficial politeness, than that, while this last flatters, in order to extort in return more praise than its due, humility, like the divine principle from which it springs, seeketh not even its own.'

In answer to some further remark of mine, with an air of infinite modesty, she said, 'I have been betrayed, sir, into saying too much. It will, I trust, however, have the good effect of preventing you from thinking better of me than I deserve. In general, I hold it indiscreet to speak of the state of one's mind. I have been taught this piece of prudence by my own indiscretion. I once lamented to a lady the fault of which we have been speaking, and observed how difficult it was to keep the heart right. She so little understood the nature of this inward corruption, that she told in confidence to two or three friends, that they were all much mistaken in Miss Stanley, for though her character stood so fair with the world, she had secretly confessed to her that she was a great sinner.'

I could not forbear repeating, though she had chid me for it before, how much I had been struck with several instances of her indifference to the world, and her superiority to its pleasures. 'Do you know,' continued she, smiling, 'that you are more my enemy than the lady of whom I have been speaking? She only defamed my principles, but you are corrupting them. The world, I believe, is not so much a place as a nature. It is possible to be religious in a court, and worldly in a monastery. I find that the thoughts may be engaged too anxiously about so petty a concern as a little family arrangement ; that the mind may be drawn off from better pursuits, and engrossed by things too trivial to name, as much as by objects more apparently wrong. The country is certainly favourable to religion, but it would be hard on the millions who are doomed to live in towns if it were exclusively favourable. Nor must we lay more stress on the accidental circumstance than it deserves. Nay, I almost doubt if it is not too pleasant to be quite safe. An enjoyment which assumes a sober shape may deceive us, by making us believe we are practising a duty when we are only gratifying a taste.'

'But do you not think,' said I, 'that there may be merit in the taste itself? May not a succession of acts, forming a habit, and that habit a good one, induce so sound a way of thinking, that it may become difficult to distinguish the duty from the taste, and to separate the principle from the choice? This I really believe to be the case in minds finely wrought and vigilantly watched.'

I observed, that however delightful the country might be a great part of the year, yet there were a few winter months, when I feared it might be dull, though not in the degree Sir John's Richmond lady had found it.

With a smile of compassion at my want of taste, she said, 'she perceived I was no gardener.' ' To me,' added she, ' the winter has charms of its own. If I were not afraid of the light habit of introducing Providence on an occasion not sufficiently important, I would say that He seems to reward those who love the country well enough to live in it the whole year, by making the greater part of the winter the busy season for gardening operations. If I happen to be in town a few days only, every sun that shines, every shower that falls, every breeze that blows, seems wasted, because I do not see their effect upon my plants.' ' But surely,' said I, ' the winter at least suspends your enjoyment. There is little pleasure in contemplating vegetation in its torpid state, in surveying

The naked shoots, barren as lances,

as Cowper describes the winter-shrubbery.'

'The pleasure is in the preparation,' replied she. ' When all appears dead and torpid to you idle spectators, all is secretly at work ; nature is busy in preparing her treasures under ground, and art has a hand in the process. When the blossoms of summer are delighting you mere amateurs, then it is that we professional people,' added she, laughing, ' are really idle. The silent operations of the winter now produce themselves—the canvas of nature is covered—the great Artist has laid on His colours—then we petty agents lay down our implements, and enjoy our leisure in contemplating *His* work.'

I had never known her so communicative ; but my pleased attention, instead of drawing her on, led her to check herself. Phœbe, who had been busily employed in trimming a flaunting yellow azalia, now turned to me, and said : ' Why, it is only the Christmas month that our labours are suspended, and then we have so much pleasure that we want no business ; such in-door festivities and diversions, that that dull month is with us the gayest in the year.' So saying, she called Lucilla to assist her in tying up the branch of an orange-tree, which the wind had broken.

I was going to offer my services when Mrs. Stanley joined us before

I could obtain an answer to my question about these Christmas diversions. A stranger, who had seen me pursuing Mrs. Stanley in her walks, might have supposed that not the daughter, but the mother, was the object of my attachment. But with Mrs. Stanley I could always talk of Lucilla, with Lucilla I durst not often talk of herself.

The fond mother and I stood looking with delight on the fair gardeners. When I had admired their alacrity in these innocent pursuits, their fondness for retirement, and their cheerful delight in its pleasures ; Mrs. Stanley replied, ' Yes, Lucilla is half a nun. She likes the rule, but not the vow. Poor thing ! her conscience is so tender that she oftener requires encouragement than restraint. While she was making this plantation, she felt herself so absorbed by it, that she came to me one day, and said that her gardening work so fascinated her, that she found whole hours passed unperceived, and she began to be uneasy by observing that all cares and all duties were suspended while she was disposing beds of carnations, or knots of anemones. Even when she tore herself away, and returned to her employments, her flowers still pursued her, and the improvement of her mind gave way to the cultivation of her geraniums.

' " I am afraid," said the poor girl, " that I must really give it up." I would not hear of this. I would not suffer her to deny herself so pure a pleasure. She then suggested the expedient of limiting her time, and hanging up her watch in the conservatory, to keep her within her prescribed bounds. She is so observant of this restriction, that when her allotted time is expired, she forces herself to leave off, even in the midst of the most interesting operation. By this limitation a treble end is answered. Her time is saved, self-denial is exercised, and the interest which would languish by protracting the work is kept in fresh vigour.' I told Mrs. Stanley that I had observed her watch hanging in a citron tree the day I came, but little thought it had a moral meaning. She said, ' it had never been left there since I had been in the house, for fear of causing interrogatories.' Here Mrs. Stanley left me to my meditations.

It is wisely ordered that all mortal enjoyments should have some alloy. I never tasted a pleasure since I had been at the Grove, I never witnessed a grace, I never heard related an excellence of Lucilla, without a sigh that my beloved parents did not share my happiness. ' How would they,' said I, ' delight in her delicacy, rejoice in her piety, love her benevolence, admire her humility, her usefulness ! Oh, how do children feel, who wound the peace of *living* parents by an unworthy choice, when not a little of my comfort springs from the certainty that the departed would rejoice in mine ! Even from their blessed abode, my grateful heart seems to hear them say, " This is the creature we would have chosen for thee ! This is the creature with whom we shall rejoice with thee through all eternity !" '

Yet such was my inconsistency, that, charmed as I was that so young and lovely a woman could be so cheaply pleased, and delighted with that simplicity of taste, which made her resemble my favourite heroine of Milton in her amusements, as well as in her domestic pursuits ; still I longed to know what those Christmas diversions, so slightly hinted

at, could be ; diversions which could reconcile these girls to their
absence, not only from their green-house, but from London. I could
hardly fear, indeed, to find at Stanley Grove what the newspapers pertly
call *private theatricals.* Still I suspected it might be some gay dissipation not quite suited to their general character, nor congenial to their
usual amusements. My mother's favourite rule of *consistency* strongly
forced itself on my mind, though I tried to repel the suggestion as unjust
and ungenerous.

Of what meannesses will not love be guilty ! It drove me to have
recourse to my friend Mrs. Comfit, to dissipate my doubts. From her
I learnt that that cold and comfortless season was mitigated at Stanley
Grove by several feasts to the poor of different classes and ages.
' Then, sir,' continued she, ' if you could see the blazing fires, and the
abundant provisions ! the roasting, and the boiling, and the baking.
The house is all alive ! On those days, the drawers and shelves of
Miss Lucilla's store-room are completely emptied. 'Tis the most
delightful bustle, sir, to see our young ladies tying on the good women's
warm cloaks, fitting their caps and aprons, and sending home blankets
to the infirm who cannot come themselves : the very little ones kneeling
down on the ground to try on the poor girls' shoes ; even little Miss
Celia ; and she is so tender to fit them exactly, and not hurt them !
Last feast-day, not finding a pair small enough for a poor little girl, she
privately slipped off her own, and put on the child. It was some time
before it was discovered that she herself was without shoes. We are
all alive, sir. Parlour, and hall, and kitchen, all is in motion ! Books,
and business, and walks, and gardening, all is forgotten for these few
happy days.'

How I hated myself for my suspicion ! And how I loved the charming creatures who could find in these humble but exhilarating duties an
equivalent for the pleasures of the metropolis ! ' Surely,' said I to
myself, ' my mother would call *this* consistency, when the amusements
of a religious family smack of the same flavour with its business and its
duties. My heart was more than easy ; it was dilated, while I congratulated myself in the thought that there *were* young ladies to be
found, who could spend a winter not only unrepiningly, but cheerfully
and delightedly, in the country.

I am aware that, were I to repeat my conversations with Lucilla, I
should subject myself to ridicule by recording such cold and spiritless
discourse on my own part. But I had not yet declared my attachment.
I made it a point of duty not to violate my engagement with Mr.
Stanley. I was not addressing declarations, but studying the character
of her on whom the happiness of my life was to depend. I had
resolved not to show my attachment by any overt act. I confined the
expression of my affection to that *series of small, quiet attentions,* which
an accurate judge of the human heart has pronounced to be the surest
avenue to a delicate mind. I had, in the meantime, the inexpressible
felicity to observe a constant union of feeling, as well as a general con-
sonancy of opinion between us. Every sentiment seemed a reciprocation
of sympathy, and every look, of intelligence. This unstudied correspondence enchanted me the more, as I had always considered that a

conformity of tastes was nearly as necessary to conjugal happiness as a conformity of principles.

Chapter XXXIV.

NE morning I took a ride alone to breakfast at Lady Aston's, Mr. Stanley having expressed a particular desire that I should cultivate the acquaintance of her son. ' Sir George is not quite twenty,' said he, ' and your being a few years older, will make him consider your friendship as an honour to him ; I am sure it will be an advantage.'

In her own little family circle, I had the pleasure of seeing Lady Aston appear to more advantage than I had yet done. Her understanding is good, and her affections are strong. She had received a too favourable prepossession of my character from Mr. Stanley, and treated me with as much openness as if I had been his son.

The gentle girls, animated by the spirit of their brother, seemed to derive both happiness and importance from his presence : while the amiable young baronet himself won my affection by his engaging manners, and my esteem by his good sense, and his considerable acquirements in everything which becomes a gentleman.

This visit exemplified a remark I had sometimes made, that shy characters, who from natural timidity are reserved in general society, open themselves with peculiar warmth and frankness to a few select friends, or to an individual of whom they think kindly. A distant manner is not always, as is suspected, the result of a cold heart, or a dull head ; nor is gaiety necessarily connected with feeling. High animal spirits, though they often evaporate in mere talk, yet by their warmth and quickness of motion obtain the credit of strong sensibility ; a sensibility, however, of which the heart is not always the fountain : while in the timid, that silence, which is construed into pride, indifference, or want of capacity, is often the effect of keen feelings. Friendship is the genial climate in which such hearts disclose themselves ; ·they flourish in the shade, and kindness alone makes them expand. A keen discerner will often detect, in such characters, qualities which are not always connected with

> The rattling tongue
> Of saucy and audacious eloquence

When people who have seen little of each other are thrown together, nothing brings on free communication so quickly, or so pleasantly, as their being both intimate with a third person, for whom all parties entertain one common sentiment. Mr. Stanley seemed always a point of union between his neighbours and me.

After various topics had been discussed, Lady Aston remarked, that she could now trace the goodness of Providence in having so ordered events, as to make those things which she had so much dreaded at the time work out advantages which could not have been otherwise obtained for her.

'I had a singular aversion,' added she, 'to the thoughts of removing to this place, and quitting Sir George's estate in Warwickshire, where I had spent the happiest years of my life. When I had the misfortune to lose him,' (here a tear quietly strayed down her cheeks,) 'I resolved never to remove from the place where he died. I had fully persuaded myself that it was a duty to do all I could to cherish grief. I obliged myself, as a law, to spend whole hours every day in walking round the place where he was buried. These melancholy visits, the intervals of which were filled with tears, prayers, and reading a few good but not well-chosen books, made up the whole round of my sad existence. I had nearly forgotten that I had any duties to perform, that I had any mercies left. Almost all the effect which the sight of my children produced in me was, by their resemblance to their father, to put me in mind of what I had lost.

'I was not sufficiently aware how much more truly I should have honoured his memory, by training his living representatives in such a manner as he, had he been living, would have approved. My dear George,' added she, smiling at her son through her tears, 'was glad to get away to school ; and my poor girls, when they lost the company of their brother, lost all the little cheerfulness which my recluse habits had left them. We sunk into total inaction, and our lives became as comfortless as they were unprofitable.'

'My dear madam,' said Sir George, in the most affectionate tone and manner, 'I can only forgive myself, from the consideration of my being then too young and thoughtless to know the value of the mother, whose sorrows ought to have endeared my home to me, instead of driving me from it.'

'They are *my* faults, my dear George, and not yours, that I am relating. Few mothers would have acted like me ; few sons differently from you. Your affectionate heart deserved a warmer return than my broken spirits were capable of making you. But I was telling you, sir,' said she, again addressing herself to me, 'that the event of my coming to this place, not only became the source of my present peace, and of the comfort of my children, but that its result enables me to look forward with a cheerful hope to that state where there is neither sin, sorrow, nor separation. The thoughts of death which used to render me useless, now make me only serious. The reflection that "the night cometh," which used to extinguish my activity, now kindles it.

'Forgive me, sir,' added she, wiping her eyes, 'these are not such tears as I then shed. These are tears of gratitude, I had not said of joy. In the family at the Grove, Providence had been providing for me friends, for whom, I doubt not, I shall bless Him in eternity.

'I had long been convinced of the importance of religion. I had always felt the insufficiency of the world to bestow happiness ; but I had never before beheld religion in such a form. I had never been furnished with a proper substitute for the worldly pleasures which I yet despised. I did right in giving up diversions, but I did wrong in giving up employment, and in neglecting duties. I knew something of religion as a principle of fear, but I had no conception of it as a motive to the love of God, and as the spring of active duty : nor did I consider it as a source of inward peace. Books had not been of any great service to me, for I had no one to guide me in the choice, or to assist me in the perusal. I went to my daily task of devotion with a heavy heart, and returned from it with no other sense of comfort but that I had not omitted it.

'My former friends and acquaintance had been decent and regular ; but they had adopted religion as a form, and not as a principle. It was compliance, and not conviction. It was conformity to custom, and not the persuasion of the heart. Judge then how I must have been affected, in a state when sorrow and disappointment had made my mind peculiarly impressible, with the conversation and example of Mr. and Mrs. Stanley ! I saw in them, that religion was not a formal profession, but a powerful principle. It ran through their whole life and character. All the Christian graces were brought into action in a way, with a uniformity, and a beauty, which nothing but Christian motives could have effected.

'The change which took place in my own mind, however, was progressive. The strict consonance which I observed between their sentiments and actions, and those of Dr. Barlow and Mr. Jackson, strengthened and confirmed mine. This similarity in all points was a fresh confirmation that they were all right. The light of religion gradually grew stronger, and the way more smooth. It was literally a "lamp to my feet," for I walked more safely as I saw more clearly. My difficulties insensibly lessened, and my doubts disappeared. I still indeed continue hourly to feel much cause to be humbled, but none to be unhappy.'

When Lady Aston had done speaking, Sir George said, 'I owe a thousand obligations to my mother, but not one so great as her introduction of me to Mr. Stanley. He has given a bent and bias to my sentiments, habits, and pursuits, to which I trust every day will add fresh strength. I look up to him as my model : happy if I may, in any degree, be able to form myself by it ! Till I had the happiness of knowing you, sir, I preferred the company of Dr. Barlow and Mr. Stanley, to that of any *young* man with whom I am acquainted.'

After some further conversation, in which Sir George, with great credit to himself, bore a considerable part, Miss Aston took courage to ask me if I would accompany them all into the garden, as she wished me to carry home intelligence to Miss Stanley of the flourishing state of some American plants, which had been raised under her direction. To speak the truth, I had for some time been trying to bring Lucilla on the tapis, but had not found a plausible pretence. I now inquired if Miss Stanley directed their gardening pursuits.—'She directs *all* our pursuits,' said the two bashful, blushing girls, who now, for the first time in their lives, spoke both at once ; the subject kindling an energy in their affectionate hearts, which even their timidity could not rein in.

'I thought, Clara,' said Sir George, 'that Miss *Phœbe* Stanley too had assisted in laying out the flower-garden. Surely she is not behind her sister in anything that is kind, or anything that is elegant.' His complexion heightened as he spoke, and he expressed himself with an emphasis, which I had not before observed in his manner of speaking.

I stole a glance at Lady Aston, whose meek eye glistened with pleasure at the earnestness with which her son spoke of the lovely Phœbe. My rapid imagination instantly shot forward to an event, which some years hence will probably unite two families so worthy of each other. Lady Aston, who already honours me with her confidence, afterwards confirmed my suspicions on a subject, about which nothing but the extreme youth of both parties made her backward to express the secret hope she fondly entertained.

In our walk round the gardens, the Miss Astons continued to vie with each other, who should be warmest in the praise of their young friends at the Grove. To Miss Stanley, they gratefully declared, they owed any little taste, knowledge, or love of goodness, which they themselves might possess.

It was delightful to observe these quiet girls warmed and excited by a subject so interesting. I was charmed to see them so far from feeling any shadow of envy at the avowed superiority of their young friends, and so unanimously eloquent in the praise of merit so eclipsing.

After having admired the plants, of which I promised to make a favourable report, I was charged with a large and beautiful bouquet for the young ladies at the Grove. They then drew me to the prettiest spot in the grounds. While I was admiring it, Miss Clara, with a blush, and some hesitation, begged leave to ask my advice about a little rustic building, which she and her sisters were just going to raise in honour of the Miss Stanleys. It was to be dedicated to them, and called the Temple of Friendship. 'My brother,' said she, 'is kindly assisting us. The materials are all prepared, and we have now only to fix them up.'

She then put into my hands a little plan. I highly approved it; venturing, however, to suggest some trifling alterations, which I told them I did, in order to implicate myself a little in the pleasant project. How proud was I when Clara added, 'that Miss Stanley had expressed a high opinion of my general taste!'—They all begged me to look in on them in my rides, and assist them with my farther counsel; adding that, above all things, I must keep it a secret at the Grove.

Lady Aston said, 'that she expected our whole party to dine at the hall some day next week.' Her daughters entreated that it might be postponed till the latter end, by which time they doubted not their little edifice would be completed. Sir George then told me, that his sisters had requested him to furnish an inscription, or to endeavour to procure one from me. He added his wishes to theirs that I would comply. They all joined so earnestly in the entreaty, that I could not withstand them, 'albeit unused to the *rhyming* mood.'

After some deliberation, Friday, in the next week, was fixed upon for the party at the Grove to dine at Aston Hall, and I was to carry the invitation. I took a respectful leave of the excellent lady of the mansion, and an affectionate one of the young people; with whom the familiar intercourse of this quiet morning had contributed to advance my friendly acquaintance, more than could have been done by many ceremonious meetings.

When I returned to the Grove, which was but just in time to dress for dinner, I spoke with sincere satisfaction of the manner in which I had passed the morning. It was beautiful to observe the honest delight, the ingenuous kindness, with which Lucilla heard me commend the Miss Astons. No little disparaging hint on the one hand, gently to let down her friends, nor, on the other, no such exaggerated praise as I have sometimes seen employed as a screen for envy, or as a trap to make the hearer lower what the speaker had too highly raised.

I dropped in at Aston Hall two or three times in the course of the week, as well to notice the progress of the work, as to carry my inscription, in which, as Lucilla was both my subject and my muse, I succeeded rather better than I expected.

On the Friday, according to appointment, our whole party went to dine at the Hall. In our way, Mr. Stanley expressed the pleasure it gave him, that Lady Aston was now so convinced of the duty of making home agreeable to her son, as delightedly to receive such of her friends as were warmly disposed to become his.

Sir George, who is extremely well bred, did the honours admirably for so young a man, to the great relief of his excellent mother, whom long retirement had rendered habitually timid in a party, of which some were almost strangers.

The Miss Astons had some difficulty to restrain their young guests from running directly to look at the progress of the American plants ; but as they grew near the mysterious spot, they were not allowed to approach it before the allotted time.

After dinner, when the whole party were walking in the garden, Lady Aston was desired by her daughters to conduct her company to a winding grass-walk, near the little building, but from whence it was not visible. While they were all waiting at the appointed place, the two elder Miss Astons gravely took a hand of Lucilla, Sir George and I each presented a hand to Phœbe, and in profound silence, and great ceremony, we led them up the turf steps into this simple, but really pretty temple. The initials of Lucilla and Phœbe were carved in cypher over a little rustic window, under which was written,

'Sacred to Friendship.'

In two niches prepared for the purpose, we severally seated the two astonished nymphs, who seemed absolutely enchanted. Above was the inscription in large Roman letters.

The Astons looked so much alive, that they might have been mistaken for Stanleys, who, in their turn, were so affected with this tender mark of friendship, that they looked as tearful as if they had been Astons. After reading the inscription, 'My dear Clara,' said Lucilla to Miss Aston, 'where *could* you get these beautiful verses ? Though the praise they convey is too flattering to be just, it is too delicate not to please. The lines are at once tender and elegant.' 'We got them,' said Miss Aston, with a sweet vivacity, 'where we get everything that is good, from Stanley Grove,' bowing modestly to me.

How was I elated ; and how did Lucilla blush ! but though she now tried to qualify her flattery, she could not recall it. And I would not allow myself to be robbed of the pure delight it had given me. All the company seemed to enjoy her confusion and my pleasure.

I forgot to mention that as we crossed the Park, we had seen enter the house, through a back avenue, a procession of little girls neatly dressed in a uniform. In a whisper I asked Lady Aston what it meant. 'You are to know,' replied her ladyship, 'that my daughters adopt all Miss Stanley's plans, and, among the rest, that of associating with all their own indulgences some little act of charity, that while they are receiving pleasure, they may also be conferring it. The opening of the Temple of Friendship is likely to afford too much gratification, to be passed over without some such association. So my girls give to-day a little feast, with prizes of merit, to their village-school, and to a few other deserving young persons.'

When we had taken our seats in the temple, Phœbe suddenly cried out, clasping her hands in an ecstasy, 'Only look, Lucilla ! There is no end to the enchantment. It is all fairy land.' On casting our eyes as she directed, we were agreeably surprised with observing a large kind of temporary shed or booth at some distance from us. It was picturesquely fixed near an old spreading oak, and was ingeniously composed of branches of trees, fresh and green. Under the oak stood ranged the village maids. We walked to the spot. The inside of the booth was hung round with caps, aprons, bonnets, handkerchiefs, and other coarse, but neat articles of female dress. On a rustic table were laid a number of Bibles, and specimens of several kinds of coarse works, and little manufactures. The various performances were examined by the company ; some presents were given to all. But additional prizes were awarded, by the young patronesses, to the best specimens of different work ; to the best spinners, the best knitters, the best manufacturers of split straw, and the best performers in plain work, I think they called it.

Three grown-up young women, neatly dressed, and of modest manners, stood behind. It appeared that one of them had taken such good care of her young sisters and brothers since their mother's death, and had so prudently managed her father's house, that it had saved him from an imprudent second choice. Another had postponed, for many months, a marriage in which her heart was engaged, because she had a paralytic grandmother, whom she attended day and night, and whom nothing, not even love itself, could tempt her to desert. Death had now released the aged sufferer ; the wedding was to take place next Sunday. The third had for above a year worked two hours every day, over and above her set time, and applied the gains to clothe the orphan child of a deceased friend. She was also to accompany her lover to the altar on Sunday, but had made it a condition of her marrying him, that she should be allowed to continue her supernumerary hours' work for the benefit of the poor orphan. All three had been exemplary in their attendance at church, as well as in their general conduct. The fair patronesses presented each with a handsome Bible, and with a complete plain, but very neat, suit of apparel.

While these gifts were distributing, I whispered Sir John, that one such ticket as we were each desired to take for Squallini's benefit, would furnish the cottages of these poor girls. 'And it *shall*,' replied he with emphasis. 'How little a way will that sum go in superfluities, which will make two honest couple happy ! How costly is vanity, how cheap is charity !'

'Can these happy, useful young creatures be my little, inactive, insipid Astons, Charles?' whispered Mr. Stanley, as we walked away to leave the girls to sit down to their plentiful supper, which was spread on a long table under the oak, without the green booth. This group of figures made an interesting addition to the scenery, when we got back to the temple, and often attracted our attention while we were engaged in conversation.

Chapter XXXV.

THE company were not soon weary of admiring the rustic building, which seemed raised as if by the stroke of a magician's wand, so rapidly had it sprung up. They were delighted to find that their pleasure was to be prolonged by drinking tea in the temple.

While we were at tea, Mr. Stanley, addressing himself to me, said, 'I have always forgotten to ask you, Charles, if your high expectations of pleasure from the society in London had quite answered ?'

'I was entertained, and I was disappointed,' replied I. 'I always found the pleasure of the moment not heightened, but effaced by the succeeding moment. The ever restless, rolling tide of new intelligence at once gratified and excited the passion for novelty, which I found to be *le grand poisson qui mange les petits*. This successive abundance of fresh supply gives an ephemeral importance to every thing, and a lasting importance to nothing. We skimmed every topic, but dived into none. Much desultory talk, but little discussion. The combatants skirmished like men whose arms were kept bright by constant use ; who were accustomed to a flying fight, but who avoided the fatigue of coming to close quarters. What was old, however momentous, was rejected as dull ; what was new, however insignificant, was thought interesting. Events of the past week were placed with those beyond the flood ; and the very existence of occurrences which continued to be matter of deep interest with us in the country, seemed there totally forgotten.

'I found, too, that the inhabitants of the metropolis had a standard of merit of their own ; that knowledge of the town was concluded to be knowledge of the world ; that local habits, reigning phrases, temporary fashions, and an acquaintance with the surface of manners, was supposed to be knowledge of mankind. Of course, he who was ignorant of the topics of the hour, and the anecdotes of a few modish leaders, was ignorant of human nature.'

Sir John observed that I was rather too young to be a *praiser of past times*, yet he allowed that the standard of conversation was not so high as it had been in the time of my father, by whose reports my youthful ardour had been inflamed. He did not indeed suppose that men were less intellectual now, but they certainly were less colloquially intellectual. 'For this,' added he, 'various reasons may be assigned. In London man is every day becoming less of a social, and more of a gregarious animal. Crowds are as little favourable to conversation as to reflection. He finds, therefore, that he may figure in the mass with less expense of mind : and as to women, they figure at no expense at all. They find that by mixing with myriads, they may carry on the daily intercourse of life, without being obliged to bring a single idea to enrich the common stock.'

'I do not wonder,' said I, 'that the dull and the uninformed love to shelter their insignificance in a crowd. In mingling with the multitude their deficiencies elude detection. The vapid and the ignorant are like a bad play ; they owe the little figure they make to the dress, the scenery, the music, and the company. The noise and the glare take off all attention from the defects of the work. The spectator is amused, and he does not inquire whether it is with the piece, or with the accompaniments. The end is attained, and he is little solicitous about the means. But an intellectual woman, like a well-written drama, will please at home without all these aids and adjuncts—nay, the beauties of the superior piece, and of the superior woman, will rise on a more intimate survey. But you were going, Sir John, to assign other causes for the decline and fall of conversation.'

'One very affecting reason,' replied he, 'is that the alarming state of public affairs fills all men's minds with one momentous object. As every Englishman is a patriot, every patriot is a politician. It is natural that that subject should fill every mouth, which occupies every heart, and that little room should be left for extraneous matter.'

'I should accept this,' said I, 'as a satisfactory vindication, had I heard that the same absorbing cause had thinned the public places, or diminished the attraction of the private resorts of dissipation.'

'There is a third reason,' said Sir John. 'Polite literature has in a good degree given way to experimental philosophy. The admirers of science assert, that the last was the age of words, and that this is the age of things. A more substantial kind of knowledge has partly superseded these elegant studies, which have caught such hold on your affections.'

'I heartily wish,' replied I, 'that the new pursuits may be found to make men wiser ; they certainly have not made them more agreeable.'

'It is affirmed,' said Mr. Stanley, 'that the prevailing philosophical studies have a religious use, and that they naturally tend to elevate the heart to the great Author of the universe.'

'I have but one objection to that assertion,' replied Sir John, 'namely, that it is not true. This should seem, indeed, to be their direct tendency, yet experiment, which you know is the soul of philosophy, has proved the contrary.'

He then adduced some instances in our own country, which I forbear to name, that clearly evinced that this was not their necessary consequence ; adding, however, a few great names on the more honourable side. He next adverted to the Baillies, the Condorcets, the D'Alemberts, and the Lalandes, as melancholy proofs of the inefficacy of mere science to make Christians.

' Far be it from me,' said Sir John, ' to undervalue philosophical pursuits. The modern discoveries are extremely important, especially in their application to the purposes of common life : but where these are pursued exclusively, I cannot help preferring the study of the great classic authors, those exquisite masters of life and manners, with whose spirit conversation, twenty or thirty years ago, was so richly impregnated.'

' I confess,' said I, ' that there may be more matter, but there is certainly less mind in the reigning pursuits. The reputation of skill, it is true, may be obtained at a much less expense of time and intellect. The comparative cheapness of the acquisition holds out the powerful temptation of more credit with less labour. A sufficient knowledge of botany or chemistry to make a figure in company is easily obtained, while a thorough acquaintance with the historians, poets, and orators of antiquity requires much time and close application.' ' But,' exclaimed Sir John, ' can the fashionable studies pretend to give the same expansion to the mind, the same elevation to the sentiments, the same energy to the feelings, the same stretch and compass to the understanding, the same correctness to the taste, the same grace and spirit to the whole moral and intellectual man ?'

' For my own part,' replied I, ' so far from saying with Hamlet, " Man delights not me, nor woman neither ;" I confess, I have little delight in anything else. The study of the human mind, is, of merely human studies, my chief pleasure. As a man, man is the creature with whom I have to do, and the varieties in his character interest me more than all the possible varieties of mosses, and shells, and fossils. To view this compound creature in the complexity of his actions, as portrayed by the hand of those immortal masters, Tacitus and Plutarch ; to view him in the struggle of his passions, as displayed by Euripides and Shakspeare ; to contemplate him in the blaze of his eloquence, by the two rival orators of Greece and Rome, is more congenial to my feelings than the ablest disquisition of which matter was ever the subject.' Sir John, who is a passionate, and rather too exclusive, admirer of classic lore, warmly declared himself of my opinion.

' I went to town,' replied I, ' with a mind eager for intellectual pleasure. My memory was not quite unfurnished with passages which I thought likely to be adverted to, and which might serve to embellish conversation, without incurring the charge of pedantry. But though most of the men I conversed with were my equals in education, and my superiors in talent, there seemed little disposition to promote such topics as might bring our understandings into play. Whether it is that business, active life, and public debate, absorb the mind, and make men consider society rather as a scene to rest than to exercise it, I know not ; certain it is that they brought less into the treasury of conversation than I expected ; not because they were poor, but proud, or idle, and reserved their talents and acquisitions for higher occasions. The most opulent possessors, I often found the most penurious contributors.'

' *Rien de trop*,' said Mr. Stanley, 'was the favourite maxim of an author,* whom I am not apt to quote for rules of moral conduct. Yet its adoption would be a salutary check against excess in all our pursuits. If polite learning is undervalued by the mere man of science, it is, perhaps, over-rated by the mere man of letters. If it dignifies retirement, and exalts society, it is not the great business of life ; it is not the prime fountain of moral excellence.'

' Well, so much for *man*,' said Sir John ; ' but, Charles, you have not told us what you had to say of *woman*, in your observations on society.'

' As to woman,' replied I, ' I declare that I found more propensity to promote subjects of taste and elegant speculation among some of the superior class of females, than in many of my own sex. The more prudent, however, are restrained through fear of the illiberal sarcasms of men, who, not contented to suppress their own faculties, ridicule all intellectual exertion in women, though evidently arising from a modest desire of improvement, and not the vanity of hopeless rivalry.'

' Charles is always the Paladin of the reading ladies,' said Sir John. ' I do not deny it,' replied I, ' if they bear their faculties meekly. But I confess that what is sneeringly called a learned lady, is to me far preferable to a scientific one, such as I encountered one evening, who talked of the fulcrum and the lever, and the statera, which she took care to tell us was the Roman steel-yard, with all the sang-froid of philosophical conceit.'

' Scientific men,' said Sir John, ' are in general admirable for their simplicity, but in a technical woman I have seldom found a grain of taste or elegance.'

' I own,' replied I, ' I should greatly prefer a fair companion, who could modestly discriminate between the beauties of Virgil and Milton, to one who was always dabbling in chemistry, and who came to dinner with dirty hands from the laboratory. And yet I admire chemistry too ; I am now only speaking of that knowledge which is desirable in a female companion ; for knowledge I must have. But arts, which are of immense value in manufactures, won't make my wife's conversation entertaining to me. Discoveries which may greatly improve dyeing and bleaching, will add little to the delights of our summer evening's walk, or winter fireside.'

The ladies, Lucilla especially, smiled at my warmth. I felt that there was approbation in her smile, and, though I thought I had said too much already, it encouraged me to go on. ' I repeat, that, next to religion, whatever relates to human manners, is most attracting to human creatures. To turn from conversation to composition. What is it that excites so feeble an interest, in perusing that finely-written poem of the Abbé de Lille, '*Les Jardins ?*' It is because his garden has no cultivators, no inhabitants, no men and women. What confers that powerful charm on the descriptive parts of ' Paradise Lost ?'—a fascination, I will venture to affirm, paramount to all the lovely and magnificent scenery which adorns it. Eden itself, with all its exquisite

---

* Frederick the Great, King of Prussia.

landscape, would excite a very inferior pleasure, did it exhibit only inanimate beauties. It is the proprietors, it is the inhabitants, it is the *live stock*, of Eden, which seize upon the affections, and twine about the heart. The gardens, even of Paradise, would be dull without the gardeners. It is mental excellence, it is moral beauty, which completes the charm. Where this is wanting, landscape poetry, though it may be read with pleasure, yet the interest it raises is cold. It is admired, but seldom remembered ; praised, but seldom quoted. It leaves no definite idea on the mind. If general, it is indistinct ; if minute, tedious.'

' It must be confessed,' said Sir John, 'that some poets are apt to forget that the finest representation of nature is only the scene, not the object ; the canvas, not the portrait. We had, indeed, some time ago, so much of this gorgeous scene-painting, so much splendid poetical botany, so many amorous flowers, and so many vegetable courtships ; so many wedded plants ; roots transformed to nymphs, and dwelling in emerald palaces ; that, somehow or other, truth, and probability, and nature, and man, slipt out of the picture, though it must be allowed that genius held the pencil.'

' In Mason's "English Garden,"' replied I, 'Alcander's precepts would have been cold, had there been no personification. The introduction of character dramatises what else would have been frigidly didactic. Thomson enriches his landscape with here and there a figure, drawn with more correctness than warmth, with more nature than spirit, but exalts it everywhere by moral allusion and religious reference. The scenery of Cowper is perpetually animated with sketches of character, enlivened with portraits from real life, and the exhibition of human manners and passions. His most exquisite descriptions owe their vividness to moral illustration. Loyalty, liberty, patriotism, charity, piety, benevolence, every generous feeling, every glowing sentiment, every ennobling passion, grows out of his descriptive powers. His matter always bursts into mind. His shrubbery, his forest, his flower-garden, all produce

Fruits worthy of Paradise,

and lead to immortality.'

Mr. Stanley said, adverting again to the subject of conversation, it was an amusement to him to observe, what impression the first introduction to general society made on a mind conversant with books, but to whom the world was in a manner new.

' I believe,' said Sir John, 'that an overflowing commerce, and the excessive opulence it has introduced, though favourable to all the splendours of art, and mechanic ingenuity, yet have lowered the standard of taste, and debilitated the mental energies. They are advantageous to luxury, but fatal to intellect. It has added to the brilliancy of the drawing-room itself, but deducted from that of the inhabitant. It has given perfection to our mirrors, our candelabra, our gilding, our inlaying, and our sculpture, but it has communicated a torpor to the imagination, and enervated our intellectual vigour.'

' In one way,' said Mr. Stanley, smiling, ' luxury has been favourable to literature. From the unparalleled splendour of our printing, paper, engraving, illuminating, and binding, luxury has caused more books to be purchased, while, from the growth of time-absorbing dissipation, it causes fewer to be read. Even where books are not much considered as the vehicle of instruction, they are become an indispensable appendage to elegance. But I believe we were much more familiar with our native poets in their former plain garb, than since they have been attired in the gorgeous dress which now decorates our shelves.

' Poetry,' continued Mr. Stanley, ' has of late too much degenerated into personal satire, persiflage, and caricature, among one class of writers ; while, among another, it has exhibited the vagrances of genius, without the inspiration, the exuberance of fancy, without the curb of judgment, and the eccentricities of invention, without the restrictions of taste. The image has been strained, while the verse has been slackened. We have had pleonasm without fulness, and facility without force. Redundancy has been mistaken for plenitude, flimsiness for ease, and distortion for energy. An over-desire of being natural has made the poet feeble, and the rage for being simple has sometimes made him silly. The sensibility is sickly, and the elevation vertiginous.'

' To Cowper,' said Sir John, ' master of melody as he is, the mischief is partly attributable. Such an original must naturally have a herd of imitators. If they cannot attain to his excellencies, his faults are always attainable. The resemblance between the master and the scholar is found chiefly in his defects. The determined imitator of an easy writer becomes vapid ; of a sublime one, absurd. Cowper's ease appeared his most imitable charm : but ease aggravated is insipidity. His occasional negligences his disciples adopted uniformly. In Cowper there might sometimes be carelessness in the verse, but the verse itself was sustained by the vigour of the sentiment. The imitator forgot that his strength lay in the thought ; that his buoyant spirit always supported itself ; that the figure, though amplified, was never distorted ; the image, though bold, was never incongruous ; and the illustration, though new, was never false.

' The evil, however,' continued Sir John, ' seems to be correcting itself. The real genius, which exists in several of this whimsical school, I trust, will at length lead them to prune their excrescences, and reform their youthful eccentricities. Their good sense will teach them, that the surest road to fame is to condescend to tread in the luminous track of their great precursors in the art. They will see that deviation is not always improvement ; that whoever wants to be better than nature, will infallibly be worse ; that truth in taste is as obvious as in morals, and as certain as in mathematics. In other quarters, both the classic and the gothic music are emulously soaring, and I hail the restoration of genuine poetry and pure taste.'

' I must not,' said I, ' loquacious as I have already been, dismiss the subject of conversation, without remarking, that I found there was one topic, which seemed as uniformly avoided by common consent, as if it had been banished by the interdict of absolute authority ; and that some

12—2

forfeiture, or at least dishonour and disgrace, were to follow it on con-viction—I mean religion.'

' Surely, Charles,' said Sir John, 'you would not convert general con-versation into a divinity school, and friendly societies into debating clubs ?'

' Far from it,' replied I ; 'nor do I desire that ladies and gentlemen over their tea and coffee should rehearse their articles of faith, or fill the intervals of carving and eating with introducing dogmas or discussing controversies. I do not wish to erect the social table, which was meant for innocent relaxation, into an arena for theological combatants. I only wish, as people live so much together, that if, when out of the mul-titude of topics which arise in conversation, an unlucky wight happens to start a serious thought, I could see a cordial recognition of its importance ; I wish I could see a disposition to pursue it, instead of a chilling silence which obliges him to draw in, as if he had dropped something danger-ous to the state, or inimical to the general cheerfulness, or derogatory to his own understanding. I only desire, that as, without any effort on the part of the speaker, but merely from the overflowing fulness of a mind habitually occupied with one leading concern, we easily perceive that one of the company is a lawyer, another a soldier, a third a phy-sician ; I only wish that we could oftener discover from the same pleni-tude, so hard to conceal where it exists, that we were in a company of Christians.'

' We must not expect, in our days,' said Mr. Stanley, ' to see revive that animating picture of the prevalence of religious intercourse given by the prophet—" Then they that feared the Lord spake often one to another." And yet one cannot but regret that, in select society, men well informed as we know, well-principled as we hope, having one com-mon portion of being to fill, having one common faith, one common Father, one common journey to perform, one common termination to that journey, and one common object in view beyond it, should, when together, be so unwilling to advert occasionally to those great points, which doubtless often occupy them in secret ; that they should on the contrary adopt a sort of inverted hypocrisy, and wish to appear worse than they really are ; that they should be so backward to give or to gain information, to lend or to borrow lights, in a matter in which they are all equally interested ; which cannot be the case in any other possible subject.'

' In all human concerns,' said I, ' we find that those dispositions, tastes, and affections which are brought into exercise, flourish, while others are smothered by concealment.' ' It is certain,' replied Mr. Stanley, 'that knowledge which is never brought forward, is apt to decline. Some feelings require to be excited, in order to know if they exist. In short, topics of every kind, which are kept totally out of sight, make a fainter impression on the mind, than such as are occasionally introduced. Communication is a great strengthener of any principle. Feelings, as well as ideas, are often elicited by collision. Thoughts that are never to be produced, in time seldom present themselves, while mutual interchange almost creates as well as cultivates them. And as to the social affections, I am persuaded that men would love each other more cordially, good will and kindness would be inconceivably promoted, were they in the habit of maintaining that sort of intercourse which would keep up a mutual regard for their eternal interests, and lead them more to consider each other as candidates for the same immortality through the same common hope.'

Just as he had ceased to speak, we heard a warbling of female voices, which came softened to us by distance, and the undulation of the air. The little band under the oak had finished their cheerful repast, and arranged themselves in the same regular procession in which they had arrived. They stood still at a respectful distance from the temple, and in their artless manner sung Addison's beautiful version of the twenty-third Psalm, which the Miss Astons had taught them because it was a favourite with their mother.

Here the setting sun reminded us to retreat to the house. Before we quitted the temple, however, Sir George Aston ventured modestly to intimate a wish, that if it pleased the Almighty to spare our lives, the same party should engage always to celebrate this anniversary in the Temple of Friendship, which should be finished on a larger scale, and rendered less unworthy to receive such guests. The ladies smiled assentingly. Phœbe applauded rapturously. Sir John Belfield and I warmly approved the proposal. Mr. Stanley said, it could not but meet with his cordial concurrence, as it would involve the assurance of an annual visit from his valued friends.

As we walked into the house, Lady Aston, who held by my arm, in answer to the satisfaction I expressed at the day I had passed, said, ' We owe what little we are and do, under Providence, to Mr. Stanley. You will admire his discriminating mind, when I tell you that he recommends these little exhibitions for my daughters far more than to his own. He says, that they, being naturally cheerful and habitually active, require not the incentive of company to encourage them. But that for my poor timid inactive girls, the support and animating presence of a few chosen friends just give them that degree of life and spirit, which serves to warm their hearts, and keep their minds in motion.'

Chapter XXXVI.

ISS SPARKES came to spend the next day, according to her appointment. Mr. Flam, who called accidentally, stayed to dinner, Mr. and Mrs. Carlton had been previously invited. After dinner, the conversation chanced to turn upon domestic economy, a quality which Miss Sparkes professed to hold in the most sovereign contempt.

After some remark of Mrs. Stanley in favour of the household virtues, Mr. Carlton said, ' Mr. Addison in the *Spectator*, and Dr. Johnson in the *Rambler*, have each given us a lively picture of a vulgar, ungentle-woman-like, illiterate housewife. The notable woman of the one suffocated her guests at night with drying herbs in their chamber, and tormented them all day with plans of economy and lectures on manage-

ment. The economist of the other ruined her husband by her parsi-
monious extravagance, if I may be allowed to couple contradictions ;
by her tent-stitch hangings for which she had no walls, and her embroidery for which she had no use. The poor man pathetically laments
her detestable catalogue of made-wines, which hurt his fortune by their
profusion, and his health by not being allowed to drink them till they
were sour. Both ladies are painted as domestic tyrants, whose
husbands had no peace, and whose children had no education.'

'Those coarse housewives,' said Sir John, 'were exhibited as *warn-
ings*. It was reserved for the pen of Richardson to exhibit *examples*.
This author, with deeper and juster views of human nature, a truer
taste for the proprieties of female character, and a more exact intuition
into real life than any other writer of fabulous narrative, has given in
his heroines exemplifications of elegantly cultivated minds, combined
with the sober virtues of domestic economy. In no other writer of
fictitious adventures has the triumph of religion and reason over the
passions, and the now almost exploded doctrines of filial obedience,
and the household virtues, their natural concomitants, been so successfully blended. Whether the works of this most original, but by no
means faultless writer, were cause or effect, I know not ; whether these
well-imagined examples induced the ladies of that day " to study
household good ;" or whether the then existing ladies, by their
acknowledged attention to feminine concerns, furnished Richardson
with living models, I cannot determine. Certain it is, that the novel
writers of the subsequent period have in general been as little disposed
to represent these qualities as forming an indispensable part of the
female character, as the contemporary young ladies themselves have
been to supply them with patterns. I a little fear that the predominance of this sort of reading has contributed its full share to bring such
qualities into contempt.'

Miss Sparkes characteristically observed, that 'the meanest understanding and most vulgar education were competent to form such a
wife as the generality of men preferred. That a man of talents, dreading a rival, always took care to secure himself by marrying a fool.'

'Always excepting the present company, madam, I presume,' said
Mr. Stanley, laughing. 'But pardon me, if I differ from you. That
many men are sensual in their appetites, and low in their relish of
intellectual pleasures, I confess. That many others, who are neither
sensual, nor of mean attainments, prefer women whose ignorance will
favour their indolent habits, and whom it requires no exertion of mind
to entertain, I allow also. But permit me to say, that men of the
most cultivated minds, men who admire talents in a woman, are still
of opinion, that *domestic* talents can never be dispensed with : and I
totally dissent from you in thinking that these qualities infer the
absence of higher attainments, and necessarily imply a sordid or a
vulgar mind.

'Any ordinary art, after it is once discovered, may be practised by a
very common understanding. In this, as in everything else, the kind
arrangements of Providence are visible, because, as the common arts
employ the mass of mankind, they could not be universally carried on,

if they were not of easy and cheap attainment. Now, cookery is one of these arts, and I agree with you, madam, in thinking that a mean understanding, and a vulgar education, suffice to make a good cook. But a cook or housekeeper, and a lady qualified to wield a considerable establishment, are two very different characters. To prepare a dinner, and to conduct a great family, require talents of a very different size : and one reason why I would never choose to marry a woman ignorant of domestic affairs is, that she who wants, or she who despises this knowledge, must possess that previous bad judgment which, as it prevented her from seeing this part of her duty, would be likely to operate on other occasions.'

'I entirely agree with Mr. Stanley,' said Mr. Carlton. 'In general, I look upon the contempt or the fulfilment of these duties as pretty certain indications of the turn of mind from which the one or the other proceeds. I allow, however, that *with* this knowledge a lady may unhappily have overlooked more important acquisitions ; but *without* it I must ever consider the female character as defective in the texture, however it may be embroidered and spangled on the surface.'

Sir John Belfield declared, that, though he had not that natural antipathy to a wit which some men have, yet, unless the wildness of a wit was tamed like the wildness of other animals, by domestic habits, he himself would not choose to venture on one. He added, that he should pay a bad compliment to Lady Belfield, who had so much higher claims to his esteem, if he were to allege that these habits were the determining cause of his choice, yet had he seen no such tendencies in her character, he should have suspected her power of making him as happy as she had done.

'I confess with shame,' said Mr. Carlton, 'that one of the first things which touched me with any sense of my wife's merit, was the admirable good sense she discovered in the direction of my family. Even at the time that I had most reason to blush at my own conduct, she never gave me cause to blush for hers. The praises constantly bestowed on her elegant yet prudent arrangements, by my friends, flattered my vanity, and raised her in my opinion, though they did not lead me to do her full justice.'

The two ladies who were thus agreeably flattered, looked modestly grateful. Mr. Stanley said, 'I was going to endeavour at removing Miss Sparkes's prejudices, by observing how much this domestic turn brings the understanding into action. The operation of good sense is requisite in making the necessary calculations for a great family, in a hundred ways. Good sense is required to teach that a perpetually recurring small expense is more to be avoided, than an incidental great one ; while it shows that petty savings cannot retrieve an injured estate. The story told by Johnson of a lady, who, while ruining her fortune by excessive splendour and expense, yet refused to let a two-shilling mango be cut at her table, exemplifies exactly my idea. Shabby curtailments, without repairing the breach which prodigality has made, discredit the husband, and bring the reproach of meanness on the wife. Retrenchments, to be efficient, must be applied to great objects. The true economist will draw in by contracting the outline, by narrowing the bottom, by cutting off with an unsparing hand costly superfluities, which affect not comfort but cherish vanity.'

' " Retrench the lazy vermin of thine hall," was the wise counsel of the prudent Venetian, to his thoughtless son-in-law,' said Sir John, ' and its wisdom consisted in its striking at one of the most ruinous and prevailing domestic evils, an overloaded establishment.'

If Miss Sparkes had been so long without speaking, it was evident by her manner and turn of countenance, that contempt had kept her silent, and that she thought the topic under discussion as unworthy of the support of the gentlemen as of her own opposition.

' A discreet woman,' said Mr. Stanley, ' adjusts her expenses to her revenues. Everything knows its time, and every person his place. She will live within her income, be it large or small : if large, she will not be luxurious ; if small, she will not be mean. Proportion and propriety are among the best secrets of domestic wisdom ; and there is no surer test both of integrity and judgment than a well-proportioned expenditure.

' Now the point to which I would bring all this verbiage,' continued he, ' is this,—will a lady of a mean understanding, or a vulgar education, be likely to practise economy on this large scale ? And is not such economy a field in which a woman of the best sense may honourably exercise her powers ?'

Miss Sparkes, who was always a staunch opposer in moral as well as in political debate, because she said it was the best side for the exertion of wit and talents, comforted herself, that though she felt she was completely in the minority, yet she always thought that was rather a proof of being right than the contrary ; for if it be true, that the generality are either weak or wicked, it follows that the inferior number is most likely to be neither.

' Women,' said Mr. Carlton, ' in their course of action describe a smaller circle than men ; but the perfection of a circle consists not in its dimensions, but in its correctness. There may be,' added he, carefully turning away his eyes from Miss Sparkes, ' here and there a soaring female, who looks down with disdain on the paltry affairs of " this dim speck called earth," who despises order and regularity as indications of a grovelling spirit ; but a sound mind judges directly contrary. The larger the capacity, the wider is the sweep of duties it takes in. A sensible woman loves to imitate that order which is stamped on the whole creation of God. All the operations of nature are uniform even in their changes, and regular in their infinite variety. Nay, the great Author of nature himself disdains not to be called the God of order.'

' I agree with you,' said Sir John. ' A philosophical lady may " read Malebranche, Boyle, and Locke :" she may boast of her intellectual superiority ; she may talk of abstract and concrete ; of substantial forms and essences ; complex ideas and mixed modes ; of identity and relation ; she may decorate all the logic of one sex with all the rhetoric of the other ; yet if her affairs are *delabrés*, if her house is disorderly, her servants irregular, her children neglected, and her table ill-arranged, she will indicate the want of the most valuable faculty of the human mind, a sound judgment.'

'It must, however, be confessed,' replied Mr. Stanley, 'that such instances are so rare, that the exceptions barely serve to establish the rule. I have known twenty women mismanage their affairs, through a bad education, through ignorance, especially of arithmetic, that grand deficiency in the education of women, through a multiplicity of vain accomplishments, through an excess of dissipation, through a devotedness to personal embellishments, through an absorption of the whole soul in music—for one who has made her husband metaphysically miserable.'

'What marks the distinction,' said Mr. Carlton, 'between the judicious and the vulgar economist is this : the narrow-minded woman succeeds tolerably in the filling up, but never in the outline. She is made up of detail, but destitute of plan. Petty duties demand her whole grasp of mind, and after all the thing is incomplete. There is so much bustle and evident exertion in all she does ! she brings into company a mind so exhausted with her little efforts ! so overflowing with a sense of her own merits ! looking up to her own performances as the highest possible elevation of the human intellect, and looking down on the attainments of more highly gifted women, as so many obstructions to their usefulness ; always drawing comparisons to her own advantage, with the cultivated and the refined, and concluding that because she possesses not their elegance, they must necessarily be deficient in her art : while economists of a higher strain (I draw from living and not absent instances,' added he, looking benignantly round him) 'execute their well-ordered plan as an indispensable duty, but not as a superlative merit. They have too much sense to omit it, but they have too much taste to talk of it. It is their business, not their boast. The effect is produced, but the hand which accomplishes it is not seen. The mechanism is set at work, but it is behind the scenes. The beauty is visible, the labour is kept out of sight.'

'The misfortune is,' said Mr. Stanley, 'that people are apt to fancy, that judgment is a faculty only to be exercised on great occasions ; whereas it is one that every hour is calling into exercise. There are certain habits, which though they appear inconsiderable when examined individually, are yet of no small importance in the aggregate. Exactness, punctuality, and the other minor virtues, contribute, more than many are aware, to promote and to facilitate the exercise of the higher qualities. I would not erect them into a magnitude beyond their real size—as persons are too apt to do who are *only* punctual, and are deficient in the higher qualities—but, by the regular establishment of these habits in a family, it is inconceivable to those who have not made the experiment, how it saves, how it amplifies time, that canvas upon which all the virtues must be wrought. It is incredible how an orderly division of the day gives apparent rapidity to the wings of time, while a stated devotion of the hour to its employment really lengthens life. It lengthens it by the traces which solid occupation leaves behind it : while it prevents tediousness by affording, with the successive change, the charm of novelty, and keeping up an interest which would flag, if any one employment were too long pursued. Now, all these arrangements of life, these divisions of time, and these selections and appropria-

tions of the business to the hour, come within the department of the
lady. And how much will the cares of a man of sense be relieved, if
he choose a wife who can do all this for him !'

'In how many of my friends' houses,' said Mr. Carlton, 'have I observed the contrary habits produce contrary effects ! A young lady
bred in total ignorance of family management, transplanted from the
house of her father, where she has learnt nothing, to that of her husband,
where she is expected to know everything, disappoints a prudent man :
his affection may continue, but his esteem will be diminished ; and
with his happiness, his attachment to home will be proportionably
lessened.'

'It is perfectly just,' said Sir John, 'and this comfortless deficiency
has naturally taught men to inveigh against that higher kind of knowledge which they suppose, though unjustly, to be the cause of ignorance
in domestic matters. It is not entirely to gratify the animal, as Miss
Sparkes supposes, that a gentleman likes to have his table well appointed ; but because his own dignity and his wife's credit are involved
in it. The want of this skill is one of the grand evils of modern life.
*From the heiress of the man of rank, to the daughter of the opulent
tradesman, there is no one quality in which young women are so generally deficient as in domestic economy.* And when I hear learning contended for on one hand, and modish accomplishments on the other, I
always contend for this intermediate, this valuable, this neglected
quality, so little insisted on, so rarely found, and so indispensably
necessary.'

'Besides,' said Mr. Carlton, addressing himself to Miss Sparkes,
'you ladies are apt to consider versatility as a mark of genius. She,
therefore, who can do a great thing well, ought to do a small one
better ; for, as Lord Bacon well observes, "He who cannot contract his
mind as well as dilate it, wants one great talent in life."'

Miss Sparkes, condescending at length to break a silence which she
had maintained with evident uneasiness, said, 'All these plodding employments cramp the genius, degrade the intellect, depress the spirits,
debase the taste, and clip the wings of imagination. And this poor,
cramped, degraded, stinted, depressed, debased creature is the very
being whom men, men of reputed sense too, commonly prefer to the
mind of large dimensions, soaring fancy, and aspiring tastes.'

'Imagination,' replied Mr. Stanley, 'well directed, is the charm of
life ; it gilds every object, and embellishes every scene : but allow me
to say, that where a woman abandons herself to the dominion of this
vagrant faculty, it may lead to something worse than a disorderly table ;
and the husband may find that the badness of his dinner is not the only
ill-consequence of her super-lunary vagaries.'

'True enough,' said Mr. Flam, who had never been known to be so
silent, or so attentive ; 'true enough, I have not heard so much sense
for a long time. I am sure 'tis sense, because 'tis exactly my own way
of thinking. There is my Bell, now. I have spent seven hundred
pounds, and more money, for her to learn music and whim-whams,
which all put together are not worth sixpence. I would give them all
up to see her make such a tansy-pudding as that which the widow in

the *Spectator* helped Sir Roger to at dinner : why, I don't believe Bell knows whether pie-crust is made with butter or cheese ; or whether a venison pasty should be baked or boiled. I can tell her, that when her husband, if she ever gets one, comes in sharp-set from hunting, he won't like to be put off with a tune instead of a dinner. To marry a singing girl, and complain she does not keep you a good table, is like eating nightingales, and finding fault that they are not good tasted. They sing, but they are of no further use ;—to *eat* them, instead of listening to them, is applying to one sense the gratification which belongs to another.'

In the course of conversation, Miss Sparkes a little shocked the delicate feelings of the ladies, of Lucilla especially, by throwing out some expressions of envy at the superior advantages which men possess for distinguishing themselves. ' Women,' she said, ' with talents not inferior, were allowed no stage for display, while men had such a reach for their exertions, such a compass for exercising their genius, such a range for obtaining distinction, that they were at once the objects of her envy for the means they possessed, and of her pity for turning them to no better account. There were indeed,' she added, ' a few men who redeemed the credit of the rest, and for their sakes she gloried, since she could not be of their sex, that she was at least of their species.'

'I know, madam,' said Mr. Stanley, ' your admiration of heroic qualities and manly virtues—courage for instance. But there are still nobler ways of exercising courage than even in the field of battle. There are more exalted means of showing spirit than by sending or accepting a challenge. To sustain a fit of sickness, may exhibit as true heroism as to lead an army. To bear a deep affliction well, calls for as high exertion of soul as to storm a town ; and to meet death with Christian resolution is an act of courage, in which many a woman has triumphed, and many a philosopher, and even some generals, have failed.'

I thought I saw in Miss Sparkes's countenance a kind of civil contempt, as if she would be glad to exchange the patient sickness and heroic death-bed for the renown of victory and the glory of a battle : and I suspected that she envied the fame of the challenge, and the spirit of the duel, more than those meek and passive virtues which we all agreed were peculiarly Christian, and peculiarly feminine.

Chapter XXXVII.

N the afternoon, when the company were assembled in the drawing-room, the conversation turned on various subjects. Mr. Flam, feeling as if he had not sufficiently produced himself at dinner, now took the lead. He was never solicitous to show what he called his learning, but when Miss Sparkes was present, whom it was his grand delight to *set down*, as he called it, then he never failed to give broad hints that if he was now no great student, it was

not from ignorance, but from the pressure of more indispensable avoca-
tions.

He first rambled into some desultory remarks on the absurdity of the
world, and the preposterousness of modern usages, which perverted the
ends of education, and exalted things which were of least use into most
importance.

'You seem out of humour with the world, Mr. Flam,' said Mr.
Stanley. 'I hate the world,' returned he. 'It is indeed,' replied Mr.
Stanley, 'a scene of much danger, because of much evil.'

'I don't value the danger a straw,' rejoined Mr. Flam; 'and as to
he evil, I hope I have sense enough to avoid that : but I hate it for its
folly, and despise it for its inconsistency.'

'In what particulars, Mr. Flam !' said Sir John Belfield.

'In everything,' replied he. 'In the first place, don't people educate
their daughters entirely for holidays, and then wonder that they are of
no use? Don't they charge them to be modest, and then teach them
everything that can make them bold ? Are we not angry that they don't
attend to great concerns, after having instructed them to take the most
pains for the least things ! There is my Fan, now—they tell me she
can dance as well as a posture mistress, but she slouches in her walk
like a milkmaid. Now, as she seldom dances, and is always walking,
would it not be more rational to teach her to do that best which she is
to do oftenest ? She sings like a syren, but 'tis only to strangers. I,
who paid for it, never hear her voice. She is always warbling in a
distant room, or in every room where there is company ; but if I have
the gout and want to be amused, she is as dumb as a dormouse.'

'So much for the errors in educating our daughters,' said Sir John :
'now for the sons.'

'As to our boys,' returned Mr. Flam, 'don't we educate them in one
religion, and then expect them to practise another ? Don't we cram
them with books of heathen philosophy, and then bid them go and be
good Christians ? Don't we teach them to admire the heroes and gods
of the old poets, when there is hardly one hero, and certainly not one
god, who would not in this country have been tried at the Old Bailey,
if not executed at Tyburn ? And as to the goddesses, if they had been
brought before us on the bench, brother Stanley, there is scarcely one
of them but we should have ordered to the house of correction. The
queen of them, indeed, I should have sent to the ducking-stool for a
scold.

'Then again, don't we tell our sons when men that they must admire
a monarchical government, after every pains have been taken when
they were boys to fill them with raptures for the ancient re-
publics ?'

'Surely, Mr. Flam,' said Sir John, 'the ancient forms of government
may be studied with advantage. were it only to show us by contrast
the superior excellence of our own.'

'We might,' said Miss Sparkes in a supercilious accent, 'learn some
things from them which we much want. You have been speaking of
economy. These Republicans, whom Mr. Flam is pleased to treat
with so much contempt, he must allow, had some good, clever contri-

vances to keep down the taxes, which it would do us no harm to imitate. Victories are much better bargains to them than they are to us. A few laurel leaves or a sprig of oak was not quite so dear as a pension.'

'But you will allow, madam,' said Sir John, smiling, 'that a triumph was a more expensive reward than a title?'

Before she had time to answer, Mr. Flam said : 'Let me tell you, Miss Sparkes, that as to triumphs, our heroes are so used to them at sea, that they would laugh at them at home. Those who obtain triumphs as often as they meet their enemies, would despise such holiday play among their friends. We don't, to be sure, reward them as your ancients did. We don't banish them, nor put them to death for saving their country, like your Athenians. We don't pay them with a trumpery wreath, like your Romans. We English don't put our conquerofs off with leaves ; we give them fruits, as cheerfully bestowed as they are fairly earned. God bless them ! I would reduce my table to one dish, my hall to one servant, my stable to one saddle-horse, and my kennel to one pointer, rather than abridge the preservers of Old England of a feather.'

'Signal exploits, if nationally beneficial,' said Sir John, ' deserve substantial remuneration ; and I am inclined to think that public honours are valuable not only as rewards but incitements. They are as politic as they are just. When Miltiades and his illustrious ten thousand gained their immortal victory, would not a Blenheim erected on the plains of Marathon have stimulated unborn soldiers more than the little transitory columns which barely recorded the names of the victors?'

'What warrior,' said Mr. Carlton, 'will hereafter visit the future Palace of Trafalgar without reverence? A reverence, the purity of which will be in no degree impaired by contemplating such an additional motive to emulation.'

In answer to some further observations of Miss Sparkes, on the superiority of the ancient to British patriotism, Mr. Flam, whose indignation now provoked him to display his whole stock of erudition, eagerly exclaimed—'Do you call that patriotism in your favourite Athenians, to be so fond of raree-shows, as not only to devote the money of the state to the play-house, but to make it capital to divert a little of it to the wants of the gallant soldiers who were fighting their battles? I hate to hear fellows called patriots, who preferred their diversions to their country.'

Then, erecting himself, as if he felt the taller for being an Englishman, he added—'What, Madam Sparkes, would your Greeks have said to a Patriotic Fund, by private contribution, of nearly half a million, in the midst of heavy taxes and a tedious war, voluntarily raised and cheerfully given to the orphans, widows, and mothers of their brave countrymen who fell in their defence? Were the poor soldiers who fought under your Cimons, and your———, I forget their names, ever so kindly remembered? Make it out that they were—show such a spirit among your ancients—and I'll turn Republican to-morrow.'

Miss Sparkes having again said something which he thought tended to exalt the ancient states at the expense of our own country, Mr. Flam indignantly replied — 'Tell me, madam, did your Athens, or your Sparta, or your Rome, ever take in seven thousand starving priests, driven from a country with which they were at war ; a country they had reason to hate, of a religion they detested ? Did they ever receive them, I say, maintain them like gentlemen, and caress them like friends ? If you can bring me one such instance, I will give up Old England, and turn Greek, or Roman, or —— anything but Frenchman.'

'I should be inclined,' said Mr. Stanley, 'to set down that noble deed to the account of our national religion, as well as of our national generosity.'

Miss Sparkes said, 'In one respect, however, Mr. Flam imitates the French whom he is abusing. He is very apt to triumph where he has gained no victory. If you hear his account of a defeat, you would take it, like theirs, for a conquest.' She added, however, that there were illustrious men in other countries besides our own, as their successes testified. For her part, she was a citizen of the world, and honoured heroes wherever they were found, in Macedon, in Sweden, or even in France.

'True enough,' rejoined Mr. Flam, 'the rulers of other countries have gone about and delivered kingdoms as we are doing ; but there is this difference—they free them from mild masters, to make them their own slaves ; we neither get them for ourselves or our minions, our brothers or cousins, our Jeromes or Josephs. *We* raise the weak, *they* pull down the prosperous. If *we* redeem kingdoms, 'tis to bestow them on their own lawful kings. If we help this nation, 'tis to recall one sovereign from banishment ; if we assist that, 'tis to deliver another from captivity.'

'What a scene for Spain,' said Sir John, 'to behold in us their own national Quixotism soberly exemplified and rationally realized ! the generous theory of their romantic knight-errant brought into actual practice ; the fervour without the absurdity ; the sound principle of justice without the extravagance of fancy ! Wrongs redressed and rights restored, and upon the grandest scale ! Deliverance wrought, not for imaginary princesses, but for deposed and imprisoned monarchs ! Injuries avenged—not the ideal injuries of ridiculous individuals, but the substantial wrongs of plundered empires !'

Sir John, who was amused with the oddities of Mr. Flam, was desirous of still provoking him to talk : much effort indeed was not required, to induce him to do what he was fond of doing, whenever there was an opportunity of contradicting Miss Sparkes.

'But, Mr. Flam,' said Sir John, 'you were interrupted as you began to enumerate the inconsistencies which you said had put you out of love with the world.'

'Why, it makes me mad,' replied he, 'to hear men who make the loudest outcry about the dangers of the state, cramming their houses with French governesses, French cooks, and French valets ; is not this adding flame to the fire ? Then I have no patience to see people who pretend great zeal for the church, delighted that an Italian singer should have a larger revenue than the highest of our own bishops. Such patriots might have done well enough for Athenians,' added he, looking insultingly at Miss Sparkes, ' but they make miserable Englishmen. Then I hate to see fellows who pay least taxes, complaining most of the burden—those who most lament the hardness of the times, spending money in needless extravagance, and luxury increasing in exact proportion as means diminish.

' Then I am sick of the conceit of the boys and girls. Do but observe how much their vanity imposes on their understanding, and how names disguise things. My son would start if I were to desire him to go to London in the *stage coach*, but he *puts himself into the mail* with great coolness. If I were to talk to Fan about living in a *small house*, she would not give me the hearing, whereas she is quite wild to live in a *cottage.*'

' I do not quite agree with you, Mr. Flam,' said Sir John, smiling, ' as to the inconsistency of the world ; I rather lament its dull uniformity. If we may rely upon those living chronicles, the newspapers, all is one faultless scene of monotonous perfection. Were it otherwise, I presume those frugal philologers would not keep a set of phrases ready cut and dried, in order to apply them universally in all cases. For instance, is not every public place, from St. James's to Otaheite, or the Cape, invariably " crowded with beauty and fashion?" Is not every public sermon pronounced to be " excellent ?" Is not every civic speech, every provincial harangue, " neat and appropriate ?" And is not every military corps, from the veteran regiment of regulars, to the volunteer company of a month's standing, always declared to be " in the highest state of discipline ?"'

Before the company went away, I observed that Mrs. Carlton gave Lucilla a significant glance, and both withdrew together. In spite of my thorough belief of the injustice and absurdity of my suspicion, a pang darted through my heart, at the bare possibility that Lord Staunton might be the subject of this secret conference. I was perfectly assured that Miss Stanley would never accept him while he retained his present character, but that character might be improved. She had rejected him for his principles ; if these principles were changed, there was no other reasonable ground of objection. He might be reformed. Dare I own, even to myself, that I dreaded to hear of his reformation ? I hated myself for the thought. I will, said I faintly, endeavour to rejoice if it be so. I felt a conflict in my mind between my principles and my passion, that distressed me not a little. My integrity had never before been so assailed.

At length they returned. I earnestly examined their countenances. Both looked cheerful, and even animated ; yet it was evident from the redness of their eyes that both had been weeping. The company immediately took their leave ; all our party, as it was a fine evening, attended them out to their carriages, except Miss Stanley : she only pressed the hand of Mrs. Carlton, smiled, and, looking as if she durst not trust herself to talk to her, withdrew to the bow-window from whence she could see them depart. I remained in the room.

As she was wiping her eyes to take away the redness, which was a sure way to increase it, I ventured to join her, and inquired, with an interest I could not conceal, what had happened to distress her. 'These are not tears of distress,' said she, sweetly smiling. 'I am quite ashamed that I have so little self-control ; but Mrs. Carlton has given me so much pleasure ! I have caught the infection of her joy, though my foolish sympathy looks more like sorrow.' Surely, said I, indignantly, to myself, she will not own Staunton's love to my face !

All frank and open as Miss Stanley was, I was afraid to press her. I had not courage to ask what I longed to know. Though Lord Staunton's renewed addresses might not give them so much pleasure, yet his reformation I knew would. I now looked so earnestly inquisitive at Lucilla, that she said, ' Oh, he is all we could wish. He is a thoroughly converted man !' Indignation and astonishment made me speechless. Is this the modest Lucilla, said I to myself? It is all over. She loves him to distraction. As I attempted not to speak, she at length said, ' My poor friend is at last quite happy. I know you will rejoice with us. Mr. Carlton has for some time regularly read the Bible with her. He condescends to hear, and to invite her remarks, telling her, that if he is the better classic, she is the better Christian, and that their assistance in the things which each understands must be reciprocal. If he is her teacher in human literature, he says, she must be his in that which is divine. He has been very earnest to get his mind imbued with scriptural knowledge.' How inexpressible was now my joy ! As I was still silent she went on. ' But this is not all :

' Last Saturday he said to her, " Henrietta, I have but one complaint to make of you ; and it is for a fault which I always thought would be the last I should ever have to charge you with. It is selfishness." Mrs. Carlton was a little shocked, though the tenderness of his manner mitigated her alarm. " Henrietta," resumed he, " you intend to go to heaven without your husband. I know you always retire to your dressing-room, not only for your private devotions, but to read prayers to your maids. What have your men-servants done, what has your husband done, that they should be excluded ? Is it not a little selfish, my Henrietta," added he, smiling, " to confine your zeal to the eternal happiness of your own sex ? Will you allow me and our men-servants to join you ? To-morrow is Sunday ; we will then, if you please, begin in the hall. You shall prepare what you would have read : and I will be your chaplain. A most unworthy one, Henrietta, I confess ; but you will not only have a chaplain of your own making, but a Christian also. Yes, my angelic wife, I am a Christian upon the truest, deepest conviction."

' " Never, my dear Lucilla," continued Mrs. Carlton, " did I know what true happiness was till that moment. My husband, with all his faults, had always been remarkably sincere. Indeed, his aversion from hypocrisy had made him keep back his right feelings and sentiments, till he was assured they were well established in his mind. He has for some time been regular at church, a thing, he said, too much taken up as a customary form to be remarkable, and which therefore involved not much ; but family prayer, adopted from conviction of its being a duty, rather pledged a man to consistent religion. Never, I hope, shall I forget the joy I felt, nor my gratitude to that Being 'from whom all holy desires proceed,' when, with all his family kneeling solemnly around him, I heard my once unhappy husband with a sober fervour begin :

' " ' To the Lord our God belong mercies and forgivenesses, though we have rebelled against him, neither have we obeyed the voice of the Lord our God, to walk in his laws which he set before us.'

' " He evidently struggled with his own feelings ; but his manly mind carried him through it with an admirable mixture of dignity and feeling. He was so serenely cheerful the rest of the evening, that I felt he had obtained a great victory over himself, and his heart was at peace within him. Prayer with him was not a beginning form, but a consummation of his better purposes." '

The sweet girl could not forbear weeping again, while she was giving me this interesting account. I felt as if I had never loved her till then. To see her so full of sensibility, without the slightest tincture of romance, so feeling, yet so sober-minded, enchanted me. I could now afford to wish heartily for Lord Staunton's reformation, because it was not likely to interfere with my hopes. And now the danger was over, I even endeavoured to make myself believe that I *should* have wished it in any event ; so treacherous will the human heart be found by those who watch its motions. And it proceeds from not watching them, that the generality are so little acquainted with the evils which lurk within it.

Before I had time to express half what I felt to the fair narrator, the party came in. They seemed as much puzzled at the position in which they found Lucilla and myself, she wiping her eyes, and I standing by in admiration, as I had been at her mysterious interview with Mrs. Carlton. The Belfields knew not what to make of it. The mother's looks expressed astonishment and anxiety. The father's eye demanded an explanation. All this mute eloquence passed in an instant. Miss Stanley gave them not time to inquire. She flew to her mother, and eagerly repeated the little tale, which furnished matter for grateful joy and improving conversation the rest of the evening.

Mr. Stanley expressed a thorough confidence in the sincerity of Carlton. ' He had always,' continued he, ' in his worst days, an abhorrence of deceit, and such a dread of people appearing better than they are, that he even commended that most absurd practice of Dean Swift, who, you know, used to perform family prayer in a garret, for fear any one should call in and detect him in the performance.' Carlton defended this as an honourable instance of Swift's abhorrence of ostentation in his religion. I opposed it on the more probable ground of his being ashamed of it. For allowing, what, however, never can be allowed, that an ordinary man might have some excuse for the dread of being sneered at, as wanting to be thought righteous overmuch ; yet in a churchman, in a dignified churchman, family prayer would be expected as a customary decency, an indispensable appendage to his situation ; which, though it might be practised without piety, could not be omitted without disgrace, and which even a sensible infidel, considering it merely as a professional act, could not say was a custom

More honoured in the breach than the observance,

Chapter XXXVIII.

NE evening, which Mr. Tyrrel happened to spend with us, after Mr. Stanley had performed the family devotions, Mr. Tyrrel said to him, 'Stanley, I don't much like the prayer you read. It seems, by the great stress it lays on holiness, to imply that a man has something in his own power. You did indeed mention the necessity of faith, and the power of grace ; but there was too much about making the life holy, as if that were all in all. You seem to be putting us so much upon working and doing, that you leave nothing to do for the Saviour.'

'I wish,' replied Mr. Stanley, 'as I am no deep theologian, that you had started this objection before Dr. Barlow went away, for I know no man more able or more willing for serious discussion.'

' No,' replied Tyrrel, 'I see clearly by some things which he dropped in conversation, as well as by the whole tenor of his sermons, that Barlow and I should never agree. He means well, but knows little. He sees something, but feels nothing. More argument than unction. Too much reasoning, and too little religion ; a little light, and no heat. He seems to me so to " overload the ship with duties," that it will sink by the very means he takes to keep it afloat. I thank God my own eyes are opened, and I at last feel comfortable in my mind.'

' Religious comfort,' said Mr. Stanley, 'is a high attainment. Only it is incumbent on every Christian to be assured that if he is happy it is on safe grounds.'

' I have taken care of that,' replied Mr. Tyrrel. ' For some years after I had quitted my loose habits, I attended occasionally at church, but found no comfort in it, because I perceived so much was to be *done*, and so much was to be *sacrificed*. But the great doctrines of faith, as opened to me by Mr. H—n, have at last given me peace and liberty, and I rest myself without solicitude on the mercy so freely offered in the Gospel. No mistakes or sins of mine can ever make me forfeit the Divine favour.'

' Let us hear, however,' replied Mr. Stanley, ' what the Bible says ; for as that is the only rule by which we shall be judged hereafter, it may be prudent to be guided by it here. God says by the prophet, " I will put my Spirit within you :" but he does this for some purpose ; for he says, in the very next words, " I will cause you to *walk* in my statutes." And for fear this should not plainly enough inculcate holiness, he goes on to say, " And ye shall *keep* my judgments, and *do* them." Show me, if you can, a single promise made to an impenitent, unholy man.'

Tyrrel. 'Why, is not the mercy of God promised to the wicked in every part of the Bible ?'

Stanley. 'It is. But that is, "if he forsake his way."'

Tyrrel. 'This fondness for works is, in my opinion, nothing else but setting aside the free grace of God.'

Stanley. 'Quite the contrary : so far from setting it aside, it is the way to glorify it, for it is by that grace alone that we are enabled to perform right actions. For myself, I always find it difficult to answer persons, who, in flying to one extreme, think they cannot too much degrade the opposite. If we give faith its due prominence, the mere moralist reprobates our principles, as if we were depreciating works. If we magnify the beauty of holiness, the advocate for exclusive faith accuses us of being its enemy.'

Tyrrel. 'For my own part, I am persuaded that unqualified trust is the only ground of safety.'

Stanley. 'He who cannot lie has indeed told us so. But trust in God is humble dependence, not presumptuous security. The Bible does not say, trust in the Lord and sin on, but, "Trust in the Lord, and be doing good." We are elsewhere told that, "God works in us to will and to do." There is no getting over that little word *to do.* I suppose you allow the necessity of prayer?'

Tyrrel. 'Certainly I do.'

Stanley. 'But there are conditions to our prayers also, "If I regard iniquity in my heart, the Lord will not hear me."'

Tyrrel. 'The Scriptures affirm that we must live on the promises.'

Stanley. 'They are indeed the very aliment of the Christian life. But what are the promises?'

Tyrrel. 'Free pardon and eternal life to them that are in Christ Jesus.'

Stanley. 'True. But who are they that *are* in Christ Jesus? The apostle tells us, "They who walk not after the flesh, but after the spirit." Besides, is not holiness promised as well as pardon? "A new heart will I give you, and a new spirit will I put within you."'

Tyrrel. 'Surely, Stanley, you abuse the grace of the Gospel, by pretending that man is saved by his own righteousness.'

Stanley. 'No, no, my dear Tyrrel, it is you who abuse it, by making God's mercy set aside man's duty. Allow me to observe, that he who exalts the grace of God with a view to indulge himself in any sin, is deceiving no one but himself; and he who trusts in Christ, with a view to spare himself the necessity of watchfulness, humility, and self-denial, that man depends upon Christ for more than he has promised.'

Tyrrel. 'Well, Mr. Stanley, it appears to me that you want to patch up a convenient accommodating religion, as if Christ were to do a little, and we were to do the rest : a sort of partnership salvation, and in which man has the larger share.'

Stanley. 'This, I fear, is indeed the dangerous creed of many worldly Christians. No ; God may be said to do all, because He gives power for all, strength for all, grace for all. But this grace is a principle, a vital energy, a life-giving spirit to quicken us, to make us abound in holiness. He does not make His grace abound, that we may securely live in sin, but that we may subdue it, renounce it, live above it.'

Tyrrel. 'When our Saviour was upon earth, there was no one quality He so uniformly commended in those who came to be healed by Him, as faith.'

13—2

Stanley. ' It is most true. But we do not meet in any of them with such a presumptuous faith, as led them to rush into diseases on purpose to show their confidence in His power of healing them, neither are we to "continue in sin, that grace may abound." You cannot but observe, that the faith of the persons you mention, was always accompanied with an earnest desire to get rid of their diseases. And it is worth remarking, that to the words, "Thy faith has made thee whole," is added, " *Sin no more*," lest a worse thing come unto thee.'

Tyrrel. You cannot persuade me that any neglect, or even sin of mine, can make void the covenant of God.'

Stanley. ' Nothing can set aside the covenant of God, which is sure and steadfast. But as for him who lives in the allowed practice of any sin, it is clear that he has no part nor lot in the matter. It is clear that he is not one of those whom God has taken into the covenant. That God will keep His word is most certain, but such a one does not appear to be the person to whom that word is addressed. God as much designed that you should apply the faculties, the power, and the will He has given you, to a life of holiness, as he meant, when He gave you legs, hands, and eyes, that you should walk, work, and see. His grace is not intended to exclude the use of His gifts, but to perfect, exalt, and ennoble them.'

Tyrrel. ' I can produce a multitude of texts to prove that Christ has done everything, and of course has left nothing for me to do, but to believe on him.'

Stanley. ' Let us take the general tenor and spirit of Scripture, and neither pack single texts together, detached from the connection in which they stand ; nor be so unreasonable as to squeeze all the doctrines of Christianity out of every single text, which perhaps was only meant to inculcate one individual principle. How consistently are the great leading doctrines of faith and holiness balanced and reconciled in every part of the Bible ! If ever I have been in danger of resting on a mere dead faith, by one of those texts on which you exclusively build, in the very next sentence, perhaps, I am roused to active virtue, by some lively example, or absolute command. If again I am ever in danger, as you say, of sinking the ship with my proud duties, the next passage calls me to order, by some powerful injunction to renounce all confidence in my miserably-defective virtues, and to put my whole trust in Christ. By thus assimilating the Creed with the Commandments, the Bible becomes its own interpreter, and perfect harmony is the result. Allow me also to remark, that this invariable rule of exhibiting the doctrines of Scripture in their due proportion, order and relative connection, is one of the leading excellencies in the service of our Church. While no doctrine is neglected or undervalued, none is disproportionately magnified at the expense of the others. There is neither omission, undue prominence, nor exaggeration. There is complete symmetry and correct proportion.'

Tyrrel. ' I assert that we are freed by the Gospel from the condemnation of the law.'

Stanley. ' But where do you find that we are free from the obligation of obeying it ? For my own part, I do not combine the doctrine of

grace, to which I most cordially assent, with any doctrine which practically denies the voluntary agency of man. Nor, in my adoption of
the belief of that voluntary agency, do I, in the remotest degree, presume to abridge the sovereignty of God. I adopt none of the metaphysical subtilties, none of the abstruse niceties, of any party, nor do I
imitate either in the reprobation of the other, firmly believing that
heaven is peopled with the humble and the conscientious out of every
class of real Christians.'

Tyrrel. 'Still I insist that if Christ has delivered me from sin, sin
can do me no harm.'

Stanley. 'My dear Mr. Tyrrel, if the king of your country were a
mighty general, and had delivered the land from some powerful enemy,
would it show your sense of the obligation, or your allegiance as a
subject, if you were to join the enemy he had defeated? By so doing,
though the country might be saved, you would ruin yourself. Let us
not then live in confederacy with sin, the power of which, indeed, our
Redeemer has broken, but both the power and guilt of which the individual is still at liberty to incur.'

Tyrrel. 'Stanley, I remember when you thought the Gospel was all
in all.'

Stanley. 'I think so still : but I am now as I was then, for a sober
consistent Gospel, a Christianity which must evidence itself by its
fruits. The first words of the Apostle after his conversion were, "Lord,
what wilt Thou have me to do?" When he says, "so run that ye may
obtain," he could never mean that we could obtain by sitting still ; nor
would he have talked of "labouring *in vain*," if he meant that we should
not labour at all. We dare not persist in anything that is wrong, or
neglect anything that is right, from an erroneous notion that we have
such an interest in Christ as will excuse us from doing the one or persisting in the other.'

Tyrrel. 'I fancy you think that a man's salvation depends on the
number of good actions he can muster together.'

Stanley. 'No, it is the very spirit of Christianity not to build on this
or that actual work, but sedulously to strive for that temper, and those
dispositions, which are the seminal principle of all virtues ; and where
the heart struggles and prays for the attainment of this state, though
the man should be placed in such circumstances as to be able to do
little to promote the welfare of mankind, or the glory of God, in the
eyes of the world ; this very habitual aim and bent of the mind, with
humble sorrow at its low attainments, is, in my opinion, no slight degree
of obedience.'

Tyrrel. 'But you will allow that the Scriptures affirm that Christ
is not only a sacrifice, but a refuge, a consolation, a rest.'

Stanley. 'Blessed be God, He is indeed all these. But He is a
consolation only to the heavy-laden, a refuge to those alone who forsake
sin. The rest He promises is not a rest from labour, but from evil.
It is a rest from the drudgery of the world, but not from the service of
God. It is not inactivity, but quietness of spirit ; not sloth, but peace.
He draws men indeed from slavery to freedom, but not a freedom to do
evil, or to do nothing. He makes His service easy, but not by lower-

ing the rule of duty, nor by adapting His commands to the corrupt inclinations of our nature. He communicates His grace, gives fresh and higher motives to obedience, and imparts peace and comfort, not by any abatement in His demands, but by this infusion of His own grace, and this communication of His own Spirit.'

Tyrrel. 'You are a strange fellow. According to you, we can neither be saved by good works, nor without them.'

Stanley. 'Come, Mr. Tyrrel, you are nearer the truth than you intended. We cannot be saved by the merit of our good works, without setting at nought the merits and death of Christ ; and we cannot be saved without them, unless we set at nought God's holiness, and make Him a favourer of sin. Now, to this the doctrine of the atonement, properly understood, is most completely hostile. That this doctrine *favours* sin, is one of the false charges which worldly men bring against vital Christianity, because they do not understand the principle, nor inquire into the grounds, on which it is adopted.'

Tyrrel. ' Still, I think you limit the grace of God, as if people must be very good first, in order to deserve it, and then He will come and add His grace to their goodness. Whereas grace has been most conspicuous in the most notorious sinners.'

Stanley. ' I allow that the grace of God has never manifested itself more gloriously than in the conversion of notorious sinners. But it is worth remarking, that all such, with St. Paul at their head, have ever after been eminently more afraid than other men of falling again into sin ; they have prayed with the greatest earnestness to be delivered from the power of it, and have continued to lament most deeply the remaining corruption of their hearts.'

In the course of the conversation Mr. Tyrrel said, 'he should be inclined to entertain doubts of that man's state who could not give an accurate account of the time and the manner in which he was first awakened, and who had had no sensible manifestations of the Divine favour.'

' I believe,' replied Mr. Stanley, 'that my notions of the evidence of being in the favour of God differ materially from yours. If a man feel in himself a hatred of all sin, without sparing his favourite corruption ; if he rest for salvation on the promise of the Gospel alone ; if he maintain in his mind such a sense of the nearness and immeasurable importance of eternal things, as shall enable him to use temporal things with moderation, and anticipate their end without dismay ; if he delight in the worship of God, is zealous for his service, making *his* glory the end and aim of all his actions ; if he labour to fulfil his allotted duties conscientiously ; if he love his fellow-creatures as the children of the same common Father, and partakers of the same common hope ; if he feel the same compassion for the immortal interests, as for the worldly distresses of the unfortunate ; forgiving others, as he hopes to be forgiven ; if he endeavour, according to his measure and ability, to diminish the vice and misery with which the world abounds, *that* man has a solid ground of peace and hope, though he may not have those sensible evidences which afford triumph and exultation. In the meanwhile, the man of a heated imagination, who boasts of mysterious communications within, is perhaps exhibiting, outwardly, unfavourable marks of his real state, and holding out, by his low practice, discouragements unfriendly to that religion of which he professes himself a shining instance.

'The sober Christian is as fully convinced, that only He who made the heart, can new make it, as the enthusiast. He is as fully persuaded that his natural dispositions cannot be changed nor his affections purified, but by the agency of the Divine Spirit, as the fanatic. And though he presume not to limit omnipotence to a sudden or a gradual change, yet he does not think it necessary to ascertain the day, and the hour, and the moment, contented to be assured that whereas he was once blind he now sees. If he do not presume in his own case to fix the *chronology of conversion*, he is not less certain as to its effects. If he cannot enumerate dates, and recapitulate feelings, he can and does produce such evidences of his improvement, as virtuous habits, a devout temper, an humble and charitable spirit, "repentance towards God, and faith in our Lord Jesus Christ;" and this gives an evidence less equivocal, as existing more in the heart than on the lips, and more in the life than in the discourse. Surely if a plant be flourishing, the branches green, and the fruit fair and abundant, we may venture to pronounce these to be indications of health and vigour, though we cannot ascertain the moment when the seed was sown, or the manner in which it sprung up.'

Sir John, who had been an attentive listener, but had not yet spoken a word, now said, smiling, 'Mr. Stanley, you steer most happily between the two extremes. This exclusive cry of grace in one party of religionists, which drives the opposite side into as unreasonable a clamour against it, reminds me of the Queen of Louis Quatorze. When the Jesuits, who were of the court-party, made so violent an outcry against the Jansenists, for no reason but because they had more piety than themselves, her majesty was so fearful of being thought to favour the oppressed side, that in the excess of her party zeal, she vehemently exclaimed, "Oh, fie upon grace! fie upon grace!"'

Mr. Stanley. 'Party violence thinks it can never recede far enough from the side it opposes.'

Tyrrel. 'But how then is our religion to be known, except by our making a profession of truths, which the irreligious are either ignorant of, or oppose?'

Stanley. 'There is, as I have already observed, a more infallible criterion. It is best known by the effects it produces on the heart, and on the temper. A religion, which consists in opinions only, will not advance us in our progress to heaven: it is apt to inflate the mind with the pride of disputation; and victory is so commonly the object of debate, that eternity slides out of sight. The two cardinal points of our religion, justification and sanctification, are, if I may be allowed the term, correlatives; they imply a reciprocal relation, nor do I call that state Christianity, in which either is separately and exclusively maintained. The union of these manifests the dominion of religion in the heart, by increasing its humility, by purifying its affections, by setting it above the contamination of the maxims and habits of the world, by detaching it from the vanities of time, and elevating it to a desire for the riches of eternity.'

Tyrrel. 'All the exhortations to duties, with which so many sermons abound, are only an infringement on the liberty of a Christian. A true believer knows of no duty but faith, no rule but love.'

Stanley. 'Love is indeed the fountain and principle of all practical virtue. But love itself requires some regulation to direct its exertions; some law to guide its motions; some rule to prevent its aberrations; some guard to hinder that which is vigorous from becoming eccentric. With such a regulation, such a law, such a guard, the divine ethics of the Gospel have furnished us. The word of God is as much our rule, as His Spirit is our guide, or His Son our "way." This unerring rule alone secures Christian liberty from disorder, from danger, from irregularity, from excess. Conformity to the precepts of the Redeemer is the most infallible proof of having an interest in his death.'

We afterwards insensibly slid into other subjects, when Mr. Tyrrel, like a combatant who thought himself victorious, seemed inclined to return to the charge. The love of money having been mentioned by Sir John with extreme severity, Mr. Tyrrel seemed to consider it as a venial failing, and said that both avarice and charity might be constitutional.

'They may be so,' said Mr. Stanley, 'but Christianity, sir, has a constitution of its own; a superinduced constitution. A real Christian 'confers not with flesh and blood,' with his *constitution*, whether he shall give or forbear to give, when it is a clear duty, and the will of God requires it. If we believe in the principles, we must adopt the conclusions. Religion is not an unproductive theory, nor charity an unnecessary, an incidental consequence, nor a contingent left to our choice. You are a classic, Mr. Tyrrel, and cannot have forgotten that in your mythological poets, the three Pagan graces were always knit together hand in hand; the three Christian graces are equally inseparable, and the greatest of these is charity; that grand principle of love, of which alms-giving is only one branch.'

Mr. Tyrrel endeavoured to evade the subject, and seemed to intimate that true Christianity might be known without any such evidences as Mr. Stanley thought necessary. This led the latter to insist warmly on the vast stress which every part of scripture laid on the duty of charity. 'Its doctrines,' said he, 'its precepts, its promises, and its examples, all inculcate it.' 'The new commandment' of John—'the pure and undefiled religion' of James—'ye shall be recompensed at the resurrection of the just' of Luke—the daily and hourly practice of Him, who not only taught to do good, but who 'went about doing it' —'the store for a good foundation against the time to come' of Paul— nay, in the only full, solemn, and express representation of the last day, which the Gospel exhibits, charity is not only brought forward as a predominant, a distinguishing feature of the righteous, but a specific recompense seems to be assigned to it when practised on true Christian grounds. And it is not a little observable, that the only posthumous quotation from the sayings of our Divine Saviour which the scripture has recorded, is an encouragement to charity—'Remember the words of the Lord Jesus, how he said it is more blessed to give than to receive.'

Chapter XXXIX.

HE next afternoon, when we were all conversing together, I asked Mr. Stanley what opinion he held on a subject which had lately been a good deal canvassed, the propriety of young ladies learning the dead languages, particularly Latin. He was silent. Mrs. Stanley smiled. Phœbe laughed out-right. Lucilla, who had nearly finished making tea, blushed excessively. Little Celia, who was sitting on my knee while I was teaching her to draw a bird, put an end to the difficulty, by looking up in my face and crying out,—'Why, sir, Lucilla reads Latin with papa every morning.' I cast a timid eye on Miss Stanley, who, after putting the sugar into the cream pot, and the tea into the sugar basin, slid out of the room, beckoning Phœbe to follow her.

'Poor Lucilla,' said Mr. Stanley, 'I feel for her! Well, sir,' continued he, 'you have discovered by external, what I trust you would not have soon found by internal evidence. Parents who are in high circumstances, yet from principle abridge their daughters of the pleasures of the dissipated part of the world, may be allowed to substitute other pleasures ; and if the girl has a strong inquisitive mind, they may direct it to such pursuits as call for vigorous application, and the exercise of the mental powers.'

'How does that sweet girl manage,' said Lady Belfield, 'to be so utterly void of pretension ? So much softness and so much usefulness strip her of all the terrors of learning.'

'At first,' replied Mr. Stanley, 'I only meant to give Lucilla as much Latin as would teach her to grammaticize her English, but her quickness in acquiring led me on, and I think I did right ; for it is superficial knowledge that excites vanity. A learned language, which a discreet woman will never produce in company, is less likely to make her vain, than those acquirements which are always in exhibition. And, after all, it is a hackneyed remark, that the best instructed girl will have less learning than a schoolboy ; and why should vanity operate in her case more than in his ?'

'For this single reason, sir,' said I, 'that every boy knows that which very few girls are taught. Suspect me not, however, of censuring a measure which I admire. I hope the example of your daughters will help to raise the tone of female education.'

'Softly, softly,' interrupted Mr. Stanley, 'retrench your plural number. It is only one girl out of six who has deviated from the beaten track. I do not expect many converts, to what I must rather call my practice in one instance, than my general opinion. I am so convinced of the prevailing prejudice, that the thing has never been named out of the family. If my gay neighbour Miss Rattle knew that Lucilla had learnt Latin, she would instantly find out a few moments to add that language to her innumerable acquirements, because her mother can afford to pay for it, and because Lady Di Dash has never learnt it. I assure you, however,' (laughing as he spoke,) 'I never intend to smuggle my poor girl on any man, by concealing from him this unpopular attainment, any more than I would conceal any personal defect.'

'I would honestly confess,' said Sir John, who had not yet spoken, 'that had I had to judge the case *a priori*, had I met Miss Stanley under the terrifying persuasion that she was a scholar, I own I should have met her with a prejudice ; I should have feared she might be forward in conversation, deficient in feminine manners, and destitute of domestic talents. But having had such a fair occasion of admiring her engaging modesty, her gentle and unassuming tone in society, and, above all, having heard from Lady Belfield how eminently she excels in the true science of a lady—domestic knowledge—I cannot refuse her that additional regard which this solid acquirement, so meekly borne, deserves. Nor, on reflection, do I see why we should be so forward to instruct a woman in the language spoken at Rome in its present degraded state, in which there are comparatively few authors to improve her, and yet be afraid that she should be acquainted with that which was its vernacular tongue, in its age of glory, two thousand years ago, and which abounds with writers of supreme excellence.'

I was charmed at these concessions from Sir John, and exclaimed, with a transport which I could not restrain : 'In our friends, even in our common acquaintance, do we not delight to associate with those whose pursuits have been similar to our own, and who have read the same books ? How dull do we find it, when civility compels us to pass even a day with an illiterate man ? Shall we not then delight in the kindred acquirements of a dearer friend ? Shall we not rejoice in a companion who has drawn, though less copiously, perhaps, from the same rich sources with ourselves ; who can relish the beauty we quote, and trace the allusion at which we hint ? I do not mean that *learning* is absolutely necessary, but a man of taste who has an ignorant wife, cannot in her company think his own thoughts, nor speak his own language ; his thoughts he will suppress, his language he will debase —the one from hopelessness, the other from compassion. He must be continually lowering and diluting his meaning, in order to make himself intelligible. This he will do for the woman he loves, but in doing it he will not be happy. She, who cannot be entertained by his conversation, will not be convinced by his reasoning ; and at length he will find out that it is less trouble to lower his own standard to hers, than to exhaust himself in the vain attempt to raise hers to his own.'

'A fine high-sounding *tirade*, Charles, spoken *con amore*,' said Sir John : 'I really believe, though, that one reason why women are so frivolous, is, that the things they are taught are not solid enough to fix the attention, exercise the intellect, and fortify the understanding. They learn little that inures to reasoning, or compels to patient meditation.'

'I consider the difficulties of a solid education,' said Mr. Stanley, 'as a sort of preliminary course, intended perhaps by Providence as a gradual preparative for the subsequent difficulties of life ; as a prelude to the acquisition of that solidity and firmness of character which actual trials are hereafter to confirm. Though I would not make instruction unnecessarily harsh and rugged, yet I would not wish to increase its facilities to such a degree as to weaken that robustness of mind which it should be its object to promote, in order to render mental discipline subservient to moral.'

'How have you managed with your other girls, Stanley?' said Sir John ; 'for though you vindicate general knowledge, you profess not to wish for general learning in the sex.'

'Far from it,' replied Mr. Stanley. 'I am a gardener, you know, and accustomed to study the genius of the soil before I plant. Most of my daughters, like the daughters of other men, have some one talent, or at least propensity ; for parents are too apt to mistake inclination for genius. This propensity I endeavour to find out, and to cultivate. But if I find the natural bias very strong, and not very safe, I then labour to counteract, instead of encouraging the tendency, and try to give it a fresh direction. Lucilla having a strong bent to whatever relates to intellectual taste, I have read over with her the most unexceptionable parts of a few of the best Roman classics. She began at nine years old, for I have remarked, that it is not learning much, but learning late, which makes pedants.

'Phœbe, who has a superabundance of vivacity, I have in some measure tamed, by making her not only a complete mistress of arithmetic, but by giving her a tincture of mathematics. Nothing puts such a bridle on the fancy as demonstration. A habit of computing steadies the mind, and subdues the soarings of imagination. It sobers the vagaries of trope and figure, substitutes truth for metaphor, and exactness for amplification. This girl, who, if she had been fed on poetry and works of imagination, might have become a Miss Sparkes, now rather gives herself the airs of a calculator, and a grave computist. Though, as in the case of the cat in the fable, who was metamorphosed into a lady, nature will break out as soon as the scratching of a mouse is heard ; and all Phœbe's philosophy can scarcely keep her in order, if any work of fancy comes in her way.

'To soften the horrors of her fate, however, I allowed her to read a few of the best things in her favourite class. When I read to her the more delicate parts of Gulliver's Travels, with which she was enchanted, she affected to be angry at the voyage to Laputa, because it ridicules philosophical science. And in Brobdignag, she said the proportions were not correct. I must, however, explain to you, that the use which I made of these dry studies with Phœbe, was precisely the same which the ingenious Mr. Cheshire makes of his steel machines for defective shapes, to straighten a crooked tendency, or strengthen a weak one. Having employed these means to set her mind upright, and to cure a wrong bias, as that skilful gentleman discards his apparatus as soon as the patient becomes straight, so have I discontinued these pursuits, for I never meant to make a mathematical lady. Jane has a fine ear and a pretty voice, and will sing and play well enough for any girl who is not to make music her profession. One or two of the others sing agreeably.

'The little one, who brought the last nosegay, has a strong turn for natural history, and we all of us generally botanize a little of an evening, which gives a fresh interest to our walks. She will soon draw plants and flowers pretty accurately. Louisa also has some taste in designing, and takes tolerable sketches from nature. These we encourage, because they are solitary pleasures, and want no witnesses. They all are too eager to impart somewhat of what they know to your little favourite, Celia, who is in danger of picking up a little of everything, the sure way to excel in nothing.

'Thus each girl is furnished with some one source of independent amusement. But what would become of them, or rather what would become of their mother and me, if every one of them was a scholar, a mathematician, a singer, a performer, a botanist, a painter? Did we attempt to force all these acquirements and a dozen more on every girl, all her *time* would be occupied about things which will be of no value to her in *eternity*. I need not tell you that we are carefully communicating to every one of them that general knowledge which should be common to all gentlewomen.

'In unrolling the vast volume of ancient and modern history, I ground on it some of my most useful instructions, and point how the truth of Scripture is illustrated by the crimes and corruptions which history records, and how the same pride, covetousness, ambition, turbulence, and deceit, which bring misery on empires, destroy the peace of families. To history, geography and chronology are such indispensable appendages, that it would be superfluous to insist on their usefulness. As to astronomy, while "the heavens declare the glory of God," it seems a kind of impiety not to give young people some insight into it.'

'I hope,' said Sir John, 'that you do not exclude the modern languages from your plan.' 'As to the French,' replied Mr. Stanley, 'with that thorough inconsistency which is common to man, the demand for it seems to have risen in exact proportion as it ought to have sunk.* I would not, however, rob my children of a language in which, though there are more books to be avoided, there are more that deserve to be read, than in all the foreign languages put together.'

'If you prohibit Italian,' said Sir John, laughing, 'I will serve you as Cowper advised the boys and girls to serve Johnson for depreciating Henry and Emma; I will join the musical and poetical ladies in tearing you to pieces, as the Thracian damsels did Orpheus, and send your head with his

Down the swift Hebrus to the Lesbian shore.'

'You remember me, my dear Belfield,' replied Mr. Stanley, 'a warm admirer of the exquisite beauties of Italian poetry. But a father feels or rather judges differently from the mere man of taste, and as a father I cannot help regretting that what is commonly put into the hands of our daughters is so amatory, that it has a tendency to soften those minds which rather want to be invigorated.

* See an ingenious little treatise entitled 'Latium Redivivum,' or the modern use of the Latin language, and the prevalence of the French.

'There are few things I more deprecate for girls than a poetical education, the evils of which I saw sadly exemplified in a young friend of Mrs. Stanley's. She had beauty and talents. Her parents, enchanted with both, left her entirely to her own guidance. She yielded herself up to the uncontrolled rovings of a vagrant fancy. When a child she wrote verses, which were shown in her presence to every guest. Their flattery completed her intoxication. She afterwards translated Italian sonnets, and composed elegies, of which love was the only theme. These she was encouraged by her mother to recite herself, in all companies, with a pathos and sensibility which delighted her parents, but alarmed her more prudent friends.

'She grew up with the confirmed opinion that the two great and sole concerns of human life were love and poetry. She considered them as inseparably connected, and she resolved in her own instance never to violate so indispensable a union. The object of her affection was unhappily chosen, and the effects of her attachment were such as might have been expected from a connexion formed on so slight a foundation. In the perfections with which she invested her lover, she gave the reins to her imagination, when she thought she was only consulting her heart. She picked out and put together all the fine qualities of all the heroes of all the poets she had ever read, and into this finished creature her fancy transformed her admirer.

'Love and poetry commonly influence the two sexes in a very disproportionate degree. With men, each of them is only one passion among many. Love has various and powerful competitors in hearts divided between ambition, business, and pleasure. Poetry is only one amusement in minds distracted by a thousand tumultuous pursuits ; whereas in girls of ardent tempers, whose feelings are not curbed by restraint and regulated by religion, love is considered as the great business of their earthly existence. It is cherished, not as the " cordial drop," but as the whole contents of the cup ; the remainder is considered only as froth or dregs. The unhappy victim not only submits to the destructive dominion of a despotic passion, but glories in it. So at least did this ill-starred girl.

'The sober duties of a family had early been transferred to her sisters, as far beneath the attention of so fine a genius ; while she abandoned herself to studies, which kept her imagination in a fever, and to a passion which those studies continually fed and inflamed. Both together completed her delirium. She was ardent, generous, and sincere ; but violent, imprudent, and vain to excess. She set the opinion of the world at complete defiance, and was not only totally destitute of judgment and discretion herself, but despised them in others. Her lover and her muse were to her instead of the whole world.

'After having for some years exchanged sonnets, under the names of Laura and Petrarch, and elegies under those of Sappho and Phaon ; the lover, to whom all this had been mere sport, the gratification of vanity, and the recreation of an idle hour, grew weary :

> Younger and fairer he another saw.

He drew off. Her verses were left unanswered, her reproaches unpitied. Laura wept and Sappho raved in vain.

' The poor girl, to whom all this visionary romance had been a serious occupation, which had swallowed up cares and duties, now realised the woes she had so often admired and described. Her upbraidings only served to alienate still more the heart of her deserter ; and her despair, which he had the cruelty to treat as fictitious, was to him a subject of mirth and ridicule. Her letters were exposed, her expostulatory verses read at clubs and taverns, and the unhappy Sappho was toasted in derision.

' All her ideal refinements now degenerated into practical improprieties. The public avowal of her passion drew on her from the world charges which she had not merited. Her reputation was wounded, her health declined, her peace was destroyed. She experienced the dishonours of guilt without its turpitude, and in the bloom of life fell, the melancholy victim to a mistaken education and an undisciplined mind.'

Mrs. Stanley dropped a silent tear to the memory of her unhappy friend, the energies of whose mind she said would, had they been rightly directed, have formed a fine character.

' But none of the things of which I have been speaking,' resumed Mr. Stanley, ' are the great and primary objects of instruction. The inculcation of fortitude, prudence, humility, temperance, self-denial—this-is education. These are things which we endeavour to promote far more than arts or languages. These are tempers, the habit of which should be laid in early, and followed up constantly, as there is no day in life which will not call them into exercise ; and how can that be practised which has never been acquired ?

' Perseverance, meekness, and industry,' continued he, ' are the qualities we most carefully cherish and commend. For poor Laura's sake I make it a point never to extol any indications of genius. Genius has pleasure enough in its own high aspirings. Nor am I indeed overmuch delighted with a great blossom of talents. I agree with good Bishop Hall, that it is better to thin the blossoms, that the rest may thrive ; and that in encouraging too many propensities, one faculty may not starve another.'

Lady Belfield expressed herself grateful for the hints Mr. Stanley had thrown out, which could not but be of importance to her, who had so large a family. After some further questions from her, he proceeded :

' I have partly explained to you, my dear madam, why, though I would not have every woman learn everything, yet why I would give every girl, in a certain station of life, some one amusing accomplishment. There is here and there a strong mind, which requires a more substantial nourishment than the common education of girls affords. To such, and to such only, would I furnish the quiet resource of a dead language as a solid aliment which may fill the mind without inflating it.

' But that no acquirement may inflate it, let me add, there is but one sure corrective. Against learning, against talents of every kind, nothing can steady the head, unless you fortify the heart with real Christianity. In raising the moral edifice, we must sink deep in proportion as we build high. We must widen the foundation if we extend the superstructure. Religion alone can counteract the aspirings of genius, can regulate the pride of talents.

'And let such women as are disposed to be vain of their comparatively petty attainments, look up with admiration to those two contemporary shining examples, the venerable Elizabeth Carter, and the blooming Elizabeth Smith. I knew them both, and to know was to revere them. In *them*, let our young ladies contemplate profound and various learning chastened by true Christian humility. In *them*, let them venerate acquirements which would have been distinguished in a university, meekly softened, and beautifully shaded by the gentle exertion of every domestic virtue, the unaffected exercise of every feminine employment.'

Chapter XL.

EVER since Mr. Tyrrel had been last with us, I had observed an unusual seriousness in the countenance of Sir John Belfield, though accompanied with his natural complacency. His mind seemed intent on something he wished to communicate. The first time we were both alone in the library with Mr. Stanley, Sir John said, 'Stanley, the conversations we have lately had, and especially the last with Tyrrel, in which you bore so considerable a part, have furnished me with agreeable matter for reflection. I hope the pleasure will not be quite destitute of profit.'

'My dear Sir John,' replied Mr. Stanley, 'in conversing with Mr. Tyrrel, I labour under a disadvantage common to every man, who, when he is called to defend some important principle which he thinks attacked or undervalued, is brought into danger of being suspected to undervalue others, which, if they in their turn were assailed, he would defend with equal zeal. When points of the last importance are slighted as insignificant, in order exclusively to magnify one darling opinion, I am driven to appear as if I opposed that important tenet, which, if I may so speak, seems pitted against the others. Those who do not previously know my principles, might almost suspect me of being an opposer of that prime doctrine, which I really consider as the leading principle of Christianity.'

'Allow me to say,' returned Sir John, 'that my surprise has been equal to my satisfaction. Those very doctrines which you maintained, I had been assured, were the very tenets you rejected. Many of our acquaintance who do not come near enough to judge, or who would not be competent to judge if they did, ascribe the strictness of your practice to some unfounded peculiarities of opinion, and suspect that the doctrines of Tyrrel, though somewhat modified, a little more rationally conceived, and more ably expressed, are the doctrines held by you, and by every man who rises above the ordinary standard of what the world calls religious men. And what is a little absurd and inconsequent, they ascribe to these supposed dangerous doctrines his abstinence from the diversions, and his disapprobation of the manners and maxims, of the world. *Your* opinions, however, I always suspected could not be very pernicious, the effects of which, from the whole tenor of your life, I knew to be so salutary.'

' My dear Belfield,' said Mr. Stanley, 'men of the world are guilty of a striking inconsistency in the charge they bring against religious men. They accuse them at once of maintaining doctrines which lead to licentiousness, and of over-strictness in their practice. One of them may be true : both cannot be so.'

' I now find, upon full proof,' replied Sir John, ' that there is nothing in your sentiments, but what a man of sense may approve ; nothing but what, if he be really a man of sense, he will without scruple adopt. May I be enabled more fully, more practically, to adopt them ! You shall point out to me such a course of reading, as may not only clear up my remaining difficulties, but, what is infinitely more momentous than the solution of any abstract question, may help to awaken me to a more deep and lively sense of my own individual interest in this great concern !'

Mr. Stanley's benevolent countenance was lighted up with more than its wonted animation. He did not attempt to conceal the deep satisfaction with which his heart was penetrated. He modestly referred his friend to Doctor Barlow, as a far more able casuist, though not a more cordial friend. For my own part, I felt my heart expand towards Sir John, with new sympathies and an enlarged affection. I felt nobler motives of attachment, an attachment which I hoped would be perpetuated beyond the narrow bonds of this perishable world.

' My dear Sir John,' said Mr. Stanley, ' it is among the daily but comparatively petty trials of every man who is deeply in earnest to secure his immortal interests, to be classed with low and wild enthusiasts whom his judgment condemns, with hypocrites against whom his principles revolt, and with men, pious and conscientious I am most willing to allow, but differing widely from his own views ; with others, who evince a want of charity in some points, and a want of judgment in most. To be identified, I say, with men so different from yourself, because you hold in common some great truths which all real Christians have held in all ages, and because you agree with them in avoiding the blameable excesses of dissipation—is among the sacrifices of reputation, which a man must be contented to make, who is earnest in the great object of a Christian's pursuit. I trust, however, that, through Divine grace, I shall never renounce my integrity for the praise of men, who have so little consistency, that though they pretend their quarrel is with your faith, yet who would not care how extravagant your belief was, if your practice assimilated with their own. I trust, on the other hand, that I shall always maintain my candour towards those with whom we are unfairly involved ; men, religious though somewhat eccentric, devout though injudicious, and sincere though mistaken ; but who, with all their errors, against which I protest, and with all their indiscretion, which I lament, and with all their ill-judged, because irregular zeal, which I blame, I shall ever think—always excepting hypocrites and false pretenders—are better men, and in a safer state, than their revilers.'

' I have often suspected,' said I, ' that under the plausible pretence of objecting to your Creed, men conceal their quarrel with the Commandments.'

'My dear Stanley,' said Sir John, 'but for this visit I might have continued in the common error, that there was but one description of religious professors ; that a fanatical spirit, and a fierce adoption of one or two particular doctrines, to the exclusion of all the rest, with a total indifference to morality, and a sovereign contempt of prudence, made up the character against which, I confess, I entertained a secret disgust. Still, however, I loved *you* too well, and had too high an opinion of your understanding, to suspect that you would ever be drawn into those practical errors, to which I had been told your theory inevitably led. Yet I own I had an aversion to this dreaded enthusiasm which drove me into the opposite extreme.'

'How many men have I known,' replied Mr. Stanley, smiling, ' who, from their dread of a burning zeal, have taken refuge in a freezing indifference ! As to the two extremes of heat and cold, neither of them is the true climate of Christianity ; yet the fear of each drives men of opposite complexions into the other, instead of fixing them in the temperate zone which lies between them, and which is the region of genuine piety.

' The truth is, Sir John, *your* society considers earnestness in religion as the fever of a distempered understanding, while in inferior concerns they admire it as the indication of a powerful mind. Is zeal in politics accounted the mark of a vulgar intellect ? Did they consider the unquenchable ardour of Pitt, did they regard the lofty enthusiasm of Fox, as evidences of a feeble or a disordered mind ? Yet I will venture to assert, that ardour in religion is as much more noble than ardour in politics, as the prize for which it contends is more exalted. It is beyond all comparison superior to the highest human interests, the truth and justice of which, after all, may possibly be mistaken, and the objects of which must infallibly have an end.'

Dr. Barlow came in, and seeing us earnestly engaged, desired that he might not interrupt the conversation. Sir John in a few words informed him what had passed, and with a most graceful humility spoke of his own share in it, and confessed how much he had been carried away by the stream of popular prejudice, respecting men who had courage to make a consistent profession of Christianity. ' I now,' added he, ' begin to think with Addison, that singularity in religion is heroic bravery, " because it only leaves the species by soaring above it." '

After some observations from Dr. Barlow, much in point, he went on to remark that the difficulties of a clergyman were much increased by the altered manners of the age. ' The tone of religious writing,' said he, ' but especially the tone of religious conversation, is much lowered. The language of a Christian minister in discussing Christian topics will naturally be consonant to that of Scripture. The Scripture speaks of a man being *renewed in the spirit of his mind*, of his being *sanctified by the grace of God*. Now, how much circumlocution is necessary for us in conversing with a man of the world, to convey the sense, without adopting the expression ; and what pains must we take to make our meaning intelligible without giving disgust, and to be useful without causing irritation !'

14

Sir John. ' But, my good doctor, is it not a little puritanical to make use of such solemn expressions in company ?'

Dr. Barlow. ' Sir, it is worse than puritanical, it is hypocritical, where the principle itself does not exist ; and even where it does, it is highly inexpedient to introduce such phrases into general company at all. But I am speaking of serious private conversation, when, if a minister is really in earnest, there is nothing absurd in his prudent use of Scripture expressions. One great difficulty, and which obstructs the usefulness of a clergyman, in conversation with many persons of the higher class, who would be sorry not to be thought religious, is, that they keep up so little acquaintance with the Bible, that from their ignorance of its venerable phraseology, they are offended at the introduction of a text, not because it is Scripture (for that, they maintain a kind of general reverence), but because, from not reading it, they do not know that it *is* Scripture.

' I once lent a person of rank and talents an admirable sermon, written by one of our first divines. Though deeply pious, it was composed with uncommon spirit and elegance, and I thought it did not contain one phrase which could offend the most fastidious critic. When he returned it, he assured me that he liked it much on the whole, and should have approved it altogether, but for one methodistical expression. To my utter astonishment he pointed to the exceptionable passage, " There is now no condemnation to them that are in Christ Jesus, who walk not after the flesh but after the spirit." The chapter and verse not being mentioned, he never suspected it was a quotation from the Bible.'

' This is one among many reasons,' said Mr. Stanley, ' why I so strenuously insist that young persons should read the Scriptures, unaltered, unmodernized, unmutilated, unabridged. If parents do not make a point of this, the peculiarities of sacred language will become really obsolete to the next generation.'

In answer to some further remarks of Sir John, Mr. Stanley said, smiling, ' I have sometimes amused myself with making a collection of certain things, which are now considered and held up by a pretty large class of men as the infallible symptoms of methodism. Those which at present occur to my recollection are the following : Going to church in the afternoon, maintaining family prayer, not travelling, or giving great dinners or other entertainments on Sundays, promoting the religious instruction of the poor at home, subscribing to the Bible Society, and contributing to establish Christianity abroad. These, though the man attend no eccentric clergyman, hold no one enthusiastic doctrine, associate with no fanatic, is sober in his conversation, consistent in his practice, correct in his whole deportment, will infallibly fix on him the charge of methodism. Any *one* of these will excite suspicion, but all united will not fail absolutely to stigmatize him. The most devoted attachment to the establishment will avail him nothing, if not accompanied with a fiery intolerance towards all who differ. Without intolerance, his charity is construed into unsoundness, and his candour into disaffection. He is accused of assimilating with the principles of every weak brother whom, though his judgment compels him to blame, his candour forbids him to calumniate. Saint and hypocrite are now, in the scoffer's lexicon, become convertible terms ; the last being always implied where the first is sneeringly used.'

'It has often appeared to me,' said I, 'that the glory of a tried Christian somewhat resembles that of a Roman victor, in whose solemn processions, among the odes of gratulation, a mixture of abuse and railing made part of the triumph.'

'Happily,' resumed Mr. Stanley, 'a religious man knows the worst he is likely to suffer. In the present established state of things, he is not called, as in the first ages of Christianity, to be made a spectacle to the world, and to angels, and to men ; but he must submit to be assailed by three different descriptions of persons. From the first, he must be contented to have principles imputed to him which he abhors, motives which he disdains, and ends which he deprecates. He must submit to have the energies of his well-regulated piety confounded with the follies of the fanatic, and his temperate zeal blended with the ravings of the insane. He must submit to be involved in the absurdities of the extravagant, in the duplicity of the designing, and in the mischiefs of the dangerous ; to be reckoned among the disturbers of that Church which he would defend with his blood, and of that government which he is perhaps supporting in every possible direction. Every means is devised to shake his credit. From such determined assailants no prudence can protect his character, no private integrity can defend it, no public service rescue it.'

'I have often wondered,' said Sir John, 'at the success of assaults which seemed to have nothing but the badness of the cause to recommend them. But the assailant, whose object it is to make good men ridiculous, well knows that he has secured to himself a large patronage in the hearts of all the envious, the malignant, and the irreligious, who, like other levellers, find it more easy to establish the equality of mankind by abasing the lofty, than by elevating the low.'

'In my short experience of life,' said I, when Sir John had done speaking, 'I have often observed it as a hardship, that a man must not only submit to be condemned for doctrines he disowns, but also for consequences which others may draw from the doctrines he maintains, though he himself both practically and speculatively disavows any such consequences.'

'There is another class of enemies,' resumed Mr. Stanley. 'To do them justice, it is not so much the individual Christian, as Christianity itself, which *they* hope to discredit ; *that* Christianity which would not only restrain the conduct, but would humble the heart ; which strips them of the pride of philosophy, and the arrogant plea of merit ; which would save, but will not flatter them. In this enlightened period, however, for men who would preserve any character, it would be too gross to attack religion itself, and they find they can wound her more deeply and more creditably through the sides of her professors.'

'I have observed,' said I, 'that the uncandid censurer always picks out the worst man of a class, and then confidently produces him as being a fair specimen of it.'

'From our more thoughtless, but less uncharitable acquaintance, the

14—2

gay and the busy,' resumed Mr. Stanley, 'we have to sustain a gentler
warfare. A little reproach, a good deal of ridicule, a little suspicion of
our designs, and not a little compassion for our gloomy habits of life,
an implied contempt of our judgment, some friendly hints that we carry
things too far, an intimation that being righteous over-much in the
practice has a tendency to produce derangement in the faculties—
these are the petty but daily trials of every man who is seriously in
earnest ; and petty indeed they are to him whose prospects are well
grounded, and whose hope is full of immortality.'

'This hostility, which a real Christian is sure to experience,' said I,
'is not without its uses. It quickens his vigilance over his own heart,
and enlarges his charity toward others, whom reproach perhaps may
as unjustly stigmatize. It teaches him to be on his guard, lest he
should really deserve the censure he incurs ; and what I presume is of
no small importance, it teaches him to sit loose to human opinion ; it
weakens his excessive tenderness for reputation, makes him more
anxious to deserve, and less solicitous to obtain it.'

'It were well,' said Dr. Barlow, 'if the evil ended here. The established Christian will evince himself to be such by not shrinking from
the attack. But the misfortune is, that the dread of this attack keeps
back well-disposed but vacillating characters. They are intimidated
at the idea of partaking the censure, though they know it to be false.
When they hear the reputation of men of piety assailed, they assume
an indifference which they are far from feeling. They listen to
reproaches cast on characters which they inwardly revere, without
daring to vindicate them. They hear the most attached subjects
accused of disaffection, and the most sober-minded churchmen of
innovation, without venturing to repel the charge, lest they should be
suspected of leaning to the party. They are afraid fully to avow that
their own principles are the same, lest they should be involved in the
same calumny. To efface this suspicion, they affect a coldness which
they do not feel, and treat with levity what they inwardly venerate.
Very young men, from this criminal timidity, are led to risk their
eternal happiness through the dread of a laugh. Though they know
that they have not only religion but reason on their sides, yet it requires
a hardy virtue to repel a sneer, and an intrepid principle to confront
a sarcasm. Thus their own mind loses its firmness, religion loses
their support, the world loses the benefit which their example would
afford, and they themselves become liable to the awful charge which
is denounced against him who is ashamed of his Christian profession.'

'Men of the world,' said Sir John, 'are extremely jealous of whatever
may be thought *particular;* they are frightened at everything that has
not the sanction of public opinion, and the stamp of public applause.
They are impatient of the slightest suspicion of censure in what may
be supposed to affect the credit of their judgment, though often indifferent enough as to any blame that may attach to their conduct.
They have been accustomed to consider strict religion as a thing which
militates against good taste, and to connect the idea of something
unclassical and inelegant, something awkward and unpopular, something uncouth and ill-bred, with the peculiar doctrines of Christianity ;

doctrines which, though there is no harm in believing, they think there
can be no good in avowing.'

'It is a little hard,' said Mr. Stanley, 'that men of piety, who are
allowed to possess good sense on all other occasions, and whose judgment is respected in all the ordinary concerns of life, should not have
a little credit given them in matters of religion, but that they should
be at once transformed into idiots or madmen, in that very point which
affords the noblest exercise to the human faculties.'

'A Christian, then,' said I, 'if human applause be his idol, is of all
men most miserable. He forfeits his reputation every way. He is
accused by the men of the world of going too far ; by the enthusiast,
of not going far enough. While it is one of the best evidences of his
being right, that he is rejected by one party for excess, and by the
other for deficiency.'

'What then is to be done?' said Doctor Barlow. 'Must a discreet
and pious man give up a principle because it has been disfigured by
the fanatic, or abused by the hypocrite, or denied by the sceptic, or
reprobated by the formalist, or ridiculed by the men of the world?
He should rather support it with an earnestness proportioned to its
value ; he should rescue it from the injuries it has sustained from its
enemies, and the discredit brought on it by its imprudent friends. He
should redeem it from the enthusiasm which misconceives, and from
the ignorance or malignity which misrepresents it. If the learned and
the judicious are silent in proportion as the illiterate and the vulgar
are obtrusive and loquacious, the most important truths will be abandoned by those who are best able to unfold and to defend them, while
they will be embraced exclusively by those who misunderstand, degrade,
and debase them. Because the unlettered are absurd, must the able
cease to be religious? If there is to be an abandonment of every
Christian principle, because it has been unfairly, unskilfully, or in-
adequately treated, there would, one by one, be an abandonment of
every doctrine of the New Testament.'

'I felt myself bound,' said Mr. Stanley, 'to act on this principle in
our late conversation with Mr. Tyrrel. I would not refuse to assert
with him the doctrines of grace, but I endeavoured to let him see that
I had adopted them in a scriptural sense. I would not try to convince
him that he was wrong, by disowning a truth because he abused it. I
would cordially reject all the bad use he makes of any opinion, without
rejecting the opinion itself, if the Bible will bear me out in the belief
of it. But I would scrupulously reject all the other opinions which he
connects with it, and with which I am persuaded it has no connection.'

'The nominal Christian,' said Dr. Barlow, 'who insists that religion
resides in the understanding only, may contend that love to God,
gratitude to our Redeemer, and sorrow for our offences, are enthusiastic
extravagances ; and effectually repress, by ridicule and sarcasm, those
feelings which the devout heart recognizes, and which scripture sanc-
tions. On the other hand, those very feelings are inflamed, exaggerated,
distorted, and misrepresented, as including the whole of religion, by
the intemperate enthusiast, who thinks reason has nothing to do in the
business ; but who, trusting to tests not warranted by scripture, is
governed by fancies, feelings, and visions of his own.

'Between these pernicious extremes, what course is the sober Christian to pursue? Must he discard from his heart all pious affections because the fanatic abuses them, and the fastidious deny their existence? This would be like insisting, that because one man happens to be sick of a dead palsy, and another of a frenzy fever, there is therefore in the human constitution no such temperate medium as sound health.'

Chapter XLI.

SINCE the conversation which had accidentally led to the discovery of Miss Stanley's acquirements, I could not forbear surveying the perfect arrangements of the family, and the completely elegant but not luxurious table, with more than ordinary interest. I felt no small delight in reflecting that all this order and propriety were produced without the smallest deduction from mental cultivation. I could not refrain from mentioning this to Mrs. Stanley. She was not displeased with my observation, though she cautiously avoided saying anything which might be construed into a wish to set off her daughter. As she seemed surprised at my knowledge of the large share her Lucilla had in the direction of the family concerns, I could not, in the imprudence of my satisfaction, conceal the conversation I had had with my old friend Mrs. Comfit.

After this avowal she felt that any reserve on this point would look like affectation, a littleness which would have been unworthy of her character. 'I am frequently blamed by my friends,' said she, 'for taking some of the load from my own shoulders, and laying it on hers. "Poor thing, she is too young!" is the constant cry of the fashionable mothers. My general answer is, "You do not think your daughters of the same age too young to be married, though you know marriage must bring with it these, and still heavier cares. Surely then Lucilla is not too young to be initiated into that useful knowledge which will hereafter become no inconsiderable part of her duty. The acquisition would be really burdensome then, if it were not lightened by preparatory practice now." I have, I trust, convinced my daughters, that though there is no great merit in possessing this sort of knowledge, yet to be destitute of it is highly discreditable.'

In several houses where I had visited, I had observed the forwardness of the parents, the mother especially, to make a display of the daughter's merits—'So dutiful! so notable! such an excellent nurse!' The girl was then called out to sing or play, and was thus, by that *inconsistency* which my good mother deprecated, kept in the full exhibition of those very talents which are most likely to interfere with nursing and notableness. But since I had been on my present visit, I had never once heard my friends extol their Lucilla, or bring forward any of her excellencies. I had, however, observed their eyes fill with delight, which they could not suppress, when her merits were the subject of the praise of others,

I took notice of this difference of conduct to Mrs. Stanley. 'I have often,' said she, 'been so much hurt at the indelicacy to which you allude, that I very early resolved to avoid it. If the girl in question does not deserve the commendation, it is not only disingenuous but dishonest. If she does, it is a coarse and not very honourable stratagem for getting her off. But if the daughter be indeed all that a mother's partial fondness believes,' added she, her eyes filling with tears of tenderness, 'how can she be in such haste to deprive herself of the solace of her life? How can she by gross acts wound that delicacy in her daughter, which, to a man of refinement, would be one of her chief attractions, and which will be lowered in his esteem, by the suspicion that she may concur in the indiscretion of the mother.

'As to Lucilla,' added she, 'Mr. Stanley and I sometimes say to each other, "Little children, keep yourselves from idols !" Oh, my dear young friend ! it is in vain to dissemble her unaffected worth and sweetness. She is not only our delightful companion, but our confidential friend. We encourage her to give us her opinion on matters of business, as well as of taste ; and having reflected as well as read a good deal, she is not destitute of materials on which to exercise her reasoning powers. We have never repressed her natural vivacity, because we never saw it, like Phœbe's, in danger of carrying her off from the straight line.'

I thanked Mrs. Stanley for her affectionate frankness, with a warmth which showed the cordial interest I took in her who was the object of it ; company coming in interrupted our interesting tête-à-tête.

After tea, I observed the party in the saloon to be thinner than usual, Sir John and Lady Belfield having withdrawn to write letters ; and that individual having quitted the room, whose presence would have reconciled me to the absence of all the rest, I stole out to take a solitary walk. At the distance of a quarter of a mile from the park-gate, on a little common, I observed, for the first time, the smallest and neatest cottage I ever beheld. There was a flourishing young orchard behind it, and a little court full of flowers in front. But I was particularly attracted by a beautiful rose tree in full blossom, which grew against the house, and almost covered the clean white walls. As I knew this sort of rose was a particular favourite of Lucilla's, I opened the low wicket which led into the little court, and looked about for some living creature, of whom I might have begged the flowers. But seeing no one, I ventured to gather a bunch of the roses, and the door being open, walked into the house, in order to acknowledge my theft, and make my compensation. In vain I looked round the little neat kitchen ; no one appeared.

I was just going out, when the sound of a soft female voice over-head arrested my attention. Impelled by a curiosity which, considering the rank of the inhabitants, I did not feel it necessary to resist, I softly stole up the narrow stairs, cautiously stooping as I ascended, the lowness of the ceiling not allowing me to walk upright. I stood still at the door of a little chamber, which was left half open to admit the air. I gently put my head through. What where my emotions when I saw Lucilla Stanley kneeling by the side of a little clean bed, a large old Bible spread open on the bed before her, out of which she was reading one of the penitential psalms to a pale emaciated female figure, who lifted up her failing eyes, and clasped her feeble hands in solemn attention !

Before the two little bars, which served for a grate, knelt Phœbe, with one hand stirring some broth which she had brought from home, and with the other fanning with her straw bonnet the dying embers, in order to make the broth boil ; yet seemingly attentive to her sister's reading. Her dishevelled hair, the deep flush which the fire, and her labour of love, gave her naturally animated countenance, formed a fine contrast to the angelic tranquillity and calm devotion which sat on the face of Lucilla.   Her voice was inexpressibly sweet and penetrating, while faith, hope, and charity seemed to beam from her fine uplifted eyes.   On account of the closeness of the room, she had thrown off her hat, cloak, and gloves, and laid them on the bed ; and her fine hair, which had escaped from its confinement, shaded that side of her face which was next the door, and prevented her seeing me.

I scarcely dared to breathe, lest I should interrup such a scene.   It was a subject not unworthy of Raphael.   She next began to read the forty-first Psalm, with the meek yet solemn emphasis of devout feeling. ' Blessed is he that considereth the poor and needy, the Lord shall deliver him in the time of trouble.' Neither the poor woman nor myself could hold out any longer.   She was overcome by her gratitude, and I by my admiration, and we both at the same moment involuntarily exclaimed Amen !   I sprang forward with a motion I could no longer control.   Lucilla saw me, started up in confusion, and blushed
                              Celestial rosy red.

Then, eagerly endeavouring to conceal the Bible, by drawing her hat over it, ' Phœbe,' said she, with all the composure she could assume, ' is the broth ready ?' Phœbe, with her usual gaiety, called out to me to come and assist, which I did, but so unskilfully, that she chid me for my awkwardness.

It was an interesting sight to see one of these blooming sisters lift the dying woman in her bed, and support her with her arm, while the other fed her, her own weak hand being unequal to the task.   At that moment, how little did the splendours and vanities of life appear in my eyes !   and how ready was I to exclaim with Wolsey,

Vain pomp and glory of the world, I hate you !

When they had finished their pious office, I inquired if the poor woman had no attendant.   Phœbe, who was generally the chief speaker, said, ' She has a good daughter, who is out at work by day, but takes care of her mother at night ; but she is never left alone, for she has a little granddaughter who attends her in the mean time ; but as she is obliged to go once a day to the Grove to fetch provisions, we generally contrive to send her while we are here, that Dame Alice may never be left alone.'

While we were talking, I heard a little weary step painfully climbing up the stairs, and looked round, expecting to see the granddaughter ; but it was little Kate Stanley, with a lap full of dry sticks, which she had been collecting for the poor woman's fire.   The sharp points of the sticks had forced their way in many places through the white muslin frock, part of which, together with her bonnet, she had left in the hedge which she had been robbing. At this loss she expressed not much concern, but lamented not a little that sticks were so scarce ; that she feared the broth had been spoiled, from her being so long in pick- ing them, but *indeed* she could not help it. I was pleased with these under allotments, these low degrees in the scale of charity.

I had gently laid my roses on the hat of Miss Stanley, as it lay on the Bible, and before we left the room, as I drew near the good old dame to slip a couple of guineas into her hand, I had the pleasure of seeing Lucilla, who thought herself unobserved, retire to the little window, and fasten the roses into the crown of her hat like a garland. When the granddaughter returned loaded with the daily bounty from the Grove, we took our leave, followed by the prayers and blessings of the good woman.

As we passed by the rose-tree, the orchard, and the court, Phœbe said to me, 'Aren't you glad that poor people can have such pleasures ?' I told her it doubled my gratification to witness the enjoyment, and to trace the hand which conferred it ; for she had owned it was *their* work. 'We have always,' said Phœbe, 'a particular satisfaction in observing a neat little flower-garden about a cottage, because it holds out a comfortable indication that the inhabitants are free from absolute want, before they think of these little embellishments.'

'It looks, also,' said Miss Stanley, 'as if the woman, instead of spending her few leisure moments in gadding abroad, employed them in adorning her little habitation, in order to make it more attractive to her husband. And we know more than one instance in this village in which the man has been led to give up the public-house, by the inno- cent ambition of improving on her labours.'

I asked her what first inspired her with such fondness for gardening, and how she acquired so much skill and taste in this elegant art? She blushed, and said, ' She was afraid I should think her romantic, if she were to confess that she had caught both the taste and the passion, as far as she possessed either, from an early and intimate acquaintance with the " Paradise Lost," of which she considered the beautiful de- scriptions of scenery and plantations as the best precepts for landscape gardening. Milton,' she said, ' both excited the taste and supplied the rules. He taught the art, and inspired the love of it.'

From the gardens of Paradise the transition to its heroine was easy and natural. On my asking her opinion of this portrait, as drawn by Milton, she replied, ' That she considered Eve, in her state of inno- cence, as the most beautiful model of the delicacy, propriety, grace, and elegance of the female character which any poet ever exhibited. Even after her fall,' added she, ' there is something wonderfully touch- ing in her remorse, and affecting in her contrition.'

' We are probably,' replied I, ' more deeply affected with the beauti- fully contrite expressions of repentance in our first parents, from being so deeply involved in the consequences of the offence which occa- sioned it.'

' And yet,' replied she, ' I am a little affronted with the poet, that

while, with a noble justness, he represents Adam's grief at his expul
sion as chiefly arising from his being banished from the presence of his
Maker, the sorrows of Eve seem too much to arise from being banished
from her flowers. The grief, though never grief was so beautifully eloquent, is rather too exquisite, her substantial ground for lamentation
considered.'

Seeing me going to speak, she stopped me with a smile, saying, ' I
see by your looks that you are going, with Mr. Addison, to vindicate
the poet, and to call this a just appropriation of the sentiment to
the sex ; but surely the disproportion in the feeling here is rather too
violent, though I own the loss of her flowers *might* have aggravated
any common privation. There is, however, no female character in
the whole compass of poetry in which I have ever taken so lively
an interest, and no poem that ever took such powerful possession of
my mind.'

If anything had been wanting to my full assurance of the sympathy
of our tastes and feelings, this would have completed my conviction.
It struck me as the Virgilian lots formerly struck the superstitious. Our
mutual admiration of the ' Paradise Lost,' and of its heroine seemed to
bring us nearer together than we had yet been. Her remarks, which
I gradually drew from her in the course of our walk, on the construction of the fable, the richness of the imagery, the elevation of the language, the sublimity and just appropriation of the sentiments, the
artful structure of the verse, and the variety of the characters, convinced me that she had imbibed her taste from the purest sources. It
was easy to trace her knowledge of the best authors, though she
quoted none.

' This,' said I exultingly to myself, ' is the true learning for a lady ; a
knowledge that is rather detected than displayed, that is felt in its
effects on her mind and conversation ; that is seen, not by her citing
learned names, or adducing long quotations, but in the general result,
by the delicacy of her taste, and the correctness of her sentiments.'

In our way home I made a merit with little Kate, not only by
rescuing her hat from the hedge, but by making a little provision of
wood under it, of larger sticks than she could gather, which she joyfully
promised to assist the granddaughter in carrying to the cottage.

I ventured with as much diffidence as if I had been soliciting a
pension for myself, to entreat that I might be permitted to undertake
the putting forward Dame Alice's little girl in the world, as soon as she
shall be released from her attendance on her grandmother. My proposal was graciously accepted, on condition that it met with Mr. and
Mrs. Stanley's approbation.

When we joined the party at supper, it was delightful to observe that
the habits of religious charity were so interwoven with the texture of
these girls' minds, that the evening which had been so interesting to
me, was to them only a common evening, marked with nothing particular. It never occurred to them to allude to it ; and once or twice
when I was tempted to mention it, my imprudence was repressed by
a look of the most significant gravity from Lucilla.

I was comforted, however, by observing that my roses were transferred from the hat to the hair. This did not escape the penetrating eye of Phœbe, who archly said, ' I wonder, Lucilla, what particular charm there is in Dame Alice's faded roses. I offered you some fresh ones since we came home. I never knew you prefer withered flowers before.' Lucilla made no answer, but cast down her timid eyes, and out-blushed the roses on her head.

Chapter XLII.

AFTER breakfast next morning the company all dropped off one after another, except Lady Belfield, Miss Stanley, and myself. We had been so busily engaged in looking over the plan of a conservatory, which Sir John proposed to build at Beechwood, his estate in Surrey, that we hardly missed them.

Little Celia, whom I call the Rosebud, had climbed up my knees, a favourite station with her, and was begging me to tell her another pretty story. I had before told her so many, that I had exhausted both my memory and my imagination. Lucilla was smiling at my impoverished invention, when Lady Belfield was called out of the room. Her fair friend rose mechanically to follow her. Her ladyship begged her not to stir, but to employ the five minutes of her absence in carefully criticising the plan she held in her hand, saying, she would bring back another which Sir John had by him ; and that Lucilla, who is considered as the last appeal in all matters of this nature, should decide to which the preference should be given, before the architect went to work.

In a moment I forgot my tale, and my rosebud, and the conservatory, and everything but Lucilla, whom I was beginning to address, when little Celia, pulling my coat, said : ' Oh, Charles ' (for so I teach all the little ones to call me), ' Mrs. Comfit tells me very bad news. She says that your new curricle is come down, and that you are going to run away. Oh ! don't go ; I can't part with you,' said the little charmer, throwing her arms round my neck.

' Will you go with me, Celia ?' said I, kissing her rosy cheek. ' There will be room enough in the curricle.'—' Oh, I should like to go,' said she, ' if Lucilla may go with us. Do, dear Charles, do, let Lucilla go to the Priory. She will be very good : won't you, Lucilla ?' I ventured to look at Miss Stanley, who tried to laugh without succeeding, and blushed without trying at it.

On my making no reply, for fear of adding to her confusion, Celia looked up piteously in my face, and cried : ' And so you won't let Lucilla go home with you? I am sure the curricle will hold us all nicely ; for I am very little, and Lucilla is not very big.'—' Will *you* persuade her, Celia ?' said I.—' Oh,' said she, ' she does not want persuading ; she is willing enough, and I will run to papa and mamma and ask their leave, and then Lucilla will go, and glad : won't you, Lucilla ?'

So saying she sprung out of my arms, and ran out of the room ; Lucilla would have followed and prevented her. I respectfully detained her. How could I neglect such an opportunity? Such an opening as the sweet prattler had given me it was impossible to overlook. The impulse was too powerful to be resisted ; I gently replaced her on her seat, and in language, which if it did any justice to my feelings, was the most ardent, tender, and respectful, poured out my whole heart. I believe my words were incoherent ; I am sure they were sincere.

She was evidently distressed. Her emotion prevented her replying. But it was the emotion of surprise, not of resentment. Her confusion bore no symptom of displeasure. Blushing and hesitating, she at last said—' My father, sir—my mother.' Here her voice failed her. I recollected with joy, that on the application of Lord Staunton, she had allowed of no such reference, nay, she had forbidden it.

' I take your reference joyfully,' said I, ' only tell me that if I am so happy as to obtain their consent, you will not withhold yours.' She ventured to raise her timid eyes to mine, and her modest but expressive look encouraged me almost as much as any words could have done.

At that moment the door opened, and in came Sir John with the other drawing of the conservatory in his hand. After having examined us both with his keen, critical eye, ' Well, Miss Stanley,' said he, with a look and tone which had more meaning than she could well stand, ' here is the other drawing. As you look as if you had been *calmly* examining the first, you will now give me your *cool, deliberate* opinion of the merits of both.' He had the cruelty to lay so much stress on the words cool, calm, and deliberate, and to pronounce them in so arch a manner, and so ironical a tone, as clearly showed, he read in her countenance that no epithets could possibly have been so ill-applied.

Lady Belfield came in immediately after. ' Well, Caroline,' said he, with a significant glance, ' Miss Stanley has deeply considered the subject since you went ; I never saw her look more interested about anything. I don't think she is dissatisfied, on the whole. General approbation is all she now expresses. She will have time to spy out faults hereafter : she sees none at present. All is beauty, grace, and proportion.'

As if this was not enough, in ran Celia quite out of breath—' Oh, Lucilla,' cried she, ' papa and mamma won't let you go with Charles, though I told them you begged and prayed to go.' Lucilla, the pink of whose cheeks was become crimson, said angrily, ' How, Celia ! what do you mean ?' ' Oh, no,' replied the child ; ' I mean to say, that I begged and prayed, and I thought you looked as if you would like to go—though Charles did not ask you, and so I told papa.'

This was too much. The Belfields laughed outright ; but Lady Belfield had the charity to take Lucilla's hand, saying, ' Come into my dressing-room, my dear, and let us settle this conservatory business. This prattling child will never let us get on.' Miss Stanley followed, her face glowing with impatience—Celia, whom I detained, called after her —' Papa only said there was not room in the curricle for three, but if 'tis only a little way, I am sure we could sit—could not we, Lucilla ?' Lucilla was now happily out of hearing.

Though I was hurt that her delicacy had suffered so much, yet I own I hugged the little innocent author of this confusion with additional fondness. Sir John's raillery, now that Lucilla could be no longer pained by it, was cordially received, or rather, I was inattentive to every object but the one of which my heart was full. To be heard, to be accepted, though tacitly, to be referred to parents who I knew had no will but hers,

> Was such a sacred and homefelt delight,
> * Such sober certainty of waking bliss,
> As I ne'er felt till now.

During the remainder of the day I found no means of speaking to Mr. Stanley. Always frank and cheerful, he neither avoided nor sought me, but the arrival of company prevented our being thrown together. Lucilla appeared at dinner as usual : a little graver and more silent, but always unaffected, natural, and delicate. Sir John whispered me that she had entreated her mother to keep Celia out of the way, till this curricle business was a little got out of her head.

Chapter XLIII.

THE next morning, as soon as I thought Mr. Stanley had retreated to his library, I followed him thither. He was busy writing letters. I apologised for my intrusion. He laid his papers aside, and invited me to sit by him.

'You are too good, sir,' said I, 'to receive with so much kindness a culprit who appears before you ingenuously to acknowledge the infraction of a treaty into which he had the honour of entering with you. I fear that a few days are wanting of my prescribed month. I had resolved to obey you with the most religious scrupulousness ; but a circumstance trifling in itself has led almost irresistibly to a declaration' which in obedience to your commands I had resolved to postpone. But though it is somewhat premature, I hope, however, you will not condemn my precipitancy. I have ventured to tell your charming daughter how necessary she is to my happiness. She does not reject me. She refers me to her father.'

'You have your peace to make with my daughter, I can tell you, sir,' said Mr. Stanley, looking gravely ; 'I fear you have mortally offended her.' I was dreadfully alarmed. 'You know not how you afflict me, sir,' said I ; 'how have I offended Miss Stanley ?' 'Not Miss Stanley,' said he, smiling, 'but Miss Celia Stanley, who extremely resents having been banished from the drawing-room yesterday evening.'

'If Celia's displeasure is all I have to fear, sir, I am most fortunate. Oh, sir, my happiness, the peace of my future life, is in your hands. But first tell me you forgive the violation of my promise.'

'I am willing to believe, Charles,' replied he, 'that you kept the spirit of your engagement, though you broke it in the letter ; and for an unpremeditated breach of obligation of this nature, we must not, I believe, be too rigorous. Your conduct since your declaration to me has confirmed the affection which your character had before excited. You were probably surprised and hurt at my cold reception of your proposal; a proposal which gave me a deeper satisfaction than I can express. Yet I was no dissembler in suppressing the pleasure I felt at an address so every way desirable. My dear Charles, I know a little of human nature. I know how susceptible the youthful heart is of impressions. I know how apt these impressions are to be obliterated —a new face, a more advantageous connection——'—' Hold, sir,' said I, indignantly interrupting him, 'you cannot think so meanly of me. You cannot rate the son of your friend so low.'

'I am very far indeed,' replied he, 'from rating you low. I know you abhor mercenary considerations; but I know also that you are a young man, lively, ardent, impressible. I know the rapid effect which leisure, retirement, rural scenes, daily opportunities of seeing a young woman not ugly, of conversing with a young woman not disagreeable, may produce on the heart, or rather on the imagination. I was aware that seeing no other, conversing with no other, none at least that, to speak honestly, I could consider as a fair competitor, hardly left you an unprejudiced judge of the state of your own heart. I was not sure but that this sort of easy commerce might produce a feeling of complacency which might be mistaken for love. I could not consent that mere accident, mere leisure, the mere circumstance of being thrown together, should irrevocably entangle either of you. I was desirous of affording you time to see, to know, and to judge. I would not take advantage of your first emotions. I would not take advantage of your friendship for me. I would not take advantage of your feeling ardently, till I had given you time to judge temperately and examine fairly.'

I assured him I was equally at a loss to express my gratitude for his kindness, and my veneration of his wisdom; and thanked him in terms of affectionate energy.

'My regard for you,' said he, 'is not of yesterday. I have taken a warm interest in your character and happiness almost ever since you have been in being, and in a way more intimate and personal than you can suspect.'

So saying he arose, unlocked the drawer of a cabinet which stood behind him, and took out a large packet of letters. He then resumed his seat, and holding out the direction on the covers, asked me if I was acquainted with the hand-writing. A tear involuntarily started into my eye as I exclaimed—'It is the well-known hand of my beloved father.'

'Listen to me attentively,' resumed he. 'You are not ignorant that never were two men more firmly attached by all the ties which ever cemented a Christian friendship than your lamented father and myself. Our early youth was spent in the same studies, the same pleasures, the same society. "We took sweet counsel together, and went to the house of God as friends." He condescendingly overlooked my being five or six years younger than himself. After his marriage with your excellent mother, the current of life carried us different ways, but without causing any abatement in the warmth of our attachment.

'I continued to spend one month every year with him at the Priory, till I myself married. You were then not more than three or four years old; and your engaging manners and sweet temper laid the foundation of an affection which has not been diminished by time, and the reports of your progress. Sedentary habits on the part of your father, and a rapidly increasing family on mine, kept us stationary at the two extremities of the kingdom. I settled at the Grove, and both as husband and father have been happiest of the happy.

'As soon as Lucilla was born, your father and I simultaneously formed a wish that it might be possible to perpetuate our friendship by the future union of our children.'

When Mr. Stanley uttered these words, my heart beat so fast, and the agitation of my whole frame was so visible, that he paused for a moment; but perceiving that I was all ear, and that I made a silent motion for him to proceed, he went on.

'This was a favourite project with us. We pursued it, however, with the moderation of men who had a settled sense of the uncertainty of all human things, of human life itself; and with a strong conviction of the probability that our project might never be realized.

'Without too much indulging the illusions of hope, we agreed that there could be no harm in educating our children for each other; in inspiring them with corresponding tastes, similar inclinations, and especially with an exact conformity in their religious views. We never indulged the presumptuous thought of counteracting providential dispensations, of conquering difficulties which time might prove to be insuperable, and, above all, we determined never to be so weak, or so unjust, as to think of compelling their affections. We had both studied the human heart long enough to know that it is a perverse and wayward thing. We were convinced that it would not be dictated to in a matter which involved its dearest interests, we knew that it liked to pick out its own happiness in its own way.'

As Mr. Stanley proceeded, my heart melted with grateful love for a father, who, in making such a provision for my happiness, had generously left my choice so free. But while my conscience seemed to reproach me as if I had not deserved such tenderness, I rejoiced that my memory had no specific charge to bring against it.

'For all these reasons,' continued Mr. Stanley, 'we mutually agreed to bury our wishes in our own bosoms; to commit the event to Him by whom all events are governed; never to name you to each other but in a general way; to excite no factitious liking, to elicit no artificial passion, and to kindle neither impatience, curiosity, nor interest. Nothing more than a friendly family regard was ever manifested, and the names of Charles and Lucilla were never mentioned together.

'In this you have found your advantage. Had my daughter been accustomed to hear you spoken of with any particularity; had she been conscious that any important consequences might have attached to your visit, you would have lost the pleasure of seeing her in her native simplicity of character. Undesigning and artless, I trust she would have been, under any circumstance, but to have been unreserved and open would have been scarcely possible; nor might you, my dear

Charles, with your strong sense of filial piety, have been able exactly to discriminate how much of your attachment was choice, how much was duty. The awkwardness of restraint would have diminished the pleasure of intercourse to both.

'Knowing that the childish brother-and-sister sort of intimacy was not the most promising mode for the development of your mutual sentiments, we agreed that you should not meet till within a year or two of the period when it would be proper that the union, if ever, might take place.

'We were neither of us of an age or character to indulge very romantic ideas of the doctrine of sympathies. Still we saw no reason for excluding such a possibility. If we succeeded, we knew that we were training two beings in a conformity of Christian principles, which, if they did not at once attract affection, would not fail to insure it, should inferior motives first influence your mutual liking. And if it failed, we should each have educated a Christian, who would be likely to carry piety and virtue into two other families. Much good would attend our success, and no possible evil could attend our failure.

'I could show you, I believe, near a hundred letters on each side, of which you were the unconscious subject. Your father, in his last illness, returned all mine, to prevent a premature discovery, knowing how soon his papers would fall into your hands. If it will give you pleasure, you may peruse a correspondence, of which, for almost twenty years, you were the little hero. In reading my letters, you will make yourself master of the character of Lucilla. You will read the history of her mind; you will mark the unfolding of her faculties, and the progress of her education. In those of your father, you will not be sorry to trace back your own steps.'

Here Mr. Stanley making a pause, I bowed my grateful acceptance of his obliging offer. I was afraid to speak, I was almost afraid to breathe, lest I should lose a word of a communication so interesting.

'You now see,' resumed Mr. Stanley, 'why you were sent to Edinburgh. Cambridge and Oxford were too near London, and of course too near Hampshire, to have maintained the necessary separation. As soon as you left the university, your father proposed accompanying you on a visit to the Grove. Like fond parents, we had prepared each other to expect to see a being just such a one as each would have wished for the companion of his child.

'This was to be merely a visit of experiment. You were both too young to marry. But we were impatient to place you both in a post of observation; to see the result of a meeting; to mark what sympathy there would be between two minds formed with a view to each other.

'But vain are all the projects of man. "Oh! blindness to the future!" You doubtless remember, that just as everything was prepared for your journey southwards, your dear father was seized with the lingering illness of which he died. Till almost the last, he was able to write to me, in his intervals of ease, short letters on the favourite topic. I remember with what joy his heart dilated, when he told me of your positive refusal to leave him, on his pressing you to pursue the plan already settled, and to make your visit to London and

the Grove without him. I will read you the passage from his letter.'—
He read as follows :

' " In vain have I endeavoured to drive this dear son for a short time
from me. He asked, with the indignant feeling of affronted filial piety,
if I could propose to him any compensation for his absence from my
sick couch ? ' I make no sacrifice to duty,' said he, ' in preferring you.
If I make any sacrifice, it is to pleasure.' " '

Seeing my eyes overflow with grateful tenderness, Mr. Stanley said,
' If I can find his last letter I will show it you.' Then, looking over the
packet—' Here it is,' said he, putting it into my hands with visible
emotion. Neither of us had strength of voice to be able to read it
aloud. It was written at several times.

' Priory, Wednesday, March 18, 1807.

' STANLEY—I feel that I am dying. Death is awful, my dear friend,
but it is neither surprising nor terrible. I have been too long accustomed steadily to contemplate it at a distance, to start from it now it
is near.

' As a man, I have feared death. As a Christian, I trust I have
overcome this fear. Why should I dread that, which mere reason
taught me is not an extinction of my being, and which revelation has
convinced me will be an improvement of it ? An improvement, oh,
how inconceivable !

' For several years I have habituated myself every day to reflect for
some moments on the vanity of life, the certainty of death, the awful-
ness of judgment, and the duration of eternity.

" The separation from my excellent wife is a trial from which I should
utterly shrink, were I not sustained by the Christian hope. When we
married, we knew that we were not immortal. I have endeavoured to
familiarise to her and to myself the inevitable separation, by constantly
keeping up in the minds of both the idea that one of us *must* be the
survivor. I have endeavoured to make that idea supportable by the
conviction that the survivorship will be short—the re-union certain—
speedy—eternal. *O præclarum diem!** etc., etc. How gloriously does
Christianity exalt the rapture, by ennobling the objects, of this sublime
apostrophe !'

' Friday, 20.

' As to the union of my son with Lucilla, you and I, my friend, have
long learned, from an authority higher than that classical one, of which
we have frequently admired the expression and lamented the application, that long views, and remote hopes, and distant expectations become
not so short-sighted, so short-lived a creature as man.† I trust, however, that our plans have been carried on with a complete conviction of
this brevity, with an entire acquiescence in the will of the great Arbiter
of life and death. I have told Charles, it is my wish that he should

---

* See this whole beautiful passage in ' Cicero de Senectute.'

† Horace, in speaking of the brevity and uncertainty of life, seldom fails to
produce it as an incentive to sensual indulgence. See particularly the fourth and
eleventh Odes of the first book.

visit you soon after my death. I durst not command it—for this incomparable youth, who has sacrificed so much to his father—will find that he has a mother worthy of still greater sacrifices. As soon as he can prevail, on himself to leave her, you will see him. May he and your Lucilla behold each other with the eyes, with which each of us views his own child ! If they see each other with indifference, never let them know our wishes. It would perplex and hamper those to whom we wish perfect freedom of thought and action. If they conceive a mutual attachment, reveal our project. In such minds, it will strengthen that attachment. The approbation of a living, and the desire of a deceased parent will sanctify their union.

'I must break off through weakness.'

'*Monday*, 23.

'I resume my pen, which I thought I had held for the last time. May God bless and direct our children ! Infinite wisdom permits me not to see their union. Indeed my interest in all earthly things weakens. Even my solicitude for this event is somewhat diminished. The most important circumstance, if it have not God for its object, now seems comparatively little. The longest life, with all its concerns, shrinks to a point in the sight of a dying man whose eye is filled by eternity ! oh my friend, eternity ! Eternity is a depth which no geometry can measure, no arithmetic calculate, no imagination conceive, no rhetoric describe. The eye of a dying Christian seems gifted to penetrate depths hid from the wisdom of philosophy. It looks athwart the dark valley without dismay, cheered by the bright scene beyond it. It looks with a kind of chastened impatience to that land where happiness will be only holiness perfected. There all the promises of the gospel will be accomplished. There afflicted virtue will rejoice at its past trials, and acknowledge their subservience to its present bliss. There the secret self-denials of the righteous shall be recognised and rewarded—and all the hopes of the Christian shall have their complete consummation.

'*Saturday*, 28.

' My weakness increases—I have written this at many intervals. My body faints, but in the Lord Jehovah is everlasting strength. Oh, Stanley ! if pain is trying, if death is awful, to him who knows in whom he has trusted, how is pain endured, how is death encountered, by those who have no such support ?'

'*Tuesday*, 31st.

' I am better to-day.—If I experience little of that rapture which some require as the sign of their acceptance, I yet have a good hope through grace. Nay, there are moments when I rejoice with joy unspeakable. I would not produce this joy as any certain criterion of my safety, because, from the nature of my disease, there are also moments when my spirits sink, and this might equally furnish arguments against my state, to those who decide by frames and feelings. I think my faith as sound, my pardon as sure, when these privileges are withdrawn, as when I enjoy them. No depression of spirits can make my evidences less solid, though it may render the review of them less delightful.'

'Friday, April 3.

' Stanley ! my departure is at hand.   My eternal redemption draweth nigh.   My hope is full of immortality.   This is my comfort—not that my sins are few or small, but that they are, I humbly trust, pardoned through him who loved me, and gave himself for me.   Faithful is HE that has promised, and HIS promises are not too great to be made good —for Omniscience is my promiser, and I have Omnipotence itself for my security.   Adieu !

*   *   *   *   *

On the cover was written, in Mr. Stanley's hand—' He died three days after !'

*   *   *   *   *

It is impossible to describe the mingled and conflicting emotions of my soul, while I perused this letter.   Gratitude that I had possessed such a father—sorrow that I had lost him—transport in anticipating an event which had been his earnest wish for almost twenty years—regret that he was not permitted to witness it, devout joy that he was in a state so superior to even *my* sense of happiness,—a strong feeling of the uncertainty and brevity of *all* happiness,—a solemn resolution that I would never act unworthily of such a father,—a fervent prayer that I might be enabled to keep that resolution :—all these emotions so agitated and divided my whole mind, as to render me unfit for any society, even for that of Lucilla.   I withdrew, gratefully pressing Mr. Stanley's hand ; he kindly returned the pressure, but neither of us attempted to speak.

He silently put my father's packet into my hands.   I shut myself into my apartment, and read for three hours, letters for which I hope to be the better in time and in eternity.   I found in them a treasure of religious wisdom, excellent maxims of human prudence, a thorough acquaintance with life and manners, a keen insight into human nature in the abstract, and a nice discrimination of individual characters ; admirable documents for general education, the application of those documents to my particular turn of character, and diversified methods for improving it.—The pure delight to which I look forward in reading these letters with Lucilla, soon became my predominant feeling.

I returned to the company with a sense of felicity, which the above feelings and reflections had composed into a soothing tranquillity.   My joy was sobered without being abated.   I received the cordial congratulations of my friends.   Mrs. Stanley behaved to me with increased affection, she presented me to her daughter, with whom I afterwards passed two hours.   This interview left me nothing to desire, but that my gratitude to the Almighty Dispenser of happiness might bear some little proportion to his blessings.

As I was passing through the hall after dinner, I spied little Celia peeping out of the door of the children's apartment, in the hope of seeing me pass.   She flew to me, and begged I would take her in to the company.   As I knew the interdict was taken off, I carried her into the saloon where they were sitting.   She ran into Lucilla's arms, and said, in a voice which she meant for a whisper, but loud enough to be heard by

15—2

the whole company, 'Do, dear Lucilla, forgive me, I will never say another word about the curricle; and you shan't go to the Priory, since you don't like it.' Lucilla found means to silence her by showing her the pictures in the 'Peacock at Home;' and, without looking up to observe the general smile, contrived to attract the sweet child's attention to this beautiful little poem, in spite of Sir John, who did his utmost to widen the mischief.

Chapter XLIV.

THE next day in the afternoon Dr. Barlow called on us. By the uncommon seriousness of his countenance I saw something was the matter. 'You will be shocked,' said he, 'to hear that Mr. Tyrrel is dying, if not actually dead. He was the night before last seized with a paralytic stroke. He lay a long time without sense or motion; a delirium followed. In a short interval of reason, he sent, earnestly imploring to see me. Seldom have I witnessed so distressing a scene.

'As I entered the room he fixed his glassy eyes full upon me, quite unconscious who I was, and groaned out, in an inward hollow voice, "Go to now, ye rich men, weep and howl, for your miseries are come upon you." I asked how he did: he replied still from St. James— "How? why, my gold and silver are cankered; the rust of them shall witness against me; they eat up my flesh as it were fire."

'I was astonished,' continued Dr. Barlow, 'to see so exact a memory coupled with so wild an imagination. "Be composed, sir," said I, seeing he began to recollect me, "this deep contrition is a favourable symptom." "Dr. Barlow," replied he, grasping my hand with a vehemence which corresponded with his look, "have you never heard of riches kept by the owner thereof to his hurt? Restitution! Doctor, restitution!—and it must be immediate, or it will be too late." I was now deeply alarmed. "Surely, sir," said I, "you are not unhappily driven to adopt St. James's next words—forgive me—but you cannot surely have 'defrauded.'" "Oh, no, no," cried he, "I have been what the world calls honest, but not what the Judge of quick and dead will call so. The restitution I must make is not to the rich, for anything I have *taken* from them, but to the poor, for what I have *kept* from them. Hardness of heart would have been but a common sin, in a common man; but I have been a professor, Doctor, I will not say a hypocrite, for I deceived myself as much as others. But, oh! how hollow has my profession been!"

'Here, seeing him ready to faint,' continued Dr. Barlow, 'I imposed silence on him, till he had taken a cordial. This revived him, and he went on.

'"I was miserable in my early course of profligacy. I was disappointed in my subsequent schemes of ambition. I expected more from the world than it had to give. But I continued to love it with all its disappointments. Under whatever new shape it presented its temptations, it was still my idol. I had always loved money; but other passions more turbulent had been hitherto predominant. These I at length renounced. Covetousness now became my reigning sin. Still it was to the broken cistern that I cleaved. Still it was on the broken reed that I leaned. Still I was unhappy, I was at a loss whither to turn for comfort. Of religion I scarcely knew the first principles.

' " In this state I met with a plausible, but ill-informed man. He had zeal, and a sort of popular eloquence ; but he wanted knowledge, and argument, and soundness. I was, however, struck with his earnestness, and with the importance of some truths which, though common to others, were new to me. But his scheme was hollow and imperfect, and his leading principle subversive of all morality."

' Here Mr. Tyrrel paused. I entreated him to spare himself ; but after a few deep groans he proceeded :

' " Whether his opinions had made *himself* immoral I never inquired. It is certain they were calculated to make his hearers so. Instead of lowering my spiritual disease, by prescribing repentance and humility, he inflamed it by cordials. All was high—all was animating—all was safe ! On no better ground than my avowed discontent, he landed me at once in a security so much the more fatal, as it laid asleep all apprehension. He mistook my uneasiness for a complete change. My talking of sin was made a substitute for my renouncing it. Proud of a rich man for a convert, he led me to mistake conviction for conversion. I was buoyed up with an unfounded confidence. I adopted a religion which promised pardon without repentance, happiness without obedience, and heaven without holiness. I had found a short road to peace. I never inquired if it were a safe one."

' The poor man now fell back, unable to speak for some minutes. Then, rallying again, he resumed, in a still more broken voice :

' " Here I stopped short. My religion had made no change in my heart, it therefore made none in my life. I read good books, but they were low and fanatical in their language, and antinomian in their principle. But my religious ignorance was so deplorable, that their novelty caught strong hold of me."

' I now desired him,' continued Dr. Barlow, ' not to exhaust himself farther. I prayed with him. He was struck with awe at the holy energy in the office for the sick, which was quite new to him. He owned he had not suspected the Church to be so evangelical. This is no uncommon error. Hot-headed and superficial men, when they are once alarmed, are rather caught by phrases than sentiments, by terms than principles. It is this ignorance of the doctrines of the Bible and of the Church, in which men of the world unhappily live, that makes it so difficult for us to address them under sickness and affliction. We have no common ground on which to stand ; no intelligible medium through which to communicate with them. It is having both a language and a science to learn at once.'

In the morning Dr. Barlow again visited Mr. Tyrrel. He found him still in great perturbation of mind. Feeling himself quite sensible, he had begun to make his will. He had made large bequests to several charities. Dr. Barlow highly approved of this ; but reminded him, that though he himself would never recommend charity as a commuta-tion or a bribe ; yet some immediate acts of bounty, while there was a possibility of his recovery, would be a better earnest of his repentance, than the bequeathing his whole estate when it could be of no further use to himself. He was all acquiescence.

He desired to see Mr. Stanley. He recommended to him his nephew, over whose conduct Mr. Stanley promised to have an eye. He made him and Dr. Barlow joint executors.. He offered to leave them half his fortune. With their usual disinterestedness they positively refused to accept it, and suggested to him a better mode of bestowing it.

He lifted up his hands and eyes, saying, 'This is indeed Christianity —pure and undefiled religion ! If it be not faith, it is its fruits. If it be not the procuring cause of salvation, it is one evidence of a safe state. Oh, Mr. Stanley, our last conversation has sunk deep into my heart. You had begun to pull the veil from my eyes ; but nothing tears the whole mask off, like the hand of death, like impending judgment. How little have I considered eternity ! Judgment was not in all my thoughts—I had got rid of the terrors of responsibility ! Oh, Dr. Barlow, is there any hope for me ?'

' Sir,' replied the Doctor, ' your sin is not the greater because you feel it : so far from it, your danger diminishes in proportion as it is discerned. Your condition is not worse, but better, because you are become sensible of your own sins and wants. I judge far more favourably of your state now, than when you thought so well of it. Your sense of the evil of your own heart is the best proof of your sincerity ; your repent-ance towards God is the best evidence of your faith in our Lord Jesus Christ.'

' Doctor, it is too late,' replied the sick man. ' How can I show that my repentance is sincere ? In this miserable condition, how can I glorify God ?'

' Sir,' replied Dr. Barlow, ' you must lay anew the whole foundation of your faith. That Saviour whom you had unhappily adopted as a substitute for virtue, must be received as a propitiation for sin. If you recover, you must devote yourself, spirit, soul, and body, to His service. You must adorn His gospel by your conduct ; you must plead His cause in your conversation ; you must recommend His doctrines by your humility ; you must dedicate every talent God has given you to His glory. If He continue to visit you with sickness, this will call new and more difficult Christian graces into exercise. If by this severe affliction you lose all ability to do God actual service, you may perhaps glorify Him more effectually by casting yourself entirely on Him for support, by patient suffering for His sake who suffered everything for yours. You will have an additional call for trusting in the Divine promises ; an additional occasion of imitating the Divine example ; a stronger motive for saying practically, The cup which my Father has given me, shall I not drink it ?'

' Oh, Doctor,' said the unhappy man, ' my remorse arises not merely from my having neglected this or that moral duty, this or that act of charity, but from the melancholy evidence which that neglect affords that my religion was not sincere.'

'I repeat, sir,' said Dr. Barlow, 'that your false security and unfounded hope were more alarming than your present distress of mind. Examine your own heart, fear not to probe it to the bottom ; it will be a salutary smart. As you are able, I will put you into a course of reading the Scriptures with a view to promote self-examination. Try yourself by the straight rule they hold out. Pray fervently that the Almighty may assist you by His Spirit, and earnestly endeavour to suffer as well as to do His whole will.'

Dr. Barlow says he thinks there is now as little prospect of his perfect recovery as of his immediate dissolution ; but as far as one human creature can judge of the state of another, he believes the visitation will be salutary.

Chapter XLV.

S we were sitting at supper, after Dr. Barlow had left us, Lady Belfield, turning to me, said, 'She had had a governess proposed to her from a quarter I should little expect to hear.' She then produced a letter, informing her that Mr. Fentham was lately found dead in his bed of an apoplexy ; that he had died insolvent ; and that his large income ceasing with his life, his family were plunged into the utmost distress ; that Mrs. Fentham experienced the most mortifying neglect from her numerous and noble friends, who, now that she could no longer amuse them with balls, concerts, and suppers, revenged themselves by wondering what she could ever mean by giving them at all, and declaring what a bore it had always been to them to go to her parties. They now insisted that people ought to confine themselves to their own station, and live within their income, though they themselves had lifted her above her station, and had led her to exceed her income.

'The poor woman,' continued Lady Belfield, 'is in extreme distress. Her magnificently furnished house will go but a very little way towards satisfying her creditors. That house, whose clamorous knocker used to keep the neighbourhood awake, is already reduced to utter stillness. The splendid apartments, brilliant with lustres and waxlights, and crowded with company, are become a frightful solitude, terrifying to those to whom solitude has not one consolation or resource to offer. Poor Mrs. Fentham is more wounded by this total desertion of those whom she so sumptuously entertained, and so obsequiously flattered, than by her actual wants.'

'It is,' said Sir John, 'a fine exemplification of the friendships of the world,
Confederacies in vice, or leagues in pleasure.'

'Lady Denham, when applied to,' resumed Lady Belfield, 'said, that she was extremely sorry for them ; but as she thought extravagance the greatest of all faults, it would look like an encouragement to imprudence if she did anything for them. Their extravagance, however, had never been objected to by her, till the fountain which supplied it was stopped ; and she had for years made no scruple of winning money almost nightly from the woman whose distresses she now refused to relieve. Lady Denham farther assigned the misery into which the elopement of her darling child with Signor Squallini had brought her, as an additional reason for withholding her kindness from Mrs. Fentham.'

' It is a reason,' said I, interrupting Lady Belfield, ' which, in a rightly-turned mind, would have had a directly contrary operation. When domestic calamity overtakes ourselves, is it not the precise moment for holding out a hand to the wretched ? for diminishing the misery abroad, which at home may be irretrievable ?'

' Lady Bab Lawless, to whom Mrs. Fentham applied for assistance, coolly advised her to send her daughters to service, saying, " that she knew of no acquirement they had which would be of any use to them, except their skill in hair-dressing." '

' It seemed a cruel reproach from a professed friend,' said Sir John, ' and yet it is a literal truth. I know not what can be done for them, or for what they are fit. Their accomplishments might be turned to some account if they were accompanied with real knowledge, useful acquirements, or sober habits. Mrs. Fentham wishes us to recommend them as governesses. But can I conscientiously recommend to others, girls with whom I could not trust my own family ? Had they been taught to look no higher than the clerks of their father, who had been a clerk himself, they might have been happy ; but those very men will now think them as much beneath themselves, as the young ladies lately thought they were above them.'

' I have often,' said Mr. Stanley, ' been amused, with observing what a magic transformation the same event produces on two opposite classes of characters. The misfortunes of their acquaintance convert worldly friends into instantaneous strictness of principle. The faults of the distressed are produced as a plea for their over hard-hearted covetousness. While that very misfortune so relaxes the strictness of good men, that the faults are forgotten in the calamity ; and they who had been perpetually warning the prodigal of his impending ruin, when that ruin comes, are the first to relieve him ; the worldly friend sees only the errors of the sufferer, the Christian sees only his distress.'

It was agreed among us, that some small contribution must be added to a little sum, that had been already raised for their immediate relief : but that nothing was so difficult, as effectually to serve persons whose views were so disproportioned to their deserts, and whose habits would be too likely to carry corruption into families who might receive them from charitable motives.

The conversation then fell insensibly on the pleasure we had enjoyed since we had been together ; and on the delights of rational society and confidential intercourse such as ours had been, where minds mingled, and affection and esteem were reciprocal. Mr. Stanley said many things which evinced how happily his piety was combined with the most affectionate tenderness of heart. Indeed, I had always been delighted to observe in him a quality which is not so common as it is thought to be—a thorough capacity for friendship.

' My dear Stanley,' said Sir John, ' it is of the very essence of human enjoyments, that they must have an end. I observe with regret, that the time assigned for our visit is more than elapsed. We have prolonged it beyond our intention, beyond our convenience : but we have, I trust, been imbibing principles, stealing habits, and borrowing plans, which will ever make us consider this visit as an important æra in our lives.

' My excellent Caroline is deeply affected with all she has seen and heard at the Grove. We must now leave it, though not without reluctance. We must go and endeavour to imitate what, six weeks ago, we almost feared to contemplate. Lady Belfield and I have compared notes. On the most mature deliberation, we agree that we have lived long enough to the world. We agree that it is time to begin to live to ourselves, and to Him who made us. We propose in future to make our winters in London much shorter. We intend to remove early every spring to Beechwood, which we will no longer consider as a temporary residence, but as our home ; we will supply it with everything that may make it interesting and improving to us all. We are resolved to educate our children in the fear of God. Our fondness for them is rather increased than diminished ; but in the exercise of that fondness, we will remember that we are to train them for immortality. We will watch over them as creatures for whose eternal well-being a vast responsibility will attach to ourselves.

' In our new plan of life, we shall have fewer sacrifices to make than most people in our situation, for we have long felt a growing indifference for things which we appeared to enjoy. Of the world, we are only going to give up that part which is not worth keeping, and of which we are really weary. In securing our real friends, we shall not regret if we drop some acquaintance by the way. The wise and the worthy we shall more than ever cherish. In your family, we have enjoyed those true pleasures which entail no repentance. That cheerfulness which alone is worthy of accountable beings, we shall industriously maintain in our own. I bless God if we have not so many steps to tread back as some others have, who are entering, upon principle, on a new course of life.

' We have always endeavoured, though with much imperfection, to fill some duties to each other, to our children, to our friends, and to the poor. But of the prime duty, the main spring of action and of all moral goodness, duty to God, we have not been sufficiently mindful. I hope we have at length learnt to consider him as the fountain of all good, and the gospel of his Son as the fountain of all hope. This new principle, I am persuaded, will never impair our cheerfulness, it will only fix it on a solid ground. By purifying the motive, it will raise the enjoyment.

' But if we have not so many bad habits to correct as poor Carlton had, I question if we have not as many difficulties to meet in another way. His loose course was discreditable. His vices made him stand ill with the world. He would therefore acquire nothing but credit in changing his outward practice. Lady Belfield and I, on the contrary, stand rather too well with the world. We had just that external regularity, that cool indifference about our own spiritual improvement, and the wrong courses of our friends, which procure regard, because they do not interfere with others, nor excite jealousy for ourselves. But we have now to encounter that censure which we have perhaps hitherto been too solicitous to avoid. It will still be our trial, but I humbly trust that it will be no longer our snare. Our morality pleased, because it seemed to proceed merely from a sense of propriety ; our strictness will offend, when it is found to spring from a principle of religion.

'To what tendency in the heart of man, my dear Stanley, is it owing, that religion is commonly seen to excite more suspicion than the want of it ? When a man of the world meets with a gay, thoughtless, amusing person, he seldom thinks of inquiring whether such a one be immoral, or an unbeliever, or a profligate, though the bent of his conversation leans that way. Satisfied with what he finds him, he feels little solicitude to ascertain what he really is. But no sooner does actual piety show itself in any man, than your friends are putting you on your guard ; there is instantly a suggestion, a hint, a suspicion. " Does he not carry things too far ?" " Is he not righteous over much ?" " Is he not intemperate in his zeal ?" " Above all this, is he *sincere* ?" And in short, for that is the centre in which all the lines of suspicion and reprobation meet, " *Is he not a Methodist ?*"

' I trust, however, that, through divine grace, our minds will be fortified against all attacks on this our weak side ; this pass, through which the sort of assaults most formidable to *us* will be likely to enter. I was mentioning this danger to Caroline this morning. She opened her Bible, over which she now spends most of her solitary time, and, with an emphasis foreign from her usual manner, read—

' " Cease ye from man, whose breath is in his nostrils, for wherein is he to be accounted of ?" '

As Sir John repeated these words, I saw Lucilla, who was sitting next Lady Belfield, snatch one of her hands, and kiss it with a rapture which she had no power to control. It was evident that nothing but our presence restrained her from rising to embrace her friend. Her fine eyes glistened, but seeing that I observed her, she gently let go the hand she held, and tried to look composed. I cannot describe the chastened, but not less fervent, joy of Mr. and Mrs. Stanley. Their looks expressed the affectionate interest they took in Sir John's honest declaration. Their hearts overflowed with gratitude to Him without whom 'nothing is strong, nothing is holy.' For my own part, I felt myself raised

Above this visible diurnal sphere.

Sir John afterwards said, ' I begin more and more to perceive the scantiness of all morality which has not the love of God for its motive. *That* virtue will not carry us safely, and will not carry us far, which looks to human estimation as its reward. As it was a false and inadequate principle which first set it a-going, it will always stop short of the true ends of goodness. Do not think, my dear Stanley,' continued he, ' that I fancy it is only our habits which want improving. Dr. Barlow has convinced me that there must be *a mutation of the whole man ;* that the change in our practice must grow out of a new motive ;

not merely out of an amended principle, but a new principle; not an improvement in some particular, but a general, determining change.'

'My dear Belfield,' replied Mr. Stanley, 'all reformation short of this, though it may obtain credit, brings neither peace nor acceptance. This change shows itself gradually perhaps, but unequivocally, by enlightening the understanding, awakening the conscience, purifying the affections, subduing the will, reforming the life.'

Lady Belfield expressed, with a sweet humility, her deep conviction of the truth of these remarks. After some farther discussion, she said, 'Sir John, I have been seriously thinking that I ought not to indulge in the expense of this intended conservatory. We will, if you please, convert the money to the building a charity-school. I cannot consent to incur such a superfluous expense merely for my amusement.'

'My dear Caroline,' replied Sir John, 'through the undeserved goodness of God, my estate is so large, and through your excellent management it is so unimpaired, that we will not give up the conservatory, unless Mr. Stanley thinks we ought to give it up. But we will adopt Lucilla's idea of combining a charity with an indulgence—we will associate the charity-school with the conservatory. This union will be a kind of monument to our friends at the Grove, from whom you have acquired the love of plants, and I of religious charity.'

We all looked with anxious expectation at Mr. Stanley. He gave it as his opinion, that as Lady Belfield was now resolved to live the greater part of the year in the country, she ought to have some amusements in lieu of those she was going to give up. 'Costly decorations and expensive gardens,' continued he, 'at a place where the proprietors do not so much as *intend* to reside, have always appeared to me among the infatuations of opulence. To the expenses which they do not *want*, it is adding an expense which they do not *see*. But surely at a mansion where an affluent family actually live, all reasonable indulgences should be allowed. And where a garden and greenhouse are to supply to the proprietor the place of the abdicated theatre and ball-room, and especially when it is to be a means in her hands of attaching her children to the country, and of teaching them to love home, I declare myself in favour of the conservatory.'

Lucilla's eyes sparkled, but she said nothing.

'It would be unfair,' continued Mr. Stanley, 'to blame too severely those who, living constantly in the country, give in a little to its appropriate pleasures. The real objects of censure seem to be those who, grafting bad taste on bad habits, bring into the country the amusements of the town, and superadd to such as are local, and natural, and innocent, such as are foreign, artificial, and corrupt.'

'My dear Stanley,' said Sir John, 'we have resolved to indemnify our poor neighbours for two injuries which we have been doing them. The one is, by our having lived so little among them : for I have now learnt that the mere act of residence is a kind of charity even in the uncharitable, as it necessarily causes much money to be spent, even where little is given. The other is that we will endeavour to make up

for our past indifferemce to their spiritual concerns, by now acting as
if we aware that the poor have souls as well as bodies ; and that, in
the great day of account, the care of both will attach to our responsibility.'

Such a sense of sober joy seemed to pervade our little party, that
we were not aware that the night was far advanced. Our minds were
too highly wrought for much loquacity, when Phœbe suddenly exclaimed, 'Papa, why is it that happiness does not make one merry? I
never was half so happy in my life, and yet I can hardly forbear crying ; and I believe it is catching, sir, for look, Lucilla is not much wiser
than myself.'

The next day but one after this conversation, our valuable friends
left us. Our separation was softened by the prospect of a speedy
meeting. The day before they set out, Lady Belfield made an earnest
request to Mr. and Mrs. Stanley, that they would have the goodness to
receive Fanny Stokes into their family for a few months, previous to
her entering theirs as governess. 'I can think of no method so likely,'
continued she, 'to raise the tone of education in my own family, as
the transfusion into it of your spirit, and the adoption of your regulations.' Mr. and Mrs. Stanley most cheerfully acceded to the proposal.

Sir John said, 'I was meditating the same request, but with an
additional clause tacked to it, that of sending our eldest girl with
Fanny, that the child also may get imbued with something of your
family spirit, and be broken into better habits than she has acquired
from our hitherto relaxed discipline.' This proposal was also cordially
approved.

———

Chapter XLVI.

DR. BARLOW came to the Grove to take leave of our friends.
He found Sir John and I sitting in the library with Mr.
Stanley. 'As I came from Mr. Tyrrel's,' said the Doctor, 'I
met Mr. Flam going to see him. He seemed so anxious
about his old friend, that a wish strongly presented itself to my mind
that the awful visitation of the sick man might be salutary to him.

'It is impossible to say,' continued he, 'what injury religion has
suffered from the opposite characters of these two men. Flam, who
gives himself no concern about the matter, is kind and generous ;
while Tyrrel, who has made a high profession, is mean and sordid.
It has been said—of what use is religion, when morality has made Mr.
Flam a better man than religion makes Mr. Tyrrel? Thus men of the
world reason ! But nothing can be more false than their conclusions.
Flam is naturally an open, warm-hearted man, but incorrect in many
respects, and rather loose in his principles. His natural good propensities religion would have improved into solid virtues, and would
have cured the most exceptionable parts of his character. But from
religion he stands aloof.

'Tyrrel is naturally narrow and selfish. Religion has not made, but found him such. But what a religion has he adopted! A mere assumption of terms ; a dead, inoperative, uninfluencing notion, which he has taken up ; not, I hope, with a view to deceive others, but by which he has grossly deceived himself. He had heard that religion was a cure for an uneasy mind ; but he did not attend to the means by which the cure is effected, and it relieved not him.

'The corrupt principle whence his vices proceeded was not subdued. He did not desire to subdue it, because in the struggle he must have parted with what he was resolved to keep. He adopted what he believed was a cheap and easy religion ; little aware that the great fundamental scripture doctrine of salvation by Jesus Christ was a doctrine powerfully opposing our corruptions, and involving in its comprehensive requirements a new heart and a new life.'

At this moment Mr. Flam called at the Grove. 'I am just come from Tyrrel,' said he ; 'I fear it is nearly over with him. Poor Ned! he is very low, almost in despair. I always told him that the time would come when he would be glad to exchange notions for actions. I am grieved for him. The remembrance of a kind deed or two done to a poor tenant would be some comfort to him now, at a time when every man stands in need of comfort.'

'Sir,' said Dr. Barlow, 'the scene which I have lately witnessed at Mr. Tyrrel's makes me serious. If you and I were alone, I am afraid it would make me bold. I will, however, suppress the answer I was tempted to give you, because I should not think it prudent or respectful to utter before company what, I am persuaded, your good sense would permit me to say were we alone !'

'Doctor,' replied the good-tempered, but thoughtless man, 'don't stand upon ceremony. You know I love a debate, and I insist on your saying what was in your mind to say. I don't fear getting out of any scrape you can bring me into. You are too well-bred to offend, and, I hope, I am too well-natured to be easily offended. Stanley, I know, always takes your side. Sir John, I trust, will take mine ; and so will the young man here, if he is like most other young men.'

'Allow me then to observe,' returned Dr. Barlow, 'that if Mr. Tyrrel has unhappily deceived himself, by resting too exclusively on a mere speculative faith ; a faith which by his conduct did not evince itself to be of the right sort ; yet, on the other hand, a dependence for salvation on our own benevolence, on our own integrity, or any other good quality we may possess, is an error not less fatal and far more usual. Such a dependence does as practically set at nought the Redeemer's sacrifice as the avowed rejection of the infidel. Honesty and benevolence are among the noblest qualities ; but where the one is practised for reputation, and the other from mere feeling, they are sadly delusive as to the ends of practical goodness. They have both indeed their reward : integrity in the credit it brings, and benevolence in the pleasure it yields. Both are beneficial to society ; both, therefore, are politically valuable. Both sometimes lead me to admire the ordinations of that over-ruling power which often uses as instruments of public good, men who, acting well in many respects, are essentially useful to others ; but who, acting from motives merely human, forfeit for themselves that

high reward which those virtues would obtain, if they were evidences
of a lively faith, and the results of Christian principle. Think me not
severe, Mr. Flam. To be personal is always extremely painful to me.'
'No, no, Doctor,' replied he, 'I know you mean well. 'Tis your
trade to give good counsel ; and your lot I suppose to have it seldom
followed. I shall hear you without being angry. You in your turn
must not be angry, if I hear you without being better.'
'I respect you, sir, too much,' replied Dr. Barlow, 'to deceive you in
a matter of such infinite importance. For one man who errs on Mr.
Tyrrel's principle, a hundred err on yours. His mistake is equally
pernicious, but it is not equally common. I must repeat it : for one
whose soul is endangered through an unwarranted dependence on the
Saviour, multitudes are destroyed not only by the open rejection, but
through a fatal neglect of the salvation wrought by Him. Many more
perish through a presumptuous confidence in their own merits, than
through an unscriptural trust in the merits of Christ.'
'Well, Doctor,' replied Mr. Flam, 'I must say, that I think an ounce
of morality will go farther towards making up my accounts, than a ton
of religion, for which no one but myself would be the better.'
'My dear sir,' said Doctor Barlow, 'I will not presume to determine
between the exact comparative proportions of two ingredients, both of
which are so indispensable in the composition of a Christian. I dare
not hazard the assertion, which of the two is the more perilous state,
but I think I am justified in saying which of the two cases occurs most
frequently.'
Mr. Flam said, 'I should be sorry, Dr. Barlow, to find out at this
time of day, that I have been all my life long in an error.'
'Believe me, sir,' said Dr. Barlow, 'it is better to find it out now,
than at a still later period. One good quality can never be made to
supply the absence of another. There are no substitutes in this warfare.
Nor can all the good qualities put together, if we could suppose them
to unite in one man, and to exist without religion, stand proxy for the
death of Christ. If they could so exist, it would be in the degree only,
and not in the perfection required by that law which says, *do this and
live.* So kind a neighbour as you are, so honest a gentleman, so
generous a master, as you are allowed to be, I cannot, sir, think without pain of your losing the reward of such valuable qualities, by your
placing your hope of eternal happiness in the exercise of them.
Believe me, Mr. Flam, it is easier for a compassionate man, if he be
not religious, to "give all his goods to the poor," than to bring every
thought, "nay, than to bring *any* thought," into captivity to the obedience of Christ ! But be assured, if we give ever so much with our
hands, while we withhold our hearts from God, though we may do
much good to others, we do none to ourselves.'
'Why surely,' said Mr. Flam, 'you don't mean to insinuate that I
should be in a safer state if I never did a kind thing ?'
'Quite the contrary,' replied Dr. Barlow, 'but I could wish to see
your good actions exalted, by springing from a higher principle, I
mean the love of God ; ennobled by being practised to a higher end,
and purified by your renouncing all self-complacency in the performance.'

'But is there not less danger, sir,' said Mr. Flam, 'in being somewhat proud of what one really *does*, than in doing nothing? And is it not more excusable to be a little satisfied with what one really *is*, than in hypocritically pretending to be what one is *not ?*'

'I must repeat,' returned Dr. Barlow, 'that I cannot exactly decide on the question of relative enormity between two opposite sins. I cannot pronounce which is the best of two states so very bad.'

'Why now, Doctor,' said Mr. Flam, 'what particular sin can you charge me with ?'

'I erect not myself into an accuser,' replied Dr. Barlow ; 'but permit me to ask you, sir, from what motive is it that you avoid any wrong practice? Is there any one sin from which you abstain through the fear of offending your Maker ?'

'As to that,' replied Mr. Flam, 'I can't say I ever considered about the motive of the thing. I thought it was quite enough not to do it. Well but, Doctor, since we are gone so far in the catechism, what duty to my neighbour can you convict me of omitting ?'

'It will be well, sir,' said the doctor, 'if you can indeed stand so close a scrutiny as that to which you challenge me, even on your own principles. But tell me, with that frank honesty which marks your character, does your kindness to your neighbour spring from the true fountain, the love of God? That you do many right things, I am most willing to allow. But do you perform them from a sense of obedience to the law of your Maker? Do you perform them because they are commanded in His word, and conformable to His will ?'

'I can't say I do,' said Mr. Flam, 'but if the thing be right in itself, that appears to me to be all in all. It seems hard to encumber a man of business like me with the action and the motive too. Surely if I serve a man, it can make no difference to him, *why* I serve him.'

'To yourself, my dear sir,' said the Doctor, 'it makes all the difference in the world. Besides, good actions, performed on any other principle than obedience, are not only spurious as to their birth, but they are defective in themselves ; they commonly want something in weight and measure.'

'Why, Doctor,' said Mr. Flam, 'I have often heard you say in the pulpit that the best are not perfect. Now, as this is the case, I will tell you how I manage. I think it a safe way to average one's good qualities, to throw a bad one against a good one, and if the balance sinks on the right side, the man is safe.'

Doctor Barlow shook his head, and was beginning to express his regret as such delusive casuistry, when Mr. Flam interrupted him by saying, 'Well, doctor, my great care in life has been to avoid all suspicion of hypocrisy.'

'You cannot do better,' replied Dr. Barlow, 'than to avoid its *reality*. But, for my own part, I believe religious hypocrisy to be rather a rare vice among persons of your station in life. Among the vulgar, indeed, I fear it is not so rare. In neighbourhoods where there is much real piety, there is no small danger of some false profession. But among the higher classes of society, serious religion confers so little credit on him who professes it, that a gentleman is not likely to put on appearances from which he knows he is far more likely to lose reputation than to acquire it. When such a man, therefore, assumes the character of piety, I own I always feel disposed to give him full credit for possessing it. His religion may indeed be mistaken ; it may be defective ; it may even be unsound ; but the chances are very much in favour of its not being insincere. Where piety is genuine, it cannot be altogether concealed. Where " the fruits of the Spirit abound, they will appear." '

'Now, my dear Doctor,' replied Mr. Flam, 'is not that cant ? What do you mean by the fruits of the Spirit ? Would it not have been more worthy of your good sense to have said mortality or virtue ? Would not these terms have been more simple and intelligible ?'

'They might be so,' rejoined the Doctor, 'but they would not rise quite so high. They would not take in my *whole* meaning. The fruit of the Spirit, indeed, always includes *your* meaning, but it includes much more. It is something higher than worldly morality, something holier than mere human virtue. I rather conceive morality, in your sense, to be the effect of natural temper, natural conscience, or worldly prudence, or perhaps a combination of all three. The fruit of the Spirit is the morality of the renewed heart. Worldly morality is easily satisfied with itself. It sits down contented with its own meagre performances—with legal honesty, with bare-weight justice. It seldom gives a particle " that is not in the bond." It is always making out its claim to doubtful indulgences ; it litigates its right to every inch of contested enjoyment ; and is so fearful of not getting enough, that it commonly takes more than its due. It is one of the cases where " the letter killeth, but the Spirit giveth life."

' It obtains, however, its worldly reward. It procures a good degree of respect and commendation ; but it is not attended by the silent train of the Christian graces, with that " joy, peace, long-suffering, gentleness, goodness, faith," which are the fruits of the Spirit, and the evidences of a Christian. These graces are calculated to adorn all that is right with all that is amiable, " whatsoever things are honest and just," with " whatsoever things are lovely and of good report." And, to crown all, they add the deepest humility and most unfeigned self-abasement, to the most correct course of conduct ; a course of conduct which, though a Christian never thinks himself at liberty to neglect, he never feels himself permitted or disposed to be proud of !'

'Well, well, Doctor,' said Mr. Flam, 'I never denied the truth of Christianity, as Carlton formerly did. 'Tis the religion of the country, by law established. And I often go to church, because that too is established by law, for which you know I have a great veneration. 'Tis the religion of my ancestors ; I like it for that too.'

' But, sir,' said the Doctor, 'would you not show your veneration for the church more fully if you attended it twice, instead of once ? and your veneration for the law, if, instead of going sometimes, you went every Sunday, which you know both the law of God and man enjoins.'

'Why, unluckily,' returned Mr. Flam, 'the hour of service interferes with that of dinner.'

'Sir,' said Dr. Barlow, smiling, 'hours are so altered, that I believe if the church were to new-model the calendar, she would say that dinners ought to be placed among the *movable feasts.* An hour earlier or later would accommodate the difference, liberate your servants, and enable you to do a thing right in itself, and beneficial in its example.'

Mr. Flam not being prepared with an answer, went on with his confession of faith. ' Doctor,' said he, ' I am a better Christian than you think. I take it for granted that the Bible is true, for I have heard many men say, who examine for themselves, which I cannot say I have ever had time or inclination to do, that no opposer has ever yet refuted the Scripture account of miracles and prophecies. So if you don't call this being a good Christian, I don't know what is.'

Dr. Barlow replied : ' Nothing can be better, as far as it goes. But allow me to say, that there is another kind of evidence of the truth of our religion, which is peculiar to the real Christian. I mean that evidence which arises from his individual conviction of the efficacy of Christianity in remedying the disorders of his own nature. He who has had his own temper improved, his evil propensities subdued, and his whole character formed anew, by being cast into the mould of Christianity, will have little doubt of the truth of a religion which has produced such obvious effects in himself. The truths for which his reason pleads, and in which his understanding, after much examination, is able to rest, having had a purifying influence on his heart, become established principles, producing in him at the same time holiness of life and peace of conscience. The stronger evidence a man has of his own internal improvement, the stronger will be his conviction of the truth of the religion he professes.'

' There are worse men than I am, doctor,' said Mr. Flam, rather seriously.

' Sir,' replied he, ' I heartily wish every gentleman had your good qualities. But as we shall be judged positively and not comparatively ; as our characters will be finally decided upon, not by our superiority to other men, nor merely by our inferiority to the Divine rule, but by our departure from it, I wish you would begin to square your life by that rule now, which, in order that you may do, you should begin to study. While we live in a total neglect of the Bible, we must not talk of our deficiencies, our failings, our imperfections, as if these alone stood between us and the mercy of God. That, indeed, is the language and the state of the devout Christian. Stronger terms must be used to express the alienation of heart of those who, living in the avowed neglect of Scripture, may be said (forgive me, sir), " to live without God in the world." Ignorance is no plea in a gentleman. In a land of light and knowledge, ignorance itself is a sin.'

Here Dr. Barlow being silent, and Mr. Flam not being prepared to answer, Mr. Stanley said : ' That the pure and virtuous dispositions which arise out of a sincere belief of Christianity, are not more frequently seen in persons professing themselves to be Christians, is, unhappily, one of the strongest arguments against us that can be urged by unbelievers. Instances, however, occur, which are too plain to be denied, of individuals who, having been led by divine grace cordially to receive Christianity, have exhibited in their conduct a very striking proof of its excellence ; and among these are some who, like our friend

16

Carlton, had previously led very corrupt lives. The ordinary class of Christians, who indeed scarcely deserve the name, as well as sceptics and unbelievers, would do well to mark the lives of the truly religious, and to consider them as furnishing a proof which will come powerfully in aid of that body of testimony with which Christianity is intrenched on all sides. And these observers should remember, that though they themselves may not yet possess that best evidence in favour of Christianity, which arises from an inward sense of its purifying nature, they may nevertheless aspire after it ; and those who have any remaining doubts should encourage themselves with the hope, that if they fully yield themselves to the doctrines and precepts of the gospel, a salutary change will in time be effected in their own hearts, which will furnish them with irresistible evidence of its truth.'

I could easily perceive, that though Mr. Stanley and Dr. Barlow entertained small hopes of the beneficial effect of their discourse on the person to whom it was directed, yet they prolonged it with an eye to Sir John Belfield, who sat profoundly attentive, and encouraged them by his looks.

As to Mr. Flam, it was amusing to observe the variety of his motions, gestures, and contortions, and the pains he took to appear easy and indifferent, and even victorious—sometimes fixing the end of his whip on the floor, and whirling it round at full speed ; then working it into his boot ; then making up his mouth for a whistle, but stopping short to avoid being guilty of the incivility of interruption.

At length, with the same invincible good nature, and with the same pitiable insensibility to his own state, he arose to take leave. He shook us all by the hand, Dr. Barlow twice, saying : ' Doctor, I don't think the worse of you for your plain speaking. He is a knave or a fool that is angry with a good man for doing his duty. 'Tis my fault if I don't take his advice ; but 'tis his fault if he does not give it. Parsons are paid for it, and ought not to be mealy-mouthed when there is a proper opening, such as poor Tyrrel's case gave you. I challenged *you*. I should perhaps have been angry if you had challenged *me*. It makes all the difference in the event of a duel which is the challenger. As to myself, it is time enough for me to think of the things you recommend. Thank God, I am in excellent good health and spirits, and am not yet quite fifty. " There is a time for all things." Even the Bible allows that.'

The doctor shook his head at this sad misapplication of the text. Mr. Flam went away, pressing us all to dine with him next day : he had killed a fine buck, and he assured Dr. Barlow that he should have the best port in his cellar. The doctor pleaded want of time, and the rest of the party could not afford a day, out of the few which remained to us ; but we promised to call on him. He nodded kindly at Dr. Barlow, saying : ' Well, doctor, as you won't come to the buck, one of his haunches shall come to you ; so tell madam to expect it.'

As soon as he had left the room, we all joined in lamenting that the blessings of health and strength should ever be produced as arguments for neglecting to secure those blessings which have eternity for their object.

'Unhappy man!' said Dr. Barlow, 'little does he think that he is, if possible, more the object of my compassion than poor Mr. Tyrrel. Tyrrel, it is true, is lying on a sick, probably a dying bed. His body is in torture. His mind is in anguish. He has to look back on a life, the retrospect of which can afford him no ray of comfort. But he *knows* his misery. The hand of God is upon him. His proud heart is brought low. His self-confidence is subdued. His high imaginations are cast down. His abasement of soul, as far as I can judge, is sincere. He abhors himself in dust and ashes. He sees death at hand. He feels that the sting of death is sin. All subterfuge is at an end. He is at last seeking the only refuge of penitent sinners, I trust on right grounds. His state is indeed perilous in the extreme : yet, awful as it is, he *knows* it. He will not open his eyes on the eternal world in a state of delusion. But what shall awaken poor Mr. Flam from his dream of security? His high health, his unbroken spirits, his prosperous circumstances and various blessings, are so many snares to him. He thinks that "to-morrow shall be as this day, and still more abundant." Even the wretched situation of his dying friend, though it awakens compassion, awakens not compunction. Nay, it affords matter of triumph rather than humiliation. He feeds his vanity with comparisons, from which he contrives to extract comfort. His own offences being of a different kind, instead of lamenting them, he glories in being free from those which belong to an opposite cast of character. Satisfied that he has not the vices of Tyrrel, he never once reflects on his own unrepented sins. Even his good qualities increase his danger. He wraps himself up in that constitutional good-nature which, being partly founded on vanity and self-approbation, strengthens his delusion, and hardens him against reproof.'

Chapter XLVII.

IN conversing with Mr. Stanley on my happy prospects, and my future plans, after having referred all concerns of a pecuniary nature to be settled between him and Sir John Belfield, I ventured to entreat that he would crown his goodness, and my happiness, by allowing me to solicit his daughter for an early day.

Mr. Stanley said, the term *early* was relative ; but he was afraid that he should hardly consent to what I might consider even as a late one. 'In parting with such a child as Lucilla,' added he, 'some weaning time must be allowed to the tenderest of mothers. The most promising marriage, and surely none can promise more happiness than that to which we are looking, is a heavy trial to fond parents. To have trained a creature with anxious fondness, in hope of her repaying their solicitude hereafter by the charms of her society, and then, as soon as she becomes capable of being a friend and companion, to lose her for ever, is such a trial that I sometimes wonder at the seeming impatience of parents to get rid of a treasure, of which they best know the value. The

16—2

sadness which attends the consummation even of our dearest hopes on these occasions, is one striking instance of that *vanity of human wishes,* on which Juvenal and Johnson have so beautifully expatiated.

'A little delay indeed I shall require, from motives of prudence as well as fondness. Lucilla will not be nineteen these three months and more. You will not, I trust, think me unreasonable if I say, that neither her mother nor myself can consent to part with her, before that period.'

'Three months!' exclaimed I, with more vehemence that politeness. 'Three months! It is impossible.'

'It is very possible,' said he, smiling, 'that you can wait, and very certain that we shall not consent sooner.'

'Have you any doubts, sir,' said I, 'have you any objections which I can remove, and which, being removed, may abridge this long probation?'

'None,' said he, kindly. 'But I consider even nineteen as a very early age; too early indeed, were not my mind so completely at rest about you on the grand points of religion, morals, and temper, that no delay could, I trust, afford me additional security. You will, however, my dear Charles, find so much occupation in preparing your affairs, and your mind, for so important a change, that you will not find the time of absence so irksome as you fancy.'

'Absence, sir!' replied I. 'What, then, do you intend to banish me?'

'No,' replied he, smiling again. 'But I intend to send you *home.* A sentence indeed which in this dissipated age is thought the worst sort of exile. You have now been absent six or seven months. This absence has been hitherto justifiable. It is time to return to your affairs, to your duties. Both the one and the other always slide into some disorder by too long separation from the place of their legitimate exercise. Your steward will want inspection, your tenants may want redress, your poor always want assistance.'

Seeing me look irresolute, 'I must, I find,' added he, with the kindest look and voice, 'be compelled to the inhospitable necessity of turning you out of doors.'

'Live without Lucilla three months!' said I. 'Allow me, sir, at least to remain a few weeks longer at the Grove.'

'Love is a bad calculator,' replied Mr. Stanley, 'I believe he never learnt arithmetic. Don't you know, that, as you are enjoined a three months' banishment, that, the sooner you go, the sooner you will return? And that, however long your stay is, your three months' absence will still remain to be accomplished. To speak seriously, Lucilla's sense of propriety, as well as that of Mrs. Stanley, will not permit you to remain much longer under the same roof, now that the motive will become so notorious. Besides that an act of self-denial is a good principle to set out upon, business and duties will fill up your active hours, and an intercourse of letters with her you so reluctantly quit, will not only give an interest to your leisure, but put you both still more completely in possession of each other's character.'

'I will set out to-morrow, sir,' said I, earnestly, 'in order to begin to hasten the day of my return.'

'Now you are as much too precipitate on the other side,' replied he. 'A few days, I think, may be permitted, without any offence to Lucilla's delicacy. This even her.mother pleads for.'

'With what excellence will this blessed union give me an alliance !' replied I ; 'I will go directly, and thank Mrs. Stanley for this goodness.'

I found Mrs. Stanley and her daughter together, with whom I had a long and interesting conversation. They took no small pains to convince my judgment that my departure was perfectly proper. My will, however, continued rebellious. But as I had been long trained to the habit of submitting my will to my reason, I acquiesced, though not without murmuring, and, as they told me, with a very bad grace.

I informed Mrs. Stanley of an intimation I had received from Sir George Aston of his attachment to Phœbe, and of his mother's warm approbation of his choice, adding, that he alleged her extreme youth as the ground of his deferring to express his hope, that his plea might one day be received with favour.'

'He forgot to allege his own youth,' replied she, 'which is a reason almost equally cogent.'

Miss Stanley and I agreed that a connection more desirable in all respects could not be expected.

'When I assure you,' replied Mrs. Stanley, 'that I am quite of your opinion, you will think me inconsistent if I add, that I earnestly hope such a proposal will not be made by Sir George, lest his precipitancy should hinder the future accomplishment of a wish which I may be allowed remotely to indulge.'

'What objection,' said I, 'can Mr. Stanley possibly make to such a proposal, except that his daughter is too young.'

'I see,' replied she, 'that you do not yet completely know Mr. Stanley ; or rather you do not know all that he has done for the Aston family. His services have been very important, not only in that grand point which you and I think the most momentous, but he has also very successfully exerted himself in settling Lady Aston's worldly affairs, which were in the utmost disorder. The large estate, which had suffered by her own ignorance of business, and the dishonesty of a steward, he has not only enabled her to clear, but put her in the way greatly to improve. This skill and kindness in worldly things so raised his credit in the eyes of the guardian, young Sir George's uncle, that he declared he should never again be so much afraid of religious men, whom he always understood to be without judgment, or kindness, or disinterestedness.

'Now,' added Mrs. Stanley, 'don't you perceive that not only the purity of Mr. Stanley's motives, but religion itself would suffer, should we be forward to promote this connection? Will not this Mr. Aston say that sinister designs influenced all this zeal and kindness, and that Sir George's estate was improved with an eye to his own daughter? It will be said that these religious people always know what they are about—that when they seem to be purely serving God, they are resolved not to serve him for nothing, but always keep their own interest in view. Should Sir George's inclination continue, and his principles stand the siege which the world will not fail to lay to a man of his fortune—some years hence, when he is complete master of his actions, his character formed, and his judgment ripened to direct his choice, so as to make it evident to the world, that it was not the effect of influence—this connection is an event to which we should look forward with much pleasure.'

' Never,' exclaimed I, ' no, not once, have I been disappointed in my expectation of consistency in Mr. Stanley's character. Oh, my beloved parents, how wise was your injunction that I should make *consistency the test of true piety !* It is thus that Christians should always keep the credit of religion in.view, if they would promote its interests in the world.'

When I communicated to Miss Stanley my conversation with *her* father, and read over with her the letters of *mine*, how tenderly did she weep ! How were my own feelings renewed ! To be thus assured that she was selected for their son by my deceased parents, seemed, to her pious mind, to shed a sacredness on our union. How did she venerate their virtues ! How feelingly regret their loss !

Before I left the country, I did not omit a visit of civility to Mr. Flam. The young ladies, as Sir John predicted, had stepped back into their natural character, and natural *un*-dress ; though he was too severe when he added, that their hopes in assuming the other were now at an end.

They both asked me, if I was not moped to death at the Grove : the Stanleys, they said, were a *good sort* of people, but quite *mauvais ton*, as everybody must be who did not spend half the year in London. Miss Stanley was a fine girl enough, but knew nothing of the world, wanted manner, which two or three winters in town would give her. ' Better as she is,' interrupted Mr. Flam, ' better as she is. She is a pattern daughter, and will make a pattern wife. *Her* mother has no care nor trouble ; I wish I could say as much of all mothers. I never saw a bad humour or a bad dinner in the house. She is always at home, always employed, always in spirits, and always in temper. She is as cheerful as if she had no religion, and as useful as if she could not spell her own receipt book.'

I was affected with this generous tribute to my Lucilla's virtues : and when he wished me joy, as he cordially shook me by the hand, I could not forbear saying to myself, why will not this good-natured man go to heaven ?

I next paid a farewell visit to Mr. and Mrs. Carlton, to the amiable family at Aston Hall, and to Dr. Barlow. How rich has this excursion made me in valuable friendships, to say nothing of the inestimable connection at the Grove ! I did not forget to assure Dr. Barlow, that if anything could add a value to the blessing which awaited me, it was that his hand would consecrate it.

Through the good doctor I received a message from Mr. Tyrrel, requesting me to make him a visit of charity before I quitted the neighbourhood. I instantly obeyed the summons. I found him totally changed in all respects—a body wasted by disease, a mind apparently full of contrition, and penetrated with that deep humility, in which he had been so eminently deficient.

He earnestly entreated my prayers, adding, 'Though it is presumption in so unworthy a being as I am, to suppose his intercession may be heard, I will pray for a blessing on your happy prospects. A connection with such a family is itself a blessing. Oh! that my nephew had been worthy of it! It is to recommend that poor youth to your friendship, that I invited you to this melancholy visit. I call him poor, because I have neglected to enrich his mind; but he will have too much of this world's goods. May he employ well what I have risked my soul to amass! Counsel him, dear sir; admonish him. Recall to his mind his dying uncle. I would now give my whole estate, nay, I would live upon the alms I have refused, to purchase one more year, though spent in pain and misery, that I might prove the sincerity of my repentance. Be to Ned what my blessed friend Stanley would have been to me. But my pride repelled his kindness. I could not bear his superiority. I turned away my eyes from a model I could not imitate.' I now entreated him to spare himself, but after a few minutes' pause he proceeded :

'As to Ned, I trust he is not ill-disposed, but I have neither furnished his mind for solitude, nor fortified his heart for the world. I foolishly thought that to keep him ignorant, was to keep him safe. I have provided for him the snare of a large fortune, without preparing him for the use of it. I fell into an error not uncommon, that of grudging the expenses of education to a relation for whom I designed my estate. I have thus fitted him for a companion to the vulgar, and a prey to the designing. I thought it sufficient to keep him from actual vice, without furnishing him with arguments to combat it, or with principles to abhor it.'

Here the poor man paused for want of breath. I was too much affected to speak.

At length he went on. 'I have made over to Doctor Barlow's son two thousand pounds for completing his education. I have also given two thousand pounds apiece to the two elder daughters of Mr. Stanley, in aid of their charities. I have made a deed of gift of this, and of a large sum for charitable purposes, at the discretion of my executors. This I hoped would prove my sincerity more than a legacy, as it will be paid immediately. A refusal to accept it, will greatly distress me. Ned still will have too much left, unless he employs it to better purposes than I have done.'

Though deeply moved, I hardly knew what to reply. I wished to give him comfort, but distrusted my own judgment as to the manner. I promised my best services to his nephew.

'Oh, good young man !' cried he, 'if ever you are tempted to forget God, as I did for above thirty years, or to mock him by an outward profession, as I have lately done, think of me. Think of one who, for the largest portion of his life, lived as if there were no God ; and who, since he has made a profession of Christianity, deceived his own soul, no less by the religion he adopted, than by his former neglect of all religion. My delusion was this, I did not choose to be good, but I chose to be saved. It was no wonder, then, that I should be struck with a religion, which I hoped would free me from the discipline of moral rectitude, and yet deliver me from the punishment of having neglected it. Will God accept my present forced submission? Will he accept a penitence of which I may have no time to prove the sincerity? Tell me—you are a Christian.' I was much distressed. I thought it neither modest nor prudent for me to give a decisive answer. He grasped my hand. 'Then,' said he, 'you think my cause hopeless. You think the Almighty cannot forgive me.' Thus pressed, I ventured to say, 'To doubt his will to pardon, and his power to save, would, as it appears to me, sir, be a greater fault than any you have committed.'

'One great comfort is left,' replied he, 'the mercy I have abused is infinite. Tell Stanley I now believe, with him, that if we pretend to trust in God, we must be governed by Him; if we truly believe in Him, we shall obey Him; if we think He sent His Son to save sinners, we shall hate sin.'

I ventured to congratulate him on his frame of mind; and seeing him quite overcome, took leave of him with a heart deeply touched with this salutary scene. The family at the Grove were greatly moved with my description, and with the method poor Tyrrel had found out of eluding the refusal of his liberal-minded executors to accept of legacies.

The day fixed for my departure too soon arrived. I took a most affectionate leave of Mr. and Mrs. Stanley, and a very tender one of Lucilla, who gratified my affection by the emotion she evidently felt, and my delicacy by the effort she made to conceal it. Phœbe wept outright. The children all hung about me, each presenting me some of her flowers, saying, they had nothing else to give me; and assuring me that Rachel should be no loser by it. Little Celia was clamorous in her sorrow, when she saw me ascend the curricle, in which neither she nor Lucilla was to have a place. I took the sweet child up in the carriage, placed her by me, and gently drove her through the park, at the gate of which I consigned her to the arms of her father, who had good-naturedly walked by the side of the carriage, in order to carry her back. I drove off, enriched with his prayers and blessings, which seemed to insure me protection.

Though this separation from all I loved threw a transient sadness around me, I had abundant matter for delightful reflection and pious gratitude. I experienced the truth of Phœbe's remark, that happiness is a serious thing. While pleasure manifests itself by extravagant gaiety, exuberant spirits, and overt acts, happiness retreats to its own proper region, the heart. There concentrating its feelings, it contemplates its treasures, meditates on its enjoyments, and still more fondly on its hopes: counts up its mercies, and feels the consummation of them in looking to the Fountain from whence they flow: feels every blessing immeasurably heightened by the heart-cheering reflection, that the most exquisite human pleasures are not the perfection of his nature, but only a gracious earnest, a bounteous prelibation, of that blessedness which is without measure, and shall be without end.

Chapter XLVIII.

EFORE the Belfields had quitted us, it was stipulated that we should, with submission to the will of a higher power, all meet for six weeks every other summer at Stanley Grove, and pass a month together every intermediate year, either at the Priory, or at Beechwood.

I passed through London, and spent three days in Cavendish Square, my friends having kindly postponed their departure for the country on my account. Lady Belfield voluntarily undertook whatever was necessary for the internal decoration of the Priory ; while Sir John took on himself the friendly office of arranging for me all preliminaries with Mr. Stanley, whose largeness of heart, and extreme disinterestedness, I knew I durst not trust, without some such check as I placed in the hands of our common friend.

As soon as all personal concerns were adjusted, Lady Belfield said, ' I have something to communicate, in which I am persuaded you will take a lively interest. On my return to town, I found, among my visiting tickets, several of Lady Melbury's. The porter told me she had called every day for the last week, and seemed very impatient for my return. Finding she was still in town, I went to her immediately. She was not at home, but came to me within an hour. She expressed great joy at seeing me. She looked more beautiful than ever, at least, the blush of conscious shame, which mingled with her usual sweetness, rendered her more interesting.

' She was at a loss how to begin. With a perplexed air she said, " Why did you stay so long? I have sadly wanted you. Where is Sir John ? I have wanted counsellors—comforters, friends. I have never had a friend."

' I was affected at an opening só unexpected. Sir John came in. This increased her confusion. At length, after the usual compliments, she thus addressed him : " I am determined to conquer this false shame. There is not a worse symptom in human nature than that we blush to own what we have not been afraid to do. From you, Sir John, I heard the first remonstrance which ever reached my ears. You ought to be informed of its effect. You cannot have forgotten our conversation in my coach,* after we had quitted the scene which filled you with contempt for me, and me with anguish for the part I had acted. You reasonably supposed that my remorse would last no longer than the scene which had inspired it. You left me alone. My lord dined abroad. I was abandoned to all the horrors of solitude. I wanted somebody to keep me from myself. Mrs. Stokes dying ! her husband dead ! the sweet flower-girl pining for want—and I perhaps the cause of all ! The whole view presented such a complication of misery to my mind, and of guilt to my heart, as made me insupportable to myself.

* See page 5.

' " It was Saturday. I was of course engaged to the opera. I was utterly unfit to go, but wanted courage to frame an excuse. Fortunately Lady Bell Finley, whom I had promised to chaperon, sent to excuse herself. This set my person at liberty, but left my mind upon the rack. Though I should have rejoiced in the company even of my own chambermaid, so much did I dread being left to my own thoughts, yet I resolved to let no one in that night. I had scarcely passed a single evening out of the giddy circle for several years. For the first time in my life I was driven to look into myself. I took a retrospect of my past conduct ; a confused and imperfect one indeed. This review aggravated my distress. Still I pursued my distracting self-inquisition. Not for millions would I pass such another night !

' " I had done as wrong things before, but they had never been thus brought home to me. My extravagance must have made others suffer, but their sufferings had not been placed before my eyes. What was not seen, I had hoped might not be true. I had indeed heard distant reports of the consequences of my thoughtless expense, but they might be invented—they might be exaggerated. At the flower-maker's I *witnessed* the ruin I had made—I *saw* the fruits of my unfeeling vanity —I *beheld* the calamities I had caused. Oh, how much mischief would such actual observation prevent ! I was alone. I had no dependent to qualify the deed, no sycophant to divert my attention to more soothing objects. Though Sir John's honest expostulation had touched me to the quick, yet I confess, had I found any of my coterie at home, had I gone to the opera, had a joyous supper succeeded, all together would have quite obliterated the late mortifying scene. I should, as I have often done before, have soon lost all sense of the Stokes' misery, and of my own crime."

' Here,' pursued Lady Belfield, 'the sweet creature looked so contrite, that Sir John and I were both deeply affected.

' " You are not accustomed, Sir John," resumed she with a faint smile, " to the office of a confessor, nor I to that of a penitent. But I make it a test to myself of my own sincerity to tell you the whole truth.

' I wandered from room to room, fancying I should be more at ease in any other than that in which I was. I envied the starving tenant of the meanest garret. I envied Mrs. Stokes herself. Both might have pitied the pangs which rent my heart, as I roamed the decorated apartments of our spacious house. In the gayest part of London I felt the dreariness of a desert. Surrounded with magnificence, I endured a sense of want and woe, of which a blameless beggar can form no idea.

' " I went into the library : I took up a book which my lord had left on the table. It was a translation from a Roman classic. I opened it at the speech of the tragedian to Pompey : ' *The time will come that thou shalt mourn deeply, because thou didst not mourn sooner !'* I was struck to the heart. ' Shall a pagan,' said I, ' thus forcibly reprove me ; and shall I neglect to search for truth at the fountain ?'

' " I knew my lord would not come home from his club till the morning. The struggle in my soul between principle and pride was severe ; but after a bitter conflict, I resolved to employ the night in writing him a long letter. In it I ingenuously confessed the whole state of my mind, and what had occasioned it. I implored his permission for my setting out next morning for Melbury Castle. I entreated him to prevail on his excellent aunt, Lady Jane, whom I had so shamefully slighted, to accompany me. I knew she was a character of that singular class, who would be glad to revenge herself for my ill-treatment by doing me a service. Her company would be at once a pledge to my lord of the purity of my intentions, and to myself a security against falling into worse society. I assured him that I had no safeguard but in flight. An additional reason which I alleged for my absence was, that as I had promised to give a grand masquerade in a fortnight, the evading this expense would nearly enable me to discharge the debt which sat so heavy on my conscience.

'" I received a note from him as soon as he came home. With his usual complaisance, he complied with my request. With his usual nonchalance, he neither troubled me with reproaches, nor comforted me with approbation.

'" As he knew that Lady Jane usually rose about the hour he came home from St. James's Street, he obligingly went to her at once. I had not been in bed. He came to my dressing-room, and informed me that his aunt had consented at the first word. I expressed my gratitude to them both, saying, that I was ready to set out that very day.

'" ' You must wait till to-morrow,' said he. ' There is no accounting for the oddities of some people. Lady Jane told me she could not possibly travel on a Sunday. I wondered where was the impossibility. Sunday, I assured her, was the only day for travelling in comfort, as the road was not obstructed by waggons and carts. She replied, with a gravity which made me laugh, " that she should be ashamed to think that a person of her rank and education should be indebted, for her being able to trample with more convenience on a Divine law, to the piety of the vulgar who durst not violate it." Did you ever hear anything so whimsical, Matilda?' I said nothing, but my heart smote me. Never will I repeat this offence.

'" On the Monday we set out, I had kept close the preceding day, under pretence of illness. This I also assigned as an excuse in the cards sent to my invited guests, pleading the necessity of going into the country for change of air. Shall I own I dreaded being shut up in a barouche, and still more in the lonely castle, with Lady Jane? I looked for nothing every moment but ' the thorns and briars of reproof.' But I soon found that the woman whom I had quizzed as a methodist was a most entertaining companion. Instead of austerity in her looks, and reproach in her language, I found nothing but kindness and affection, but vivacity and elegance. While she soothed my sorrows, she strengthened my better purposes. Her conversation gradually revived in my mind tastes and principles which had been early sown in it, but which the world seemed completely to have eradicated.

'" In the neighbourhood of the Castle, Lady Jane carried me to visit the abodes of poverty and sickness. I envied her large but discriminating liberality, and the means she possessed of gratifying it, while I shed tears at the remembrance of my own squandered thousands.   I had never been hard-hearted, but I had always given to importunity, rather than to want or merit.   I blushed, that while I had been absurdly profuse to cases of which I knew nothing, my own village had been perishing with a contagious sickness.

'"While I amused myself with drawing, my aunt often read to me some rationally entertaining book, occasionally introducing religious reading and discourse, with a wisdom and moderation which increased the effect of both.   Knowing my natural levity, and wretched habits, she generally waited till the proposal came from myself.   At first, when I suggested it, it was to please her ; at length I began to find a degree of pleasure in it myself.

'" You will say I have not quite lost my romance : a thought struck me, that the first use I made of my pencil should serve to perpetuate at least one of my offences.   You know I do not execute portraits badly. With a little aid from fancy, which I thought made it allowable to bring separate circumstances into one piece, I composed a picture.   It consisted of a detached figure in the background, of poor Stokes, seen through the grate of his prison on a bed of straw ; and a group, composed of his wife in the act of expiring, Fanny bending over a wreath of roses withered with the tears she was shedding, and myself in the horrors in which you saw me :

> Spectatress of the mischief I had made.

'" Wherever I go, this picture shall always be my companion.   It hangs in my closet.   My dear friends," added she, with a look of infinite sweetness, " whenever I am tempted to contract a debt, or to give in to any act of vanity or dissipation which may lead to debt, if after having looked on this picture I can pursue the project, renounce me, cast me off for ever !

'" You know Lady Jane's vein of humour.   One day, as we were conversing together, I confessed that, at the very time I was the object of general notice, and my gaiety the theme of general envy, I had never known happiness.   ' I do not wonder at it,' said she.   'Those who greedily pursue admiration, would be ashamed to sit down with so quiet a thing as happiness.'   'My dear. Lady Jane,' said I, ' correct me, counsel me, instruct me—you have been too lenient, too forbearing.' ' Well,' said she, with a cheerful tone, 'as you appoint me your physician, as you disclose your case, and ask relief, I will give you a prescription, which, though the simplest thing in the world, will, I am certain, go a great way towards curing you.   As you are barely six-and-twenty, your disease, I trust, is not inveterate.   If you will be an obedient patient, I will answer for your recovery.'

'" I assured her of my willing adoption of any remedy she might prescribe, as I was certain she would consider my weakness, and adapt her treatment, not so much to what my case absolutely required, as to what my strength was able to bear.

'"' Well then,' said she, ' but pray observe, I am no quack.   I do not undertake to restore you instantaneously.   Though my medicine will work surely, it will work slowly.   You know,' added she, smiling, 'the success of all alteratives depends on the punctuality with which they are taken, and the constancy with which they are followed up. Mine must be taken two or three times a day, in small quantities at first, the dose to be enlarged as you are able to bear it. I can safely assert, with the advertising doctors, that it may be used full or fasting, in all weathers, and all seasons ; but I cannot add with them, that *it requires no confinement.*'

'" I grew impatient, and begged she would come to the point. ' Softly, Matilda,' said she, ' softly ; I must first look into my receipt-book, for fear I should mistake any of my ingredients. This book,' said she, opening it, 'though written by no charlatan, contains a cure for all diseases. It exhibits not only general directions, but specified cases.' Turning over the leaves as she was speaking, she at length stopped, saying : 'Here is your case, my dear, or rather your remedy.' She then read very deliberately—' COMMUNE WITH YOUR OWN HEART— AND IN YOUR CHAMBER—AND BE STILL.'

'" I now found her grand receipt-book was the Bible. I arose, and embraced her : 'My dear aunt,' said I, 'do with me whatever you please. I will be all obedience. I pledge myself to take your alterative regularly, constantly. Do not spare me. Speak your whole mind.'

'" 'My dear Matilda,' said she, ' ever since your marriage, your life has been one continued opposition to your feelings. You have lived as much below your understanding as your principles. Your conduct has been a system of contradictions. You have believed in Christianity, and acted in direct violation of its precepts. You knew that there was a day of future reckoning, and yet neglected to prepare for it. With a heart full of tenderness, you have been guilty of repeated acts of cruelty. You have been faithful to your husband, without making him respectable or happy. You have been virtuous, without the reputation or the peace which belongs to virtue. You have been charitable without doing good, and affectionate without having ever made a friend. You have wasted those attentions on the worthless, which the worthy would have delighted to receive, and those talents on the frivolous, which would have been cherished by the enlightened. You have defeated the use of a fine understanding by the want of common prudence, and robbed society of the example of your good qualities by your total inability to resist and oppose. Inconsideration and vanity have been the joint cause of your malady. At your age, I trust it is not incurable. As you have caught it by keeping infected company, there is no possible mode of cure but by avoiding the contagious air they breathe. You have performed your quarantine with admirable patience. Beware, my dearest niece, of returning to the scene where the plague rages, till your antidote has taken its full effect.'

'" 'I will *never* return to it, my dear Lady Jane,' cried I, throwing myself into her arms. ' I do not mean that I will never return to town. My duty to my lord requires me to be where he is, or where he wishes me to be. My residence will be the same, but my society will be changed.'

'" 'You please me entirely,' replied she. ' In resorting to religion, take care that you do not dishonour it. Never plead your piety to God as an apology for your neglect of the relative duties. If the one is soundly adopted, the others will be correctly performed. There are those who would delight to throw such a stigma on real Christianity, as to be able to report that it had extinguished your affections, and soured your temper. Disappoint them, my sweet niece ; while you serve your Maker more fervently, you must be still more patient with your husband. But while you bear with his faults, take care you do not connive at them. If you are in earnest, you must expect some trials. He who prepares these trials for you, will support you under them, will carry you through them, will make them instruments of his glory, and of your own eternal happiness.'

'" 'Lord Melbury's complaisance to my wishes,' replied I, 'has been unbounded. As he never controlled my actions when they required control, I trust he will be equally indulgent now they will be less censurable. Alas ! we have too little interfered with each other's concerns —we have lived too much asunder—who knows but I may recall him ?' My tears would not let me go on—nor will they now," added she, wiping her fine eyes.

' Sir John and I were too much touched to attempt to answer her ; at length she proceeded.

'" By adhering to Lady Jane's directions, I have begun to get acquainted with my own heart. Little did I suspect the evil that was in it. Yet I am led to believe that the incessant whirl in which I have lived, my total want of leisure for reflection, my excessive vanity, and complete inconsiderateness, are of themselves causes adequate to any effects which the grossest vices would have produced.

'" Last week my lord made us a visit at the Castle. I gave him a warm reception ; but he seemed rather surprised at the cold one which I gave to a large cargo of new French novels and German plays, which he had been so good as to bring me. I did not venture to tell him that I had changed my course of study. Lady Jane charged me to avoid giving him the least disgust by any unusual gravity in my looks, or severity in my conversation. I exerted myself to such good purpose, that he declared he wanted neither cards nor company. I tried to let him see, by my change of habits, rather than by dry documents or cold remonstrances, the alteration which had taken place in my sentiments. He was pleased to see me blooming and cheerful. We walked together, we read together ; we became lovers and companions. He told Lady Jane he never saw me so pleasant. He did not know I was so agreeable a woman, and was glad he had had this opportunity of getting acquainted with me. As he has great expectations from her, he was delighted at the friendship which subsisted between us.

'" He brought us up to town. As it was now empty, the terrors of the masquerade no longer hung over me, and I cheerfully complied with his wishes. I drove immediately to Mrs. Stokes's with such a portion of my debt as my retirement had enabled me to save. I feasted all the way on the joy I should have in surprising her with this two hundred pounds. How severe, but how just was my punishment, when, on knocking at the door, I found she had been dead these two months ! No one could tell what was become of her daughter. This shock operated almost as powerfully on my feelings as the first had done. But if it augmented my self-reproach, it confirmed my good resolutions. My present concern is how to discover the sweet girl whom, alas! I have helped to deprive of both her parents."

'Here I interrupted her,' continued Lady Belfield. 'You have not far to seek; Fanny Stokes is in this house. She is appointed governess to our children.

' Poor Lady Melbury's joy was excessive at this intelligence, and she proceeded : " That a too sudden return to the world might not weaken my better purposes, I was preparing to request my lord's permission to go back to the Castle, when he prevented me, by telling me that he had an earnest desire to make a visit to the brave patriots in Spain, and to pass the winter among them, but feared he must give it up, as the state of the Continent rendered it impossible for me to accompany him.

' " This filled my heart with joy. I encouraged him to make the voyage, assured him I would live under Lady Jane's observation, and that I would pass the whole winter in the country."

" Then you shall pass it with us at Beechwood, my dear Lady Melbury," cried Sir John and I, both at once; " we will strengthen each other in every virtuous purpose. We shall rejoice in Lady Jane's company. "

' She joyfully accepted the proposal, not doubting her lord's consent ; and kindly said, that she should be doubly happy in a society at once so rational and so elegant.

' It was settled that she should spend with us the three months that Fanny Stokes and little Caroline are to pass at Stanley Grove. She desired to see Fanny, to whom she behaved with great tenderness. She paid her the two hundred pounds, assuring her she had no doubt of being able to discharge the whole debt in the spring.

' I received a note from her the next day, informing me of her lord's cheerful concurrence, as well as that of Lady Jane. She added, that when she went up to dress, she had found on her toilette her diamond necklace, which her dear aunt had redeemed and restored to her, as a proof of her confidence and affection.—As Lady Melbury has for ever abolished her coterie, I have the most sanguine hopes of her perseverance. All her promises would have gone for nothing, without this practical pledge of her sincerity.'

When Lady Belfield had finished her little tale, I expressed, in the strongest terms, the delight I felt at the happy change in this charming woman. I could not forbear observing to Sir John, that as Lady Melbury had been the 'glass of fashion' while her conduct was wrong, I hoped she would not lose all her influence by its becoming right. I added, with a smile, ' In that case, I shall rejoice to see the fine ladies turn their talent for drawing to the same moral account with this fair penitent. Such a record of their faults as she has had the courage to make of hers, hanging in their closets, and perpetually staring them in the face, would be no unlikely means to prevent a repetition, especially if the picture is to be as visible as the fault had been.'

Chapter XLIX.

THE next morning I resumed my journey northwards, and on the fourth day I reached the seat of my ancestors. The distant view of the Priory excited strong but mingled emotions in my bosom. The tender sorrow for the loss of the beloved society I had once enjoyed under its roof, was a salutary check to the abundant joy arising from the anticipation of the blessings which awaited me there. My mind was divided between the two conflicting sentiments, that I was soon to be in possession of every material for the highest happiness—and that the highest happiness is short! May I ever live under the influence of that act of devout gratitude, in which, as soon as I entered the house, I dedicated the whole of my future life to its Divine Author, solemnly consecrating to his service my time, my talents, my fortune ; all I am, and all I have !

I next wrote to Lucilla, with whom I continued to maintain a regular and animated correspondence. Her letters gratify my taste, and delight my heart, while they excite me to everything that is good. This interchange of sentiment sheds a ray of brightness on a separation that every day is diminishing.

Mr. Stanley also has the goodness to write to me frequently. In one of my letters to him, I ventured to ask him how he had managed to produce in his daughter such complete satisfaction in his sober and correct habits of life ; adding, that her conformity was so cheerful, that it did not look so much like acquiescence as choice.

I received from Mr. Stanley the answer which follows :

'Stanley Grove, Sept., 1808.

'MY DEAR CHARLES,
'As I wish to put you in possession of whatever relates to the mind of Lucilla, I will devote this letter to answer your inquiries respecting her cheerful conformity to what you call our " sober habits of life ;" and her indifference to those pleasures which are usually thought to constitute the sole happiness of young women of a certain rank.

' Mrs. Stanley and I are not so unacquainted with human nature, as to have pretended to impose on her understanding, by attempting to breed her up in entire ignorance of the world, or in perfect seclusion from it. She often accompanied us to town for a short time. The occasional sight of London, and the frequent enjoyment of the best society, dissipated the illusions of fancy. The bright colours with which young imagination, inflamed by ignorance, report, and curiosity, invests unknown and distant objects, faded under actual observation. Complete ignorance and complete seclusion form no security from the dangers incident to the world, or for correct conduct at a distance from it. Ignorance may be the safety of an idiot, and seclusion the security of a nun ; Christian parents should act on a more large and liberal principle, or what is the use of observation and experience ? The

French women of fashion, under the old régime, were bred in convents ; and what women were ever more licentious than many of them, as soon as marriage had set them at liberty ?

'I am persuaded that the best-intended formation of character, if founded on ignorance or deceit, will never answer. As to Lucilla, we have never attempted to blind her judgment. We have never thought it necessary to leave her understanding out of the question while we were forming her heart. We have never told her that the world is a scene absolutely destitute of pleasure : we have never assured her that there is no amusement in the diversions which we disapprove. Even if this assurance had not been deceitful, it would have been vain and fruitless. We cannot totally separate her from the society of those who frequent them, who find their happiness in them, and whom she would hear speak of them with rapture.

'We went upon other grounds. We accustomed her to reflect that she was an intellectual creature ; that she was an immortal creature ; that she was a Christian. That to an intellectual being diversions must always be subordinate to the exercise of the mental faculties ; that to an immortal being, born to higher hopes than enjoyments, the exercise of the mental faculties must be subservient to religious duties. That in the practice of a Christian, self-denial is the turning point, the specific distinction. That as to many of the pleasures which the world pursues, Christianity requires her votaries to live above the temptations which they hold out. She requires it the more especially, because Christians in our time, not being called upon to make great and trying sacrifices, of life, of fortune, and of liberty, and having but comparatively small occasions to evidence their sincerity, should the more cheerfully make the petty but daily renunciation of those pleasures which are the very element in which worldly people exist.

'We have not misled her by unfair and flattering representations of the Christian life. We have not, with a view to allure her to embrace it on false pretences, taught her that when religion is once rooted in the heart, the remainder of life is uninterrupted peace and unbroken delight ; that all shall be perpetually smooth hereafter, because it is smooth at present.

'This would be as unfair as to show a raw recruit the splendours of a parade-day, and tell him it was actual service. We have not made her believe that the established Christian has no troubles to expect, no vexations to fear, no storms to encounter. We have not attempted to cheat her into religion, by concealing its difficulties, its trials, no, nor its unpopularity.

'We have been always aware, that to have enforced the most exalted Christian principles, together with the necessity of a corresponding practice, ever so often and so strongly, would have been worse than foolish, had we been impressing these truths one part of the day, and had, in the other part, been living ourselves in the actual enjoyment of the very things against which we were guarding her. My dear Charles, if we would talk to young people with effect, we must, by the habits of which we set them the example, dispose them to listen, or our documents will be something worse than fruitless. It is really hard upon girls to be tantalised with religious lectures, while they are at the same time tempted to everything against which they are warned, while the whole bent and bias of the family practice are diametrically opposite to the principles inculcated.

'In our own case, I think I may venture to affirm that the plan has answered.

'We have endeavoured to establish a principle of right, instead of unprofitable invective against what was wrong. Perhaps there can scarcely be found a religious family in which so few anathemas have been denounced against this or that specific diversion, as in ours.

'We aimed to take another road. The turn of mind, the tendency of the employment, the force of the practice, the bent of the conversation, the spirit of the amusement, have all leaned to the contrary direction, till the habits are gradually worked into a kind of nature.

'It would be cruel to condemn a creature to a retired life, without qualifying her for retirement : next to religion, nothing can possibly do this but mental cultivation in women who are above the exercise of vulgar employments. The girl who possesses only the worldly acquirements —the singer and the dancer—when condemned to retirement, may reasonably exclaim with Milton's Adam, when looking at the constellations :

> Why all night long shine these ?
> Wherefore, if none *behold* ?/

'Now the woman who derives her principles from the Bible, and her amusements from intellectual sources, from the beauties of nature, and from active employment and exercise, will not pant for beholders. She is no clamorous beggar for the extorted alms of admiration. She lives on her own stock. Her resources are within herself. She possesses the truest independence. She does not wait for the opinion of the world to know if she is right, nor for the applause of the world to know if she is happy.

'Too many religious people fancy that the infectious air of the world is confined to the ball-room or the play-house, and that when you have escaped from these, you are got out of the reach of its contagion. But the contagion follows wherever there is a human heart left to its natural impulse.

'And though I allow that places and circumstances greatly contribute to augment or diminish the evil ; and that a prudent Christian will always avoid an atmosphere which he thinks not quite wholesome ; yet whoever lives in the close examination of his own heart, will still find something of the morbid mischief clinging to it, which will require constant watching, whatever be his climate or his company.

'I have known pious persons, who would on no account allow their children to attend places of gay resort, who were yet little solicitous to extinguish the spirit which these places are calculated to generate and nourish.

' This is rather a geographical than a moral distinction. It is thinking more of the place than of the temper. They restrain their persons, but are not careful to expel from their hearts the dispositions which excite the appetite, and form the very essence of danger. A young creature cannot be happy who spends her time at home in amusements destined for exhibition, while she is forbidden to be exhibited.

' But while we are teaching them that Christianity involves an heroic self-denial, that it requires some things to be done, and others to be sacrificed, at which mere people of the world revolt ; that it directs us to renounce some pursuits because they are wrong, and others because they are trifling—we should, at the same time, let them see and feel, that to a Christian the region of enjoyment is not so narrow and circumscribed, is not so barren and unproductive, nor the pleasures it produces so few and small, as the enemies of religion would insinuate. While early habits of self-denial are giving firmness to the character, strengthening the texture of the mind, and hardening it against ordinary temptations, the pleasures and employments which we substitute in the stead of those we banish, must be such as tend to raise the taste, to invigorate the intellect, to exalt the nature, and enlarge the sphere of enjoyment ; to give a tone to the mind, and an elevation to the sentiments, which shall really reduce to insignificance the pleasures that are prohibited.

' In our own instance I humbly trust, that, through the Divine blessing, perseverance has been its own reward. As to Lucilla, I firmly believe that right habits are now so rooted, and the relish of superior pleasures so established in her mind, that had she the whole range of human enjoyment at her command, had she no higher consideration, no fear of God, no obedience to her mother and me, which forbad the ordinary dissipations, she would voluntarily renounce them, from a full persuasion of their empty, worthless, unsatisfying nature, and from a superinduced taste for higher gratifications.

' I am as far from intending to represent my daughter as a faultless creature, as she herself is from wishing to be so represented. She is deeply conscious, both of the corruption of her nature, and the deficiencies of her life.

' This consciousness, I trust, will continue to stimulate her vigilance, without which all religion will decline, and to maintain her humility, without which all religion is vain.

' My dear Charles ! a rational scene of felicity lies open before you both.

' It is lawful to rejoice in the fair perspective, but it is safe to rejoice with trembling. Do not abandon yourself to the chimerical hope that life will be to you, what it has never yet been to any man— a scene of unmingled delight. This life, so bright in prospect, will have its sorrows. This life, which at four-and-twenty seems to stretch itself to an indefinite length, will have an end. May its sorrows correct its illusions ! May its close be the entrance on a life which shall have no sorrows and no end !

' I will not say how frequently we talk of you, nor how much we

17—2

miss you. Need I tell you, that the person who says least on the subject, is not the one who least feels your absence? She writes by this post.

'Adieu, my dear Charles! I am with great truth your attached friend, and hope before Christmas to subscribe myself your affectionate father,

'FRANCIS STANLEY.'

    *   *   *   *   *   *   *   *

Delightful hope! as Miss Stanley, when that blessed event takes place, will resign her name, I shall resume mine, and joyfully renounce for ever that of

CŒLEBS.

THE END

ALSO AVAILABLE FROM THOEMMES PRESS

For Her Own Good – A Series of Conduct Books

Cœlebs in Search of a Wife
Hannah More
With a new introduction by Mary Waldron
ISBN 1 85506 383 2 : 288pp : 1808–9 edition : £14.75

Female Replies to Swetnam the Woman-Hater
Various
With a new introduction by Charles Butler
ISBN 1 85506 379 4 : 336pp : 1615–20 edition : £15.75

A Complete Collection of Genteel and Ingenious
Conversation
Jonathan Swift
With a new introduction by the Rt Hon. Michael Foot
ISBN 1 85506 380 8 : 224pp : 1755 edition : £13.75

Thoughts on the Education of Daughters
Mary Wollstonecraft
With a new introduction by Janet Todd
ISBN 1 85506 381 6 : 192pp : 1787 edition : £13.75

The Young Lady's Pocket Library, or Parental
Monitor
Various
With a new introduction by Vivien Jones
ISBN 1 85506 382 4 : 352pp : 1790 edition : £15.75

Also available as a 5 volume set : ISBN 1 85506 378 6
Special Set Price: £65.00

Her Write His Name

Old Kensington *and* The Story of Elizabeth
Anne Isabella Thackeray
With a new introduction by Esther Schwartz-McKinzie
ISBN 1 85506 388 3 : 496pp : 1873 & 1876 editions : £17.75

Shells from the Sands of Time
Rosina Bulwer Lytton
With a new introduction by Marie Mulvey Roberts
ISBN 1 85506 386 7 : 272pp : 1876 edition : £14.75

Platonics
Ethel Arnold
With a new introduction by Phyllis Wachter
ISBN 1 85506 389 1 : 160pp : 1894 edition : £13.75

The Continental Journals 1798-1820
Dorothy Wordsworth
With a new introduction by Helen Boden
ISBN 1 85506 385 9 : 472pp : New edition : £17.75

Her Life in Letters
Alice James
Edited with a new introduction by Linda Anderson
ISBN 1 85506 387 5 : 320pp : New : £15.75

Also available as a 5 volume set : ISBN 1 8556 384 0
Special set price : £70.00

Subversive Women

The Art of Ingeniously Tormenting
Jane Collier
With a new introduction by Judith Hawley
ISBN 1 8556 246 1 : 292pp : 1757 edition : £14.75

Appeal of One Half the Human Race, Women, Against the Pretensions of the Other Half, Men, to Retain them in Political, and thence in Civil and Domestic, Slavery
William Thompson and Anna Wheeler
With a new introduction by the Rt Hon. Michael Foot and Marie Mulvey Roberts
ISBN 1 85506 247 X : 256pp : 1825 edition : £14.75

A Blighted Life: A True Story
Rosina Bulwer Lytton
With a new introduction by Marie Mulvey Roberts
ISBN 1 85506 248 8 : 178pp : 1880 edition : £10.75

The Beth Book
Sarah Grand
With a new introduction by Sally Mitchell
ISBN 1 85506 249 6 : 560pp : 1897 edition : £18.75

The Journal of a Feminist
Elsie Clews Parsons
With a new introduction and notes by Margaret C. Jones
ISBN 1 85506 250 X : 142pp : New edition : £12.75

Also available as a 5 volume set : ISBN 1 85506 261 5
Special set price : £65.00

MARY WALDRON
teaches literature part-time in the Department of
Continuing Education at the University of Essex. Her
research interests are mainly among women writers of
the late eighteenth and early nineteenth centuries. She
has completed a book-length study of the life and
writings of Ann Yearsley, milkwoman and poet of
Bristol. She has also discussed the status of this writer
and her relationship with Hannah More in an essay,
'Ann Yearsley and the Clifton Records' which
appeared in *Age of Johnson* III in 1990.
The attitude of Jane Austen to *Cœlebs in Search of a
Wife* and to the Evangelicals generally is explored in
another essay, 'The Frailties of Fanny: *Mansfield Park*
and the Evangelical Movement', published in the
April 1994 issue of *Eighteenth-Century Fiction*.

Marie Mulvey Roberts is a Senior Lecturer in literary
studies at the University of the West of England and is
the author of *British Poets and Secret Societies* (1986),
and *Gothic Immortals* (1990). From 1994 she has been
the co-editor of a Journal: 'Women's Writing; the
Elizabethan to the Victorian Period', and the General
Editor for three series: *Subversive Women*, *For Her
Own Good*, and *Her Write His Name*. The volumes
she has co-edited include: *Sources of British Feminism*
(1993), *Perspectives on the History of British Feminism*
(1994), *Controversies in the History of British
Feminism* (1995) and *Literature and Medicine during
the Eighteenth Century* (1993). Among her single
edited books are, *Out of the Night: Writings from
Death Row* (1994), and editions of Rosina Bulwer
Lytton's *A Blighted Life* (1994) and *Shells from the
Sands of Time* (1995).

COVER ILLUSTRATION
Pursuit on the North Bridge *by John Kay*
Cover designed by Dan Broughton